11/'82

Dear Mimi —

Although I've never before
seen you ride, I hope that
this book will help to instill
an even greater love & enjoyment
of horses in you —

Happy 10th birthday, love!
(Two digits — that's a biggie)

Our love,
Aunt Donna,
Uncle Teddy,
Danielle & Brett

The Complete Book of
The Horse

The Complete Book of
The Horse

edited by Candida Geddes

octopus

First published 1978 by Octopus Books Limited, 59 Grosvenor Street, London W1
© 1978 Octopus Books Limited   ISBN 0 7064 0743 1
Produced by Mandarin Publishers Limited, 22a Westlands Road, Quarry Bay, Hong Kong   Printed in Singapore

CONTENTS

One of the most interesting things about the horse, it has always seemed to me, is the story of its relationship with man. Ever since the days that man first realized he might benefit more from the horse by using it than by eating it, the horse has been inextricably involved in man's own development. Except for true desert peoples, for whom the camel was as important an animal, and peoples of the sea, almost every race and civilization has been affected by the horse. Assyrians, Greeks, Romans and barbarians, the Crusaders (on heavy horses) and their Muslim enemies under Saladin (on the fleet-footed Arab types), the Spanish *conquistadores* and the Indians they conquered – all these and many more fought with the horse, and sometimes even for the horse. But the horse has contributed more to the story of man than is told by the history of warfare alone. From large-scale migrations to individual exploration, horses have travelled with man; the cultural cross-fertilization which plays such a large part in the development of ideas and technical advance has been helped by them; trade over much of the world's great landmasses was for centuries conducted using the horse; the horse is the proud symbol of kingly power, and the helper of the peasant ploughman. Only recently has the horse become primarily a pleasure animal in many parts of the world, rather than being an essential element in the everyday working life of people in all kinds and varieties of occupations.

It is for this reason that the choice of material for this book has deliberately been slanted towards the cultural and historical aspects of the horse and man, rather than dealing exclusively with the modern horse and how to ride and care for it. There is an infinity of books which give detailed practical information on individual aspects of horsemanship and horsemastership as they are practised today; while these topics are covered in the present book, the emphasis is on a broader conspectus: the enduring, unique relationship man has with this most versatile and delightful animal, the horse.

Candida Geddes

The Horse in History

8 THE HORSE IN HISTORY

THE DOMESTICATION OF THE HORSE

The Pre-Domestic Horse

Before Darwin perfected his theory of evolution all that was known about the origin of the horse, so far as the average horseman was concerned, was contained in the story of Noah and the Ark. From this, a belief that *Equus caballus* was of one single origin was a logical conclusion. Darwin himself was, therefore, no innovator in this respect. He demonstrated his tenets of evolution and the origin of species by natural selection, largely by reference to successive equine ancestors in *one line*.

The only pre-Darwinian theory that can still command respect is that of Hamilton Smith, who had postulated several wild species of horses contributing to the make-up of *Equus caballus*. He thought they were principally differentiated by coat-colour, which explained the wide spectrum of extant coat colours. That part of his theory, however, cannot be upheld in the light of our present knowledge.

The discovery of the Przewalski horse in 1881 caused it to be hailed as the only begetter of domestic horses, thus supporting, again, the theory of single origin.

It was not until about the turn of the nineteenth century that the single origin theory, so widely held, suffered a reverse through the discoveries made by J. Cossar Ewart of Edinburgh. He made a series of hybridization experiments with Equidae at Pennicuik not far from that city, the results of which, and of his study of 'primitive' horses and ponies in Britain and overseas, he best summarized in an article in *Nature* (21 April 1904). He it was who coined the phrase 'Celtic pony' to indicate one of the wild equine sub-species ancestral to the domestic horse. Another heavier, northern sub-species he called the Norse horse. Other separate ancestors he recognized were the wild horse of Mongolia, *Equus przewalskii*, and two more-than-pony-sized races, one with a ram head and one with a straight profile, which he did not endow with names. He did not assign the Arab or related breeds to a separate race, deeming them merely the most easterly representatives of the 'cline' (as it is now called) of which the Exmoor and the Welsh pony were the westernmost. From this it will be seen that he regarded the geographical distribution of all these races as very wide, and that he envisaged two or three or more of them co-existing in the same district . . . 'as Africa now contains several species of zebras, Europe at the beginning of the Pleistocene period was inhabited by several species of horses'.

Monophylists or partisans of the single-ancestor school still flourish, notably among equine psychologists, professional or amateur, who seek to explain behaviour in terms of situations to which the wild ancestor was exposed: and it is always one kind of wild ancestor, exclusively grass-eating, dwelling on a boundless prairie with neither mountain nor forest in sight.

In my view, the most articulate, the most logical, and the best-equipped with evidence among prehistorians of the horse are the latter-day followers of Ewart, Speed (also of Edinburgh), Skorkowski in Poland, and Ebhardt in Germany. They have the advantage of being equipped with aids not available to Ewart, such as radiology and the technique of carbon-14 dating, and the results of some archaeological finds of the first importance, such as the Pazyryk horse burials of the Altai which have been made since his day.

Their classifications of post-glacial Old World horses available to the first domesticators are not dignified by the name of species but as 'Types', as under:

1) substantially, Ewart's Celtic pony, better called the Atlantic pony. The modern breeds most resembling it are the Exmoor and a certain strain of Icelandic.

2) substantially, Ewart's Norse horse and those inhabiting northern Eurasia. Modern breeds most resembling it are the Norwegian Fjord pony, a certain type of Highland pony, and the Noriker heavy horse of the sub-Alpine region.

3) a horse, not a pony, with a Central Asian habitat. Modern breeds most resembling it are the clay-coloured Sorraia horse of the Spanish–Portuguese border, and, in a more elegant form, the Akhal-Teké of Central Asia and the Karabakh, both of which are golden-dun. This was the ancestor of the Nisaean and Bactrian breeds and, to the extent of about 50 per cent through the 'Turks', the Bactrian and the Andalusian, of the Thoroughbred.

4) a pony-sized horse of western Asia. The modern breed most resembling it is the Caspian pony, thought to be the ancestor of the Arabian and a small handful of allied breeds found chiefly in Persia. But in part this type is bred into a multitude of domestic races, endowing them with many of its qualities, not the least of which is beauty.

Excluded is Przewalski's horse, because of a factor not known in Ewart's day. This is that a species is characterized by an embryonic cell structure peculiar to it, the cell nuclei containing a given number of chromosomes – 'rod-like structures . . . regarded as the bearers of hereditary factors' (R. Geurts). The chromosome count of Przewalski's horse differs from that of all domestic horses.

Included is the Tarpan, the wild horse of eastern Europe and western Russia. Extinct in its pure form since the last century but now 're-constituted' in the Polish Tarpan herds, it is regarded as a hybrid occurring in the wild at the point where the habitats of Types 1 and 4 once joined. The Tarpan was the basis of stock used by all the chariot-driving nations of the eastern Mediterranean from the Hittites to the Greeks, and originally of the Celtic tribes. It is the principal ancestor of the small 'peasants' horses' in east central Europe and the Balkans. Many individuals of these breeds resemble it closely: the Hungarian Goral, the Romanian Huçul, the Polish Konik and the Bosniak of Yugoslavia, etc., but even closer facsimiles have been 'back-bred' in Poland and Bavaria for scientific purposes.

If we had no evidence at all from fossil bones and teeth, it would still be apparent to anyone with an eye for a horse, from the evidence of European cave paintings alone, that in the Old Stone Age a great variety of wild horse types roamed Europe. In the Dordogne there is the cave of Rouffignac, the roof of which is covered with drawings that depict identically the present-day Exmoor ponies. Not far away, at Les Combarelles, there is a drawing of an obese, ram-headed, Clydesdale-looking specimen. At Niaux in the Pyrenees, there is a quite credible Fell pony. At Font de Gaume, near Les Eyzies, there is a New Forest pony in the act of leaping. Go over the mountains into Cantabrian Spain and yet further recognizable types can be seen in these prehistoric galleries, including horses of great quality – virtually 'oriental'.

In speaking of domestic horses the over-worked phrase 'pure-bred' is a relative term. At the head of every pedigree stands an imported stallion of whose history and ancestry in his 'old country', nothing of consequence is known, and a country-bred mare of unrecorded ancestry. 'Pure breeding' occurred only in the wild ancestors: and then, it seems, not absolutely.

Domestication and the Early Horse Peoples

The preceding section, concerning the pre-domestic horse, might be thought to be within the province of the naturalist. He could be either a biologist or a zoologist, but would be accustomed to working in the past rather than the present. He would be well-grounded in ecology, and thus able to consider the horse against the background of its environment; the effect on it of climate and vegetation; its own effect on the vegetation; and its relations to other living creatures, be they vegetarians which constituted competition for grazing, or predators which controlled its numbers. These are its 'natural enemies', chief among whom, up to the moment of domestication, is Man.

Of qualified experts in this field there is no lack; the academic staffs of veterinary schools abound in them. But to make any progress in this relatively new discipline, the history of the horse as a domestic animal, and by implication the history of horse-breeding and horse-borne peoples, requires a different set of qualifications altogether, and they would be outside the experience of the pure naturalist. Ideally, in addition to the knowledge of the equine prehistorian, some acquaintance with practical horsemanship and horsemastership, the former to include driving as well as riding, is essential. Then something must also

be known about soldiering and agriculture, as well as
wainwrightship, enough at least to realize what is practicable and
what is not in the way of vehicle design. Likewise some historical
grasp of the technical aspects of shipbuilding at certain crucial
times and places, enough to determine whether it was viable in,
say, 200 BC, to transport horses across, say, 200 km (125 miles) of
open sea.

In earlier days it all seemed so simple, at least up to the time
when Darwin wrote his *Origin of Species*. All literate persons in
the West at that time were acquainted with Holy Writ, at least in
Protestant countries. The educated class in Europe and North
America, both Catholic and Protestant, was well read in Greek
and Latin authors. All that had to be done was to assemble the
requisite quotations from the Bible and the classics, arrange them
in the right order, and the back of the work was broken. As for
the practical implications of what the literary sources said, they
were easily, and mostly correctly, interpreted, because up to the
invention of the passenger-carrying railway, and to a certain
extent from then until the birth of the internal combustion engine,
almost all competent middle-class males knew how to persuade a
horse to convey them from point A to point B by one means or
another. Not to be able to do this was not simply the equivalent
of being unable to drive a car: it was more like not being able to
ride a bicycle. To this extent Dr Syntax and his like could cope
more adequately with this involved subject than their modern
counterparts.

It might appear simple but in fact it was not so. No one took
account of the fact that the Old Testament was written by and for a
people who had a taboo against horses. Up to the time of King
Solomon, this was about as virulent as the one they had against
dogs or pigs. The pious Hebrew looked back to respected
patriarchs who rode camels and asses, but horses never. To him the
horse was inseparably associated with foreign imperialists –
Assyrians or Egyptians or Persians. Hence the Old Testament is
an indifferent historical source for this subject, and can tell us
virtually nothing about it before about 900 BC, by which time we
have plenty of alternative evidence anyway.

The same objections apply, though to a lesser degree, to classical
authors, whose voices speak to us from about 800 BC onwards of
the great civilizations of the Mediterranean. But the horse was not
first domesticated about 800 BC, nor in the Mediterranean region.

When was the horse domesticated, and where? To the first there
is no quick or certain answer, only that it was certainly as early as
the third millennium BC and that as evidence from archaeology
slowly accumulates, the favoured date recedes ever further
towards the opening centuries of that millennium. As to where, the
certainty is that it was in a region north-east of the Mediterranean,
at least as far distant as the Oxus (Amu Darya) basin, and perhaps
as distant as the far end of Siberia, along the shores of the Bering

Strait. Or anywhere along that diagonal line. But 'when?' and 'where?' are closely related questions. Just as there are monophylists who believe in a single wild ancestor of the horse, and polyphylists who postulate several of them, so there are diffusionists who believe that the horseman was born in one centre and one only, from which the horse culture spread over all the world. In addition there are those who maintain that horses could be, and in fact were, domesticated not necessarily in imitation of other tribes but by several peoples, not in contact with each other, living in separate regions where wild horses were found.

So, to be able to read Xenophon in the original is not enough. To be able to interpret the exact practical implications of the Hebrew text of the Book of Job is not enough. A knowledge of ancient Egyptian and Babylonian texts would be a help and mastery of the languages current in the Hittite Empire about 1400 BC more useful still. . . .

That will bring us back to the earliest written text of any significance concerning horses, *The Chariot Training Manual* of Kikkulis the Mittanite. And yet we have irrefutable evidence of the use of horses in various regions of the Old World more than sixteen centuries earlier than that. This is the testimony of pictorial art and the remains of artifacts belonging to illiterate peoples, *one* of whom – but which? – first domesticated the horse. The interpretation of this evidence is a branch of archaeology. It can be supplemented by the oral traditions of the peoples dwelling along that diagonal line between the Oxus basin and the Pacific coast of Siberia, a study of which, in the original, demands familiarity with several languages, some of them Indo-European but mostly belonging to the Turkic, Ural-Altaic and Mongolian groups. Oral tradition is valuable because legends contain a core of what once in the remote past was historical fact. But they need interpreting: to take a Western example, the legend of horses being bestowed on some hero by a god of the sea, such as the Greek Poseidon, or the Irish Mananaan Mac Lir, may signify in mundane terms that horses, or more likely a superior breed of horse, were first brought to Hellas or to Eire by sea. And to arrive at the right interpretation of such legends demands, in the first instance, an anthropologist or a folklorist.

And where will we find the historian possessed of all these skills? Nowhere, for there is no such person. So the task must fall inevitably to those who have much knowledge in some areas, and less in others, or who have some knowledge in most areas. They must take other men's translations and interpretations at their face value, and rely on someone else's summary and exposition for the layman of highly technical reports of research in various natural sciences, from geology to genetics. If we are to construct a prehistory, and an early history, of the horse before and after domestication, it must be built of bricks made of other men's straw and other men's clay, baked in a kiln fired with other men's fuel, and bound with mortar made by yet others. There is no other way. This is the extent of the problem and it must, therefore, preclude any single definitive explanation.

Let us now consider the fortunes of the domestic horse over the first thirty centuries or so, still considering them, in the main, under the headings of the four local races which were defined and discussed in the preceding section.

Type 1, which Ewart called the Celtic pony, was probably not first domesticated by the Celtic peoples, but by the peoples who preceded them in north-west Europe; in Scotland, for example, by the Picts. Being capable of a very fast trot with a sweeping action it was admirably adapted for chariot work in pairs, and some years ago a practical demonstration was given by two Exmoor mares harnessed to a replica of an ancient British chariot, discovered at Llyn Cerig Bach in Wales. The mares performed admirably, although in fact such a team would in ancient times have consisted of stallions, who could have done much better. The rock drawings of Scandinavia which date from the Bronze Age include many pictures of pairs of ponies harnessed to chariots, and these are likely to have been of the same Type 1. Here domestication was not the work of the aboriginal Lapps, who retained the reindeer, but of Indo-European invaders – ancestors of the Norse – who brought sheep, goats, cattle and crop-farming to the north.

The Celts themselves originally lived not on the Atlantic coast but in the lower Danube valley, where the prevalent wild horse was not this type, but the Tarpan. In the early stages of their equestrian history, therefore, the chariots would have been horsed with Tarpans, which as we have seen were a cross between Type 1 and Type 4. But the great Celtic migration, which came about the middle of the first millenium BC, led up that valley and along the axis Swabia–Burgundy–Brittany. Conquering as they went, they inevitably acquired great numbers of horses along the route, and these would include, as the most important element, the more substantial horses of the Alpine foothills as they skirted around the northern edge of the massif. Thus when they stood poised on the Channel shore for the invasion of Britain, it would already have been inaccurate to describe their horses as 'pure-bred'. What awaited them on the other side of the Channel was a more uniform stock, consisting only of Type 1 with a small admixture of Type 2. Once they had established themselves and begun putting their own stallions to the aboriginal mares, therefore, the 'ancient British horse' would already have contained elements of three out of four types of the primeval wild stock.

Type 2, whatever its exact relationship to Przewalski's horse may be, is probably the first to have been domesticated. Its habitat overlapped that of the reindeer, and it may well be that in north-east Asia (where it lived) it was first domesticated as a substitute for the reindeer. At least one tribe in that region, the Yakuts, seems

to have remained in a transitional stage to this day, riding horses
and reindeer alike. At a primitive level of culture, it is probably
easier for a reindeer-keeping people to start taming horses from
scratch than it would be for anyone else. For instance, in certain
weather conditions it might be feasible for men mounted on
reindeer or in light reindeer-drawn sledges like the Lapps' *pulkka*
to overtake, or get within lasso-range of, horses hampered by snow
(this might also be done on skis, or on snow-shoes, but hardly by
any other means). Again, reindeer-keepers are the people most
likely to be familiar with the use of the lasso. If the hunt took
place in summer-time, all, or the majority of, the animals captured
intact would be unweaned foals. Next to camel-keepers, reindeer
herders would have the readiest adequate supply of milk that can
be digested by a foal (cow's milk cannot).

The wheel was unknown in north-east Asia long after its
invention in south-west Asia, and the newly-domesticated horses
could only have been put to work under the pack or the riding
saddle or in front of the sleigh. Their performance in the first two
roles would have been inferior to that of reindeer in the winter
months. In the summer the sleigh could not
be used, but the slide-car, a wheelless
conveyance called a 'travois' in North

America, could be drawn by either horses or reindeer (it was originally drawn by dogs).

However, it was under the saddle that the horse bestowed the greatest mobility on the herdsmen of Mongolia, Manchuria, and eastern Siberia. Its adoption began the long series of horse-borne invasions by archers armed with the double-curved laminated bow, which culminated in the invasion of Europe by the Turks – a tide that did not begin to recede until the end of the seventeenth century of our era.

Again, this cycle began with the taming, almost exclusively, of Type 2, but as the flood of conquering horse-archers rolled steadily west and south other varieties were added to the remount herds, just as they were to be later with the Celts. The disturbances spread outwards from the vortex of Mongolia like ripples in a pond, and the first impact on Europe was chiefly felt in the invasions of Indo-European ('Aryan') and Turkic charioteers, moving westward under pressure from the Mongol horse-archers. Then came other Indo-Europeans, riding and armed with the Tartar-type composite bow. The most famous of these people are the Scythians, and probably it was they who drove the Celts out of the Danube valley and set in train the Celtic pilgrimage to the Atlantic shore. The particular wave threatening to engulf Europe at the dawn of the Christian era consisted of Parthians. They it is whom St John had in mind when he wrote: 'And I looked, and behold a pale horse, and his name that sat on him was Death.' The word rendered as 'pale' in the Authorized version could also be rendered 'light dun', the characteristic colour of Types 2 and 3.

Type 3, beginning with the Persian invasions which were checked at Marathon and Salamis, now began to appear in Europe in considerable numbers. They included the famous Nisaean breed that was so much taller than any mount available to the Greeks of Xenophon's time. That they were all in enemy hands was a position reversed only by Alexander the Great's conquest of Persia, accomplished not alone by the redoubtable Macedonian infantry but also by auxiliary horsemen from the conquered kingdom of Bactria (northern Afghanistan). After the take-over of the Persian Empire it became possible to bring back these Bactrian horses to Macedon to upgrade the Tarpan-type local stock.

Type 4: The same applies to specimens of this type, although from a military point of view this Proto-Arab, as it then was, had the grave disadvantage of being too small for a charger. But certainly it was in the Hellenistic period when Alexander's successors were ruling his fragmented empire in Europe and Asia – and not, as is commonly supposed, in Roman times – that these horses were first available in any considerable numbers in Mediterranean Europe. It was to be many centuries before they were to be called Arabian.

If we conclude that the Caspian pony is *not* the unmodified descendant of Type 4, the Proto-Arab, or that the latter never existed in the wild, then we shall have to look for another possible ancestor for the Arab and its close relations among early domestic stock. This brings us back inevitably to Professor Ridgeway and his *Multiple Origins of the Thoroughbred*.

Ridgeway's intuitive guess was that the Proto-Arab was a hybrid, arising from the union of the Asiatic Wild Horse, or rather its domestic descendants, with some species of zebra that was formerly, but is not now, domesticated, and that this cross could only have come about in North Africa. The chromosome count of a hybrid is the sum of the count of both parents divided by two. If this 'average' comes to an odd number (as most of the feasible ones do) then the hybrid is sterile (e.g. the mule). But in the few cases where it comes to an even number, hybrid can mate fruitfully with hybrid and a new species – or at least sub-species – can be born. The Hungarian author, Miklos Jankovich, has pointed out in a work not yet published in English that, in terms of species now living, not all Equidae have had their chromosome count established. Of those whose count is known, there is a species of zebra whose chromosome count added to that of Przewalski's horse and divided by two is identical with that of the domestic horse. Jankovich therefore has demonstrated, without consciously wishing to reinforce Ridgeway, that in terms of the mechanics – that is the arithmetic – of genetics, his theory of equine origins is perfectly feasible. He refuses to speculate on how such a cross could have arisen, but it could not have occurred in the wild, in view of what is known about the distribution of the Asiatic Wild Horse and the various species of zebra. Ridgeway lost the trick by assuming that the horse came to the zebra and not vice versa.

We know from many modern instances that zebras *can* be tamed to ride and drive, but it has never been claimed that they are as good to drive as a horse, and there is ample testimony that they are a worse ride, since they have no withers. Suppose that in late prehistoric times men came down the Nile Valley leading pack-laden zebras, to cross the isthmus of Suez and journey through Sinai and Palestine. Somewhere in the latitude of the Caspian Sea we might expect them to meet men riding or driving or leading the domesticated version of Przewalski's horse. Ridgeway's theory foundered on the archaeological rock; no identifiable remains of horses of the required antiquity could be found in North Africa to prove his point. Likewise no such remains of zebras have been found in western Asia. But then, for *certain* identification of Equidae a good deal of material is required for autopsy, the minimum being a skull with both jaws intact, and one fore and one hind limb below the knee or hock. For this much to remain of one skeleton over several thousand years, along a migration route that is mostly through desert country, is too much to be hoped, yet only the bones can tell the true story. Neither the striped hide, nor the huge trumpet-like ears of the zebra, nor yet its chromosomes, could possibly be preserved.

The fact that very occasionally zebra-like markings are found on the legs, and more rarely still on other parts of the body, of new-born Arabian foals is neither here nor there. So they are in horses of all breeds, and they are merely an atavistic reminder of the stripes that are believed to have occurred in most Equidae before the Ice Age. Whatever the origin of the horses now called Arabian, they only just fail to be considered in this section, which does not extend beyond the beginning of the Christian era. Classical Greek authors do not mention Arabian horses, and no Latin author up to the time of Augustus does so, in the sense that there was then a recognized Arabian breed. European authors writing in antiquity give the impression rather that the Arab peoples used donkeys almost exclusively in peace-time and camels in war. Horses in Arabia at the beginning of the Christian era were very scarce and this was still the case in the lifetime of Mohammed, who in his holy wars demonstrated their superiority over camels for military purposes. It was the compulsion to spread the faith of Islam by force of arms that led to the expansion of horse-breeding among the desert tribes to its widest feasible limits. Although the Koran might exhort the faithful to produce as many foals as possible for service against the infidel, in the Arabian peninsula this could only be done by the same means as had been practised in pre-Islamic times. And so these limits remained fairly narrow. Horses cannot live on camel-thorn; the number that could be reared was in direct proportion to the amount of barley that could be acquired from the Fertile Crescent bordering the desert zone, and the amount of dates that the oases could produce surplus to human consumption. The only requisite that was available more or less *ad lib* was camel's milk, essential for weaning foals under conditions in which the mare only lactated for a couple of months at best.

Horse-breeding and horse-keeping began, in Arabia itself, as a prestige symbol, associated only with the rich and powerful. When it became a religious duty incumbent also on the less rich and less powerful this must have meant three things. First, that other livestock kept by the Bedouin – his sheep, goats, camels – would have to content themselves with a smaller share of available drinking water and even grittier grazing than before. Second, that breeders themselves would have to make do with less dates, less barley, less camel's milk and even less fish, since in certain parts of Arabia near the coast, protein in the diet of horses is supplied by dried sprats from which the oil is first extracted. Third, that the slogan 'quality before quantity' would be hammered home in no uncertain fashion. If piety compels a man to bankrupt himself and starve his family and flocks in order to breed horses, he might as well breed good ones. One cannot but reflect, contemplating the enormously inflated numbers of Arabs bred outside Arabia today, that some such economic stringency and consequent pruning of numbers would be of the greatest benefit to modern Western breeders.

EUROPEAN HORSES SINCE CLASSICAL TIMES

The tribes whom Julius Caesar subdued seldom fought on horse-back, though the Britons still used war-chariots which the civilized world had discarded centuries earlier. It seems likely that the horses of northern Europe were small ponies similar to our native breeds, and that the Romans brought with them larger, better bred animals. For it was from the countries around the Mediterranean – Thrace, Syria, North Africa and Spain – that the largest, fastest and best bred horses came. It is customary to attribute this to the potent Arabian strain; but Strabo, an accurate geographer writing at the beginning of the Christian era, states definitely that there were then no horses in Arabia, and no archaeological or other finds have weakened his evidence. But innumerable Assyrian, Egyptian, Greek and Spanish artists have shown that the horse of those regions was, as a result of two thousand years of domestication, selective breeding and grain feeding, a light, well-bred looking animal of 14·2 to 15 hands; and it was this horse which the Romans brought to Gaul and Britain.

These speculations are partially confirmed by excavations at Newstead, in the Scottish lowlands, which in the third and fourth centuries AD was a frontier post garrisoned by a regiment of Gallic horse. Most of the equine remains are of light ponies about 12·2 hands; evidently the troopers were mounted on these and, though too small for combat, they would be useful in reconnaisance and the pursuit of Pict raiders. There were also the bones of some heavier, coarser animals of about the same height – probably pack-ponies. Finally the post had a few well-bred horses between 14 and 15 hands, almost certainly officers' chargers of some Mediterranean stock.

The inventions of the saddle-tree and the stirrup reached Europe from the East during the fourth and sixth centuries respectively, and revolutionized the art of war. Cavalry could now, for the first time, charge home and fight in a melée without fear of falling off. The heavy, armoured lancer now dominated the European battlefield, establishing a measureless superiority over infantry. Only in England and Scandinavia did those who could afford horses stick to the old-fashioned habit of riding to battle, then dismounting to fight on foot. The inference is that they were not good horsemen (Harold almost had a mutiny when he tried to make his Saxons fight on horseback against the Welsh) and that they had few good horses. Both suppositions are partially confirmed by chroniclers: the Venerable Bede says that it was rare for Saxons to ride before the mid-seventh century, and no king of England employed a Master of Horse before Alfred (871–901). His successor, Athelstan (925–940) forbade the export of horses, which suggests that he took more interest in them; but at Hastings (1066) the Saxon army fought wholly on foot. Such ponies as they had, for carrying them on the marsh, are shown in the Bayeux tapestry as much smaller, meaner animals than the destriers of the Norman knights.

About the knights' charger there has been much nonsense written, based on the assumption that the 'Great Horse' required to carry an armoured knight in battle had to be a great, lumbering carthorse. The expression 'Great Horse' or destrier simply means a knight's charger, and his size must have varied from century to century according to the weight he had to carry. From the eleventh to the fourteenth century the knight was clad in mail over a padded leather or wollen gambeson, and his horse was unarmoured. He was, by modern standards, a smallish man, turning the scales at perhaps ten stone. His mail hauberk would hardly have weighed more than twenty-five to thirty pounds. Surviving saddles of the fifteenth century weigh about forty pounds, but the twelfth-century saddle probably weighed less because it carried less. Add a few pounds for helm, gambeson, lance, sword and shield, and one comes to the conclusion that the knight's charger of the early Middle Ages need not have carried more than sixteen stone. British cavalry horses of 1914 carried between seventeen and a half and eighteen stone, assuming that the rider weighed eleven stone; French and German horses carried much more. One therefore concludes that there was no need for the knight to ride an enormous weight-carrier; what he needed was something very like the ordinary twentieth-century cavalry horse, of about 15·2 hands, well bred and able to gallop.

This is precisely what the Bayeux tapestry and other contemporary illustrations show; the Norman knights' destriers were well-bred, hunter-type horses, if one makes allowance for the convention that an artist must show men proportionately much bigger than horses or inanimate objects – ships are depicted as about the size of rowing boats, and horses as donkeys. Curiously enough, all were stallions. It was not until the late eighteenth century that the cavalryman of western Europe realized that geldings and mares, because they are more tractable and more silent, make better cavalry horses.

At the time of the battle of Hastings, Normans had conquered southern Italy and Sicily, and some of William's mercenaries came from those distant lands, no doubt bringing their horses with them. William himself is reputed to have ridden a Spanish horse. The Mediterranean countries were still the source of the best horses, and the Arabian strains must by now have been strong there. For in the centuries after Strabo the Bedouin had discovered that for war the horse was a far better animal than the camel. A hard nomadic existence with sparse limestone grazing, little water and occasional feeds of barley from an oasis allowed only the fittest to survive, but mares and foals were treated by the dwellers in goathair tents almost like their own children, and fed with camel's milk even when their riders went short. Centuries of this life produced the steed which carried Islam from the Hedjaz to the Pyrenees, an animal renowned for beauty, gentleness and fire, for iron-hard hooves, solid ivory bones, steely sinews, lovely arched neck, delicate head with small ears and wide nostrils, high tail carriage and unlimited courage and endurance – the Arabian horse. One of his characteristics is his prepotency, by which he transmits his best qualities to coarser breeds, and there can be little doubt that by the eleventh century the best horses in Europe had a strain of Arabian blood. Obviously this would be stronger in the south, but a picture of a Swedish king hunting in the eleventh century shows him riding a horse with obvious Arab blood.

Nevertheless, the pure-bred Arab was probably a bit light for an armoured knight, and Crusaders, who had plenty of opportunity to acquire Arabian horses, generally preferred something larger though with a strong Arab strain. Richard Lionheart's two favourite chargers were a Cypriot and a Turcoman; and the Franks who settled in the kingdom of Jerusalem for nearly two hundred years preferred to import Spanish horses. None of these animals bore any resemblance to the large and heavy Great Horses described by so many historians.

Of course there were other types of horse besides the knight's charger. The rules of the Knights Templar laid down that each knight should be provided with three chargers and a hack (or palfrey): there are mentioned also pack horses, presumably heavier and slower, and jades for menial tasks such as drawing water. It is recorded that running horses (*equites cursores*) were imported into England in the twelfth century. Were these ambling hacks or race-horses? Probably the latter, used for the king's messengers and as hunters by wealthy nobles. Richard Lionheart had two such, Favell and Lyard, described as being swifter than dromedaries and destriers, which he said he would not sell for a thousand pounds. There is, however, no record of his actually being offered and refusing such an enormous sum.

We know that King John imported a hundred large stallions from the Continent. Coming from north Germany and the Low Countries, they were probably bought to improve the size rather than the quality of English horses. A hundred years later we find owners claiming compensation for horses killed at the battle of Falkirk; among them the most valuable was a 'bay charger with a white hind foot, value a hundred marks', the property of Sir Eustace de la Heccke; the least valuable, a black Hackney of the younger brother of Sir John Botetorte, value eight marks. (A mark was nearly 35 pence but, of course, worth many times the present value of that sum.) Chargers or destriers are all valued at sixty marks or more, hacks at ten marks or less. There is on the list an animal non-committally described just as a black horse, valued at

This statue of the great second century AD Roman Emperor, Marcus Aurelius, dominates the surrounding area from Rome's Piazza del Campidoglio. The piazza was designed by Michelangelo.

Much early horsemanship was first developed among the peoples of Asia. The Chinese, in particular, realized the value of horses – they even went to war to obtain some of the large horses of the Ferghana Basin. There are many studies of horses in the arts of China, of which this porcelain piece is a fine example.

OPPOSITE ABOVE: The Japanese cavalry played an important part in the country's turbulent history. This eighteenth-century screen painting shows a general dressed in full battle regalia at the battle of the Uji River in 1184.

OPPOSITE BELOW: A relief of the Roman Imperial Period, probably representing Alexander the Great on his famous black steed – Bucephalus.

twenty-four marks.

In the early fourteenth century the art of war was transformed by the dramatic appearance in the battlefields of Scotland and France of the deadliest weapon yet devised by man, the longbow. This was not a super-accurate marksman's weapon, but a cheap instrument of mass destruction. With it a few companies of bowmen could create a beaten zone through which, under the arrow-hail, nothing could pass. Hundreds of clothyard shafts, plunging down from the sky, pierced mail like paper, and transfixed horses, killing or driving them mad with pain and fear. The long supremacy of the armoured knight was over.

The chivalry of France tried to counter this in two ways. First, like the Vikings of old, they dismounted before battle, left their horses in the rear ready for a pursuit (in either direction) and fought on foot. This did not work because, by the time they had plodded forward four or five hundred yards in their heavy mail, shields up, shoulders hunched against the arrows which beat down upon them, they were in no fit state for a hand-to-hand fight against the enemy, fresh and in a position of vantage, who were waiting for them; they certainly could not withstand a cavalry counter-attack.

Next they tried, by piling plate armour on themselves and their unfortunate horses, to purchase immunity from the hail of arrows. But the heavy bodkin-pointed arrow took some stopping: if enough arrows rained down one would surely find a chink, a joint, or a weak spot in the armour. So plate armour became more and more elaborate, expensive and heavy, until by the late fifteenth century the knight's armour weighed as much as 45 kg (100 lbs) and the horse's 36 kg (80 lbs). Add the weight of the saddle, now a massive affair with a pommel built up into a shield, the weapons, and the rider himself who was probably heavier than his ancestors, and you find that by 1500 the charger had to carry anything up to thirty-two stone. A horse bred to carry such a weight was an elephantine creature who could barely break into a ponderous, earth-shaking trot. Successive English kings, culminating in Henry VIII, took strong measures to make horses larger and heavier, importing Great Horses from Flanders and ordering the slaughter, spaying or castration of breeding stock under 15 hands. The knight had succeeded in making himself invulnerable as a tortoise – and as innocuous.

By this time gunpowder was known and even plate-armour was not proof against musket balls, so the Great Horse was almost banished from the battlefield, and relegated to the tiltyard. The tournament itself, once a bloody miniature battle, became a gorgeous spectator-sport, hardly more dangerous than football. The contestants, heavily armoured, their horses protected also by great pads of straw, approached one another at a dignified trot, a barrier between them to prevent a collision, and the saddle was made without a cantle so that the rider, struck fair and square by a blunt lance, could roll off his horse without being hurt.

The four noble horses in front of the façade of Venice's most famous church, St Mark's, are one of the city's familiar landmarks. They are, however, in such urgent need of restoration that they are to be removed.

Nevertheless there developed in the sixteenth and seventeenth centuries, under the aegis of those great *maestri* Federico Grisone of Naples, Antoine de Pluvinel of France and the Duke of Newcastle a highly scientific school of manège riding which was supposed to make a Great Horse handy. The object of all this was to make the Great Horse easy to stop and turn in a melée, and then to teach him various 'airs above the ground' which were supposed to be of use in combat. The curvet, for instance, in which a horse marks time behind while raising his forehand in a half-rear, was said to be 'very necessary to make him keep his head towards an enemy'. Turning on his haunches, the volte, was 'most in use in service, especially in that manner of fight which our English soldiers term fighting at the croup'. By a half-pirouette a horse could clear a space for himself among a crowd of foot soldiers, while he un-manned a crafty enemy creeping up to hamstring him by the *capriole*, a goat-like leap into the air accompanied by a kick with both hind legs. But all this was nonsense: cavalry actions are won not by 'airs above the ground' but by mobility, seizing the fleeting opportunity and the timing and impetus of a charge; and manège training of this kind destroyed all forward impulse. Who, inquired Thomas Blundeville, an English rider with a critical mind, wants a horse which, spurred forward in battle, 'falls a-hopping and a-dancing up and down in one place?'

Cavalry was rescued from this costly futility by Gustavus Adolphus, Prince Rupert and Cromwell, who saw that the horseman's protection against musketry was not armour but speed, the ability to charge home before a second volley can be fired. For these tactics another type of horse was required. Gervase Markham, writing early in the seventeenth century, was perceptive enough, while paying lip service to the Great Horse, to suggest that 'in some kinds of service in the war (especially desperate exploits to be done suddenly, or upon occurrents or discoveries, or any other kind of service wherein either the toughness or the swiftness of the horse is to be tried)' a lighter, faster horse was required, such as was used for hunting. In the English Civil War the cavalry on both sides were mounted, not on Great Horses, but on medium-weight horses (mainly mares and geldings) of 15 to 15·2 hands, and the dragoons on 'good, squat dragoon cobs'.

Useless and far too expensive for war, the Great Horse was also useless as a hunter. For hunting and for the 'wild-goose chase' (a sort of cross-country race over obstacles, enlivened by heavy betting), one needed a horse that was 'long winded, tough, hard' and, above all, able to gallop on 'till he be in that extremity that some suppose he cannot live an hour, yet within two or three hours afterwards be so fresh and courageous as if he had never been laboured'. By the end of the seventeenth century enclosures had made it necessary, or at least desirable, for a hunter to be able to jump – a feat unknown to mediaeval horsemen.

Nor was the Great Horse much joy on a journey, for he had a

rough, uncomfortable trot. For travel, people greatly preferred a hack with comfortable paces, especially Irish 'hobbies' trained to amble. Some nobles, the Duke of Northumberland for instance, rode hobbies on journeys, but mounted a manège-schooled Great Horse for ceremonial rides through towns.

Unsuitable for the battlefield, for hunting and for travel, of what use was the Great Horse apart from providing a rich man with a costly status symbol and a nobleman with a pastime for his ample leisure hours? The Duke of Newcastle had a straight answer to this impertinent question. 'Some wag will ask, what is a horse good for that will do nothing but dance and play tricks? If these gentlemen will retrench everything that serves them either for curiosity or pleasure, and admit nothing but what is useful, they must make a hollow tree their house, and clothe themselves with fig-leaves, feed upon acorns and drink nothing but water. . . . I presume those great wits [the sneering gentlemen] will give Kings, Princes and Persons of Quality leave to love pleasure horses, as being an exercise that is very noble, and makes them appear most graceful when they show themselves to their subjects, or at the head of an army to animate it.'

So the Great Horse as a saddle horse passed into history. His

progeny were employed in the eighteenth century as heavy draught horses, very necessary until roads improved, and are seen today as the Shire, the Suffolk Punch and the Clydesdale. All that was useful in his manège work was perpetuated in High School training and is seen to perfection today in the Spanish Riding School in Vienna.

The period which saw the relegation of the Great Horse to draught work saw also the establishment of the English Thoroughbred. This, as is well known, was produced by crossing Arab stallions (sometimes known as Turks, because they were generally imported from the Ottoman Empire) with the best English hunter mares. Neither breed was itself particularly fast, though both had fine qualities, but their progeny was unbeatable as a racehorse.

Arabs, Barbs and 'Turks' had been imported into England, and even more into France, in small numbers all through the Middle Ages; but it needed Cromwell's methodical mind to systematize the improvement of light horses. His buyers scoured the Near East for likely stallions and brood mares, and all ships' captains in the Mediterranean knew the quickest way to the Lord Protector's favour. Racing had, in the eyes of his more fanatical adherents, a flavour of recusancy, and was banned by the government of the Saints, but when 'the King enjoyed his own again' Charles II, who had a passion for racing, very promptly ordered that 'the seven horses of Oliver Cromwell, said to be the best in England . . . be carried to the Mews for the service of His Majesty'. He imported Arabian mares, known as 'Royal Mares' but generally not named, as well as stallions, in large numbers: the Levant Company was commissioned to obtain annually ten of the highest quality. His expenditure on horseflesh was denounced almost as passionately as expenditure on his amours and his navy. It is to Cromwell's thoroughness and Charles II's extravagance that we owe the Thoroughbred horse.

All Thoroughbreds are descended in the direct male line from one of four Arab stallions and a number of Arab mares. Each of the stallions was of a breed recognized by Arabs as noble, but they were probably not all clean-bred. The Darley Arabian was bought in Aleppo by Thomas Darley in 1706 and brought to England three years later in the modest hope that he 'would not be too much disliked'. A bay with a 'blaze something of the largest', he is believed to be clean bred of the pure Kehilan strain. The Byerley 'Turk' was imported in 1689 and used as an officer's charger in the Irish and French wars. The Godolphin Arabian was bought in 1730 in Paris, where he was found drawing a water-cart. His name was Sham, implying that he came originally from the Damascus area, and he is believed to be of the Jilfan strain, highly respected but not quite as aristocratic as the Kehilan. Fourth of the foundation stallions was the Helmsley Turk. Every racehorse in the world, and a vast number of top class show-jumpers, hunters and event horses, are descended from these famous stallions.

THE HORSE IN THE NEW WORLD

Horses in North America

There was once an equid native to America, but he became extinct many millennia ago. In historic times the first horses in the New World were those landed by Columbus in Hispaniola on his second voyage in 1493. They were five brood mares and twenty stallions, not of the best quality, for the knights who accompanied him were understandably reluctant to risk their chargers on such a dubious enterprise and exchanged them before embarcation for 'sorry hacks'. These were, however, quite impressive enough to overawe and conquer Indians who had never seen a horse. Later imports were of better quality, and had, of course, a strong Arab and Barb strain derived from the Moorish conquest of Spain and the trade of two thousand years. It is a common phenomenon for some animals, introduced into a country where they were previously unknown but where the conditions suit them, to increase and multiply beyond all bounds. They did so on Hispaniola, and soon it was considered quite unnecessary to import any more.

The first horses to land on the North American mainland, in 1519, were eleven stallions – mounts for the cavalry with which Cortés conquered Mexico – five mares and a foal. These do not seem to have escaped and run wild, but no doubt there were plenty of escapes from the horse ranches which Cortés established after the conquest. The ancestry of the feral mustang herds of North America is also traced in romantic legend to the expedition of Hernando de Soto, a tough adventurer who in 1539 led an expedition westward from Florida in search, inevitably, of gold. Three years later, after suffering great hardships, his expedition reached the Mississippi, still vainly torturing any Indians they could catch in order to get news of the precious metal. Of the one hundred and ninety horses with which he had set out, only forty were left, in a pretty poor state, when de Soto himself died on the banks of the great river. The survivors of the expedition built boats to ship the horses downstream; but progress was so slow that they landed to butcher them and dry their meat. Hostile Indians arrived before the job was finished, the Spaniards hurriedly embarked and the four or five horses which were still left alive 'began to neigh and run up and down in such sort that the Indians for fear of them leaped into the water'.

From these, perhaps, were descended the mustang herds who, by the eighteenth century, roamed the western plains in hundreds of thousands. But it seems much more likely that mustangs were descended more prosaically, from breeding stock which had either escaped, been bought or been stolen from Mexican ranches.

Running wild, with neither selective breeding nor grain feeding, these horses lost their good looks and degenerated in size until few were over 13·2 hands. But they retained many qualities of their Arab and Spanish progenitors – toughness, self-reliance and a singular freedom from diseases of the feet and lameness of all kinds. The Indian tribes first hunted them for meat, then learned from Spanish settlers in Mexico to domesticate and ride them. They were quick to see the advantages given by the horse in war and hunting. First to take to horsemanship were the Apache of the south, who in 1680 massacred hundreds of Spaniards and made away with their horses: they even made armour of bull-hide, in imitation of breastplate, cuirass and morion. Then horsemanship spread all across the plains, through Ute, Pawnee and Comanche to the Blackfoot tribe along the Canadian border. In an astonishingly short time a whole new culture had developed, based on this new and invaluable acquisition. Braves buffalo-hunted and raided on horseback: they shampooed their long hair with horse-blood, made horse fat into tallow, and horse-sinews into bowstrings; they used the skin of the shins for leggings and the skin of the hocks for shoes. Horses were employed to draw the travois, for bride-prices, for ransoms and fines, for currency, for funeral celebrations and for sacrifice. Indian braves, particularly the Comanche, developed methods of catching and taming wild horses and a natural style of equitation as effective and graceful as any in the world.

The mustang herds and the Indian horse-culture for a long time made no contact with other types of horses and another horse culture which were spreading westward from the Atlantic seaboard. French settlers in Canada, and English and Dutch settlers in New England and Virginia, had brought with them the larger horses of northern Europe. We do not know much about them: presumably they brought the horses they used at home, the farmers their heavy carthorses, the gentry their hunters and hacks. The first Thoroughbred was landed in Virginia in 1730: Bulle Rock, reputedly sired by the Darley Arabian.

There was in the new colonies an unlimited demand for horses, unmatched by care in looking after them. A Jamestown parson in 1688 even reported to the Royal Society his parishioners' poor and callous horsemanship. 'They neither shoe nor stable them; some few gentlemen may be something more curious, but it is very rare. Yet they ride pretty smartly, a Planter's Pace is a proverb, which is a good, smart, hard gallop.' To this unsatisfactory picture a French visitor added, 'All the care they take of them at the end of a journey is to unsaddle, feed a little Indian corn and so, all covered with sweat, drive them out into the woods where they eat what they can find even though it is freezing.' Evidently horses by the late eighteenth century were plentiful and cheap.

Different conditions in the New World developed some

excellent new breeds of horse. Highly valued for long journeys was the Narragansett Pacer, perhaps bred from the Irish Hobby but now alas extinct. 'These are very spirited and carry both head and tail high. But what is most remarkable is that they amble with more speed than most horses trot, so that it is difficult to put some of them upon a gallop.' Smooth-paced and surefooted, they greatly appealed to intrepid 'females who were obliged to travel over the roots and holes in the New Countries'.

Virginian squires brought with them the aristocratic values of Royalist England, including a love of racing. But a full-scale racecourse was expensive and difficult for widely scattered planters to construct, and the dirt roads had too many twists and turns for racing. So their races became quarter-mile sprints, on private estates or down the main street of a town. (At Lexington this became such a nuisance that it had to be prohibited by law.) The sport was established before the Revolutionary War, when a traveller wrote, 'They are much attached to quarter-racing, which is always a match between two horses to run a quarter of a mile, straight out. . . . They have a breed which performs it without astounding velocity.'

'Without astounding velocity'. . . So the horses ridden in these races were at first not particularly well bred. A quick start from a standstill, rather than sustained speed, was what they needed, so a Quarter Horse has well-muscled quarters, rather heavy shoulders and a short back. He is a stockier animal altogether than the Thoroughbred, resembling more a heavyweight polo pony, or a Portuguese bullfighting horse. Indeed the horses first used for quarter-racing probably had a dash of Iberian blood from the Spanish settlements in the south. But speed was to be added to the mix, for all modern Quarter Horses are supposed to be descended from Janus, a stocky Thoroughbred stallion imported into Virginia in 1752. As the breed was only formally established by the formation of the American Quarter Horse Association in 1941, some of the pedigrees may well be taken with a grain of salt. But the Quarter Horse blood needed to be constantly refined by crossing with Thoroughbreds to correct common faults such as heavy shoulders and withers, thick, upright pasterns and, in general, a tendency to coarseness.

There was in 1795 a Vermont schoolteacher called Justin Morgan, who was also a farmer, a musician and a horseman – or at least a man with a good eye for a horse. In settlement of a bad debt he accepted a smallish bay colt named Figure, probably Thoroughbred, who made himself generally useful round the farm, won an occasional country race, made a bit of money for Justin by hauling huge logs for a wager and with all this proved to be a fast, comfortable hack. That there was nothing particular about Figure in his lifetime; that he was rather a Jack-of-all-trades and master of none is indicated by the fact that after Justin's death his new owner turned him out in the winter snow, like any other old horse, where he was eaten by wolves. What nobody realized until after his death was that poor Figure had excelled as a sire. Numerous first-class horses were identified later as Figure's get, and inherited all his versatile strength, willingness, courage and intelligence. The Morgan horse became a byword for an equine all-rounder. He is generally under 15 hands, with high head and tail carriage, a deep wide chest, shortish legs, good sloping shoulders, strong quarters and a beautiful, intelligent Arab head. He should be a dark bay. In the days of horsed cavalry he made the perfect charger, sought after by 'Yellowlegs' from General Sheridan downwards, and is now one of the most popular breeds in the United States. Thoroughbred and Quarter Horse enthusiasts both claim Figure for their own, but neither have much hard evidence to support their passionate partisanship. Figure was the perfect specimen of the horse that everyone wants – the horse which does everything and costs nothing. His progeny have proved particularly tenacious of the former quality.

The Tennessee Walking Horse is another example of a breed developed in America for a specific purpose. Southern plantation owners, especially those of riper years and ample bank balances, were not all dedicated to a life of hard physical exercise under a semi-tropical sun; they wanted a super-hack which would carry them quickly and comfortably while they rode between and inspected row upon row of crops before the first mint-julep of the day. By selective breeding from Morgan, Quarter Horse and Standardbred strains, and patient, meticulous horsemanship, they produced a horse with three gaits, of which the third is peculiar to the breed. They are an ordinary walk, set off in show horses by a cadenced nodding of the head; an easy, luxurious canter; and an extraordinary running walk, smooth and high-stepping, with which a horse carried his owner along at a comfortable nine miles an hour with a minimum of fatigue for horse and rider.

Last of the specialized eastern saddle-horses is the American Saddlebred, of Thoroughbred ancestry, somewhat similar to the Tennessee Walking Horse but without the famous running walk. The ordinary Saddlebred horse has the three natural gaits, walk trot and canter, all very accurately and elegantly performed. The 'five-gaited' horse has, in addition, two artificial gaits, which have to be taught. The 'slow gait' is something between a walk and a trot: the horse almost trots in front and walks behind. The 'rack' is a development of the slow gait, with an even rhythm and faster speed. Both are very comfortable for the rider, but tiring for the horse. Finally, there was the eastern harness-horse – the Standardbred, a fast racing trotter, also of Thoroughbred ancestry.

In their new homes, particularly in the blue grass country where the grazing has rich food value, horses flourished, as did racing. The first formal race meeting, apart from quarter-races, was held in Kentucky in 1788, and gentlemen were asked to come armed lest proceedings be rudely interrupted by Indians. In Charlestown, race meetings soon became fashionable social occasions, with ample opportunities for duelling and dalliance; 'youth anticipating its delight for weeks, lovers becoming more ardent, and young damsels setting their caps with greater taste and dexterity . . . the *quality* of the company in attendance . . . the splendid equipages . . . the gentlemen attending in fashionable London-made clothes, buckskin breeches and top-boots.' There is a curious mixture here of sophistication and simplicity, of security and peril, of an elegant social life against a background of silent forests and, perhaps only a few miles away, a painted Indian war-party moving swiftly through the trees. But 'horses and law-suits', observed the French Republican consul in 1793, 'comprise the usual topic of conversations. If a traveller happens to pass by, his horse is appreciated. If he stops, he is presented with a glass of whisky and asked a thousand questions.'

Meanwhile horses had spread all over the middle and far West. First, of course, there were the feral mustang herds and Indian ponies moving up from Mexico. In the late eighteenth century the Spaniards colonized California, bringing from Mexico their fine Spanish horses which were stolen in hundreds by Indian and, indeed, American raiders such as Pegleg Smith and Philip Nolan,

and so came east to enrich the stock of the interior. From Canada and the eastern states voyageurs, traders, farmers and soldiers moved west, taking with them their larger horses of northern Europe. So the mustang strain was strengthened even from the early days by other breeds. Nevertheless it is probably true to say that by the mid-nineteenth century, the start of the short-lived 'cattle kingdom', most Indian ponies and most cow-punchers' ponies were pure mustang; but travellers tales suggest that the best generally bore Spanish brands.

The Indian was in his way a fine horseman, but a bad and utterly callous horsemaster, who regarded ordinary horses as expendable. Believing that a raw back did not hurt a horse when it was warmed up, he thought nothing of riding an animal whose whole back was one bloody wound. He was entirely ignorant of selective breeding. Poor stallions were allowed to run wild and perpetuate their runtish stock, while good ones were reserved for riding. Only one tribe, the Flathead, gelded colts not required for stud; and only the Nez Percé made any attempt at selective breeding to produce their peculiar 'Appaloosa', a grey with black and brown spots and vertically striped hooves. His turned-in forefeet and wide heel with well-developed frog made him safe and surefooted along narrow mountain paths and over rough, slippery ground, while his thin, rat-like tail did not get caught in thorn bushes. But in most tribes the Indian pony, like the feral mustang, had sharply deteriorated from the original Spanish stock.

Nevertheless there is a school of thought which indignantly refutes any suggestion that the mustang lacked any equine virtue except, perhaps, size. It is an emotional, not an intellectual belief, akin to the nineteenth century article of faith that any red-blooded American boy could ride and shoot, particularly if he had been taught neither. But it was not an opinion much voiced in the West in 1840. No doubt there were exceptions, but the average grass-fed mustang was, from the day of his first backing, a docile slug, and small at that. It is not difficult for a six-foot man to ride the devil out of a 13·2 hands pony, which puts Indian and early Western horsemanship into proper perspective. The more realistic contemporary artists show the Western horse as he was in fact, not in glorious technicolour, but a small, quiet animal with a large, common head, a ewe-neck and falling away behind. Most travellers who praised the horses of the Comanche, Apache, Shoshoni, Nez Percé and other tribes reported many Spanish brands among them. Chiefs would pay traders good prices for Spanish or 'American' horses.

Nevertheless the mustang had some excellent qualities. He was intelligent, sure-footed, tough and abstemious; capable, although only grass-fed, of long journeys at a slow pace. Above all he seemed to have an inherited 'cow-sense', and instinctive knowledge, like a sheepdog's, of what a cow or a steer would do, and a delight in frustrating this. Cow-punchers and Indians both achieved their mobility by the 'remuda' system, a herd of spare horses accompanying those being ridden. A working cow-puncher needed for a round-up not less than seven ponies – two morning, two afternoon and two night horses, so that each rested every other day, and one spare. The US cavalry, which really knew its job and for whom the remuda system was not practicable, never rode mustangs if it could get anything else. The Royal North-West Mounted Police, the Mormon elders and most cattle barons took rapid steps to improve the horses they found in the west by the prompt introduction of Thoroughbred, Quarter Horse, Standardbred, Morgan and even Percheron stallions. Not all these experiments were successful: some crosses were too large and clumsy, some did not do well on grass, some lacked 'cow-sense'. But by the end of the nineteenth century the Western horse had been immeasurably improved.

The Western Quarter Horse, in particular, makes a very fine cutting horse and rodeo performer favoured particularly in Texas: Sam Houston was a Quarter Horse lover, and in his state Quarter Horses are sometimes called 'Copperbottoms' after his favourite stallion. Many cattlemen, particularly in California and Colorado, prefer the Thoroughbred, and comparing him with lesser breeds, hold that anything they can do, he can do better. This is probably true of rodeo performers: Jack Hammer, one of the greatest cutting horses California ever produced, is a Thoroughbred; but it may not be true of real range working horses which cannot receive the feeding and care a Thoroughbred requires.

A characteristic of American horse-culture is the great stress laid upon colour, a matter in which European horsemen are generally not much interested. Appaloosas, Palominos, Albinos, even those which are known in the United States as Pintos (in England skewbalds, piebalds or 'coloured horses') have societies dedicated to their glorification and refinement. The Appaloosa may, perhaps, qualify as a separate breed by virtue of certain peculiarities of conformation, but the others really do not, though they are often treated as though they do. Palominos may be beautiful, and therefore command a higher price than equally good horses of less glamorous colours, but that is their only advantage.

Horses in South America

Tradition has it that the foundation stock of all South American horses was a party of five mares and seven stallions imported in 1535 to what is now Buenos Aires and left to run wild when the garrison, besieged and starving, evacuated the post. By 1600, so we are told, their progeny had so increased that they could not be numbered. Tiresome historians, sceptical of legend and hungry for facts, have undermined this excellent tale: why, they ask, did the starving garrison not eat the horses? Answer comes there none. It seems, perhaps, more probable that most South American horses are descended from those brought in far larger numbers to

Peru and Chile between 1532 and 1560.

The pattern of horse breeds in South America is a trifle confused because in different countries different names are given to what is, to all intents and purposes, the same breed. All South American horses are descended mainly from the original Iberian stock, though Thoroughbred blood has been imported from Europe, North America and Australia.

The ordinary cow-horse of the pampas was a larger animal of better quality than the mustang, about 15 hands, short-backed, well ribbed up but a trifle thick and common about the head and neck. They were first-class working horses, well balanced and tractable, with legs and hooves like steel so that they generally worked unshod. Wonderfully handy, a bit of Thoroughbred blood gives them speed, and the Argentine remains about the world's best source of polo ponies – so much so that gauchos complain that their best horses are taken from them and sold at great prices to millionaires. This horse, known in Europe loosely as an Argentine, is known in that country, in Uruguay, Brazil and all over the pampas as the Criollo. He is very similar to that known in Chile as the Chileno.

The varied terrain of Peru produces three distinct types of horse. The Chola, like the Criollo, is essentially a working ranch horse, but of the hills, not the plains. He is shorter in the leg and more heavily built, very apt for scrambling up and down the mountains. The Costena is a miniature show hack, never over 14·3 hands, with a remarkably smooth, extended walk which he can maintain for very long distances at a phenomenal speed. He is wonderfully comfortable to ride, and deserves to be much better known outside his own country. Finally there is in the high Andes, living out of doors up to 13,000 feet in all weathers, a small, tough mountain pony known as the Morochuca.

The wonderful thing about horses in the Americas is the variety which flourish there in their original state or developed to suit local needs. Ireland may breed Thoroughbreds better than any in the world, the Waler is unequalled as a working horse, the best Iberian horses may be found in Spain – but in North and South America Iberian, Thoroughbred and north European working horse strains met under conditions ideal for horsebreeding. With these various breeds, refined and specialized, is found an extraordinarily varied collection of horse cultures and schools of horsemanship. Hunting, racing, showing, jumping, rodeo and ranching are all practised to a high degree of skill, and have in the Americas the horses they deserve.

THE HORSE IN WAR

'The state is founded on the horse's back' was a true saying for 4000 years. Man's domestication of the horse, coupled with his learning to ride and drive it, shaped the course of history. As soon as he combined it with the use of stones and a sling, the horse was invaluable for hunting food and for war.

The centre of the Old World was the source of the horses that regularly recur in the history of mounted warfare. It comprised a region on the mountain slopes of Afghanistan known as Ferghana and Bactria, and there is credible evidence that a type of wild horse lived there, superior to the native ponies of other parts of Asia. The area was inhabited by crop farmers, a settled people with a highly organized irrigation system, defences similar to the Great Wall of China, and with a warrior caste of armed charioteers.

Tribes of raiding nomadic herdsmen, who already practised castration, would have turned their mares out to mate with the wild stallions. Cave drawings exist that show tall, 'superior' horses coupling with small mares, and as wild strains are prepotent, the characteristics began to be distributed over the ancient world. Migrations of mounted herdsmen were limited to latitudes which provided climate and grazing to support their horses, but knowledge of the excellence of these horses spread to the grain-growing, chariot-driving settlements from the Indus to the Euphrates and the Nile.

The first specific mention of 'superior' horses comes from China, where records tell us that 'blood-sweating', 'heavenly' horses existed in Taiyuan in Turkestan. The discovery was made by Chang Ch'ien, envoy of the then emperor, Wu-ti, who journeyed in the lands west of the Kunlun and Pamirs between 138 and 126 BC. At the time there was urgent need for faster mounts than the Mongolian-type pony to carry messengers between forts along the Great Wall when smoke signals were obscured by mist. Some of these were eventually acquired by exchanging them for an emperor's daughter; more were obtained by besieging a town until the terms of surrender – a supply of horses – were honoured.

The man on a horse had, and still has, a psychological as well as a physical advantage. For kings and rulers the horse was a symbol of pomp and majesty and they sat on saddle cloths of skin. To people who had never seen a horse it was such an awesome sight it gave rise to the centaur legends, which together with depictions of horses with wings or horses rising from the sea, helped sustain fear of horsemen. A Kassite seal shows a centaur shooting arrows backwards; proof that from very early times mounted nomads used this weapon in a way perfected by the Parthians, who fired arrows over their shoulders when retreating.

Non-riding peoples had to learn equitation and, in addition, how to use a short bow or lance, and to throw a spear from horseback. The King of Assyria said to Hezekiah, King of Judah, 'I will deliver thee 2000 horses if thou be able on thy part to set men on them'. The Pharaohs were charioteers until the advances of the Medes and Persians, but the migrating tribes were born in wagons, and given horses before they could walk. They ate, slept, relieved themselves, and held all their conferences on horseback. Men, women, and children literally lived on horseback and were followed by herds of horses; they drank mare's milk, and each warrior had a spare horse to change on to, to be eaten as food (sometimes a vein was opened and men drank the blood), or to be tied together to form a defence at the rear of an army. When riding their swift, lightly-burdened horses they were a constant threat to settled peoples, even those better armed. The Assyrians and Persians boasted that they taught their children to ride, to shoot, and to tell the truth. Plato wrote 'we must mount our children on horseback to see war in order that they may learn to ride'.

Western Europe was a land of forest and swamp; Germanic tribes in the Danube basin did not use arrows but a spear, nor did they ride, since their horses were too small to carry a man and in winter had hair 12 cm (5 ins) long. Later they used horsemen – such as the Alans and Sarmatians – as mercenaries. Horses and riding spread west by two main routes: one north of the Black Sea and the Alps, the other along both shores of the Mediterranean.

The Scythians of Central Asia spread as far west as Ireland, where until the Anglo-Norman invasion they guided their horses with a crooked stick and a halter with a single rein. These Scythians took horses with them wherever they went; they could swim wide rivers with them, floating their wagons by tying hides around them. In addition they knew how to work metal. In the fourth century, Chinese charioteers began to be replaced by horsemen wearing Scythian-type helmets. Among their successors were the Parthians (the name means 'prick' or 'spur') who, like the Medes and other nomadic tribes, merged with – or became subject to – others who gained temporary ascendancy, for the existence of a horde ended when its pastures became horse-sick. Strabo said the Parthians were originally an army of slaves trained in riding and archery, who wore scale armour made from hoof and horn. Taking prisoners as slaves was always one great objective of raids.

Bactria was astride the famous Silk Route, which gradually developed into a trade route of 9650 km (6000 miles). Along it, or at least along parts of it, moved many significant influences of the civilized world, most of which depended on horses. The city badge of Bactria was a galloping horse; its coins showed armoured men on horses who carried long spears, and tribal names meant 'golden horses' and 'well-schooled horses'.

Horse-borne trade reached to the corners of the known world: Chinese and Persian objects were found in the Pazyryk burial mounds in Siberia. The Medes joined the Bactrians and struggled for centuries with the Assyrians. The Persians, who first fought from chariots, adopted riding under Cyrus, who founded their cavalry. When he failed to be adopted as overlord of Bactria he married the daughter of the defeated Median king, thus achieving his ambition. Then, with the help of Bactrian cavalry, he conquered Lydia under King Croesus by placing camels in front of the King's horsemen, which caused the Lydian horses to panic. His successor, Cambyses II, conquered Egypt and founded the Persian Empire of the sixth century BC.

The Etruscans, who inhabited an area around Rome, are thought to be of Lydian origin. Certainly sculpture from Tarquinae is of magnificent horses, with wings, and wearing simple ring snaffle bits and breastplates. The legendary Sybarites, also of Italy, taught their horses to dance to music. Their enemies, the Crotons, sent spies to learn the tunes, which they then played just before battle. The Sybarites' horses began to dance and their riders were defeated.

At a time when the Indians were still using the onager, a kind of wild ass, Persian troops wore bronze helmets; their auxiliary Bactrians had infantry weapons, and the Sagartian herdsmen were equipped with daggers and lassoes. Persian 'Nisaean' horses – from Nisaea, the lower parts of Bactria – were so much coveted that after an Assyrian victory a tribute to them was demanded. On a stele to commemorate an Athenian warrior, dated about 400 BC, is shown a youth on a horse that today would pass for a small Thoroughbred, such was its conformation and quality.

Horses in the Greek World
A little nucleus of states in the Aegean became Greece, and there is much evidence handed down of the importance of the horse to its civilization. There are pictures on ceramics, an important book written by Xenophon, a cavalry master (430–355 BC) on horses and horsemanship. In Homer's poems, the Greeks are reported as driving, but seldom riding, although their messengers were mounted. There is a story that when wild cattle came down from the hills and destroyed the crops, the King of Thessaly offered a big reward to anyone who could drive them off. Some youths unharnessed chariot horses, never before ridden, and chased the cattle away, whereupon they realized the value of riding, became bandits, and attacked the king.

Xenophon was a follower of Socrates and belonged to the Equestrian class, who provided their own horses and equipment. A picture on a vase shows young men being examined vaulting on their horses with a spear, as a scribe writes down their marks. Xenophon wrote his *Hippike* for his two sons, both of whom served in the cavalry, one being killed in action.

After taking part in the Peloponnesian War (431–404 BC), Xenophon joined a Greek army going to aid Persia, primarily as an historian. After their defeat, however, he was elected to lead a retreat of 10,000 which took two years to reach the Black Sea, passing over the ruins of Sennacherib palace. Xenophon was able to study the weaknesses and strength of the Persian army, as well as the horsemanship of other lands. He said the Persians galloped their horses downhill and they were as sound as Greek horses; he also noted the method of 'mounting Persian fashion' when a servant or prisoner offered his back for his master to step on, which he thought useful for the wounded.

Alexander the Great may have profited by Xenophon's knowledge of Persian cavalry. At the age of twenty, having inherited his father's Macedonian cavalry, he defeated the Thebans, took Asia Minor from the Persians, and conquered Egypt before defeating Darius and bringing the Persian Empire to an end. A Pompeian mosaic shows Alexander in a high war chariot with saw-tooth wheels, but it was with cavalry that he was a master of strategy, using mounted archers and lancers. He was a great admirer of the Bactrian horse, mounting his army on them on his way to India. He chose his charger from some young horses brought by dealers for his father to choose. Its broad, concave forehead and large eyes must have seemed bovine to western eyes, which was why it was given its name – Bucephalus (Ox-face). Bucephalus carried Alexander in his Asian campaigns, dying in India in 326 BC.

When the Greeks colonized southern Italy they took thousands of horses to Taranto, and when they colonized Cyrenaica they took Bactrian horses. The Libyans became noted horse breeders and trainers, copying the quadriga method of harnessing chariot horses (i.e. four horses abreast). When Darius conquered Barka in Cyrenaica he transferred the population back to Bactria, thus distributing more horses.

Romans and Barbarians

The Romans were at first a land army of charioteers and infantry. Their roads were so good they could drive through much of the Empire. In Asia Minor they employed auxiliary cavalry, but on one occasion were defeated by the Parthians; when they extended the Empire to North Africa they were obliged to use mounted soldiers against the Carthaginians. Numidian horses were descendants of the Bactrian type. The Numidian people, who at first supported the Carthaginian, Hannibal, changed sides as a result of Roman diplomacy after the battle of Cannae, in which the Romans were defeated, and back in North Africa, they supported the Romans.

It was the Celts, heirs to the Iron Age, who brought their skills in working metal and building forts when they spread from Asia Minor to the Rhine and on to Gaul. Three waves continued to the

British Isles. The 'Celtic pony' was native to the Celtic areas but had bigger relatives; it was Julius Caesar's express intention to conquer Britain for gold and chariot horses, and no doubt Gaul had excellent chariot horses, for their chiefs were buried sitting up in their chariots. This is a description of what Caesar thought ideal tactics for charioteers: 'At the first onset the warriors drove the cars in all directions, hurled their javelins and by the din and clatter of horses and wheels, commonly threw the ranks of the enemy into disorder. Then making their way among them, they leaped down and fought on foot; little by little the charioteers withdrew in such a way that if hard pressed they could readily retreat, thus affording the mobility of cavalry and the steadiness of infantry. Daily practice enabled them to pull up at full speed on a slope.' In fact the chariot wheels often became clogged or jammed together, and horses stampeded.

The Romans fought dismounted at Cannae, having first tethered their horses. At first, they wore only a leather cuirass and used a leather shield, but raids by Germanic tribes resulted in their forming a cavalry corps under its own commander, which enabled them to hold their own against the Alans. These warriors threw spears but later changed to bows and arrows. After them came the

western Huns, skilful archers, who first appeared among the Goths.

The Romans developed a recognizable saddle although it had no tree. These, and wider use of the horseshoe, were landmarks in equestrian progress. At first a metal plate was bound to the hoof with a leather sock, but by the fifth century a horseshoe was in use with a wavy outline where the nailholes were punched. The ideal horse at the time had clustering locks, a flowing mane and tail, a huge crest, a small head, and a restless disposition.

After the Visigoths sacked Rome, hordes of barbarians ebbed and flowed. The Franks moved into Gaul and the last Germanic tribes, the Lombards, brought horses from Pannonia and are depicted on a shield found in Switzerland riding useful 'half-bred' horses. During these centuries western Europe was formed, as nations emerged from anonymity, and they developed their own bigger, heavier, horses.

By the time of Christ horses had spread, through the medium of commerce and war, so that suitable types for military purposes were available in most countries. The Jews were not horse owners because Moses had forbidden them to take horses to the Promised Land. (Job, whose description of war horses is so well known, was a Jordanian and wrote of Bedouin horses.) By now the light, steppe/nomad horse lived east of a line through Poland and Hungary, and the coarser type was found to the west. It began to increase in size as a result of better food as more land came under cultivation, and from crosses of 'oriental' blood.

Islam and the West

Then another horse-borne force – the Arabs – appeared transformed by the Prophet Mohammed (c. AD 570–632) from seafaring people and sheep and camel herdsmen. He promised eternal paradise to men killed in battle, and the indulgence of Allah to every sinner who gave a grain of barley to a horse, on whose back, he said, was a seat of honour. He encouraged breeding, the female line being considered the more important, and pedigrees were hung round the mares' necks. When he died his best horses were to be found in the Nejd region from whence came the Kehilan strain of Arabian horse. They were treated as household pets, slept in the tents with the family, and were fed with scraps of fish and meat. The characteristics of hard feet, great speed and courage, and exceptional temperaments still persist. A British cavalry officer wrote that Arab horsemen could gallop, turn, and halt with no saddle and only a halter, better than British dragoons could with a heavy bit. In British hands, the Arab horses pulled and hotted up. He also said that Arab grooms could restore order when horses broke loose in camp, while his own men shouted and cursed and caused further confusion.

The Saracens overran Egypt and part of Asia, then swept through North Africa to Europe. They were halted short of Paris by Charles Martel in AD 720, his knights being mounted on bigger and stronger horses. When Charlemagne defeated the Avars soon afterwards, the age of chivalry began and European horsemen regarded themselves as invincible. Unpaid knights kept themselves in readiness, modelling themselves on Charlemagne's nephew, Roland, and chivalry formed a bond where ideas were exchanged and horses and skills were tested in jousts and tournaments. A nobleman of Anjou wrote a code of rules, and he described manoeuvres such as wheeling in a closed field.

Soon western Europe was united against the threat of Islam and the Crusades began. European horses were already sizeable animals and great impetus was given to their improvement from the tenth to the fourteenth centuries as forests and swamps were replaced by fields of crops, towns, and better communications. King John imported 100 draught stallions; Saumur, Limousin and Ardennes gained reputations for fine horses, and Norman, Flemish and Danish horses increased in size to meet the demands of trade and war.

However, a glimpse of the future is seen in the itineraries of the Crusaders. 'The infidels, not being weighed down with heavy armour like our knights, were always able to outstrip them in pace and were constant trouble. When charged they were wont to fly and their horses were more nimble than any others in the world; one may liken them to swallows for swiftness.'

The Empires of Asia

In Asia, Genghis Khan built an empire, beginning with a few disciplined leaders on hardy ponies which grew to an army of 400,000. Independent corps were linked by messengers who could cover 400 km (250 miles) in twenty-four hours, preceded by spies. They excelled in tactics, fought with clouds of arrows, and taught the horses to swerve at the sound of a quiver being shaken. Hunting for food when mounted was forbidden, to save the horses. The hordes poured through a gate in China's Great Wall, left open by a bribed frontier tribe; they defeated the Persians, pursuing them as far as India, and Genghis' grandson overran Poland and Hungary, going as far as Moscow.

One hundred and fifty years later Timur (Tamerlane), with better horses and the use of lance and scimitar, built another empire. Pincer movements, relentless pursuit taking many prisoners, and a veteran guard for a final attack took his army to the river Don in Russia and as far south as Delhi. It also cut off the Ottoman emperor at Ankara, capturing him and all his supplies. This brought letters of congratulation from three Christian kings. Marco Polo described the horses he saw on the old trade routes as very swift, never shod, and able to carry a rider down hills so steep and at a speed that other horses could scarcely follow.

Islam flourished in Europe, but the Arab world was threatened by the Turks – nomads from central Asia on 'Turcoman' horses. These animals were tall and conditioned to the privations of long raids during which their only food was barley rolled into balls with sheep's fat. They endured drastic sweating under felt rugs, picketing in the open with increasing weights piled on them, douches of icy water, and days of starvation. The Circassian Turks seized power for twenty-six dynasties; in the sixteenth century Osmanli Turks prevailed. The Turks were often mercenaries; fearless horsemen mounted on horses which came to be known as 'Turks' and are some of the ancestors of the modern Thoroughbred. Under el-Nasser, the Arabs held back both Turks and Mongols. He bred horses from Syrian stock, supervised the covering of mares, and paid astronomical sums in gold for suitable bloodlines. There was stabling in Cairo for three thousand, with training grounds for cavalry, dressage arenas, and places where riders practised shooting at a dove in a cage at full gallop. Camels were ridden on the march, the riders changing onto mares (they considered stallions too noisy) for the charge.

The New World

In 1519 Cortés took fifteen horses to the New World. His successor, Pizarro, failing to reach the Inca gold until his second expedition, picked up some poor, wretched horses, refusing to put them down as he realized their value. But he did not expect the terror they instilled into a formerly aggressive army of Aztecs who fled before him. When a rider fell from his horse, the Aztecs were dumbfounded. They had thought the 'creature' was indivisible, like the centaur.

Queen Isabella did much to further riding by establishing vast studs of Andalusian horses. Her son became Charles V, who financed Columbus' expeditions to North America. The Indians he found there were of Mongolian origin and had never seen a horse, but they quickly adapted to riding, using the same style as the nomads of Asia. They had wooden saddles or a blanket and rawhide bridles, and learned to lie along the horses' side at full gallop, there protected from enemy fire. With one heel hooked in a groove in the saddle they fired arrows from under their horse's neck.

Herds of wild horses had flourished in the New World, providing a stock, later implemented by imports from Europe of heavy draught horses, carriage horses and the English Thoroughbred, which became the mounts of soldiers in the various wars that ensued. General Lee was said to have had particularly fine horses. The US cavalry was created during the Revolutionary War by Baron von Steuben. After the war the US government used mounted troops to subdue Indian tribes in the West, of which General George A. Custer's Seventh Cavalry, of 'Custer's Last Stand' fame, was the most notable. The army instituted a 'remount' breeding programme in which Thoroughbreds were crossed with other breeds and types to create a supply of suitable light cavalry horses. The role of equestrian troops in warfare declined during the century and the army abolished the mounted cavalry in 1948.

THE HORSE IN ART

With a few significant exceptions the horse and art meet only coincidentally, and with the same exceptions, there is no field of art devoted exclusively to the horse as there is, for instance, to the portrait or to landscape. Pictures of 'The Duke of Omnium on his charger Fleetfoot' abound, but pictures of 'The Duke of Omnium's charger Fleetfoot' are much more difficult to find! This is particularly true of the period before the late seventeenth century when the English horse painters began to get into their stride.

Of course, prior to the English painters, the horse did appear in art, but most usually he was playing a secondary role. In one picture he provides a convenient podium for a small man who wants to look important, in another he gives a rouch of animation to an otherwise flat landscape, while in a third he is required to paw the air to underline the marshal bearing of his rider. In all three he is a convenient prop to the main action.

Notable among the exceptions is the Chinese tradition of equine art. Strangely enough, despite his warlike connections with Huns, Mongols and Tartars, the Chinese horse is for the most part a peaceable animal. Pastoral and hunting scenes far outnumber those of battle, and although pictures of the war-horse, his ears laid back, mouth agape and one forefoot pawing the air, do exist they are nowhere near as commonplace as pictures of the small, fat, close-coupled, everyday working breed.

Sport, usually in the form of hunting, and the horse have always been closely connected in art and this is also well substantiated in Chinese art. The Chinese custom of painting on scrolls has lent its own form of dynamism to this type of picture. As the scroll is unrolled the same huntsman can be seen in a series of situations progressing up to the final excitement of the kill. These 'moving' pictures were particularly popular during the Ming dynasty (AD 1368–1644), but the zenith of Chinese equine art had come well before this, in the T'ang dynasty (AD 618–906). This was the time of the famous funerary statuettes and the pictures of Han Kan, court and horse painter to the Emperor Hsuan-tsung. Han Kan cannot have wanted for subjects, for his patron was said to have stabled more than 40,000 horses, but unfortunately, like so many of the treasures of this period, no completely authenticated examples of his work have survived. The Chinese reverence for tradition, however, with its emphasis on slavishly copying what has gone before, has ensured that Han Kan's style has not been completely lost. For many years after his death his pupils carefully and skilfully copied his work as an act of respect, thus giving us some idea of their master's genius.

The reverence for tradition has also ensured that certain themes run like a thread through many hundreds of years of Chinese art. One such theme, recurring regularly from the T'ang to the Ming dynasties, is that of horses and grooms, with one of its better exponents being the eleventh-century artist and poet, Li Lung-mien. His scroll of five western horses and their grooms captures to perfection the gentleness and power of the animal subject and does full justice to the human, while neither is subordinated to the other.

Tradition can also create stagnation, and by the Ming dynasty horse pictures were becoming marvellous, but spiritless, decorations. As works of art they had run their course, albeit an immensely long one. The time-span involved is huge, but at least it is capable of comprehension. That of the cave paintings of the limestone valleys of south-west Europe, on the other hand, is less so. Well over 10,000 years ago man, who had yet to discover bronze, iron, the wheel and a host of other aids to development, was sufficiently advanced artistically to draw and paint the bison, deer and small, clean-headed horses of Altamira and Lascaux. There is no clear reason why he did it; it cannot have been purely for artistic reasons, as the paintings are so often in places where they cannot be seen properly – even with modern lighting equipment. The most likely explanation is that they were a combination of artistic expression and ritualistic magic, probably connected with hunting. The horse figures widely in hunting scenes, but unfortunately more often as the quarry than the pursuer. At Aviege there is a picture of a bridled horse dating from about the same time, suggesting domestication, even in those early days.

The realism of the animals is uncanny. Hunger is said to sharpen the senses, so perhaps the pictures were drawn by a very unsuccessful hunter with correspondingly heightened powers of observation. Certainly the man who carved a stag's horn found in the Pyrenees had exceptional powers. In carving three running deer he captured, with almost photographic accuracy, the leg movements of the animal, something which subsequent artists were unable to recapture until the camera came to their aid. Some of them came very close and some of them went to great lengths to do so. The French artist Meissonier, for instance, constructed a miniature railway so he could ride on a trolley alongside a galloping horse to record its movements. It did not help him and he had to fall back upon the stylized forms of gallop developed down the years to represent the true movement.

The earliest edition of this style, although by no means the earliest use of it, is the form used by van Dyck in his portrait of Prince Thomas von Savoyen, by Velasquez in his portrait of King Philip IV, and by Leonardo da Vinci in his studies for the Sforza monument. In all these pictures the horse stands squarely on his back legs and rears up in an unnatural, but strangely effective, representation of the gallop.

The contemporary artist, Lionel Edwards, has questioned whether this pose was in fact even meant to be a gallop, certainly among its later examples. He points out that both van Dyck and Velasquez were living at a time when riding was an art. It would not be surprising, therefore, if these two courtiers flattered the pretentions of their sitters by placing them on a horse performing one or other of the movements of *haute école*. What has been accepted as a rather stylized form of gallop may, in fact, be the levade, that is a half-rear with bent hocks. Edwards' objection is undoubtedly reasonable, and probably in many of the later cases correct. However, substantially the same position has, without a doubt, been used both before and after van Dyck to represent the gallop.

As time went on the rear became lower and lower until it became the rocking-horse gallop beloved of such eighteenth century painters as Sartorius and Alken. In this movement the horse stretches out, but with its back feet still firmly planted on the ground. The attitude is intended to suggest movement, but it does not do so very successfully for the position of the hind feet makes it unimaginable that the horse could possibly take another step! Although van Dyck's was not a natural galloping position, it was at least one which gives an idea of movement. In an attempt to improve the rocking-horse position a minor correction was eventually made whereby the horse no longer stood all square on his hind feet, but only the tips of his hooves touched the ground.

Who finally took the plunge and lifted all four feet off the ground in the *ventre à terre* position is not known for certain, but this position is a familiar sight in the racing prints of the mid-nineteenth century. It lasted, quite effectively, until the camera of Eadweard Muybridge finally revealed all.

In an essay on art, a paragraph on a photographer may appear incongruous but the influence of Muybridge is great enough to warrant more than a passing mention. Born in Kingston-upon-Thames, England, in 1830 under the more prosaic name of Edward Muggeridge, Muybridge emigrated to America where he became involved with the experiments of the railway millionaire, Leland Stanford, to analyse the movements of a trotting horse. Using a number of cameras, the shutters of which were opened by a wire tripped by the passing horse, Muybridge was able to take a series of silhouette photographs which showed not only the sequence of the trot, but also of the canter and the gallop. His plates opened the floodgates for hundreds of 'realistic' pictures, but strangely enough there were more bad horse paintings after Muybridge than before him. This was basically for two reasons: first because the novelty of the discovery attracted many artists with little or no knowledge of conformation and who would not have otherwise attempted the subject; and, more importantly, because photographic accuracy is not necessarily a good thing, especially when trying to convey movement. A photograph freezes action and freezing is the negation of movement.

Contemporary opinion, while interested, was far from unanimous in praising the newly revealed truth. As one disillusioned viewer put it: 'The animal is seen in a series of grotesque positions, seeming at one time endeavouring to draw himself, legs and body, into a heap, and at others as if attempting to sling himself apart'. A new form of artistic gallop was needed, based on the photograph, but not absolutely copying it. While this requirement was being developed towards the end of the nineteenth century, horse art sank into a temporary decline.

Even in a subject with a merely coincidental acquaintance with the horse, a jump from the Stone Age paintings of Lascaux to the photographs of Muybridge leaves out an unjustifiable amount. For instance, it leaves out the heavily stylized horses of the Egyptian tombs, the equestrian statues of Rome and the magnificent reliefs of the Assyrians, one of the finest of which, from Kuyunjik or Nineveh, is now in the British Museum in London. This masterpiece is a triumphant presentation of bursting energy, with the horse, whether in battle or hunting, being particularly well portrayed. Here there is no question of his being a stage prop: he is as much a part of the action as his royal master, eagerly pressing forward with life and spirit. It was to be 200 years before the Greeks were to recapture such vitality, and it is questionable whether they did anything more than equal it.

The supreme example of Greek equine art is also to be found in the British Museum. It is the frieze from the Parthenon, known as the Elgin Marbles, and it contains some of the finest examples of ridden horses ever attempted. The Greeks idealized the human form, and the horsemen of the Parthenon, sitting bareback on their mounts in a wonderfully natural manner, rival the very best of the athletic statues. Here again the riders and the horses have equal artistic importance with neither one being dominant. From the Kuyunjik relief of circa 650 BC to the Athens of 438 BC the horse, for a brief moment, is given a place in Western art which was to undeservedly escape him for the next 2000 years.

European art as we know it from our galleries begins with the Florentines and Sienese of the thirteenth century. Their subjects were religious in content and, but for one man, would not play any part in this story. For all its virtues, early Italian art appears heavily stylized and formal to the modern eye. One of the reasons for this is the lack of appreciation of perspective, a fault which Paolo Uccello (1397–1475) recognized and went all out to rectify. Besides his experiments with perspective, Uccello reintroduced the profane into art. His battle picture, *Sant' Egidio*, otherwise known as *The Rout of San Romano*, created the ancestors of all those thousands of canvas rocking-horses which were to follow. For some reason, Uccello painted many of his horses red.

Sant' Egidio was an early work, however, and in his later pictures he began to strive for realism. His freedom from religious artistic ties enabled him to paint one of the earliest European mounted portraits, that of the English mercenary John Hawkwood. Because of its realism, this portrait is a landmark in a style of art which had previously been rather stilted and symbolic. The horse is certainly real enough, and is based on a study of the classical bronze horses of St Mark's church in Venice. For that reason it is a magnificent animal, but with one rather disconcerting fault; it appears to be walking with both its off-fore and off-hind legs off the ground at the same time and so is in imminent danger of falling over! Considering that Uccello was working in an artistic vacuum, with no predecessors and no immediate followers, criticism of him on this score is somewhat unfair.

Uccello was a man with an enquiring mind, just like his successor Leonardo da Vinci. In fact the horse in art seems to attract the scientific enquirer. Uccello conquered the problems of perspective; much later George Stubbs was not content merely to paint horses but had to dissect them to see how they worked, and there can never have been a greater searcher after truth than Leonardo da Vinci. As a competent horseman in his own right, da Vinci had a sympathy with his equine subjects, further enhanced by his ironic contempt for man. 'Man has a great endowment of judgement, but the greater part thereof is empty and deceitful. The animals have little, but that little is useful and true.' He must have written these words in despair when, after years of work sketching and modelling in clay, he was told that his project for the Sforza equestrian statue could not proceed as the bronze was required to cast cannon.

Unfortunately very little remains of Leonardo's horses, so we cannot consider how he reflected this 'useful and true' judgement in them. What we do know, from his sketches for the Sforza monument now at Windsor Castle, is that he fully understood, and could portray accurately, the conformation of the horse. Like Stubbs, his knowledge came from a scientific study of anatomy and, again like Stubbs, he wrote and illustrated a treatise on the subject. Unfortunately this work is another casualty of time, from which only a few isolated drawings have survived. It is said to have influenced Dürer, however, and there is some evidence to show that Rubens knew of it, although whether he made any use of it is uncertain.

With Rubens (1577–1640), big women and heavy horses came into fashion. Rubens caught the vitality of his subjects, including that of his horses, as no one before him had succeeded in doing. Religion was still a predominant theme, but not so much as in the past. There was now room for secular paintings and Rubens covered them all, from landscapes to battle scenes, from portraits to hunts. In the latter it has been suggested that his choice of horse sometimes let him down, as, for instance, in *The Lion Hunt*, where demonstrably eastern riders bestride equally demonstrably Flemish mounts. The horses, however, are real, making a refreshing change from the stiff wooden animals of previous years, even if they do all originate from Rubens' own carriage horses, as has been asserted.

Rubens ran his studio on the lines of a factory, in which the essentials of the pictures were the concern of the master, but the details were left to competent workmen. In a number of the master's pictures, horses were still 'details' and as such were often contracted out to the more than competent Frans Snyders (1579–1657).
As a specialist in the hunting scene, not only was Snyders useful to Rubens but he also enjoyed quite a high reputation in his own right. Unlike the later English variety, Snyders' hunts were full of ferocity and drama, involving horses, wild boar, lions and even crocodiles. He helped to pave the way for the Woottons and the Seymours of the English shires, although his melodrama had to be somewhat watered down.

Whether or not Rubens painted all his own horses, his work has had immense influence on subsequent equine art, especially in France, where the horse has fared well, artistically speaking, in the hands of Delacroix, Morot, Géricault, Bonheur and numerous others, including the great Degas. Both Delacroix, with his *Fighting Horses*, and Géricault, with his *Charging Chasseur* show more than a trace of the impetuous dynamism of Rubens.

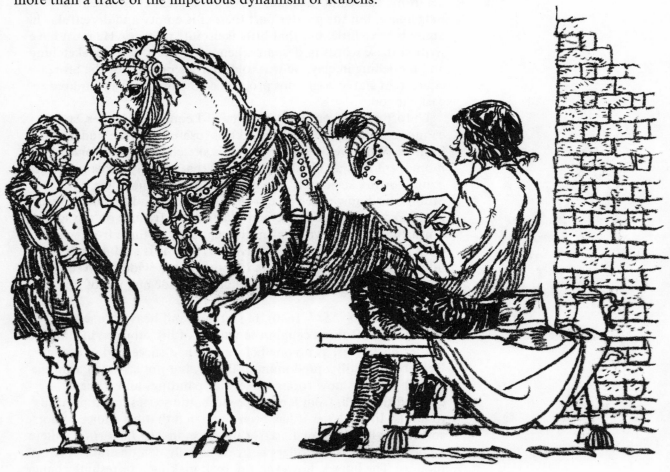

Géricault is especially interesting. His small studies of horses are visually real and his painting of the Epsom Derby ranks with the best of its kind. Additionally he was one of the first to take the step of lifting the back feet off the ground to convert the rocking-horse gallop into the *ventre à terre* method.

In speaking of French art, mention must be made of Rosa Bonheur, one of the few women to succeed in the genre of horse art. Specializing in the horse, perhaps her best known work is the painting of the apocryphal fight between Hobgoblin and the Godolphin Arabian, which was said to have given the latter his chance to become a breeding stallion rather than a 'teaser'.

Influenced by such equestrian portraits as *The Duke of Buckingham* and *Archduke Albert*, Rubens' more immediate successors, van Dyck and Velasquez, were both experts in this field; in fact it is arguable that they outstripped the master. Among van Dyck's best known works is his portrait of Charles I in the National Gallery, London. The man is still overshadowing the horse, but the horse is well portrayed, although it has an unnaturally small head. This inexplicable fault was to be repeated over many years. The technical problems of capturing the gallop are easy to understand – the action is too swift for the eye to register – but certain other conventions, such as the small head and, even more inexcusably, the eyes in the front of the head, defy understanding.

Many of Velasquez' horses also suffer from a blemish – they are immensely fat. According to his biographer, Justi, there is a reason for this. Velasquez was a court painter and in Spain it was the rule that, once a horse had been ridden by royalty, it could never be ridden by anyone else, hence: 'the royal stud, through idleness, burst with fat in the mews'. Blemishes apart, Velasquez was a better horse painter than van Dyck overall, well exhibited in the poignant portrait of King Philip's doomed and only son, Don Balthasar, riding his fat, long-haired, but obviously treasured, pony.

It is no exaggeration, then, to say that Rubens was the turning point for equestrian art. Before him was wooden convention; after him, life and movement. His personal contribution to this change appeared on canvas only in isolated instances, but through his spiritual influence of vitality, on van Dyck, Velasquez, Snyders and others, he swayed a whole movement of painters who were to bring the representation of the horse to its finest peak.

This movement became centred in England, where the English aristocracy of the late seventeenth and eighteenth centuries were, almost to a man, sport-loving. They much preferred their country estates to the court and their country pastimes to politics. Some even preferred their horses to their wives! Moreover, they were rich, so could afford to indulge their pleasures by having them recorded on canvas. Add to this that the English were in the process of creating the Thoroughbred, and it can be seen that anyone capable of competently painting a hunting scene or a race meeting was assured of a popular following and of a patron. Such a climate was sure to throw up talent, which it undoubtedly did.

The leading genius of this period was, of course, George Stubbs (1724–1806). His position is best judged by the way he stands supreme over such experts in the field as Ben Marshall, John Wootton and John Ferneley, none of them a Rubens or a Renoir, but all capable of producing work of outstanding merit. Such supremacy does not happen by accident; it has to be worked for. In Stubbs' case the work consisted of eight years hard labour, some of it in a lonely Lincolnshire farmhouse, dissecting and drawing the putrefying carcasses of long-dead horses, and culminating in 1766, in the publication of *The Anatomy of the Horse*. Not only did this labour benefit Stubbs in his own work, but it also added fuel to the sporting movement of which he was a part. Ben Marshall studied the drawings, as did Sawrey Gilpin and James Ward, and their modern relevance is shown by the fact that Sir Alfred Munnings considered himself lucky to have been able to acquire a copy.

Mention of Munnings highlights the fact that, in becoming President of the Royal Academy in 1944, he was one of the few English horse painters ever to receive professional recognition. The art establishment seems to have had a horror of them – which to be fair was cordially returned. Stubbs himself, because of some slight over the hanging of his enamels at an exhibition, consistently omitted to present a picture to the Academy, so effectively ensuring that he was never elected an Academician. Such sturdy independence is all very well, but it has resulted in most of the best examples of sporting art being in private collections and only coming on public display at specially arranged exhibitions.

Stubbs is best remembered for his hunting scenes, such as *The Grosvenor Hunt*, his portraits of racehorses, such as *Eclipse* and *Hambletonian*, and his purely lyrical studies of horses for their own sake, such as his *Mares and Foals*. For all that, he strongly resented the title of horse painter, giving rise to the jingle:

> ''Tis said that naught so much the temper rubs,
> Of that ingenious artist Mr Stubbs
> As calling him a horse painter – how strange
> That Stubbs the title should desire to change.'

John Frederick Herring (1795–1865) showed no such reluctance. He was very content to be known as a horse painter and became very rich on it. He painted every Derby winner between Mameluke (1827) and the Flying Dutchman (1849), and every St Leger winner between Filho da Puta (1815) and Sir Tatton Sykes (1846) with such scrupulous accuracy, that not only are they pleasing works of art but they are also a valuable record of the development of the Thoroughbred. Herring was a contemporary of Landseer, himself a distinguished horse painter, and suffered, like him, from what the art historian Walter Shaw Sparrow described as 'a lack of manliness'. Whereas Stubbs scorned 'to show an immortal soul in the poodle's eye', Herring allowed a certain amount of sentimentality to creep in, not by any means on the level of *The Monarch of the Glen*, but sufficient to suggest that art was beginning to take over from nature once again and the horse was slipping back to being a representation of something which it was not in reality. To Stubbs a horse was a horse; to some of his successors it had to be endowed with human qualities.

After Herring the climate, which had carried equestrian art along with it, began to change. Prince Albert died and England slipped into a gloom which rejected the sporting buck and his exploits. Moreover the artists themselves became entangled with the problems of the photograph, striving valiantly to tame the new monster. Sporting art declined and with it the horse in art, for the two were irretrievably entwined. The decline was not permanent, but Herring represented the end of an era.

In the United States, equestrian art started late, not surprisingly, as there were no horses there before the *conquistadores*. Consequently there was also no indigenous tradition to build upon, so treatment of the subject tended, in the early days, to be heavily influenced by Europe. This was really true of all American art, with the result that many of the country's more ambitious painters decided to work closer to the source and emigrated to the Old World: Benjamin West, Sargent and Whistler all left. England owes America for its Herring family, Denmark for its Alken family and Nuremburg for Sartorious, while, just to show that traffic was not all one way, America owes Geneva for Edward Troye (1808–1875).

Troye made his name in the southern states, travelling around the plantations, painting portraits of the owner's favourite Thoroughbred or Standardbred. He had as little difficulty as Stubbs and Ben Marshall in finding commissions but, unlike them, he was working very much on his own. There was no American movement of sporting art as there was in Europe, perhaps because all the energies of the United States were firmly directed towards opening up a continent, rather than to developing its culture. Troye eventually left his adopted country for Arabia, where he painted the Arab horse in its own environment.

Although not strong, the American tradition of the equine portrait has lasted down the years, one of the better recent exponents being Franklin Voss. A fascinating feature of the America of the eighteenth and nineteenth centuries, however, was primitive or folk art, said to have been evolved by itinerant sign painters. As can be imagined, in a country as horse-orientated as America, that animal often figured in these paintings, but in a fresh and uncommitted manner, free from the rules and conventions of the professional artist. Such work can either be very good, because of its originality, or very bad. An example of the former is *The*

Runaway Horse in the Whitney Museum of American Art. The artist is anonymous, but the picture was probably painted in about 1850.

America's contribution to originality in the field of horse painting comes from the talented artists who were captivated by the far West. Uninfluenced by other cultures, such men as the historical painter Charles M. Russell, Will James with his buckjumpers, and the cowboy artist Edward Borein, were able to bring a refreshing new light to bear on the horse. No longer was he underpinning an equestrian portrait, or even hunting or racing: he was now shown as a working animal. The best known of these artists is Frederic Remington, with his superb bronze of *The Bronco Buster* and his paintings of the vanishing West. Although he was given to using raw and unnatural colours, his pictures are otherwise extremely realistic and are packed with carefully observed detail. His Indian and cow ponies are especially well done, although, strangely enough, he appeared to be almost incapable of capturing any other breed; a series of pictures of polo ponies is markedly unimpressive. With his pictures of the vanishing West, however, Remington introduced to art a new type of horse to join the chargers, hunters and racehorses of earlier days.

The horse in twentieth-century art has held its own with no difficulty. Probably sporting prints and horse pictures are as popular now as they have ever been, thanks in no small measure to the many talented artists who have entered the field since the turn of the century. Equine art has progressed and developed, new avenues have been explored and new techniques used. Franz Marc, before his death at Verdun in 1917, was using the horse in symbolic form, John Skeaping has employed economy of line in impressive manner, and Jack Lawrence Miller, with his pallet knife and racing scenes, has made an enviable name for himself in America.

The Stubbs of the twentieth century must undoubtedly be Sir Alfred Munnings, with his wide range of interest in every aspect of the horse and his understanding of its conformation. Probably best known for his racecourse scenes, such as *Epsom Downs, Derby Week* and *Epsom Downs, City and Suburban Day*, he was also capable of painting first-class equestrian portraits as, for instance, *The Prince of Wales on Forest Witch*. Munnings' strong point was his use of colour, for which his fellow-artist Lionel Edwards, himself a front rank horse painter, said of him: 'Great colourists are extremely rare – Munnings is one'.

Munnings and Lionel Edwards are dead, but the tradition of painting horses lives on. The horse embodies in its great strength combined with gentleness, in its beauty combined with functionalism, all that da Vinci would call 'good and true', and as such must be a natural subject for the artist. It only remains to hope that the horse and art no longer meet only coincidentally but that they should travel side by side.

The Art of Riding

THE GROWTH OF CLASSICAL EQUITATION

The first definitive records of man riding a horse date back to 1600 BC and are depicted on the tomb of Horenhab of Egypt. There are plaques still in existence from long before this, however, which show man sitting on the quarters of an onager. This horse-like animal is now rare, but was in fact domesticated long before the horse. The next recorded horsemen of any note were the Assyrians, great hunters of the 800s BC; they sat in the centre of the horse's back as opposed to perching on his quarters, and were, in turn, followed by the Persians. But it was a Greek cavalry officer, Xenophon, who provided the first landmark in classical equitation.

Born in Athens in 430 BC, Xenophon's two books, *Hippike* and *Hipparchikos*, provide a wealth of information on a system of riding that is just as applicable today as it was when it was written, and which formed the base of the classical equestrian art. They cover breaking, buying and schooling young horses, and Xenophon trained his horses in most of the movements that we know today. As well as balancing and suppling exercises involving changes of pace and direction, turns and circles, he also taught his horses to jump collectedly off their hocks, and enjoyed hunting and cross-country riding when he was able to put his manège work into practice.

Xenophon also studied the horse's mind and believed in a system of reward and correction, for 'if you reward him with kindness when he has done what you wish and admonish him when he disobeys, he will be most likely to do what you want. This holds good in every branch of horsemanship'. He insisted on the patient handling of horses, disapproving strongly of any form of force to get the required results, saying 'riders who force their horses by the use of the whip only increase their fear, for they then associate the pain with the thing that frightens them'. But however advanced Xenophon's thinking, his great disadvantage, as a cavalry officer, was his lack of a saddle. As befitted a Spartan officer, he rode bareback, without even a cover on the horse's back, a fact that no doubt encouraged his liking of a well-muscled back. He rode with a long leg and turned down toe, maintaining that man's naked leg gave a greater degree of adhesion to the horse's sweating coat if the two were in direct contact.

In battle, however, the adhesion was not sufficient to withstand the enemy's charge, and it was not until the invention of the saddle, built high at both pommel and cantle, and used initially by a group of Nubian mercenaries from the Nile valley, that the course of mounted warfare was changed. This was because the high cantle

The oldest recognized breed in the world, the Arab has also contributed a great deal to the development of other breeds. It has been highly valued for thousands of years for its beauty, stamina and hardiness, and combines courageous fire with an amenable temperament.

OVERLEAF: A herd of Lipizzaners, seen in more natural surroundings than those of the Riding Hall of the famous Spanish Riding School in Vienna. The origins of the Lipizzaner trace back to Spanish Andalusian horses imported into Austria by the Archduke Charles, who founded a stud at Lipizza in 1580. The blood of the Arabian stallion Siglavy made a notable contribution to the development of the breed.

provided a base against which the mounted soldier could brace his back when closing with bodies of infantry. With the invention of the stirrup, first used by the Huns of Mongolia in the fourth century AD, the use of horses advanced rapidly, although we know little of the uses to which they were put in the Dark Ages which followed.

The Middle Ages, however, saw the beginning of Charlemagne's Age of Chivalry, with jousts and tourneys between teams of knights who, initially at least, rode light Arab or Barb-type horses and wore light chain mail. The tourneys were also the beginning of an early form of musical ride or carousel which was to be seen much later. Although they now used stirrups, the knights still rode with a long leg and with their feet pushed forward. They held the reins high in their left hand together with the shield, leaving their right hand free to handle the sword. Curb bits were much in evidence, but the principal means of control was by the use of the leg. The influence of the mounted knight, ever skilful in defence but not so good in attack, persisted until 1346 when the disciplined use of the bow and arrow decimated the French troops at Crécy, forcing the knights to take measures to protect both themselves and their horses. The solution was to encase themselves and their mounts in cumbersome armour, which meant in turn that the horses had to be larger and heavier and in consequence they became slower and less mobile. Increasingly, they became virtual sitting targets, until their end came in 1525 with the Battle of Pavia.

The age of the mounted knights did, however, produce a high degree of schooling in the horse, albeit imposed by mechanical means. Long curb bits were employed and so were long, sharp spurs in order to control the quarters without necessitating the leg being moved too much. The battles and jousts continued – knights being mounted on heavy, lumbering horses – long after their influence in battle was finished. But while this form of riding was operating in the West, the cavalry of the East was in fact fast and mobile. They favoured a forward seat and rode with a loose rein on Arab-type horses.

Riding was first recognized as an art form in its own right, on an equal footing with the classical arts of music, painting, literature and so on, in the Renaissance period of about 1500 to 1600. Then no nobleman's education was considered complete until he had acquired an appreciation of the art of equitation and could ride well. Movements, in imitation of those that it was thought were practised in battle by the armoured knights, were performed, the pirouette, piaffe and passage forming the basis of the work on the ground, while the levade, courbette and the capriole formed the basics of the airs above the ground. Elegant Baroque riding halls – of which the last remaining one is the Spanish Riding School in Vienna built in 1735 by Fischer von Erlach (although first built of wood in 1572, prior to that the area it covered was laid out as a training ground in 1565) – sprang up all over Europe to house the

The Lusitano is an ancient breed whose origins are obscure, but it probably contains both oriental and Andalusian blood. Much used as a cavalry mount in the past, highly-trained Lusitano horses are now greatly valued for the bullring.

PREVIOUS PAGE: The Welsh Mountain pony shows its Arabian blood in its widely-spaced eyes and slightly dished face, as well as in its elegant freedom of movement. Thousands of years of breeding in the Welsh hills have produced a hardy, sure-footed pony as well as a beautiful one.

stately carousels performed by members of the aristocracy. Xenophon and his works were rediscovered and High School riding had begun, although the horses were, initially, rather heavy.

Although Count Cesare Fiaschi, in his book written in 1559, like Xenophon advocates the use of patience when dealing with horses, and recommends the use of hands, legs and voice used in combination, in practice it would appear that the required result was achieved by breaking the horse's resistance by any barbaric method that presented itself. Hedgehogs or cats tied to the horse's tail, a hot iron applied in the same place, or an iron bar with sharp hooks on the end to be dug into the quarters, were all used to encourage horses to go forward, and the only reward would appear to have been a relaxation of the punishment currently being inflicted. The natural aids were defined, an addition to the more usual ones being a clicking of the tongue, but considerable emphasis was given to the artificial aids or 'helps' of the bridle, the stirrup – frequently made with a sharp inner edge – the spur and the rod. Stress was laid on not harming the mouth, however, although long, severe curb bits were frequently used, as were spiked nosebands.

Fiaschi recommended the use of a mild jointed bit with no curb chain, which acted on the bars of the mouth and had no port. He taught in Naples, his most successful and best-known pupil being Federico Grisone, to whom credit is usually given for being the first Master. His book, *Gli Ordini de Cavalcare,* published in 1550 shortly before that of his tutor, and his own popularity, may well be the reason for this claim to fame. Whatever the cause, Grisone's pupils were invited to other parts of Europe where his system of training and riding was propounded and his word spread. His book was translated into English on the instructions of Queen Elizabeth I.

Grisone's successor and the most famous of his pupils was Giovanni Baptista Pignatelli, who also taught at the Academy of Naples. He developed Grisone's methods still further and incorporated some circus training and movements into his work. He observed in the methods of the circus performers that although a high degree of obedience and balance was necessary from their horses, physical force achieved by mechanical means and severe bits was not employed to get the desired result. He was not slow to see the advantages in this form of riding and training, and gradually, using some of the circus methods, the whole picture of classical riding took on a lighter appearance, and many of the more severe 'aids' were abandoned. Horses of a lighter Spanish build became popular, and to cope with the demand for this type of horse studs were set up, the best known being the stud at Lipizza. It was founded with nine stallions and 24 mares in 1580 by the emissary of Archduke Charles, the Freiherr von Khevenhiller, and it established the breed which we now know as the Lipizzaner. Pignatelli's pupils continued to disseminate the teachings of their

Master throughout Europe in the early seventeenth century. The Chevalier de St Antoine became the first Master of the Horse to James I, while Pignatelli's most famous pupil, Antoine de Pluvinel, (1555–1602) went to France to teach King Louis XIII. His book *L'Instruction du Roy* was published in 1623.

De Pluvinel carried on the teachings of his Master, all the time trying to fine down the aids so as to make them almost unnoticeable. He was a much more sympathetic teacher both with his horses and his pupils, not believing in the use of a long curb or curb chain and never introducing a bit into a horse's mouth until it was sufficiently schooled to accept it readily. His schooling methods, too, were more refined, and he used a number of suppling exercises in preparation for the more advanced movements such as passage and changes of leg at every two or three strides. Very rarely did he resort to the persuasions of whip and spur, the latter being an aid he considered 'a confession of failure'.

De Pluvinel was the first of the Masters to make use of the pillars in the manège, teaching his pupils to sit their horses without reins while they performed the high school airs. He was also a very practical horseman, realizing the importance of getting the horse fit before attempting to work him hard, and he was constantly concerned that all items of saddlery really fitted properly. He started schooling his young horses by lungeing them from the cavesson. Not until they were performing calmly were bridle and saddle introduced, and finally a lightweight rider put on top. He used educated and experienced horsemen to teach the horses their elementary schooling and laid great stress on patient handling and gentleness. Work on two tracks and figure riding on large circles and at various gaits and tempos was introduced, bringing with it a new and enlightened approach to the schooling of horse and rider.

While de Pluvinel was practising this new approach to riding and schooling in France, William Cavendish, Duke of Newcastle (1592–1676), who had been trained in the School of Naples, had started a riding school in Belgium, later transferring it to Bolsover Castle in England. Although he was a classically educated man, reading easily in Italian, French and Latin, he was a hard taskmaster and believed that horses obeyed their riders' wishes out of fear rather than respect. However, he did not often resort to severe punishment and, like de Pluvinel, made extensive use of the cavesson and lunge rein. Unlike de Pluvinel, though, he did not place much faith in the pillars as a means of teaching the horse, believing that their use stopped free forward movement. His own forte was manège work, but he expected his horses, as well as his pupils, to be masters of all trades, and indeed two of his most famous pupils, Charles II and Prince Rupert, were principally concerned with racing and cavalry respectively.

Newcastle was one of the first horsemen to realize that horses had memories and to see that this fact could be turned to advantage. He wrote in his book, *A New Method to Dress Horses*

and Extraordinary Invention and Work them According to Nature
published in 1658, that 'often repetition fortifies the memory'. He
realized equally that this memory could also be a disadvantage if
the horse was initially taught wrongly. He liked to use long spurs so
that the rider had to move very little in the saddle and he carried
two switches, one in each hand (as is still done in the Spanish Riding
School today), in order to tell his horse on which leg to strike off,
and he also used the voice extensively as an aid. The only English
Master, Newcastle found great difficulty in persuading the British
people that classical equitation was an art form and that there was
more to riding then racing and hunting – a fact that the British as a
whole have still to appreciate.

As the new enlightened approach to horsemanship spread across
Europe, the way became paved for the Frenchman who was to
become known as the father of classical equitation, François
Robichon de la Guérinière (1688–1751). This man's influence
changed the course of classical equitation, and his teachings are at
the base of modern equitation. It was largely as a result of his work
that two great streams of classical equitation sprang up in Europe,
one based on the French Schools of Versailles and Saumur, and the
other on the Spanish Riding School of Vienna. His riding school at
the Tuileries, which had housed the royal stables until they were
moved to Versailles, was founded by Louis XIV and was managed
by de la Guérinière from 1730 onwards. It was soon to become
famous all over Europe, mainly through the refinements in his
schooling methods and the better stamp of horses (mostly English
Thoroughbreds) that were used there. De la Guérinière perfected a
system of suppling and gymnastic exercises designed to cultivate
and extend the horse's natural movements and paces, and to make
it respond willingly to its rider's wishes without any form of
physical force or cruelty being inflicted. His book *Ecole de
Cavalerie*, published in 1733, describes his methods and these
suppling exercises in detail. He invented the shoulder-in and used
it extensively as a suppling exercise, also further developing two-
and four-track work as well as making extensive use of the lateral
movements. During de Pluvinel's time the aids had gradually
become more refined, and de la Guérinière furthered these
refinements in the way the seat and legs were used in combination
and in his definition and extensive use of the rein aids. He designed
a modern form of saddle in which the high pommel and cantle
that had hitherto been used were reduced and knee and thigh rolls
were incorporated. It was similar to that still used in the Spanish
Riding School today.

Meanwhile, in Versailles de Nestier, who is reported to have
exhibited on horseback the *belle assiette* of the time, had become
riding master to Louis XV, but at the outbreak of the Revolution
he, together with the Director of the Great Stables, de Salvert, and
the rest of the *écuyers*, was driven into exile. As military supremacy
became increasingly important the first cavalry school was set up

in Saumur by the Duc de Choiseul, and although it was closed down through lack of funds, another was set up in 1744 at Versailles, with one of François de Salvert's pupils, Lubersac, at its head. Seven years later a 'Military School' was created in Paris which, although it lasted only thirty-seven years, left its influence on French equitation. The first Director was d'Auvergne, who was to change the rider's position, making it less formal and stiff, and in fact making military equitation 'less academic, simpler, more natural and bolder, more military indeed and yet no less brilliantly taught and practised'.

The war years did little to further equitation in France, but with the return of Louis XVIII the School of Versailles was re-established for academic equitation under the direction of Viscount Pierre Marie d'Abzac. This man's principal claim to fame, his own talents apart, was his training of Comte d'Aure. The National School of Equitation created in 1793 at Versailles changed its name three years later to the School for Mounted Troop Instruction, its function being to train men to be officers in the shortest possible time. It did, however, train Cordier, who was later to become the first *écuyer en chef* of the School of Saumur, when the School for Mounted Troop Instruction was moved there and academic equitation again took over at Versailles. The first of the carousels for which the School of Saumur is famous was presented under Cordier in 1828. This was just two years before the School of Versailles closed its doors for ever, leaving Saumur to take over and perpetuate the traditions of the French School.

One whose ambition was to become *écuyer en chef* at Saumur after the retirement of Cordier's pupil, Novital, was a butcher's son from Versailles, François Baucher (1796–1873). Although he was never to fulfil this ambition, Baucher founded a school in Le Havre and later another in Rouen, running the two concurrently. At the same time, he wrote his book *Dictionnaire Raisonné d'Equitation*, which was published in 1833. Baucher was an obsessive seeker after truth, constantly accepting and rejecting theories until he discovered the right one. His only platform for propounding his theories was the circus ring, to which he had been introduced by Franconi. Realizing, however, that the circus was bad for his image, depicting him as an entertainer rather than as a serious teacher and trainer, he persuaded the Duc d'Orléans to let him train a couple of regiments using his own methods. The Duke agreed, but before he could complete this task d'Orléans was killed in a carriage accident, and Baucher's training programme was stopped. He returned to the circus, producing ever more outlandish acts and then, fortuitously, met Lt. l'Hotte in Lyon, to whom he expounded his pure classical teachings. It was during a rehearsal for one of his circus acts that a chandelier crashed down on him, leaving him almost crippled and without the full use of his legs. To make up for this deficiency, he invented his own 'slipper equitation', that is, 'hand without leg – leg without hand'. Baucher was undoubtedly a brilliant teacher and a genius, using a systematic training of the horse to destroy resistance. His methods and achievements have left their mark on French equitation, not least by the use of the flying change of leg at every stride which was invented by him and written off by his contemporaries as 'nothing but a cantered amble'.

Baucher's contemporary, who did in fact succeed Novital as *écuyer en chef*, was Antoine Cartier, Comte d'Aure, born in Toulouse in 1799. He was a strong and gifted horseman but did not possess Baucher's gift for teaching. He opposed resistance in the horse with resistance, thereby leading his mount mechanically into the required movements. D'Aure dispensed with many of the teachings of the School of Versailles and stopped teaching his pupils on perfectly trained horses. Instead he treated each horse as an individual and left his pupils to find out which particular aids achieved the best results on each particular horse. He also introduced racing and cross-country riding into Saumur and placed greater emphasis on the all-round performance of both horse and rider.

The man who brought the teachings of both Baucher and d'Aure together was Alexis François l'Hotte, the 'icy tin soldier' who was an admirer and pupil of Baucher's until the teacher's death, and later came under d'Aure as a cavalry officer at Saumur. He adopted d'Aure's methods as enthusiastically as he had done Baucher's, but when at the end of his first year he was warned that he would not be promoted unless he disavowed Baucher and his teachings, he refused to do so. Nevertheless, he was promoted and he taught his men and their horses in d'Aure's methods, while teaching his own horses according to Baucher. A brilliant horseman and an efficient officer, his book *Questions Equestres* was gathered from notes made after each lesson and conversation that he had with both his teachers, and it expounded his motto of 'calm, forward and straight'. He took over as *écuyer en chef* at Saumur, and by combining the teachings of d'Aure and Baucher became probably the most complete and versatile horseman not only of his day but of the century. He finally retired to run his own school at Luneville, to which selected horsemen were invited to spectate.

Another versatile, if somewhat unorthodox, horseman who performed in the circus was James Fillis, an Englishman who lived most of his time in France and who later became *écuyer en chef* at the Cavalry School in Leningrad. He was an all-round horseman who specialized in manège work and taught his pupils without stirrups in order that they might gain a deep, flexible seat. He placed great importance on balance and suppleness as opposed to grip, a point he makes clear in his book *Breaking and Riding*. Although Fillis practised a number of unorthodox movements for the circus ring, such as the reversed pirouette with the feet crossed, the passage to the rear, and the canter backwards on three legs, he also introduced jumping into his performances, for which, unlike his other movements when he used a double bridle, he used a snaffle. The position he adopted was to lean back on the descent from the jump, slip the reins to allow the horse free movement of his head, while keeping his legs in contact with the horse throughout the jump in order to obtain a *bascule*. Fillis was probably the last of the great horsemen to use this position over fences, for Federico Caprilli (1868–1908), a captain at the Italian Cavalry School at Tor di Quinto, evolved the forward seat and established its use in the cavalry school at just about the same time as Fillis died in 1900. The reason for the necessity of the forward seat, as Caprilli saw it, was in accordance with the classical principle of keeping the rider above the horse's centre of gravity when going across country at speed, and to do this his weight must be moved forward. The system of cross-country riding used today is a combination of Caprilli's system and the purely classical method.

During the nineteenth century there were frequent interchanges between the two great schools of Europe: the Comte de Montigny, for instance, commanded the Spanish Riding School from 1842 to 1845 before becoming *écuyer* at Saumur. Few documents exist concerning the early beginnings of the Spanish Riding School, but the Imperial Court in Vienna, through its associations with the Habsburg family (one member ruling over Austria and the other over Spain and Naples), had long been concerned with equitation, and horses frequently changed hands between the two sides of the family. Spanish horses were introduced in 1562 to found the Court Stud at Kladrub and three years later an exercise area was built near the Hofburg. This was later replaced by a covered school, which kept out the worst of the weather. Work was not actually started on the present School, on the corner of Josephsplatz, until 1726; the first Chief Instructor after the School's move was Adam von Weyrother. The School was officially opened by the Emperor Charles VI in September 1735 and subsequently a number of festivals, balls and exhibitions were held there in addition to the daily routine of training the horses. Carousels, too, were popular, the most spectacular being that held in November 1814 to which all the kings of Europe were invited. A brochure, published in 1833, stated that 'The Imperial Royal Court Riding School accepts trainees only by special permission of the Office of the Chief Master of the Horses, and every day you can ride your own horse there between the hours of 12 and 3 in the afternoon'. After 1894, the School was devoted solely to the training of horse and rider in *haute école,* but entrance to the School was exclusive, being restricted to officers and members of the aristocracy, and fees were high. The French Revolution and the Napoleonic Wars, while putting an end to the classical art in most European countries, did not have a similar effect on Vienna. Indeed the School continued to adhere strictly to its principles and succeeded in developing the art further during the nineteenth century under the direction of Max Ritter von Weyrother and his subsequent instructors.

The training of horse and rider at the Spanish Riding School, then as now, follows the pattern laid down by de la Guérinière, with an overlay of Field-Marshal Franz Holbein von Holbeinsberg and Chief Rider Johann Meixmer's *Directives for the Implementation of a Methodical Procedure in the Training of Riders and Horses at the Imperial Spanish Riding School*, which was drawn up in 1898. In this, it is made clear that the 'High Art of Riding' comprises three distinct parts. These are the first stage, in which the horse is ridden in 'as natural a position as possible with free forward movement along straight lines'; 'campaign riding' which involves riding the collected horse at all gaits including turns and circles in perfect balance; and riding the horse in a more collected position with the haunches deeply bent and performing all the gaits and jumps which make up the 'airs'.

With the collapse of the Austro-Hungarian monarchy in 1918 the Spanish Riding School was taken into State possession and the future of the School seemed in doubt. Due largely to the efforts of the Chief Rider, Moritz Herold, who gave lectures to visiting education societies and had postcards printed of the School's high school airs which he sold to raise funds for the ailing School, it was saved. In July 1920 the first public performance of the Spanish Riding School was given. Since then the School has given regular public performances throughout the summer, autumn and winter months, attracting visitors from all over the world to see the highly-schooled Lipizzaners performing the classical art of equitation in what is its last home in the world.

DRESSAGE IN THE TWENTIETH CENTURY

The French name dressage did not come into use to describe the principles of formal training and riding until the early eighteenth century, though the origins of training horses for this most classical form of riding can be traced back at least as far as the fourth or fifth century BC. It is derived from the French verb *dresser*, which means to train, to adjust, to straighten-out. Like many other French words adopted by the Anglo-Saxons, it could hardly be more apt for its purpose. A *dresseur* is a man who practises dressage.

Over the intervening centuries, right up to the present day, dressage has developed in a sporadic fashion in different countries, in different degrees and at different times. It has always flourished, however, only in the more advanced civilizations and social cultures, for there has never been any place for activities requiring such patience, applied intelligence and aesthetic sensitivity in poor or primitive societies. There has to be a certain amount of leisure time to turn what is desirable, but perhaps inessential, into a practical proposition.

Revived after the Dark and Middle Ages, along with all other cultural activities, in Renaissance Italy, dressage began to assume almost precisely the form in which we know it today in the late seventeenth and early eighteenth century. One major distinction between the general practice of dressage and classical riding in the twentieth century and that of all previous times has been the introduction of competition riding. This is best expressed in the international contests that lead up to and include the Olympic Games. Previously, dressage had been primarily the concern of the military, through the teaching at their cavalry schools, and also of the wealthy civilian minorities focussed round royal courts and similar centres of culture. In the military, dressage was a professional requirement, whereas among the wealthy civilians, it was a gentlemanly accomplishment, highly regarded as an integral part of a complete education. No doubt the harsh necessities of military life precluded all but a small minority of the soldiers from following dressage to its highest levels, but through them the spirit of Versailles and Vienna was kept fresh and was handed down and practised at many relatively small establishments. In the riding schools maintained at the royal courts, the dressage achievements may have reached higher levels.

By the beginning of this century, the courts were rapidly dwindling in number, and the improvement in communications and travel facilities had radically changed the life in those that remained. The cavalry schools consequently became virtually the sole bearers of the dressage torch, and they themselves were to last only for the next forty years or so. By the end of the Second World War they had all gone, and the lead passed to civilians and to the few professional or retired soldiers who had received their training before the war. Interest became more widely spread and quickly found its expression in the expanding world of competitive sport of all kinds. Dressage was first included in an Olympic programme in the Stockholm Games of 1912.

This changing pattern resulted in some variation between what was taught and practised in the secluded academy in Vienna on the one hand and what was produced by the majority of riders in the wider, and mainly amateur, world of national and international competition on the other. The artistic element in dressage is all too easily sacrificed to the need to score points or to speed up the training programme in time for the next Olympic Games or other major event. On the other hand, the changes have not all been for the worse. The periodic gatherings of dedicated dressage riders from all over the world provide an excellent and recurrent opportunity to compare standards, techniques and ideas. They also serve to bring dressage before a much larger audience than has experienced it since it was used in the sixteenth century in popular festivities. Above all they have resulted in the reintroduction of a degree of freedom of movement as an accepted standard that might have been lost for ever if twentieth century dressage had been restricted to indoor displays and academic institutions.

A very beneficial aspect of competition riding is that the riders regularly have to subject their performances to the comprehensive scrutiny of trained assessors. Their duty is to recognize and expose weak results or false techniques as well as to commend correct and admirable work. This continuous world-wide process of technical assessment cannot fail to improve and maintain the purity of contemporary dressage to an extent that could hardly be possible without the stimulus provided by competitive events. A further beneficial aspect of contemporary dressage is that in its lower echelons it has become a true leisure sport, giving pleasure to many thousands of the less ambitious riders. This is partly because of the widely felt urge to escape – even for short periods – from the stresses of modern-day living, and partly because of the ever-decreasing opportunities for long-range or cross-country riding. Paradoxically, though, in the higher competitive echelons, it is in danger of becoming very intense indeed, and very large sums of money are spent in the pursuit of fame and success in competitions.

Climatic conditions have always had a marked impact on the development and practice of dressage within different countries. Given the opportunity, mankind the world over shares the love of riding horses in some aspect, but much depends on the conditions available. In Great Britain, for example, where the winters are mild and much of the terrain is agricultural or pastoral, it is possible and pleasant to ride out of doors the whole year round. Thus the ardour of young men has often expressed itself in riding across country, usually following a hunt. In other countries, particularly Germany and central Europe, the terrain and the climate combine to keep riders indoors for large portions of the year. This has produced an atmosphere that is conducive to an interest in the skills and science of pure horsemanship rather than the more immediate and simpler excitements of hunting. It followed, therefore, that for the first forty years of this century the art of dressage riding in competitions was pursued throughout continental Europe but was hardly recognized as existing, much less understood, in Great Britain. The result is that the countries of continental Europe, with their 250-year unbroken tradition of skilled horsemanship, arrived in the present era of competitive dressage with a long start over Britain and the younger nations. This is particularly apparent when the results of major competitions are studied.

The twentieth-century transition from a mainly military or aristocratic activity to the present status of dressage as an internationally recognized and almost totally civilian sport has in practice been remarkably smooth. Although, since the mid-sixties, the sight of a military uniform in the arena has been rare and the titles rarer still, this change has not affected the sport adversely. The military establishments were superseded by riders from private domestic stables, many of whom had only modest financial backing. One significant innovation was the emergence of women riders at the highest levels. From a previous standpoint of non-participation in the sport, they were soon to show themselves well able to challenge the men on equal terms. The first woman to win an Olympic medal in dressage was Mme Liz Hartel of Denmark, a courageous lady who had been severely handicapped by poliomyelitis. Riding her horse Jubilee, Mme Hartel won the silver medals at Helsinki and Stockholm, 1952 and 1956. Frau Liselotte Linsenhoff of Germany won the bronze medal in 1956 and the gold medal in 1968. In 1972 Mme Elena Petouschkova of the USSR, then the reigning world champion, took the silver on Pepel, and in 1976 Christine Stuckelberger of Switzerland took the gold at Montreal. In the world championship competitions in Copenhagen in 1974, women riders out-numbered the men.

The influence of dressage on the general welfare of the horse must be recognized as being considerable. Taken up very widely as a sport, it has encouraged many thousands of riders all over the world to accept the challenge of improving their riding, which is clearly of great benefit to their mounts. This challenge, together with the time and concentration needed to train a dressage horse, has resulted in dressage riding becoming almost a way of life for many people, and one in which they find great interest, great pleasure and great relief from the pressures of contemporary, over-mechanized life. It also has the enormous advantage of being practicable for riders in the seventh or eighth decades of their lives, provided they have kept reasonably fit.

Apart from the private dressage riding practised and enjoyed by individuals solely for their own interest, there are two forms in which it is known and appreciated by the public. As already mentioned, one is in the world of competitive events which are governed by precise rules and conventions. The fact that the performance of each competitor has to be judged separately means that most competitions tend to be too slow and prolonged to hold the attention of large audiences except at the highest level and where major championships are involved. In addition some basic knowledge of the principles of this somewhat esoteric sport is essential for a real appreciation of its finer points. The other and more popular form is that of special and relatively short displays given by one or more riders, usually as only one item in a programme of more varied entertainment. Such displays can be enjoyed by many thousands for their aesthetic value and for the sense of rhythmical movement and precision timing that they provoke. However, as with most other activities, really top-class performers are required to ensure the full success of such a display.

Regular displays of very high quality and renown are given all over the world by the uniformed riders and white Lipizzaner horses

of the Spanish Riding School, and by a very few great masters of classical horsemanship such as Nuño Oliveira of Portugal. Some of the top competition riders also give displays. In all cases, the dressage performed conforms as closely as possible to pure classical concepts. It should not be confused with the type of exhibition normally seen in circuses which, although often of very high quality and demanding very fine horsemanship, is likely to accept a degree of licence in the interest of entertaining a possibly less critical audience. Such an audience, however, will have no difficulty in appreciating a display of fine dressage for precisely the same reasons as would influence spectators watching dancing, skating, gymnastics or other forms of physical prowess that combine skill and grace with strength and discipline.

Competition dressage covers a very wide variety of standards, from those of provincial riding club events through to continental or world championships and the Olympic Games. The same basic principles and rules apply to all of these, and competitions at all levels are controlled by the Dressage Bureau of the International Equestrian Federation founded in 1921, the headquarters of which are in Brussels. The Bureau lays down and keeps up to date the necessary rules to cover the standards of performance, the rules and guide-lines for judges and competition organizers, the qualifications for judges and all other factors that directly affect the sport. Each federated nation maintains its own national dressage bureau to control its purely national affairs and through which contact is maintained world-wide on matters of principle and method. The highest priority is given throughout the organization to maintaining the purity of the classical concept and to preventing the growth of potentially false methods of training that would lead to a lowering of standards.

There are various conventionally recognized grades of training in dressage, and contests for all or some of the grades may be held at a normal competitive event. Competitors can enter for one or more contest, and in each case will be required to perform a preordained sequence of movements in exactly the order stipulated. In the United Kingdom the grades, and thus the contests, are referred to as Preliminary, Novice, Elementary, Medium and Advanced. Each grade is further subdivided into two or more degrees of difficulty. The advanced grades in all countries are clearly distinguished from the early grades by the inclusion of flying-changes of leg and pirouettes and, at the Grand Prix or highest level, the *haute école* airs of piaffe and passage. Airs above the ground, such as the levade, courbette and others, which are the ultimate achievement at such academies as the Spanish Riding School, are never included in competitions.

The national federations are responsible for devising and publishing a set of tests for all levels of national competition. These are called National Tests. The International Federation further devises and publishes four standard International Tests, all at Advanced grade, the lowest being the Prix St Georges, which is separated from the Grand Prix at the top by the Intermediate I and the Intermediate II. These four tests form the basis of all international competitions. Five judges for each of the four tests are recommended, although this number has varied from time to time in different places. From one to three judges are normally required for national contests.

The precise content of each of the standard international tests is revised approximately every four years to prevent the horses from becoming too narrowly routined, but they always take from eight to twelve minutes to perform. The programme at an international competition also frequently includes a Free Style contest or Kur, in which competitors devise their own display, the only proviso being that they include and show all the particular movements that the organizers may prescribe.

Dressage contests are always ridden in rectangular arenas, the standard size of which is either 20 × 40 m or 20 × 60 m. The standard international tests invariably require the larger arena. All arenas use a conventional system of lettering to indicate to riders and judges where the movements to be performed should begin and end. The origins of this somewhat illogical lettering system are obscure.

Competition judges are required to allocate a mark out of a maximum of ten for each movement or combination of movements as set out on the published test sheet. To do this efficiently the judge has to criticize and evaluate the performance, and then voice his conclusions. He is always accompanied by a writer, whose duty it is to record on the judging sheet provided for each competitor the mark allotted together with a summary of the judge's comments. These sheets are later made available for perusal by the competitors. The marks allotted by each of the presiding judges are collected, checked and totalled by the secretariat and the competitor scoring the highest total is the winner.

It is obvious that a good judge must have a very thorough knowledge of the principles of dressage and of the problems involved in training a horse. It is a great advantage if he has had practical experience of those problems from the saddle. He also has to memorize the test he is judging, since he cannot afford to take his eyes off the competitor during the performance and he must know the correct point at which each mark has to be given. Quick thinking, good judgement, moral courage, integrity and experience are essential qualities for a good judge. In fact his task is almost as difficult to perform well as that of the rider!

The International Federation maintains its own panel of judges who may officiate at international competitions. Each nation maintains its own list of judges, graded according to the standard of dressage for which they are considered qualified. As a guide and aid for standardized judging, the International Federation has specified certain connotations for each of the marks from nought to ten.

These are:

0	Not performed	4	Insufficient	7	Fairly good
1	Very bad	5	Sufficient	8	Good
2	Bad	6	Satisfactory	9	Very good
3	Fairly bad			10	Excellent

To assist in maintaining a reasonably high standard of training and performance it is stipulated in the rules that no horse shall receive a prize unless he has earned at least 50 per cent of the maximum marks available. As an indication of the standard actually achieved in this century, it is a fact that there is no record of a horse ever scoring as much as 80 per cent of possible marks from all five judges. A scoring at an international Grand Prix of anything over 75 per cent is exceptional. The record is 79·5 per cent achieved by Switzerland's Christine Stuckelberger and her horse Granat at Salzburg in 1975.

In Olympic Games and in continental and world championships it is usual to award team prizes for teams of three from any one nation in addition to the individual awards.

The dressage contest at the Stockholm Olympic Games in 1912, staged in a 20 × 40 m arena, was in the form of a Free Style and the degree of difficulty was extremely modest by later standards. No lateral movements of any kind were required, no piaffe, no passage and no sequence changes of leg. A jumping section, comprising five jumps, and an obedience section were included. Eight nations competed with a total of twenty-one competitors, and Swedish riders were placed first, second, third, fifth, sixth and eighth.

By the next Games, held in Antwerp in 1920, a much more comprehensive set test had been devised, including counter-changes of hand in trot and canter and sequence changes of leg in four-, three-, two- and one-time. Various coefficients were used for what were considered the most important movements, the highest coefficient being thirty for canter circles incorporating changes of rein and without changes of leg. The coefficient of twenty was given for the counter-change of hand in trot and canter, the serpentine in canter and for the sequence changes of leg in two- and one-time.

The piaffe and passage were first introduced into the Olympic dressage test in Los Angeles and have remained since then, with the exception of the post-war Games held in London in 1948. Canter pirouettes were required for the first time in Berlin in 1936.

Despite the enormous expansion of interest in pleasure riding and the various forms of equestrian sports that have been such a feature of the mid-twentieth century, the number of truly first class international horse/rider combinations from any country (with the single exception of West Germany) remains surprisingly small. It actually seldom exceeds four or five, and with such small numbers it is hardly surprising that the representation of any one nation has been liable to fluctuate quickly and dramatically in quality. For a few years a country may show great promise or achieve outstanding success, but then, as one, or perhaps two, of their good horses retire, there may be no replacement available. Thus their team may be of little account for some years. Fortunes can also be seriously affected by the availability or otherwise of really good trainers – invaluable assets who are always in short supply. On all these counts West Germany stands alone with an apparently inexhaustible supply of trainers, good horses and skilful riders. A few countries (some of them famous in other forms of horsemanship, notably Italy) have either shown little interest in dressage or have made no significant impact internationally. This is also true of countries with relatively small populations such as Australia, New Zealand and Norway.

When one considers the principles and aims of modern dressage, it is perhaps easier to understand why most countries can boast only a few top-class horses at any one time. Firstly it is required that a horse should be active and free, but still display all the qualities of power and speed that are its inherent characteristics. It must be light in hand, allowing the rider to control and deploy its movements with no visible effort and no more than a light contact with the reins. It must be calm, but keen, so that it gives the impression of always wanting to go forward when allowed and asked to do so. It must be supple and submissive, willing to adjust its paces without resistance or resentment according to the slightest, and outwardly invisible, indications from its rider.

Other requirements are that the horse should remain perfectly straight from its head to its tail when moving on a straight line, and bent slightly in the direction in which it is travelling when on a curved line, so that full use can be made of its natural impulsion. All paces must have perfect regularity of rhythm, with the correct natural sequence of footfall at the walk, trot and canter. The horse must accept a light, but continuous, contact through the reins, remaining confident, attentive and diligent, so that in effect it gives the impression of doing of its own accord what is required of it. Together horse and rider should create an impression of elegance and total harmony.

The type of horse likely to conform to these requirements and to work successfully in the gymnastic discipline of dressage and high school will always be one that combines mental alertness and muscular freedom with a thoroughly strong, robust and symmetrical conformation. In particular it must have the potential ability to carry much of its own weight, and that of its rider, with the hindquarters. The quarters and the loins therefore have to be strongly constructed with hocks that naturally fall into place in a weight-carrying position in relation to the quarters themselves.

There has always been a tendency for certain breeds of horse to be popularly credited with possessing the best qualities for high school or, in this century, for high level competition dressage. The Spanish breeds, especially the Andalusians, which were

The Andalusian of Spain is an old-established breed, and an important one in the development of a number of other breeds, particularly the Lipizzaner. For centuries the mount of kings and emperors, the Andalusian was taken across to the New World where its blood is found in both North and South American breeds.

OVERLEAF: Named after Marshal Budyonny, who was responsible for founding the breed, the Budyonny horse was originally intended for use by the cavalry. It has become a popular riding horse in the USSR; this mare and foal belong to the State stud at Rostov, the region where the breed originated.

considered to be unusually intelligent, courageous and well balanced, were very popular in the sixteenth and seventeenth centuries. Horses of unmistakably Andalusian type were frequently chosen for important equestrian statues or paintings, the mounted statue of King Charles I in Trafalgar Square in London being an example. For similar reasons horses of Spanish blood were chosen as the breeding stock for the great school in Vienna in the late sixteenth century. It is for that reason that the school originally became known as the Spanish Riding Stable and later as the Spanish Riding School.

It was a further three hundred years before Thoroughbred blood, which did not exist until the early part of the eighteenth century, began to be used to influence the conformation and mental aspect of other breeds throughout Europe and the world. Nowadays it is renowned for its special qualities of speed, lightness of action, and beauty. Currently the most popular and successful dressage horses appear to be the German and Swedish breeds, both of which are strongly modified by Thoroughbred blood although it has only been introduced into the German breeds in quite recent years. The Hanoverian, Trakehner, Westphalian and Holstein studs all produce fine horses of substance and quality, and the breeding is carefully controlled so as to eliminate lines that do not come up to the required standards of movement and temperament. Some of the popularity of these horses as dressage mounts no doubt stems from the fame and success of the German riders in this discipline, but it cannot be denied that their horses do have many excellent qualities. They have been bred for many years essentially as riding horses, rather than for speed alone as has largely been the case with the Thoroughbred. Swedish horses have been almost as successful as their German counterparts and are mainly a mixture of German and Thoroughbred blood.

The Thoroughbred itself has not yet become widely accepted as ideal for dressage purposes, although there have been a number of pure Thoroughbreds that have earned themselves great distinction in this sphere. There is little evidence to suggest that they are physically or mentally unsuitable or incapable of even the most demanding movements such as piaffe and passage. However, their inherent intelligence and sensitiveness demands a higher degree of sympathetic handling than is essential in some coarser breeds. It is generally considered that horses of most, or at least many, breeds can become excellent dressage horses provided that they are well constructed, well handled and well ridden. Surprisingly it is also true that for competition purposes the Lipizzaner, for all his great ability and fame, is put at some disadvantage by his relatively small size combined with his naturally rather short action. Consequently the breed is not as popular as might be supposed among ambitious competition riders, though there have been one or two with distinguished careers. Notable among them was Conversano Caprice, who represented England during the sixties when ridden

The Danish Knabstrup, which can be traced back to a spotted mare called Flaebehoppen left behind by a Spanish officer stationed in Denmark during the Napoleonic wars, has always been popular as a circus horse because of its distinctive colouring.

PREVIOUS PAGE: The Akhal-Teké is renowned both for the colour of its coat and for its exceptional powers of endurance. These two horses, on a racetrack in the USSR, show the breed's typical wiriness as well as the metallic sheen of the coat.

by Mrs R. N. Hall and won a number of Grand Prix and other prizes in Europe.

With its seemingly endless supply of good horses, riders and talented professional trainers, West Germany leads the world in the field of dressage. Their impressive achievements at past Olympics show this to be a position they have enjoyed for some considerable time, and their overwhelming domination of the world dressage scene seems unlikely to change significantly during this century. The sport is undoubtedly helped by the immensely strong support given to it throughout the country, and this is further upheld by the interest shown from the government. The state-controlled school at Warendorf, for example, with its permanent establishment of school horses and trainers, acts as a controlling centre. Dressage has virtually assumed the status of a national sport in Germany, and although this is partly because of the restrictions on outdoor riding in winter, the interest is widely spread, with a high standard of connoisseurship among the population.

The very large number of competition horses that are regularly trained and ridden up to Grand Prix level throughout the country has resulted in Germany becoming the main source of supply for other countries wishing to import top quality, at least partly-trained, dressage horses. These horses command very high prices, and indeed the German riders themselves are prepared to pay large sums of money for trained horses.

Elsewhere on the Continent, dressage training in France has mainly been based at, and fostered by, the long-established, one-time cavalry school at Saumur. In recent years, however, the school's output has dwindled and is now being overtaken by individual civilians.

Switzerland has ideal conditions for dressage which it owes to wartime neutrality and a severe winter climate. The leading riders have until recently all been soldiers based on the cavalry school at Berne, but as in other countries the closure of this establishment has resulted in the balance tilting in favour of civilian riders. During the fifties and sixties, the Swiss developed a distinct style of dressage that owed more to the teaching and practice of Saumur than to that of Vienna or the more precise and forceful German style. More recently, the Swiss have tended to make use of their geographical link with Austria to liaise more closely with the Spanish Riding School.

The Swiss have always looked to other countries, Sweden in particular, for their best cavalry, and thus dressage, horses. However, one of their most successful and famous horses, Granat, owned and ridden by Christine Stuckelberger, is a Holstein, who was trained with the help of the Austrian ex-Oberbereiter of the Spanish School, Georg Wahl. Granat is considered by many to be one of the finest dressage horses in living memory.

The Scandinavian countries, notably Sweden, have long been prominent on the dressage map, and Sweden in fact held a leading role in the development of modern dressage throughout the first half of the present century. Her inspiration came from the cavalry school at Stromsholm, and her neutrality during both world wars helped to ensure a strong position when most other countries were struggling to re-establish their postwar economies. Sweden's northern climate has always encouraged indoor riding during the winter, which inevitably led to a feeling for and an interest in dressage riding.

Swedish riders completely dominated the competition world dressage arenas during the first twenty-five years of the century, and they have remained a strong force ever since. Possibly their most famous rider has been Major H. St Cyr, who took the gold medals in 1952 and 1956 riding Master Rujus and Juli. The country's well controlled and intelligent breeding system has produced a very robust and handsome type of horse that has found popularity in many other countries.

In Denmark, dressage has always enjoyed a high degree of participation in relation to the population, although the main interest comes from the small private establishments. Denmark first came to prominence in 1952 when Mme Liz Hartel took the Olympic silver medal at Helsinki on Jubilee, a horse which she herself originally trained. Subsequent progress and success can be mainly attributed to the talent of trainer Gunnar Andersen.

Participation in international dressage in the United States has been sporadic both in quality and volume. In the past, many German horses, most of them at least partly trained in Germany, have been used, but there are definite indications now of a swing in favour to the many high-quality American Thoroughbreds. Much reliance has been placed on the frequent visits of top grade professional trainers, many of whom have taken up temporary residence and are in constant demand.

As we have seen previously, Great Britain lags far behind other nations in this sport, and virtually no interest was shown until just before the Second World War. The cavalry school at Weedon, which might have provided a nucleus of skilled riders, had been abolished by the end of the war and it was left to a very small number of civilian enthusiasts to establish this form of equestrianism in a country infinitely more interested in such sports as hunting. In spite of the fact that there was little in the way of knowledgeable or professional help available, this small number included two or three with considerable talent – all of them women – who quickly assumed a place in European circles. The general lack of interest persisted, making overall progress slow, but by the sixties a substantial degree of achievement had been made, the highlight coming in 1963 when Mrs Brenda Williams and Little Model took the bronze position in the European championship. Britain has no Olympic medals for dressage to her credit.

Dressage in the USSR owes its origins to the work of the Englishman James Fillis, who was *écuyer en chef* at the cavalry school at St Petersburg from 1898 to 1910. Widely considered to be the greatest high school rider of his or any previous age, Fillis had previously been a pupil of the Frenchman Baucher, who had developed theories and techniques somewhat at variance with those of de la Guérinière and the eighteenth-century classicists. Fillis simplified and modified Baucher's teaching and set down his own ideas in his book *The Principles of Dressage and Equitation*. The sport was inevitably eclipsed by the Revolution and its after-effects, but it gradually began to be practised again after the Second World War in the state riding schools of the bigger cities. The USSR first achieved major international status in the Rome Olympics of 1960, since when they have been consistently to the fore in their annual excursions to the European championships and their participation in the Olympic Games.

THE GROWTH OF WESTERN RIDING

In the Iberian peninsula, during the late fifteenth century, there were two distinct styles of horsemanship. In the north, as in western Europe, men rode *à la brida,* straight-legged, feet rather forward, in a saddle with a high pommel and cantle. The bit was a very severe curb, with a high port and arms as much as 37 cm (15 in) long. The whole was the product of battle-tactics which had long been obsolete – the lance-charge of the heavily armoured knight. In this, he braced himself between stirrups and cantle to take the shock of impact; he needed a severe bit to control his heavyweight horse with his left hand (impeded by a shield), while his right hand was busy with a weapon. Throughout western Europe and much of North America this style of horsemanship prevailed for centuries after its original purpose had disappeared.

In the south of the peninsula, where Moorish influence was strong, men rode in the style of the steppes and desert, described by a contemporary English author as 'riding short in the Turkey fashion'. They did so because their principal weapons were the bow and the curved scimitar, both used to best effect if the rider stands up in the stirrups. Young horses were initially trained by Arabs and Moors with a bitless device acting on the nose, and only when they answered to this were they fitted with a ring-bit. The bitless bridle was known to them as a *hakma,* to Spaniards as a *jaquima,* and to us as a hackamore. The ring-bit was called *la gineta* after the name of a Moorish tribe, and the Moorish school of horsemanship, to some extent adapted by Spaniards for light cavalry, was *à la gineta.* The more accomplished Iberian horsemen could ride well 'in both saddles', i.e. *à la brida* and *à la gineta;* but at a time when Spaniards were turning their eyes towards the New World, it seems that most of them rode *à la brida.*

When Columbus first crossed the Atlantic in 1492, he took a number of gentlemen adventurers as his mounted escort. Before embarking on such a doubtful enterprise, these men exchanged their costly chargers on advantageous terms for quadrupeds which were more expendable, but even these, against Amerindians who had never seen horsemen, proved as formidable as tanks would be to an army of the eighteenth century. It is reasonable to suppose that the first horses taken to the mainland were of far better quality. For some reason unknown to us, *à la brida* equitation prevailed among the new settlers in North America, but some of those who settled in Brazil and the Argentine rode *à la gineta,* as some of their descendants still do today. There must have been some synthesis between the two schools, however, because 200 years later, Mexican riders were training young horses on the hackamore before fitting them either with a ring-bit or a very severe curb with a high port and long arms known as a spade-bit.

From the horses of the *conquistadores* descended the mustangs, through animals abandoned by early explorers or through those that strayed from ranches and missions. By the nineteenth century they were roaming in herds over the great plains west of the Mississippi. They proved a good foundation-stock, for Spanish horses, with Arab and Barb blood, had been highly prized by the Crusaders and the knights of mediaeval Europe. Mustangs had hard feet, sound legs, and were extremely tough and self-reliant. On the dry, curly buffalo-grass of the prairies they increased and multiplied, but two or three centuries of sparse grazing and hard conditions, with no selective breeding, impaired them in size and beauty. By the nineteenth century the typical mustang tended to be hammer-headed, ewe-necked, mutton-withered, roach-backed, cow-hocked and tied-in below the knee. These defects were generally ignored by artists, but cruelly displayed in early photographs.

The horse transformed the life-style of the plains Indians. Previously their efforts at cultivation had been desultory and in their efforts as hunters they had always been at a disadvantage in pursuing the animals of the open prairie on foot. Mounted, they could kill buffalo by the thousand. In addition the horse meant wealth and nobility in war; he was currency, status-symbol and bride-price. In a couple of generations the plains tribes, especially the Comanche, became horsemen as complete as Scythians, Mongols and Huns. They virtually lived on horseback, and when a war-leader died his favourite horses were sacrificed in the belief that they would accompany him to the Happy Hunting Grounds.

Some Indians rode horses stolen, or even bought, from Mexicans, using the Mexican saddle and an armour of tough bull's hide in imitation of the Spaniard's morion and cuirass. They would pay up to $300 for a good made pony. Most, however, caught and trained wild mustangs. The method was to gallop into a herd, lariat coiled over the arm, and cast it over a likely animal's neck. The rider then vaulted off his own pony and ran after the captive, letting out rope as slowly as possible until the mustang dropped, half-throttled, to the ground. Then the forelegs could be hobbled and a thong tied round the lower jaw. The lariat was loosened, giving the mustang a chance to rise to its feet, buck, rear and plunge; but the hobble and thong soon brought it under control. As the animal quietened down, the Indian advanced, hand over hand along the rope, until he could first touch, then stroke the animal's muzzle and eyes. Soon the captive lost its fear, or realized the hopelessness of further resistance; and in two or three hours after capture – according to George Catlin, an eye-witness – could be led or ridden back to camp.

Another method was to control the newly-caught mustang with a thin thong around its muzzle which, when jerked, exerted cruel pressure on the nose. The Indian first talked to the pony, his grunts, deep in the chest, apparently intriguing and soothing the terrified animal. Then he passed his hands and a blanket all over the pony's body, punishing any protest by a jerk of the thong. He rested his weight on the pony's back, then swung a leg over and was mounted in an instant.

In admiring these feats, it is well to remember that it would usually be the laggard of the herd, not the best animal, which was caught, and that the mustang was only about 13 hands high, while the Indian was a strapping young warrior.

Indians rode on the white man's saddle, on home-made imitations of it, on pads fitted with stirrup leathers, or bareback. Usually they rode with an almost straight leg, but in races the boys rode short, crouched over the pony's neck like a modern jockey. Control was by a rawhide thong, half-hitched round the lower jaw. The Spaniards adopted from the Moors, and the Indians from the Spaniards, the habit of mounting their horses from the off-side.

A trick which, according to Catlin, most young braves could do, was to drop down on the off-side of his mount, at full gallop, his left leg crooked over the horse's back and his right arm through a leather loop braided to the mane, while he shot arrows over the back or under the neck. It sounds more spectacular than lethal, for the shooting could hardly have been accurate except at point-blank range. The rider, however, was protected by the pony's barrel, and a raiding party might be taken for a wild herd until it got close enough to attack.

In general, Indians were good riders but bad horsemasters, paying not the least attention to lameness or galls so long as an animal could still be ridden. When a pony foundered, it was abandoned or killed and eaten; mustangs were plentiful – another could easily be caught. But of the Indians' mobility there is no doubt. It was based on the *remuda*, each brave on a raid having a number of spare ponies herded by boys, so that as soon as one was tired he could change to another. The disadvantaged pursuing troopers had only one horse apiece.

The only tribe noted for good horsemastership was the Nez Percé. In one of the later Indian wars this tribe, led by its famous Chief Joseph, rode 2575 km (1600 miles) to evade converging forces and escape into Canada. The women, children and baggage averaged 34 km (21 miles) a day, the men much more, besides fighting thirteen battles and skirmishes. They were finally brought to bay and surrendered almost within sight of the border.

The first American rancher was a Puritan gentleman named John Pynchon who, when Cromwell was Lord Protector of England, with his cowboys (as they were already called) drove a herd of fat cattle from his farm at Springfield down to Boston for shipment to the West Indies. Around Springfield, ranching techniques developed on a small scale, and spread to the 'cowpens' in several southern states. The cowboy's favourite tool, or weapon, was the 4·5 m (15 ft) long stock-whip with which he could kill a man, throw a steer or snap the head off a rattlesnake. Hence the expression 'Georgia cracker'.

When their manifest destiny brought Americans to Texas, they found there a different tradition of ranching, developed by the wealthy Charros and their Mexican *vaqueros*. These people were riding the progeny of Cortés' horses, on saddles which were basically those of the mediaeval knight with the pommel lengthened into a horn for roping. The cattle were lean, wild, leggy Longhorns. As immigrants flooded into the west at the close of the Civil War, it became apparent that the toughest beef would find a buyer if only it could be brought to market. It was discovered, too, that the Longhorn could survive a winter on the prairie and would put on weight as it was moved over the plains in spring and summer.

In 1867, a bold entrepreneur built a complex of stockyards on the railway at Abilene to which cattle could be driven in great herds from Texas and then railed east or west to the consumer. So began the 'cattle kingdom'. It was ended in the 1880s by over-production, a slump in prices, wire, sheep-farming, the farmers themselves and a succession of very hard winters. But on the screen and in fiction it has never ended.

The cowboys of the 1860s, apart from Mexican *vaqueros,* were nearly all Texans: indeed the two terms were almost synonymous. The ranchers, big and small, grazed their cattle on the open range; the cowboys herded them, rounded them up, branded them and drove them up the Chisholm and other trails to the railhead. Although some of the cowboys must have had experience of eastern cowpens, they copied the methods of the Mexicans, and furthermore they adopted the Mexican saddle, bridle, bit, lariat, riding gear and vocabulary of horsemanship.

Since they were sometimes derided for putting a $40 saddle on a $10 horse, it is well to have a close look at both. To begin with, most of their ponies were mustangs, captured wild or bred from captured stock. Despite its small size and common appearance, the mustang was a very good cow-pony. It had extraordinary endurance, living just on grass and a handful of oats: it seemed to be resistant to heat, cold, hunger and thirst, and though it was slow and grossly overloaded for its size, it could nevertheless cover amazing distances in a short time. As an example of its ability, one pure-bred mustang which raced against larger and faster horses from Galveston, Texas, to Rutland, Vermont – a distance of 2880 km (1800 miles) – came in two weeks before its nearest rival.

The mustang seemed to inherit, or to develop very quickly, the essential quality of 'cow-sense'; like a sheepdog, it just knew what a cow would do next, so that a pony with a rider on its back could establish an extraordinary moral ascendancy over the savage Longhorns, which would kill a man on foot. Finally the mustang, once broken, was nearly always a quiet ride. For an objective witness to this, take my ancestor J. H. Lefroy who, while surveying western Canada in the 1840s, rode nothing but mustangs. He said of them: 'Though scarcely at all broken in, these horses are good-tempered, completely free from vice and much more easily managed than our own.'

Ponies were broken by crude and cruel methods. A youngster would be 'forefooted' (roped round both forefeet) as he ran round the corral, so that he was brought down with such violence that the stuffing, and sometimes the front teeth, were knocked out of him. While on the ground he was saddled (rolled from side to side to tighten the cinch) and then he was mounted. Or he might be saddled and mounted when tied to a post or held by a strong man with a rope round the lower jaw. Once mounted, he probably started bucking, and every time he bucked he was hit on the nose with a quirt (a short, stout stick with a braided leather lash). Soon he would stop bucking, at which point he was deemed broken; and so he was, in every sense of the word, unless the bronc-buster was broken first. If a pony did not respond to these methods, he was turned loose as an outlaw, or kept on the ranch to take the 'mickey' out of the first stranger who claimed he could ride. No further training in the modern sense was considered necessary, apart from being taught the specialist tricks of the stockhorse's trade. Why bother? Broncs were cheap and expendable, and so were bronc-busters.

There were more sophisticated methods of breaking practised by professional, itinerant 'horse-tamers'. In general these were based on the tactful application of overwhelming force, so that the horse learned painlessly that resistance was futile. But horse-tamers were expensive, and often resented by cowboys who took pride in their toughness and preferred to do things the 'hard way'. One Texan rancher devised a highly efficient method of teaching unbacked ponies to walk and trot quietly by tying them to the slowly revolving arms of a threshing-machine, the gentle force of which was quite irresistible. This system worked, and produced better horses, quicker than any orthodox bronc-buster, but all the rancher's cowboys, jealous of their image, walked out on him, having been ridiculed by other outfits for riding 'machine-broken' horses.

The early Mexican and Texan stock-saddles had a flat seat. So did the McLelland, which was a simplified adaptation of the stock-saddle without the roping-horn, used by the US cavalry. But gradually the stock-saddle acquired a sharp slope from front to rear which pushed the rider's seat back against the cantle. The stirrups were slung rather far forward, so that the stockman, like the knight in armour, was braced between stirrups and cantle. Modern horsemen deprecate this, but no one then realized that for the horse's comfort and best performance, the rider's weight must be directly above the horse's centre of gravity: otherwise he is 'unbalanced'. To modern eyes, the cowboy sat too far back with his feet too far forward, but be that as it may, the early stock-saddle had undeniable advantages for indifferent riders.

'The cowboy an indifferent rider!?' Well, the average cowboy must have been, for no one is a born horseman, any more than a born electrician, although some have the physical and mental attributes to profit more from teaching and experience than others. He must have been worse than the average cavalry trooper who had six months' riding school training behind him, for it is doubtful if anyone on a ranch had much time to teach a new hand to ride. Experience for the most part meant riding slowly behind a herd, 16 km (10 miles) a day, 'eating dust' while better horsemen led the way or rode alongside the herd to prevent animals straying. In time most cowboys probably became good riders – or they became farmhands or bar-tenders – but it would have taken time.

An indifferent rider, after a few hours in the saddle, likes to rest his aching back against the cantle and push his feet forward. He feels safer in a deep seat, and from the deep-seated stock-saddle, with 'swells' to hold the thighs in place, it is almost impossible to fall, providing the horse is reasonably well behaved. The insecure rider likes to have something to grab in a crisis, and even the best modern performers will not hesitate to grab the horn if, for instance, a cutting-horse makes a sharp turn. (It is certainly far better than jerking the reins.) On a long ride in a flat saddle the beginner slides about, giving his horse a sore back; he could not slide about in a stock-saddle. The stock-saddle is criticized for standing too far off the horse's back, modern equestrians liking to sit as close to the horse as possible, but it was made that way so it would fit (over a folded blanket), horses of almost any size or conformation without galling their back or withers.

Because of its size and weight, the stock-saddle had two cinches, fore and aft, which held it firmly in place. These were made of horsehair or lamp-wick, which would not gall the belly. To take the terrific strain of roping, Americans improved the Mexican saddle by a fork and horn of tempered steel. But the great and outstanding virtue of the stock-saddle was that it and its rider's weight were distributed by the skirts over two or three times the rib-area covered by the eastern hunting-saddle. Thus, despite its weight, it was very easy on the horse for long rides. Three examples out of hundreds may be quoted to emphasize this. A constable of the North-West Mounted Police, on a 19 kg (42 lbs) stock-saddle, rode from Regina to Wood Mountain Post, 209 km (132 miles) in daylight without changing horses. Most of the cowboys and Mounted Police constables moving between Fort Macleod and Calgary covered this distance, 173 km (108 miles), in a day. Kit Carson and a party of three Mexican gentleman rode from Los Angeles to San Francisco, 960 km (600 miles), in six days without changing horses. Outlaw gangs such as the Robbers' Roost thought nothing of covering even longer distances, although they had spare horses stationed along their escape route.

The cowboy seldom galloped, except for fun, or to head back contrary steers or get round a stampeding herd. On long distances he walked, trotted and cantered in turn. His seat at the canter, feet slightly forward, leaning slightly back, was comfortable and relaxed for him, if not entirely so for his horse. Since his stirrups were, to modern eyes, slung too far forward, in order to rise at the trot, he had to balance himself by thrusting his buttocks back against the cantle and raking his body well forward – an ugly seat. Some horses were taught to amble, which was a very comfortable gait for the rider and popular among those of riper years, but a tiring one for the horse. On the rare occasions on which he was compelled to jump – perhaps over a deadfall trap, or up a bank – the roping-horn prevented him leaning forward, since any attempt to do so would drive it into his midriff, or worse! At that time eastern riders also leaned back, and not forward, for a jump, under the impression that they were helping by lightening the horse's forehand.

Generally using a severe curb or spade-bit, the cowboy rode with a loose rein and made no attempt at collection. Any pull on the reins would probably be rewarded by the horse rearing out of sheer pain, giving the rider a bloody nose. Besides, a horse ridden on a loose rein over rough ground, left to pick his own way, is less likely to stumble than one on a tight rein. The evangelist John Wesley, who rode very long distances, always bought stumblers because he could get them cheap; then he rode with a loose rein, reading the Bible as he went. Within a few weeks they ceased to stumble, and he sold them for a good price – profit and piety combined. An old-time Western horsewoman told me that with a loose rein she has ridden across ground crawling with rattlesnakes and her horse, left to himself, kept out of trouble. All Western horses were taught to neck-rein.

Although no attempt was made to supple and school a horse in the modern sense, he had of course to be taught his trade – that of remaining calm and steady under a whirling lariat, and bracing himself back against the pull of a roped steer. The star turn of any ranch was the good cutting-horse. As we have seen, mustangs were particularly good because of their 'cow-sense', and some were extraordinarily expert. A quote from a veteran rancher bears witness to this: 'If we were cutting yearlings out of a mixed herd, all I had to do was to show Old Harvey the first one. After we had brought it out, Old Harvey would go back and bring out all the others, one by one'. Down on record is another cutting-horse called Red Bird, who, on his rider's orders, worked a jack-rabbit out of a herd of cattle. A good cutting-horse had only to be shown the wanted animal, and would then do the job himself, even without a bridle.

I cannot discover if the stock-horses of the old West were usually shod. Cavalry horses, being larger, certainly were; Indian ponies, mustangs with iron-hard hooves, were not. I have found occasional reference to forges on ranches, but none to mobile forges or anvils travelling with the chuck-wagon. I am inclined to think that the boss's better horses might have been shod to work at home, but on the trail the cowboys rode unshod horses. A list of all the articles a well-equipped rider should carry on a long journey at the end of the last century did not include spare shoes, nails or tools for cold-shoeing.

Of course there were plenty of Western riders who never worked with cattle, among them the cavalry troopers, Texas rangers and other law enforcement officers, hunters, trappers, miners, prospectors, homesteaders and livery stable keepers. But all rode, and all in Western style, with Western tack, and were part of the Western tradition. Most famous were the Pony Express riders of the early 1860s. The riders were 'young, skinny, wiry fellows, not over eighteen, willing to risk death daily'. And on joining they had to swear not to get drunk, use profane language, ill-treat animals or do anything incompatible with being a gentleman. The horses were selected for speed and endurance, and bought at high prices. Although stock-saddles seem to have been used (the lighter McLelland might have been better) everything else was done to cut down weight. The Express averaged at 15 km (9 miles) an hour over 40 km (25 mile) stages, with two minutes for changing horses. A rider's round trip of 110–160 km (70–100 miles) was covered twice a week. At every staging-post were the best of oats, stables, bedding and ostlers. It was all very expensive, and eventually it became priced out of business.

With the decline of the cattle kingdom and free range, ranching conditions altered. The long trail was a thing of the past; much of a cowboy's work consisted of riding along great lengths of fence-line looking for, and repairing, breaks. Fewer horses were needed, and it became more convenient to have something faster than a 13·2 hands pony. More emphasis began to be placed on pleasure-riding, and casual contests between cowboys for fun and a few dollars developed into the highly organized rodeo industry, with full-time professionals competing for big money prizes. Later still, the internal combustion engine put many ranch-horses out of business. All this resulted in the gradual phasing-out, or breeding-up, of the mustang by imported Arabs, Morgans, Quarter Horses and Thoroughbreds. The stock-horse improved enormously in size, speed and appearance, though some would still claim that no 'improved' stock-horse can touch the mustang for cow-sense and endurance.

The old stock-saddle was altered by sloping the horn forward (making it less of a hazard to the rider's masculinity), levelling the seat and bringing back the stirrups so as to make possible a balanced seat over the horse's centre of gravity. (Not all modern saddles have been so improved.) Milder bits than the spade-bit or ring-bit were found to be perfectly suitable for Western horses. Snaffles, Pelhams, the half-breed which is a modified spade, the cutting-bit which is a mild curb with swept-back cheekpieces, even the Weymouth double bridle all came into use. The ring-bit is now rarely seen north of the Mexican border, but some spade-bit enthusiasts still maintain that what could be an instrument of torture with rough hands, is a perfect instrument for the painless and sensitive control of a horse when used by an expert.

Larger, hot-blooded horses would not respond favourably to the rugged methods of the old-time bronc-buster. Besides, they could no longer be bought for $10 nor be hired for $5 a horse. So more time, patience and skill began to be devoted to training the stock-horse. However, this was not entirely an innovation. Texans taking cattle to the West Coast a century ago were astonished at what could be achieved with time by the Californian hackamore experts. It is claimed that their methods were used by the *conquistadores,* who learned them from the Moors, and perfected by Charros who had been liquidated in Mexican revolutions but survived in California. Patience and gentleness were the keynotes of hackamore training.

The hackamore is a bitless bridle which acts on the nose, not the mouth. It is shaped rather like the frame of an old-fashioned tennis racket; wide and rounded at the end which encircles the horse's nose, and pointed at the end which lies behind the chin-groove. The rear-end is weighted by a heavy rawhide knot which acts as a counterweight to hold the noseband clear of the nose when the reins are loose: as the reins are tightened, pressure is applied to the tender skin above the nostrils. The reins are attached, together, just in front of the knot. What appears in pictures to be a third rein is actually a tie-rope, coiled on the saddle. The horse is stopped by pressure on the nose and steered by neck-reining, with no help from the rider's legs.

After about ten months, the breaking hackamore is replaced by a much lighter model known as a two-rein bosal and a bit. The rider holds all four reins in one hand, with the bit-reins very loose, so that the horse is still ridden by nose-pressure, applied now by the bosal. After another year the bosal is replaced by an even lighter model, without nose-pressure reins, and the horse is now ridden on the bit. Throughout the horse's career, however, the Californian rings the changes between bosal and bit, for if kept too long on either a horse becomes heavy on the hand or hard-mouthed. Traditionally the Californian uses the spade-bit. The Charros, themselves born with silver spoons in their mouths, believed that their horses too preferred silver and gold to steel, and used bits made of these precious metals. Now spade-bits with a copper inlay are used to serve the same purpose.

The spade-bit, with its very high port, acts on the roof as well as on the bars of the mouth, so with a really good rider the horse is kept correctly bent by these two opposing, but very light, pressures. The port is often fitted with copper rollers or 'crickets' conducive to a horse's contentment since he can play with them as he goes along, and is encouraged to hold the bit, without pain, in the correct position. The noise of the cricket is a familiar feature of spade-bit country. The horse is ridden on the very lightest of reins, controlled not so much by the ironmongery in his mouth as by respect for the reins imparted by his early training on the hackamore. This is proved by the ban, in Western riding-horse competitions, of any form of noseband, even though no reins be attached to it.

Many Westerners believe that the hackamore is a Californian affectation, and that a spade's a spade, an instrument of torture in any hands. Hackamore spade-bit riding certainly remains a specialized form of Western horsemanship, practised chiefly in California. Most Western horses now have a preliminary training – although subject to the idiosyncrasies of individual trainers – very much like that of hunters, hacks, show-jumpers, polo-ponies and event-horses. That is to say, they are lunged, long-reined, backed, ridden first in a snaffle and schooled for months to render them obedient, supple and balanced at all paces. Only then are they considered fit for specialized training in roping, cutting, barrel-racing or any other work on the ranch or at the rodeo. The end-product is a far better horse for modern purposes, and one that is pleasanter to ride, than the mustang broken by a bronc-buster in half an hour. But it is not necessarily more efficient for the purposes of a cowboy a century ago, when finesse in training was not even considered, and is certainly a lot more expensive.

A description of Western horsemanship would be incomplete without mention of the distinctive riding clothes of the West, that are so different from the breeches and narrow boots of flat-saddle riders. Whatever its present purpose (and there may now be an element of fancy-dress involved) it was developed for practical reasons. The nineteenth-century cowboy wore a wide-brimmed hat with a much flatter crown than the modern stetson. This sheltered him from sun and rain, protected his head and face when he forced his way – head down – through thorn-scrub, and served as a pillow at night. A large silk or cotton square, knotted loosely round the neck, was sweat-rag, bandage, water-filter, dust-mask and mosquito-net. A flannel shirt, with close-fitting cuffs, was as warm, yet less sweaty and constrictive, than a jacket. In winter a sheepskin coat might be necessary. The cowboy's trousers were not skin-tight as seen in 'Glorious Technicolor', but loose, tucked into boots with high heels, which could be dug into the ground to help hold a roped steer and would not slip through the wide wooden stirrups. Leather chaps gave a good grip on the saddle, were used as a groundsheet at night, and protected the legs against the friction of long-distance riding, as well as thorns, kicks, snake-bites and rain. The spurs had huge rowels, more humane than prick-spurs, making a distinctive clink which a horse would recognize as his master came to catch him at night.

The lariat was used for roping cattle, for tying between trees to make a temporary corral, for stringing up horse-thieves and any number of other purposes. It was usually made of rawhide or cotton or, sometimes, plaited horsehair. The last were very expensive, but did not kink and were believed by Mexican *vaqueros* to have the invaluable property, when laid round the bed roll, of keeping off rattlesnakes. Most cowboys wore a gun as a badge of their profession and to despatch a horse or a cow with a broken leg. Contrary to another great tradition most were very bad shots – practice ammunition was expensive.

TRAINING THE HORSE

Like the education of a human child, the young horse's schooling is divided into distinct stages. It begins with what may be termed the nursery school, which will occupy the period between birth and the age of three years. This stage is undemanding of either physical or mental effort in the pupil and acts as an introduction to the 'primary' schooling period beginning at the age of three, when the horse is sufficiently mature to perform the physical exercises which will prepare him for the acceptance of a rider's weight on his back. During the 'primary' period the horse is also accustomed to light work, acquainted with the rudiments of the 'aids' (the signals made by the rider's limbs to express his wishes) and taught the habit of obedience to his trainer. The 'primary' schooling does not exceed much more than six months, after which the horse is rested and allowed to grow on naturally until he is four, when he enters into 'secondary' education.

For the majority of horses, schooling beyond the secondary stage is unnecessary and in most cases is probably beyond their natural limitations. Only a few riders need a horse above this level and, more relevantly, would be able to do justice to a highly-schooled animal. There are even fewer trainers able to train a horse for advanced work. On the other hand, the very talented horse, like his human counterpart, will benefit from advanced schooling, which can be likened to a 'university' education. In the case of the horse, such training is designed to be a preparation for participation in one or other of the specialist disciplines, i.e. dressage, show jumping or eventing. Nonetheless, whether talented or not, every horse requires a basis of education up to secondary level if he is to lead a useful working life of reasonable duration. What is more, all horses, within the limits imposed by their individual conformation, should be able to reach an acceptable standard at this level.

It is, however, a mistake, and one that is insufficiently appreciated, to attempt to begin serious training before the ages indicated. In fact, several notable authorities would advocate delaying primary training until the age of four, arguing that the horse is then stronger and better grown and so able to work with less risk of being strained or becoming unsound. Ideally, they are right, and the extra year given at the outset will be repaid by possibly an extra two or more years of service at the end of the horse's life. Commercially, however, the practice would not be good economics and there is some truth in the assertion that a relatively unhandled four-year-old can be so strong as to present a problem.

The argument that racehorses are raced as two-year-olds does not hold any water at all. The Thoroughbred is bred to mature

The excitement and speed of the race-track: the finish of a race at Goodwood. Racing is also often referred to as 'the Turf', although in many parts of the world races are held over dirt tracks rather than the lush grass of the European courses.

OVERLEAF: A pair of quality yearlings, elegantly displaying their high breeding even while at play. Mock fights such as this will help the youngsters to develop muscle and improve their balance.

early, and is encouraged, indeed 'forced', into maturity by high feeding and even, in some areas, by the use of anabolic steroids. The results are all too evident in the annual rate of wastage which occurs in the racing industry. It will, however, continue for so long as it is commercially viable to race two-year-olds.

To outline the basic training of the riding horse it will be easier to examine the work involved under the headings of Stage 1 (the 'nursery' stage from birth to three years); Stage 2 ('primary' schooling at three years) and Stage 3 ('secondary' training involving the four-year-old). Each one of these stages is subdivided, but while it is convenient to think of the training programme in these divisions it should be stressed at the outset that each stage and each sub-division within a stage of training will, to some extent, overlap its neighbour. The success of one stage, and ultimately of the whole enterprise, depends upon the objectives of the preceding stages and sub-divisions being firmly established, thus providing a base from which further progress can be made.

Stage 1   Nursery Training
These are the objectives to be achieved in this introductory period:

1) To accustom the young foal to the presence of humans, and to being handled by them, and to establish a relationship between the two.
2) To teach the foal to be haltered and to be led. To introduce an element of discipline into the relationship and to teach the youngster the first, simple lessons in obedience.
3) To prepare the youngster for the world outside his home paddock and stable by taking him, if it is possible, on occasional excursions outside his immediate environment, e.g. to a small local show.
4) To develop natural growth by proper feeding and management.

The foal will initially learn instinctively from its mother and will copy her. If she shows no fear of humans, the foal will very soon follow suit and submit to being stroked and patted. Even so, the foal will need to be fitted with a head slip at a very early age, and then be taught to lead. This can be accomplished by brute strength, but if this method is used the foal will be frightened and the first opportunity for teaching a number of small lessons will have been lost. The foal will also have received a very bad impression of humans, which may persist for a long time. It is not advisable to attempt to fit a slip out in the paddock; it is too easy for the foal to get away and learn a bad habit by doing so. The first lessons in haltering and leading are best taught within the confines of a box, and to this end mares and their foals should be brought into a stable daily. In some instances foals can be very shy and can, indeed, only be handled within the stable. The foal will, however, always follow its dam and if the mare is led into the box the foal will go in too, so as not to be separated from her. Once in the box

Only unplaced once in all his seventy races, Arkle captured the imagination of the public and became almost a legend in his own time. This outstanding steeplechaser is a superb example of the Thoroughbred's courage, speed and stamina.

PREVIOUS PAGE: Even frosty weather does not alter this racing stable's routine of early morning exercise for a string of young horses in training.

the mare can be positioned against a wall with a helper holding her head, and the foal quietly urged to stand along its dam's near side. Once in position, the trainer's right arm can be placed around the foal's quarters and the left encircle its chest. Almost certainly the baby will try to escape, but it must be held firmly and calmed with the voice. It is quite possible that several days may have to be spent in this way before the foal will stand quietly, but it is time well spent and the foal has learnt a lesson in obedience even if one is still some way from actually fitting the head slip.

Once the foal stands quietly, close to the mare's left side so that it gains confidence from being able to touch its mother, the first lesson in leading can begin. The method employed is to have the mare led round the box and to encourage the foal to follow within the encircling arms. A push from behind will be helpful, and any sudden plunge forward can be checked by the left arm round the foal's chest. After a day or so the left arm can be replaced by a stable rubber put round the foal's neck. Once the foal is behaving calmly it should be possible to lead him with his mother to and from the field by means of the stable rubber round his neck.

These lessons should be practised each day but should only last for a few minutes. Horses are taught by repetition and by a system of minimal discomfort alternating with a reward. The foal experiences a very minimal discomfort when he is urged to follow the mare by the push of the right arm under his quarters. When he obeys the arm stops pushing and the slight discomfort is removed. It doesn't seem much of a reward, and there are occasions when rewards may be much more tangible, although not necessarily edible. (The habit of giving titbits, except on rare occasions, is to be resisted, particularly with foals. It can lead to a situation akin to that of the spoilt child who habitually expects sweets and throws a tantrum when they are not produced.) However, once the foal has been led alongside the mare he should be rewarded by a friendly scratch before being released. All foals love to be scratched, the most desirable areas being in front of the wither, on the chest and where the tail joins the quarters. In another way we can say that in order to obtain obedience to our wishes we act physically in one way or another upon the horse and we reward him the moment he obeys by ceasing to act. This system is maintained throughout the training and throughout the horse's life, and is at the very root of the 'aids' which we use when riding.

One point, however, must always be remembered. It will be no good at all to *punish* the horse for obeying us. That will only confuse him. It can happen if, because we are not sufficiently quick, we hang on to the foal's stable rubber immediately after we push his quarters to send him forward, preventing him from doing so and thus from obeying our request. The same thing can happen with the ridden horse if we urge him forward and because of his immediate response retain our balance by hanging on to the reins. It may have been unintentional but there is no way in which that can be explained to the horse, and if we do it often enough he will very sensibly cease to obey because of the discomfort which follows.

Having prepared the foal, the actual fitting of the foal slip can take place. This will require the employment of a little innocent guile – a quality to be encouraged in all trainers of horses.

If the trainer is very skilled, the fitting of the slip can be accomplished single-handed, but in the majority of cases the presence of an assistant will make the job easier and lessen the risk of the foal damaging itself by some violent reaction. The role of the assistant is to control the foal's quarters, which will be done by the usual encircling arm. So positioned, the assistant will be able to prevent the foal from rearing up in fright, and possibly coming over backwards, by urging the foal forward or by pushing the quarters to one side.

The trainer stands at the foal's near-side shoulder, holding the slip with a hand on each cheekpiece. He or she then passes the nose-piece over the foal's muzzle and brings it quietly upwards into place. All that remains to be done then is to pass the headstrap behind the ears and fasten it up to the appropriate buckle. It sounds very easy, but more often than not the foal will be frightened by the unaccustomed pressure on its head and react accordingly by trying to run backwards. If this happens then the assistant must counter the movement by pushing the foal forward, and therefore *into* the head slip.

Once the slip is in place the foal can be persuaded to move forward for a few strides by the trainer giving the command 'walk-on' and exerting a gentle pressure on the lead strap, while the assistant reinforces the order by pushing the quarters forward. Once the foal has grown used to the feel of the slip he can be led to and from the paddock alongside his dam.

Obviously, the leather of the slip must be made soft and supple by repeated applications of oil or grease well before it is put on the foal, or it will chafe and cause discomfort which may lead to a quite unnecessary rebellion.

It is of the greatest importance at this stage that the foal is taught to lead from both sides. A fundamental objective in training is to encourage equal suppleness on either side of the spine, an essential requirement for later training under saddle. Far too frequently young horses, and even mature horses, are 'one-sided', i.e. they find difficulty in turning with equal facility in both directions. Usually, horses turn more easily to the left than the right, a situation which is brought about for two reasons. First, there is a natural tendency from birth for the spine to be slightly curved and second, because this curvature is further confirmed and established by the young animal consistently being led from the near side. Habitually led in this fashion the horse carries himself virtually bent round his trainer's hand. In consequence, a block of muscle is developed on the right (off) side of the body with no corresponding development on the near side. It then becomes a matter of difficulty to bend the body to the right and we have the classic 'one-sided' horse. Teaching the young foal to lead from both sides will go a long way towards obviating this problem and will save much time and effort later in his training.

Constant handling of the foal is also necessary, and gradually it should be possible to pick up each foot while the foal stands quietly. Foals that have learnt the lesson of having their feet picked up regularly will rarely be any trouble when they have to be shod later in their lives. Grooming with a soft brush as a sequel to initial hand rubbing should also be introduced as part of the foal's training.

These lessons will take place in surroundings which are familiar to the youngster, but at some point he has to learn something of the world outside his stable and paddock. An ideal introduction is to enter the mare and foal at one or two local shows, a proceeding which will involve him in being loaded into a trailer or horse-box and having some lessons in the behaviour expected of him in the show ring. He has, for instance, to be taught to be run out independently in-hand and to allow the mare to do likewise without being too much of a nuisance.

Obviously, these lessons have to be practised at home well before the date of the show and the same is true in the case of trailer drill.

Although the foal will almost always follow its dam it is not advisable to put the mare into the trailer first in the hope that the foal will follow. It is quite probable that the foal will remain rooted to the spot at the sight of the relatively dark container into which his mother has disappeared. The mare, separated from her offspring, is then likely to panic and attempt to rush out of the trailer, setting the foal a bad example. It is more sensible and less risky to lead the foal first, cradling it between the arms of two people and propelling it into the box. The mare, anxious not to be separated from her baby, will then enter without more ado.

These elementary lessons early in the foal's life contribute very largely to his future training. If they are learned well they represent a sound foundation for the following stages. If they are not, and the foal is frightened or confused, the effect will be made evident later, and from the outset the trainer's difficulties will be increased.

A young foal must, of course, be treated gently but he should not at any time be allowed to become 'cheeky'. Normal high spirits are excusable, but nipping, kicking or standing on end to box his leader with the forefeet are to be discouraged firmly by the use of the voice and by a sharp smack delivered at the appropriate place.

Training can certainly not be neglected, but it should not occupy a disproportionate amount of time. The foal should be allowed the liberty of an ample acreage in which he can develop naturally with companions of his own age and, most important, he requires adequate supplementary feeding to ensure his full growth potential.

As a general guide a foal should receive 450 g (1 lb) of concentrate food for each month of his age up to a maximum of 2·2 to 2·7 kg (5 to 6 lb) according to his size. The feeds are given daily and should consist of nuts or cubes, bran, oats, linseed, apples, carrots, etc., and should also include powdered milk and a ration of cod-liver oil to promote bone formation. From September until the spring young horses will also require ample rations of soft meadow hay.

At the age of two years the horse should be in receipt of a daily ration of up to 3·2 g (7 lb) concentrates and by three years, when his primary training begins, he should be eating 4·1 g (9 lb) of food per day, divided into three feeds. Thus prepared, he should be ready for the more serious training of the second stage to begin.

Stage 2   Primary Training
The second stage of training begins in the horse's third year, and in Europe it is usual to bring the horse up from grass in early April and to work him lightly through the summer months to August or September, after which he can be rested until the following April when he is in his fourth year.

Once more it is advisable to define the objectives to be achieved if the training is to have a clear purpose. Recognizing that the three-year-old is as yet undeveloped in mind and body, the aims in the second stage are as follows:

1) To accustom the horse further in the acceptance of discipline and to being handled to a much greater degree than previously.
2) To prepare the horse physically to carry weight.
3) To teach him to *accept* weight on his back.
4) Having achieved his acceptance of weight to teach him *how* to carry it, which will involve his making adjustments to his natural balance.
5) To teach the rudiments of control by the rider.

These overall objectives will be achieved gradually by dividing the training into distinct phases, each having its own objectives, but all the work and the methods employed will also be directed at producing a stage of *calm* in the pupil. Without calm it will be impossible to attain the desirable triumvirate pronounced by General l'Hotte, one of the greatest of the French masters, as containing the essential principles of training. L'Hotte summed up the essentials in the three words, calm, forward, straight. Calm is a state of mind, and is not to be confused with lethargy. Once it is achieved in the horse he can then be taught to go forward, a quality which implies not only immediate and willing obedience to the leg aids, but also a positive mental attitude. True forward movement is in fact a physical manifestation of a mental attitude. For a horse to be straight means that his hind feet follow exactly the track made by the forefeet, the full propulsive effort of the hind legs being delivered directly to the front, and the effect of their thrust not lost by being directed to one side or another and away from the direction of the movement. Straightness is achieved by the equal development of muscle on either side of the horse, and the correction of the congenital curvature which has already been mentioned.

It is easy enough to appreciate the necessity for calm, but it is perhaps not so easy to understand the remaining requirements. To go forward instinctively, is, however, an essential in the riding horse and when it is not present the rider is at the mercy of his horse and loses control. An obvious example of disobedience caused by the horse ceasing to go forward is the refusal to jump a fence which is within his capacity. He then disobeys the indications of the rider's legs. Very simply, he stops because he ceases to go forward. The need for a horse to be straight is even less recognized. Clearly, the mechanical efficiency of the structure is improved by a horse tracking up correctly without any deviation of the hind legs, but there is rather more to it than that. Straightness in the horse certainly involves equal physical development on either side of the spine, etc., but it also involves the ability of the rider to position the quarters, which are the origin of directional movement, by the use of his legs. Straightness is in part achieved by inducing mobility in the quarters so that they can be moved from side to side by the action of the rider's right or left leg. It must follow that if the rider is thus able to control the shift of his horse's quarters he will not only be able to impose straightness on his horse but will also be able to prevent any unwanted movement which would result in a change of direction and a consequent loss of straightness. Given that a horse is confirmed in forward movement and is straight he must be under control, and the chances of his refusing (by ceasing to go forward) or running out at a fence (because he has shifted his quarters to enable him to make an unwanted change of direction) must be reduced to a minimum.

Early in April the young horse is stabled and made familiar with the routine of the yard. Many trainers advocate the young horse being allowed a 'free' period at liberty during a part of the day so as to allow him to stretch his legs, get rid of his high spirits and generally relax. This is a good practice, and prevents boredom and the usual antecedent of this frame of mind – mischief-making.

Circumstances may not permit an ideal routine for the stabled horse to be carried out in its entirety, but what is important is what goes on in the time devoted to grooming, exercise and stable training.

Grooming has the practical effect of cleaning the horse and contributes to his health and well-being, but it also provides an opportunity for a relationship to be established between trainer and pupil. Properly carried out it can help, too, in the formation and development of muscle. Initially it has to be done gently but by gradual stages it can become more thorough. Particular attention has to be given in these first weeks to the handling of the feet, the head and the mouth. The feet will, indeed, need to be trimmed by the farrier during this period, and if the horse has been properly prepared there is no reason why this first experience with the smith should be other than peaceful.

The handling of the head is important as a preparation for bridling the young horse; teaching the horse to allow his mouth to be opened and inspected serves a two-fold purpose. In the first place it will make the eventual introduction of a bit that much easier, and secondly it will give the trainer the opportunity of seeing the state of his pupil's teeth, which at this time and up to the age of six are in the process of being shed and replaced by permanent ones. There is nothing to be done about the teeth but a regular inspection will reveal inflammation of the gums which may cause temporary discomfort and will provide an explanation for an occasional display of fractious behaviour.

Ideally, a horse should stand quietly untied when being groomed and handled, but initially he has to be taught to submit to being tied up, and in any case there will be frequent occasions when he has to be tied. This is perhaps the first lesson in stable training and it can be accomplished, as can most things, by firmness and patience – strong-arm methods are neither necessary nor, in the long run, helpful. All that is necessary is a fairly long lead rope which is attached to the headcollar and passed through the wall ring to the trainer's hand. Holding the rope, the trainer grooms the horse with his free hand. If the horse steps back the rope is allowed to slip through the ring, after which the horse is urged forward again and once more a light tension is taken up on the rope. If the practice is repeated on a dozen or more occasions the horse will have learned how to stand still and the rope can be tied in the usual way without any fear of his running back.

An equally important lesson is for the horse to learn to 'move over' in his box in response to a request to do so. It can be taught by just bending the horse's head towards one and then tapping the flank with a stick, at the same time giving the verbal command. Gradually one can move further back towards the hip and tap and command as before. In quite a short time one should be able to stand in line with the dock and achieve the same result with no more than a pat and a word. The secret lies in the correct positioning of the body in relation to the horse's body so that he cannot misunderstand what is wanted.

Exercise in the first few weeks is undemanding, and consists of nothing more than the horse being led about the place from a lungeing cavesson and being allowed to observe the normal activities that are taking place around him. To start with an assistant can be employed to follow behind and encourage the horse to walk freely forward. As in his foal days, the horse will be taught to lead from both sides and then, towards the end of the first three or four weeks, he will be expected to walk properly in-hand. Walking in-hand is an important exercise since it forms the basis of forward movement and is a preparation for work on the lunge. The trainer teaches the lessons standing at the shoulder, holding a long whip behind his back in his free hand. He gives the command 'walk-on' and at the same time taps the horse with the whip to ensure that he steps off smartly. Quite quickly the horse will learn to move forward on the verbal command alone and he can also be taught to halt and even to trot at the spoken word.

Once the work in-hand has advanced sufficiently it is time to begin the important exercises on the lunge line, in which the horse circles the trainer to either hand. In the stable, grooming can be extended to include wisping (thumping the muscles of the neck, shoulders and quarters to assist toning and development), and by placing the horse against a wall the trainer can, by a discreet pressure on the nose and a spoken command, teach the horse to take a few steps backwards in preparation for the ultimate rein-back under saddle, though this is still a long way in the future.

Lungeing is possibly the most important and useful of the conditioning exercises, and its purposes are worth examining in some detail.

Physically, its objects are:

1) To promote the build-up of muscles without their being formed in opposition to the rider's weight; to develop the muscles equally on either side of the body.
2) To make the horse supple laterally by the equal stretching of the dorsal, neck and abdominal muscles on either side.
3) To induce a tension in the spine by the encouragement of a rounded outline, brought about by an extended carriage of head and neck accompanied by an engagement of the hind legs under the body. The latter will always be easier on the circle, as the inside leg is bound to be more actively engaged and placed further under the body.
4) To encourage an increased flexion of the joints as the result of greater and more supple muscular development.
5) To encourage the flexion of the spine, as far as this is possible, with the object of correcting its natural curvature.
6) To improve the balance – an object best achieved on the circle because of the need for greater engagement of the hocks.

Mentally, the exercise has just as much importance. It inculcates calm and accustoms the horse to the habit of discipline, teaching him obedience to the first of the aids, the voice. Finally, it teaches the horse to *go forward*.

Lungeing is, however, a demanding exercise for the young horse and initially the periods spent on the lunge should not exceed 10 to 15 minutes. As the horse becomes stronger the lessons can be extended to as long as 30 to 40 minutes, the remaining part of the exercise and work period being devoted to walking the horse to where he can see traffic, etc., leading him across country, and generally getting him used to new sights and sounds.

As the lunge training progresses the horse will be fitted with a body roller, accustoming him to the pressure of a girth round his middle. Side-reins can in time be attached to this.

The next step is to have the horse shod to prevent him from becoming footsore. No trouble should be experienced, but it will take a few days for the horse to grow used to the feel of shoes on his feet.

It is now necessary to introduce the bit to the horse's mouth, to assist the improvement of the carriage by the use of side-reins on the lunge, to fit a saddle, and then to put a rider on the horse's back, a proceeding which is known as 'backing'. To accomplish all of these things will take some weeks, depending upon the aptitude of the pupil and his development.

The bit is at first worn suspended from the lunge cavesson which, on the first occasion that it is fitted, is fastened by a strap from the off side. The bit, together with the bribe of a few sliced carrots, is then held in the palm of the hand and gently inserted into the mouth, the near-side bit ring being finally attached to the ring on the cavesson which is there for the purpose. The horse wears the bit for an hour or so each day and may even be given a small feed while it is in position. This will encourage him to 'mouth' the bit,

relaxing his jaw and making saliva. He will also wear the bit while working on the lunge so that he learns to accept its presence without showing resentment.

The type of bit used depends very much on the preference of the trainer. Some trainers prefer the 'mouthing' bit fitted with keys, which are supposed to encourage the horse to play with the bit and so relax his jaw, others will use the plain half-moon snaffle made either of rubber, which is very mild, or of nylon.

The use of side-reins is always a point of controversy, but essentially they are used to 'bring the horse together' and are shortened progressively to this end. At first side-reins will be attached from the roller to the cavesson rings, and only when the horse is used to them will they be attached to the bit itself.

Lungeing with side-reins attached to the bit teaches the horse to accept the presence of the latter but it does not, of course, teach the horse about the varying bit pressures that will be employed by the rider, nor how he is expected to respond to them. The ground for teaching the ridden hand aids can, however, be prepared in the stable. The trainer will often start by standing in front of the horse, holding a bit ring in either hand and vibrating the bit slightly upwards and to the rear. The horse responds by momentary relaxation of the lower jaw and when that happens the pressure is released and the horse rewarded. Similar pressures on one bit ring will produce a dropping of the nose and a relaxation of the corresponding side of the jaw. The lessons can be taken further in the school, where the horse can be persuaded to walk forward by an assistant while the trainer, a little in advance of the shoulder, holds a rein in either hand. A slight vibration on both reins accompanied by the command 'whoa' teaches the halt. The changes of direction are taught by the vibration of a single rein on the side towards which the turn is wanted.

Some authorities teach the rein-aids on long-reins while the horse is driven from behind. To be effective, however, long-reining requires an expert skilled in the exercise.

The fitting of the saddle is done when the horse is well used to wearing a roller, and many people will also take the precaution of placing a weighted sack over the horse's back each day before actually putting on the saddle. Prudence dictates that the first attempt will take place after the exercise period, in the stable, when the horse has rid himself of any itch in his heels and is in a co-operative frame of mind.

When the horse works on the lunge calmly, without showing any resentment towards the saddle on his back, the business of putting up a rider can begin. Once again the preparation for this event takes place in the stable after exercise. A lightweight, agile assistant is needed who will in the first instance do no more than put his or her weight across the horse's back, making no attempt actually to sit on the horse. If the horse, suitably distracted by a bowl of feed, accepts the weight calmly, then by degrees a leg can be put over his back, and the assistant is mounted. The schooling continues in the training area with the rider mounted and the horse circling the trainer on the lunge as before. At this point the rider makes no effort to control the horse at all. The object is to get the horse to accept the weight on his back.

The final phase in the three-year-old's training is concerned with teaching the horse the elementary aids, to *carry* the weight on his back at walk, trot and canter and, additionally, to introduce the first lessons in jumping.

The exercise period, or periods, since it is quite reasonable to work the horse twice during the day, must now, perforce, be extended. The lungeing exercises continue and may include the strengthening and balancing exercises practised over spaced poles on the ground and then over similarly spaced cavalletti. The ridden work will take place in the schooling area but the lessons learned there will also have to be put into practice out in the countryside. A significant proportion of the exercise will, therefore, consist of hacking excursions around quiet lanes and in the countryside. Hacking the young horse about is a most important part of his education. It introduces him to a variety of new circumstances and is the best safeguard against boredom and a loss of interest in his work. Before he ventures out into the world outside his familiar surroundings, however, he must first be taught, for his own sake as well as for that of his rider, to obey the aids.

Once he is working quietly on the lunge with the rider in the saddle, the aids can be taught by the trainer reinforcing the physical action of the rider with his voice, to which the horse has already been made obedient. To teach the aids from halt into walk, for instance, the rider, having obtained the horse's attention by a squeeze of the legs and a slight closing of the fingers on the reins, applies both legs decisively behind the girth. As he does so the trainer gives the command 'walk-on' and, if necessary, sweeps the thong of his lungeing whip behind the horse further to encourage a movement forward. It will not be long before the horse associates the squeeze of the legs with the verbal command and moves forward from their action alone. So, increasingly, control passes from the trainer to the rider, with the latter gradually assuming the major role. Once the aids for walk, trot and halt have been learned and the horse has been accustomed to the application of the rein aids on the circle, the lunge line can be removed and the horse ridden in the school under the rider's control.

How well the horse responds depends very much, of course, on the competence of the rider – the more accomplished the latter the better will be the result. At this point it is absolutely essential that the aids, often supplemented by the use of the voice, should be completely clear. If the horse is confused now there will be no chance of his learning the more advanced work in the secondary stage of training. For this reason the aids to turn should be quite unmistakable and even exaggerated. The accepted turning aids on the schooled horse are made by applying the inside leg on the girth, to maintain the impulsion; the outside leg is held slightly to the rear of the girth, supporting the action of its opposite number and preventing an outward swing of the quarters; the fingers of the inside hand close to bend the head and neck in the direction of the movement and the outside hand is opened a little so as not to oppose the bend. Used in this way the rein is employed as that of *direct opposition*, i.e. it opposes or blocks the forward movement on the side to which it is applied, and in consequence the movement is rechannelled so that the quarters, when the right rein is used, must be pushed over to the left and vice-versa.

This is far too complicated an action for a young horse to understand, let alone obey. If it is used, the pressure on one side will only confuse him, restrict his stride and cause a loss of the essential forward progression – the very last thing that is wanted at this early stage. It is, therefore, more sensible to keep the horse moving forward and to make the turn by using a simple *direct* or *opening* rein effect. To use the rein in this way the rider carries the inside hand well out to the side, pointing the thumb in the direction that is to be taken. The action will pull the horse's nose over to the left or right, according to which rein is used, and the shoulders will be shifted in the required direction. The aid is exaggerated but its intention is quite unmistakable to the horse; equally important at this stage is the fact that his forward movement is not interrupted.

So far the horse will have been ridden from his mouthing bit or from the half-moon snaffle. It is now an appropriate time to make a change to a jointed snaffle with a good fat mouthpiece. If a half-moon snaffle has been used it may not be necessary to replace it. Indeed, if the horse is going well and is happy in his mouth with this particular type of bit there is no reason to make a change just for the sake of doing so.

The school lessons will involve the execution of simple figures, changes of direction, elements of circles, transitions from one pace to another and so on. They can also include a little work over a grid of poles on the ground or low cavalletti – exercises which will have already been done on the lunge. This work will strengthen the quarters and hind legs, and help the horse to find balance under his rider's weight. They are, of course, also a very useful preliminary to jumping.

Increasingly, however, more emphasis will be placed on the hacking activity, as the ability to ride the horse outside the school area is the ultimate goal. Ideally, a young horse should be ridden out initially in company with an older and more experienced companion from whom he can draw confidence and whose example he can follow.

On the roads the older horse can shield the young one from traffic by being ridden on his outside and a little ahead of him, and as long as he is steady, the youngster will soon lose any fear he may have felt about road vehicles.

Hacking in fact provides the greatest opportunity for schooling. Crossing undulating ground, for instance, compels the horse to make constant adjustments to his balance, and short, fairly steep ascents and descents are excellent developers of muscle. It is also possible to introduce other little balancing exercises. On a good bridle-path, for instance, the horse can be asked by judicious use of hands and legs to slow down and speed up the pace, which is the beginning of the exercises designed to make him supple longitudinally. Out in the open, preferably on a slight uphill slope, the trainer has the ideal place for teaching the horse to canter, a pace that is usually too difficult for a young horse to accomplish under saddle in the confined area of the school. The early efforts at canter will not be polished performances, but the horse will be learning how to carry weight at this pace and will improve continually.

Small ditches, low logs and little streams can all be used to advantage. Given a lead by an older horse the youngster soon learns how to negotiate these obstacles, and the knowledge gained will stand him and his rider in good stead for the future.

Towards the end of this primary stage it should be possible to make a change from the use of the simple direct turning rein to the more conventional rein of direct opposition.

Finally, the horse can be asked to do a little simple jumping, over very low fences, before his primary education is concluded and he is rested over the winter months. He will already have learned on the lunge and under saddle how to cross a grid of low cavalletti, but for his first jumping lessons it will be prudent to revert to the lunge. The first jump is very simply accomplished by a rearrangement of the basic cavalletti grid. The trotting distance between each cavalletto is between 1·2 m (4 ft) and 1·8 m (6 ft), depending upon the size of the horse and the length of his stride, and usually a grid consists of four cavalletti. To make a fence, the third cavalletto in the line is placed on top of the fourth, the height of the two being about 50 cm (20 in). The horse is then lunged over the grid in the usual way at trot and will, almost always, make no trouble about hopping over the last element. Jumping without the burden of the rider's weight is obviously easier, and the horse can learn to judge his fences without interference. Once, however, he is jumping confidently and freely, the exercise can be repeated with a rider, although the lunge rein will be retained and the rider will not at first act with the bit rein. Thereafter, it should be possible to dispense with the lunge line.

Before he is rested for the winter, the horse's teeth should be examined and if necessary he should be wormed. The feed ration, of concentrates and hay, must be continued through the winter months if the horse is to be brought up in the following April in a strong condition ready for demanding work.

Stage 3   Secondary Training

There will be a pronounced difference in the physical appearance of the three- and four-year-old horse. The latter should, if he has been well fed and cared for, be big, well-grown and strong by the time he is brought up in the April following the completion of his primary education. Of the two, this secondary phase is likely to give rise to more problems than the elementary training, and not only because the work is more advanced. The young horse, more sure of himself now, may begin to assert himself and on occasions his natural exuberance may turn to outright disobedience. It is, therefore, necessary to consolidate the work done in the previous year, insisting upon obedience in the exercises already learned before attempting to teach anything new.

As in the case of the primary training, the secondary stage of education will divide naturally into phases, the whole comprising a number of subsidiary objectives leading to the desirable end product of the all-round horse.

In general, within this stage, the following are the objectives to be attained:

1) Progressive physical conditioning.
2) The furtherance of the mental development.
3) The placing of the horse 'on the bit' and 'on the hand'. (That is, the horse moving forward in response to the action of the legs to take up contact with the bit and going, as it were, between the rider's legs and hands.)
4) Increasing the lateral and longitudinal suppleness of the horse by gymnastic exercises. (In effect the aim is to produce a horse that can be likened to a spiral spring which can be compressed and extended at will and which is able to be bent laterally in either direction.)
5) Teaching the aids up to the secondary standard.
6) Inducing by the use of school figures and exercises a greater degree of straightness in the horse.
7) Continuing and extending the jumping training.
8) Introducing greater exposure to road traffic.
9) Making the first introduction to the double bridle.

The conditioning of the horse is a gradual process obtained, as before, through feeding, grooming and exercise. In the secondary stage of training a four-year-old should be able by September to be doing some two and a half hours of exercise and work each day. Approximately 45 minutes each day, excluding the early morning quartering, should be spent on grooming and wisping, and the feed ration may have risen to as much as 4·5 to 5·5 kg (10 to 12 lb) of concentrates for a horse of 16 hands or so, and about 7 to 8 kg (16 to 18 lb) of hay daily. Rations, like work, must of course be increased by gradual stages, and no hard and fast rule can be made about exact quantities as the requirements vary from individual to individual. Clearly there is no sense in putting up with an over-fresh horse unable to concentrate on his work. The solution in such a case is either to cut back the corn ration or to increase the work – or, of course, to resort to a combination of both.

The remaining objectives will be achieved by the combination of work on the lunge, a method of training retained well into the schooling programme; ridden schooling on the flat and over fences, and by hacking exercise. How the three elements are combined and in what proportion will depend upon the individual trainer and also upon the degree of talent of his pupil.

For the sake of clarity it is probably better to consider the work involved in each activity, although, of course, in practice the three would be blended into one programme.

The Lunge: In the work on the flat it should be possible to have the horse's side-reins at a shorter length for longer periods of time. The reins may also be attached higher up the roller, more nearly to the position of the hands than previously. It is usual to begin with the side-reins adjusted low down on each side of the roller to encourage the horse to lower the head, but in the final stages the head should be carried naturally in a position that allows for the reins to be fastened nearer to the withers. The work on the flat will be aimed at perfecting the rhythm and elasticity of the paces and insisting upon the horse being correctly bent from poll to tail while executing a true circle.

Additionally, the lunge can be used to improve the canter, which as yet will be undeveloped. Initially, the horse will find cantering a true circle difficult to accomplish in a collected fashion and he may also have problems in striking-off correctly from trot into the canter pace. To strike off correctly on the circle left the horse has to lead with his left, inside foreleg, and vice-versa when on the circle right. Leading with the outside foreleg is cantering 'false' and, until such time as the horse is sufficiently advanced, the canter will be unbalanced and the horse in danger of falling over his own legs if not of causing some strain to them. Later, when the balance is much improved, the horse is expected to canter with the outside leg leading and remain in balance. The exercise is then termed the 'counter' canter. But for the moment the strike-off and the subsequent circle at canter is the objective. A relatively painless method of getting the correct strike-off, followed initially by a few strides of canter, is to place a single cavalletto across the corner of the school. The horse is then lunged over the small obstacle from trot and will almost always, because of the curve imposed, land in the canter stride and on the correct lead. Once the strike-off is established, progress can be made towards the cantering of a full circle to either hand.

Jumping ability is also improved by lungeing the horse over fences. This encourages the horse's confidence and initiative. Fences should be firm and very solid but not, in the beginning, higher than 75 cm (2·5 ft) or so, and with a corresponding spread. Flimsy fences, easily knocked down, discourage good jumping. The horse soon loses respect for fences he knows will collapse at a slight knock and ceases, quite sensibly, to exert much effort in jumping them.

To help the horse judge the fence a 'distance' pole, or a low cavalletto, can be placed on the ground 9·9 m (33 ft) away. This distance allows for two non-jumping canter strides between landing over the small fence and taking off over the 'arger one. An additional advantage in using a 'distance' pole is that it helps prevent the horse from acquiring the habit of rushing at his fences.

If the horse uses himself insufficiently over a fence and makes the angle of descent too steep, a pole placed a foot or so out on the landing side will encourage him to stretch out so as to clear the additional part of the obstacle. Conversely, a horse that gets too close at take-off to his fence can be helped by a pole or cavalletto placed on the take-off side.

When the horse is jumping a simple obstacle like this one freely and with confidence, new fences can be introduced which will, because of their construction or appearance, cause different problems. It is, in fact, no bad plan to make unusual-looking fences. Coloured sacks laid over a fence, or brightly coloured fertilizer cans surmounted by coloured poles, makes fences look sufficiently unusual and give the horse something to think about.

As jumping on the lunge progresses, combination fences can be used to increase the horse's judgement of the jump involved. The fences comprising a combination should, however, be placed at exactly the correct distances, otherwise the horse is being set too difficult a problem and will be in danger of becoming confused and of losing his confidence. Between two vertical (upright) fences, 7·2 m (24 ft) from inside to inside of each fence allows for one non-jumping stride at canter; 9·9 m (33 ft) allows for two strides. In the case of a vertical to a spread fence these distances have to be shortened by between 15 cm (6 in) and 30 cm (12 in) according to the length of the horse's stride and the speed at which the combination is approached. If the combination consists of a spread to a vertical then the distance between the two fences has to be lengthened by up to 30 cm (12 in).

In general terms a good stride at canter will cover 3·3 m (11 ft), and 3·6 m (12 ft) should be allowed for the leap from take-off to landing. Distances for three non-jumping strides are 13·5 m (45 ft); for four, 16·8 m (56 ft); and for five, 20·1 m (67 ft).

When using uprights to support fences there will obviously be a danger of the lunge line becoming caught, with results that can be imagined. To avoid so disastrous an event a pole is rested on the top of the upright from the ground on the take-off side and allowed to project some 45 cm (18 in) beyond the top of the upright. The rein will then slide up the pole without restraint.

As a general rule lungeing from the bit is not recommended, and should certainly not be countenanced when jumping on the lunge. On the other hand, there are methods of using the lunge

This young foal, with its well-formed, strong limbs and no doubt with plenty of energy, will appreciate the company of other foals.

OVERLEAF: A well-grown foal and its dam at liberty. Even Thoroughbred foals benefit from the freedom of being out at grass, and will be brought in to stables only during cold weather from quite a young age.

rein from the bit which are acceptable enough in the hands of an expert and can be used beneficially. They can, indeed, replace the necessity for using long-reins since by their use the horse can be 'put on the hand'.

Ridden Work on the Flat: The initial ridden school work in this stage is relatively undemanding of the horse, and consists of establishing the pupil in the simpler school exercises – the changes of rein, shallow curves and occasional full circles using half of the the school area. But in all these the direct rein of opposition is now used in preference to the elementary direct or opening rein. The effect of this rein, which acts on the quarters to alter the direction of the forward movement, ensures that the horse is bent round a turn along the whole length of his body, thus improving the lateral suppleness.

So far the horse has learned that the aids *act* to cause one movement or another, and *yield* when the movement is obtained. It is now necessary for him to be taught the third function of the aids and to learn that they may also be used to *resist*. A simple example of a resisting aid is that of the outside leg on a turn. The leg held flat against the horse and to the rear of the girth prevents the quarters swinging too far out. It is then supporting the action of the inside leg, and by holding the quarters may be said to be resisting their movement.

Similarly, the hands can resist, even if they must do so with infinite tact. In the beginning, the hands become more definite in their action only to prepare the horse for turns or transitions of pace, but in time they are used in conjunction with the legs to shorten the outline of the horse, helping to compress him towards his centre. By practising slow-ups (shortenings) and speed-ups (lengthenings), longitudinal suppleness of the horse is improved. The method employed is for the rider to continue the action of his legs while resisting intermittently with the fingers. The legs maintain the thrust forward of the quarters at one end, while the hands hold, or resist, that impulsion at the other.

Such exercises are performed for the most part at the trot; the sitting trot is employed only when a shortening of the horse is demanded. They have the effect of raising the head, lightening the horse's forehand. This takes place because there is greater engagement of the hind legs under the body and so the horse's weight is carried more upon the quarters and less upon the forehand. The raising of the head, involving the transference of body weight and balance a little to the rear and more over the quarters, is accomplished not by any upward action of the hands but by the increasing use of the legs, causing greater engagement of the horse's hind legs.

Those exercises that stretch the neck and lower the head are not, however, to be neglected. It is only by the stretching of the neck muscles that they are made able to contract, and they must contract when the head is carried in a higher position. (A singular property

The earlier a foal is accustomed to being handled the better: this one, for example, has already been taught enough to wear its foaling slip quite happily.

PREVIOUS PAGE: Young foals playing together: company is important for all horses, and for foals in particular as they will learn a good deal while they play.

of muscle is that it can contract only to the degree that it can be stretched. It therefore follows that the horse's muscles must be stretched before they can be asked to contract effectively.) Exercises over a grid of poles or cavalletti encourage this stretching and relaxation of the neck muscles, as well as helping to strengthen the quarters.

When the more complex school exercises can be accomplished, the head carriage will improve and the trainer will work towards the third element of l'Hotte's dictum – straightness. That quality will not be achieved in its entirety during this secondary stage, but much progress can be made towards it. He will start by lightening both ends of the horse, and the root of that is in the mobility of the quarters. The horse has to be taught first to move his quarters laterally, away from the action of a single leg, and finally to move his quarters round his forelegs in a turn on the forehand, another movement which will not be accomplished perfectly in the secondary stage of training.

This turn, like the turn on the haunches, is not a natural one. It is an example of man improving upon nature to further his own purposes. Horses in freedom turn on their centres. Very occasionally, if frightened, they may execute a turn on the quarters, but never a turn on the forehand. These movements, however, mark the difference between the partially schooled horse and the much more responsive schooled one.

The reasons why mobility of the quarters is taught are, one, to lighten the quarters; two, to strengthen and make supple each hind leg individually by causing the hind legs to cross; and three, to obtain control of the quarters, the origin of directional movement and therefore of the horse himself. Most sources of resistance, perhaps surprisingly, emanate from the quarters rather than from elsewhere.

Methods used vary from trainer to trainer and from country to country but of them all the French method has the most logical appeal and is to be recommended because of its insistence on the maintenance of forward movement.

The first step is for the trainer, standing slightly to the side of the head and facing the tail, to hold the horse and then to walk backwards. He slows the horse a little, inclines the head a trifle towards him, then taps the horse low down behind the girth with his long whip. Inevitably the horse moves away from the whip and shifts the quarters over. He may, indeed, cross the hind legs once or twice. The horse is then walked forward on the line dictated by the new position of the quarters. There is no point in teaching the horse to move in this fashion at halt since it is when the horse is in movement that it is necessary to be able to control the position of his quarters. Practised to either hand, after a few days this exercise should be easily executed from the saddle and it can then be followed by riding a zig-zag down the long side of the school before moving on to the reversed half-volte, the final lead-in to the actual forehand turn. The reversed half-volte is made by leaving the track on an oblique line and returning to it by a small 6 m (24 ft) half-circle. In time the half-circle can be reduced in size until, eventually, a half-turn on the forehand can be executed.

When the head carriage is sufficiently high the horse can be taught the turn on the quarters, which will lighten the forehand just as the preceding turn lightened the quarters. Until, however, the head is carried high enough the turn cannot be attempted. A low head carriage resists any lightening effect because it will not allow enough of the weight to be moved to the rear – an essential in the execution of the turn. The French term for this high carriage of the head is *ramener* and it refers to a head carried close to the vertical with the poll at the apex. It is a position brought about by *the advance of the body towards the head,* the former being driven forward on to gently resisting hands, and it is the aim of progressive schooling. It will not be reached within the secondary education but at its completion the goal should be in sight.

The turn on the quarters follows the forehand turn because the former demands that the rider's legs must resist to hold them in place, whereas in the turn on the forehand the leg acted. It follows that an unwanted shift of the quarters cannot be opposed, and the quarters held in position for a turn to be made on them, until the horse has learned to move his quarters in obedience to the single leg as in the forehand turn. By teaching a horse to yield to a single leg the rider is provided with the means by which the horse will respond to one that resists.

The turn is taught in order, one, to eradicate the resistances of the quarters through being able to control them; two, to make supple the shoulders as the forehand turn made supple the quarters; three, to effect a rebalance of the horse. The forehand turn lightened the quarters, the turn on the quarters acts in opposite fashion to lighten the forehand. Both will therefore contribute to an overall improvement in balance.

Of the two the turn on the quarters is by far the most difficult and calls for the aids of hand and leg to be applied with exactitude and delicacy if the quarters are to be held in place and the forehand to pivot correctly round them. Nonetheless the approach to the turn, or at least to the half-turn on the quarters, can be made with a fair hope of success within the period of the secondary schooling.

As in the forehand turn the approach is made from walk, but this time into a half-volte, the opposite to the reversed half-volte. Once more, the turn can by degrees be tightened until the point is reached where a half-turn on the quarters can be executed.

The lunge work will have prepared the horse for the cantering exercises under saddle, and once the pace is established reasonably well on the lunge, the rider can begin cantering in the school area. In the beginning the horse is bound to experience some little difficulty and this may also be the case in strike-offs into canter on the correct lead. The classical aids for the strike-off are the 'diagonal' aids, i.e. for circle left the left rein and right leg (together, of course, with the supporting right rein and the left leg at the girth). In many cases it is possible to obtain a strike-off perfectly well using these aids, but if the horse has difficulty the rider must resort to the 'lateral' aids, which are not pretty but do cause the horse to strike off correctly, even if he does so from a state of imbalance. The lateral aids for a canter lead to the left are the right hand drawing the head away from the direction of the movement and the strong application of the leg on the same side. The result of moving the head to the outside is to free the horse's inside shoulder, and it is then very difficult for him to do otherwise than lead with the inside leg. As the departures into canter become more proficient the gradual change to diagonal aids can be effected and will produce a more balanced transition into canter.

Much work will need to be done to perfect the canter but it is most necessary that the pace is performed correctly, as the canter is probably the most useful pace of all for improving the longitudinal suppleness of the horse.

A simple form of control at the canter, producing either a shortening or lengthening of the posture, is easily practised by manipulating the reins. To extend the horse, for instance, the outside rein can be used to turn the nose slightly away from the directional movement. The effect will be to give greater freedom to the inside shoulder and to allow the stride made by the inside, leading, foreleg to be lengthened. To shorten the stride the inside rein must act and will by closing, or restricting, the full movement of the inside shoulder, shorten the stride. This simple technique is of great value in jumping a course of obstacles, when it will always be necessary to control the length of stride in order to cope with the demands of the course and the individual fences.

Shortening the stride causes a re-imposition of balance and checks the impulsion by the weight being moved towards the quarters. It will, however, be necessary to teach the horse a more sophisticated method of achieving the same object by means of the half-halt, a movement which can also be used when making any downward transition or to check impulsion within the other paces. This is, however, most effective when practised at canter and, apart from being a very useful exercise in obedience, has a practical application in controlling the impulsion when jumping.

A half-halt means exactly that. It is a momentary check causing a redistribution of weight by shifting this from the forehand to the quarters. It will always be followed immediately by forward movement. To make the half-halt the rider applies both legs in a strong momentary action, causing the horse to be sent further into contact with his bit. Almost simultaneously both hands are raised and turned upwards, with the palms on top. The actions involve only a second or two and, obviously, it will be essential for the horse to be in strong impulsion before they can take effect. Without impulsion there would be nothing to check, and as a result no half-halt would be possible.

Further exercises in balance are involved in practising the transitions upwards and downwards from halt. These also provide a useful solution to an over-exuberant young horse.

In this stage attention will be paid to the correctness of the 'school' halt. The 'school' halt is accomplished when the horse stands square with fore and hind legs together. Halted in this manner the horse is in a state of balance, and is able to move off smoothly from that state. Occasionally a young horse will find it easy enough to bring his forelegs into line but will carry one hind leg behind its partner. The difficulty will be overcome by making the halt on an element of a circle, when the inside hind leg will be brought further under the body. If the problem is with the left hind leg a halt on a circle to the left will be used and vice-versa.

Somewhat surprisingly, it may seem, no mention has yet been made of the rein-back, apart from the reference to the training in the stable when the horse was required to step back a pace or two from a push on his nose. The movement is delayed until this late stage for very good reasons. In the first place it is a difficult movement to perform correctly, and secondly it cannot be taught with any hope of success before the horse is in the correct form, has good engagement of the hocks and is confirmed in forward movement; nor can the horse rein-back from anything other than a square halt. Most trainers will teach the rein-back from the ground before attempting the movement from the saddle and risking the horse becoming confused. The horse is led down the side of the school, slowed down and brought to a square halt. The trainer then moves to the front, and holding the reins in either hand causes the horse to lower his head. He will then act alternately with each rein towards the rear and the horse will usually take a pace back – if he does not, a tread on the horse's toes will produce the required result. The rein-back is in 'two-time', that is, the horse moves his legs in diagonal pairs. It is *not* a walk backwards, since the walk is a pace of 'four-time'. The pace taken to the rear must, therefore, be made by a diagonal pair of legs moving in unison. Two paces are considered sufficient at this point and the horse must then be persuaded to move smartly forwards.

When the horse moves back in-hand in a straight line the exercise is carried out from the saddle, again using the wall to ensure that the quarters will not swing out in at least one direction. The horse will be ridden into halt, the legs will hold him straight and the hands will act alternately as before. Correctly done the horse should step back with the right fore and the left hind in response to the right rein and with the opposite diagonal when the left rein is applied.

Not all schools of thought will follow this method, or even agree with it, holding that if the horse is driven forward by the legs onto closed hands he must, since he cannot go forward, move backwards. It sounds logical enough but it is far, far more difficult to put into practice than the method described.

Finally the horse will learn something of the work on two tracks which will confirm the suppleness of his body. Two-track work, where the forelegs and hind legs follow separate tracks, begins with the exercise invented by the eighteenth century French Master, de la Guérinière. It is known as 'shoulder-in'. From this movement the horse will be taught the half-pass, in which he will move diagonally with his outside legs crossing over the inside ones. Two-track work has its roots in the training on the circle, with the horse correctly bent in the direction in which he is travelling, and in the turns on forehand and quarters which gave control over the quarters.

In shoulder-in the horse is bent from poll to tail with his head held *away* from the direction of the movement. He travels sideways but moves forward always in the direction of his convex side. The legs of the opposite concave side pass in front and cross over those of the convex side.

To perform the movement it is necessary to employ the more advanced rein aids, the indirect rein of opposition in front of the withers and the indirect rein of opposition behind the withers, sometimes known as the intermediary rein. The first of these acts to move the shoulders sideways, the second has the effect of moving the whole horse in a similar fashion. This latter is that most concerned with lateral work.

Shoulder-in is obtained from a circle, when the horse will already be correctly bent and prepared for the movement. In the case of left shoulder-in, a circle to the left is ridden and as the horse comes to the wall, the bend is held and the left intermediary rein applied behind the withers in the direction of the right hip, just as the forelegs are leaving the track and while the hindlegs are still on it. The right hand, after yielding initially, supports in line with the neck; the right leg, behind the girth, controls any swing of the quarters to the right while the left acts on the girth to maintain impulsion and reinforce the action of the left rein which, by opposing, is driving the quarters to the right. After a few steps have been executed the horse is pushed forward onto the circle again.

Clearly, the half-pass can be, and frequently is, taught from shoulder-in, but it is probably best approached from the movement called *travers* which in English is called head-to-the-wall or, confusingly, quarters-in. It is probably easier to return to the half-volte which led up to the half-turn on the quarters, riding the figure with quarters-in and returning to the track by a few steps at half-pass. The advantage lies in the fact that forward movement will be promoted rather than slowed down, a tendency and a failing apparent in the conventional head-to-wall exercise preceding half-pass.

The aids for half-pass to the left in this case, applied as the return to the track is begun, are right rein on the neck (the indirect rein) and right leg held behind the girth, which will push the shoulders to the left. The left rein then inclines the head to the left while the left leg on the girth maintains the impulsion.

Once half-pass is obtained in this way it can be obtained on a straight line from the conventional head-to-the-wall movement, the horse being moved obliquely at first, no more than an angle of 25 to 30 degrees, and only later increasing the angle to 45 degrees. Head-to-the-wall is then followed by tail-to-the-wall (*renvers*), the opposite way round, so that the movement can be carried out independently of the wall.

Jumping: Once more the horse has been prepared for mounted jumping by the work on the lunge, and to a large degree the ridden jumping follows the same pattern. Other exercises can, however, be practised and it is helpful if a jumping area is available where the horse can jump a variety of obstacles and where once a week or so in the later stages of training he can be asked to jump one, or at the most two, bigger fences. On two things all trainers are agreed: one, that good jumping is the result of sound, basic training on the flat; two, that within reason, the less jumping a horse does the better he will jump – it is all too easy and too tempting to over jump a horse and make him sour.

Cross-country type fences, particularly those involving jumping

from one level to another, and of course water, should be included in the jumping training. A good way to teach a horse to jump water is to lay a pole or cavalletto on the take-off side and place a pole over the centre of the spread. This will make the horse gain some height in his leap, and helps him to realize that water does, in fact, constitute a fence to be jumped.

Most schooling fences will have 'wings' or some form of side pole to prevent the horse from running out, but while wings are helpful to start with, the aim should be to dispense with them by gradual stages.

To discourage the annoying habit of rushing, and to encourage the horse to jump calmly, an exercise commencing with a single cavalletto is frequently carried out. The cavalletto is placed in the centre of the schooling area and approached from trot. The obstacle is jumped and then the horse is brought immediately to halt by the rider stretching his back upwards and inclining the shoulders a little to the rear on landing. The exercise, over two cavalletti placed one on top of the other, can be extended to the canter pace and the horse halted on landing as before.

A variation on the same theme is to construct a square of cavalletti, the length and breadth being 9·9 m (33 ft). The square can be approached at trot, the obstacle jumped and the halt made in the centre. Then the horse can be jumped out over the cavalletto immediately in front of him or, later on, he can be asked to make a right or left turn and jump out of the sides of the box.

As a practical accomplishment and one that also encourages confidence, obedience and initiative, the horse should also be taught to jump from an angle, something he will certainly be required to do if he is ever to jump seriously in competition.

As before, a cavalletto is laid in the centre of the school and jumped from a straight approach at trot. Very gradually the approach is made at an increasing angle until the horse is being ridden in a figure of eight with the cavalletto at its centre. Another cavalletto placed alongside the first to make a spread can then be jumped from canter in the same manner, the leading leg being changed at each end of the school by bringing the horse back to trot for a few paces before striking off on the appropriate leg. An extension of these exercises is possible by making use of the cavalletti square which can be jumped in a variety of ways.

The final exercise involves changing direction while jumping the fence and is obviously more difficult to accomplish. It is, however, an invaluable technique in jumping competitions. A small fence is erected, and jumped first from a straight approach and then from a slight angle. In this last instance the horse will almost always land with the correct foreleg leading since he is in effect on an element of a circle. If the fence is jumped slightly from the left the horse is on a right-handed circle and will land with the right foreleg leading. The bend can be increased by inclining the horse's head in the required direction while he is still in the air. In time, and with some practice, it will be possible to jump the fence from a straight approach and bend the horse to either direction over the obstacle according to the position of the next fence on the course.

In jumping competitions there is seldom time or opportunity for the rider to be concerned with the niceties of changing the lead; a great deal must, perforce, be left to the horse. Trained in this way, the horse will learn to change leg automatically when the direction is changed by the rider.

Hacking: Hacking during the secondary stage of training is of just as much importance as in the primary schooling. As well as relaxing the horse and keeping him interested, it provides opportunities for teaching valuable lessons which cannot be taught in the school area. In the early periods the horse will learn to canter, often over undulating ground, and towards the end of the training he will be given short gallops, not only to improve his wind but to teach him to carry his rider at this much faster pace. Road work at a steady trot improves his muscular condition, helps his wind and hardens his legs, and of course it is on the roads that he will learn about traffic. It is a wise precaution for the young horse to be accompanied by a 'school-master', but as time goes on less reliance will be placed upon the older horse and by the end of the training period the youngster should be fairly reliable in most types of traffic conditions.

The Double Bridle: Towards the end of the secondary training it will be necessary to introduce the horse to the double bridle. So far the horse will have been ridden in a plain jointed snaffle, with or without a drop noseband, but now he has to be taught to respond to the more sophisticated actions of the double bridle, which will help the flexion of the lower jaw and poll in a way that is not completely possible in a snaffle. The double bridle, indeed, will add to the polish of the educated horse. Nonetheless it is necessary for the horse to be taught to carry the bridle, and for both horse and rider to understand its actions.

The double bridle consists of a light bradoon lying in the mouth above a short-cheeked curb bit. In the trained horse, the former acts upwards upon the corners of the lips to suggest a raising of the head. The curb, when it assumes, through the pressure of the rein, an angle of some 45 degrees, acts upon three parts of the head to induce a lowering and a retraction of the nose from the poll.

The mouthpiece of the curb bit has a port in its centre to allow room for the tongue and to ensure that the bearing surface rests on the bars of the mouth. The action is a downward one and slightly to to the rear and is assisted by the curb chain acting on the curb groove. The combined effect of the two is to cause the horse to lower his head and flex the lower jaw while retracting his nose. This lowering influence of the bit is supported by pressure being applied to the *poll*. The latter occurs when rein pressure is applied, causing the eye of the bit, which is attached to the cheekpieces, to move forward, thus exerting pressure through the cheekpieces to the headpiece of the bridle.

The two bits of the double bridle, therefore, enable the rider to position the head by raising it, lowering it and bringing the nose inwards. Unless the horse is accustomed to these complexities gradually he is more likely to resist the unfamiliar pressures than to respond to them.

The first lesson, as is often the case, takes place in the stable, where the horse is fitted very carefully with the new bridle. Still wearing the bridle, he is then given a small feed. In order to eat he must relax his lower jaw, and this is the first lesson. After some three or four days of wearing his bridle while eating a small feed, the bit can be manipulated in the mouth. To prevent the horse retreating from the pressures he is placed with his quarters into a corner. The reins are passed over the head and the trainer takes the bradoon rein in the left hand, holding it some 25 cm (10 in) from the bit rings and above the nose. The curb reins are held in the right hand, the same distance from the bit, but behind the horse's chin. The head is raised a few times by the bradoon, and the curb rein is operated to make the horse drop his nose and relax his lower jaw.

When the horse understands what is wanted and is responding to the action of both reins, the lesson can be carried out in the school with the trainer holding the reins as before and walking backwards while an assistant follows the horse to keep him moving forward.

Finally, the reins are put over the neck and the trainer positions himself at the near side of the horse, with the bradoon rein in his right hand and the curb in his left. The same raising and lowering exercises are practised at the halt and, by manipulating the reins, the trainer will ask the horse to flex to the right and left. When this can be done at halt it is carried out at walk and after a week or so it should be possible to ride the horse satisfactorily in the bridle.

The methods which have been described are not common to all trainers – each will have his own ways developed from his personal experience. But if the detail differs, most trainers would agree on the general progression followed and that such training, properly carried out, will produce what every rider wants – a sound, strong, reliable all-round horse.

HORSE PSYCHOLOGY
The science of psychology investigates the mind and the reasons behind the behaviour of animals. These reasons depend very much on the physical structure of a particular animal and the environment in which it is adapted to live; so before one can really understand the behaviour of any animal, one has to study its physique, and give special attention to the structure and arrangement of its sensory organs, in order to appreciate their capabilities and particularly their limitations.

Vision
Vision, one of the most important senses to both man and animals, is the result of electrical activity in the retina, a layer of cells at the back of the eye; these cells convey impulses to the brain when stimulated by rays of light. The retina of man and of monkeys contains two different sorts of cell; some are shaped like rods, others like cones. It is the combination of these two types of cells which makes colour vision possible. A shortage of cones may indicate colour-blindness. The eyes of horses, like those of most other mammals, contain only rod cells, so it has always been assumed that they cannot see in colour. Recent research, however, may indicate otherwise.

Dr Bernard Grzimek has published the results of work in which he claims to have been able to train horses to distinguish between colours. Two horses were used in his experiments; each was led numerous times into a riding school in which were a number of mangers filled with oats. A coloured card was hung in front of one manger and in front of the others were cards of various shades of grey. The horses were allowed to eat only from the manger displaying the coloured card; whenever they tried to go to the others they were prevented from doing so. Eventually, when the horses were taken into the arena where the training had been carried out, they would invariably make for the manger with the coloured card and would ignore the others. This indicates, according to Dr Grzimek, that colour-vision in these animals is possible, even if not very often utilized.

Even if they cannot distinguish colours, there is no doubt that horses can distinguish different shades and textures, and are usually very scared of bright white or deep black objects when these are first seen. The reason for this may not lie with the nature of the colours themselves, but only with their rarity. In the temperate zones of the earth inhabited by horses, completely white objects, for instance, are seldom found in a natural setting. As anything rare is a potential danger, it will typically be treated with suspicion until it is proved to be harmless.

Fear of dark areas may be explained in a different way. It is often found that during cross-country events, the fences which are most likely to upset horses are those which involve jumping out of sunlight into shadows or woods. The reason for the upset is likely to be due to the peculiarities of a horse's vision.

It is only natural to be cautious when entering a dark place from a light one, as there is a temporary blindness which lasts until the eye adjusts to the difference in the amount of light reaching the retina. This blindness is usually very short-lived. The eye, by the process known as dark-adaptation, soon gets used to the situation, and after a short time may be able to see just as well in deep shadow as it did in the sunlight only a few minutes before. The process of dark-adaptation occurs in nearly all mammals and takes place at more or less the same rate in all the individuals of the same species, though the rate differs considerably between one species and another. In humans, the speed is comparatively fast: within a few seconds of coming into a shaded room from the sun outside, the outline of large objects can usually be distinguished, and within twenty minutes the whole adaptive process is almost completed. Curiously enough, animals such as dogs and cats, whose eyes are made to enable them to see in the dark, take longer than humans to adapt to sudden changes of illumination. Dogs, in whom the speed of dark-adaptation has been studied most carefully, seem to take nearly twice as long as man, so that if a man and his dog both enter a room at the same time, the dog will still be able to see very little when the man is seeing without difficulty.

It seems probable that horses, too, adapt very slowly to changes in the intensity of light, as their eyes are also specialized for night vision. To ask a horse, therefore, to jump from the sunlight into shadow is like asking it to jump into the unknown; and no horse, unless in such a state of excitement that personal danger is forgotten, or so completely confident in its rider that it is prepared to do whatever is asked of it, will be at its best in such circumstances.

A very important aspect of vision is that of focusing. Our eyes cannot focus simultaneously on objects at different distances. When an object in the far distance is seen clearly, those closer to hand will appear blurred; when a near object is in focus, the more distant ones are blurred. Yet a normal young person can switch over from near to distant with comparatively little difficulty.

To understand how this comes about, it is necessary to consider the structure of the eye itself. The eyes of most mammals consist of two cavities, each filled with a transparent fluid. They are divided from one another by a layer of opaque, elastic tissue – the iris – in the centre of which is the transparent lens.

Now in order that the rays of light from an object may be bent and brought to form an image exactly on the retina, the lens makes itself round and fat or flat and thin according to the distance of the object from the eye. This process is known as accommodation. As a person gets older and the elasticity of the lens decreases, accommodation becomes more difficult and extra lenses must be fitted to frames in front of his eyes in order to help him overcome that difficulty.

The lens inside a horse's eye has no elasticity or powers of accommodation. The problem of distinguishing objects at different distances is overcome by having the retina arranged on a slope or ramp, so that the bottom part is much nearer the lens than the top part. The only way a horse can focus on objects at different distances is by raising or lowering its head so that the image is brought into contact with the correct part of the retina. For a horse living in the wild state, this is an extremely practical arrangement; while its head is down feeding, both those objects at its feet and those in the distance above the horizon will be in focus at the same time. For horses that are being ridden and driven, however, it means that when they are made to hold their heads up, the objects at their feet will always be out of focus and will only be seen imperfectly. This is probably why horses often shy at close objects, and why, when they are being ridden over rough country or jumps, they should be encouraged to keep their heads low.

The manner in which a horse focuses its eyes must make it difficult for it to judge distances accurately. This difficulty is probably emphasized because horses do not possess binocular vision. There are many ways in which depth and distance can be measured visually. Humans, because their eyes are situated close together on the face, are able to take in very much the same scene with each eye. This is called binocular vision. Since each eye sees the scene from a slightly different angle, each receives a slightly different image; the two are superimposed inside the brain and the combined result is a three-dimensional picture. Binocular vision gives objects the appearance of solidity while establishing their position in space.

A horse's eyes are set wide apart on the sides of its head so that each takes in a very different view. Images do not superimpose in the same way as in the human brain. The perception of depth is, therefore, very different for horses and humans. The position of a horse's eyes, however, do give it the ability to see great distances behind as well as in front and also to see each side simultaneously. This wide-screen vision would be a most valuable asset to an animal living on an open plain and subject to attack from any direction – more valuable, perhaps, than accurate depth perception.

Hearing

The sense of hearing is sharper in most animals than in man; but the horse's sense of hearing has never been studied very systematically. We know from experience that horses quite quickly learn to distinguish the commands that are given to them when they are being trained on the lunge (provided that the commands are always given in the same way and are quite distinct from one another). It is also obvious that horses quickly learn to associate the sound of food being prepared with the anticipation of eating it, and that calls between a mare and foal will be recognized by each other. Horses do not respond to their names, even if they are being called to be fed, nor do they seem to use sound very much when communicating with one another. Beyond these few observations there is little really known about a horse's hearing or use of sound. The facts suggest that sounds are not very important to them in their natural element, as where a sense is unimportant for survival it tends to be comparatively poorly developed. One might wonder why, if this is so, the horse has such large and mobile ears. The reason is probably that the ears are used in place of voice or hands for signalling to one another rather than for focusing sound waves. This point too will be taken up again later when we come to consider communication itself.

Smell
Smell is another of the senses more important to, and therefore better developed in, animals than in man. To what extent horses use the sense of smell we do not really know, but although horses do not sniff the air as ostentatiously as dogs, most horses, especially young ones, appear to take a keen interest in smells. A youngster is never at home with a new person, in a new stable, or in front of a new piece of saddlery, until it has had a good sniff at it, after which it often raises its head and curls up its top lip in a gesture first described by Flehmen, and now often called after him the Flehmen gesture. Moreover, all horses, young and old, sniff at one another when first introduced.

Undoubtedly the most important use made of smell by those animals in which it is strongly developed is in the sphere of communication and territorial recognition, and it is therefore in this connection that a horse's sense of smell should be assessed.

Most animal species stake out their territories by 'scent-marking' them with their excreta. In horses this is the job of the stallion, who will deposit his dung in neat piles at various points over his territory. Intruders will recognize these as the signs of ownership and behave accordingly. On the other hand, mares, and to some extent geldings, spread their dung liberally over a wide area as they move, so that a lost member of the herd or family will be able to find its way back to the group by tracking them from one pile of dung to the next.

In most young horses, even after thousands of years of domestication of the species, this tendency is still well retained. A youngster out on the road for the first few times will want to stop and smell every pile of dung it comes across, as if to make sure it is not trespassing. All horses, young or old, retain the tendency to mark a freshly cleaned or newly entered stable in the natural manner by covering it with their excreta.

Finally, smell may have a very important function in telling the

horse the state of another individual. The emotions have a strong
influence on the body – especially the sweat glands – causing these
to start exuding their contents. Hence an excited, worried or fearful
animal will give out a distinctive – even if only very faint – odour,
which an animal with a well-developed sense of smell may well be
able to detect. This may be why horses can usually recognize
people who are afraid of them.

Touch
The senses dealt with so far – those of sight, hearing and smell –
have one very important function in common. They give the
individual information about things that are going on some
distance away from him and so allow him to anticipate and, if
necessary, avoid danger. But before an animal can really know what
different things are like – which are dangerous and which safe,
which pleasant and which unpleasant – he has to come into direct
contact with them: he has to touch them.

The skin is a highly specialized organ of touch. It is important,
therefore, for the skin to be able to tell the animal a good deal
about the quality of different objects. It tells the animal whether an
object is hot or cold, whether it causes pain, and whether it is hard
or soft; exactly how it differentiates between these different
sensations – touch, temperature and pain – is still a considerable
mystery. One thing only has been established with certainty. Most
of the skin is actually quite insensitive, but scattered over its surface
are minute spots, some of which will respond to one sense, some
another. Thus, a spot which responds to touch will not respond to
pain; one that responds to temperature will not necessarily respond
to pressure.

Although all areas of the skin have a certain number of these
discrete sensory spots, some areas have many more than others. In
man, the mouth, feet and hands are particularly well-equipped, and
are very much more sensitive to touch than, for instance, the middle
of the back or the forearm. In addition, some areas concentrate
much more on one type of sensation than on others: the tips of the
fingers are especially sensitive to light touch and temperature, while
comparatively insensitive to pain; the inside of the mouth, however,
is very much more sensitive to pain than to temperature. It is
possible to drink things which are too hot to hold comfortably in
the hand, although a minute pimple inside the mouth will be far
more painful than a sore of equal size on the finger.

The general pattern of sensitivity appears to be very much the
same throughout the entire animal world. The vital areas around
the mouth and extremities are always those most richly provided
with sensory spots. One has only to touch a young horse around
the mouth or try to pick up one of its feet to realise that this is so.
But sensitivity may alter with experience. In man, for instance,
it is well known that if the sense of sight is lost, the sense of touch
becomes much finer – not because nerve endings or touch spots

are developed in the skin but because the individual learns to distinguish minute details which at first he was inclined to overlook.

That the same thing happens in horses is quite plain to anyone who has ever tried to school them. When a young horse is first backed, it not only fails to understand what is required of it when its flanks and mouth are touched, but it needs considerably more pressure on these parts to make it understand what is required of it than is the case later on. Gradually, with training, the horse learns to interpret and anticipate the different signs and to respond to very much slighter pressure than was originally necessary.

The fact that sensitivity to pressure can become very keen over some areas of the horse's body is not, however, an unmixed blessing, for it is possible that the highly trained animal may finally be able to perceive the slightest and most unconscious tensions and muscular twitches in the rider. The involuntary activities of the body which accompany thoughts and emotions have long occupied the attention of psychologists, and it is now realized that almost every emotion, thought and desire which passes through the mind is reflected to some extent by activities in the body. Although it sometimes takes extremely sensitive scientific instruments to measure the psychological changes, some of them are obvious and familiar. Probably everyone has had the experience of some embarrassing situation during which, at the moment of emotional tension, he has found himself sweating or blushing. Not everyone, however, realizes that the moment he even thinks of an embarrassing moment his heart will begin to beat faster, his hands to sweat, his mouth to dry up, and his muscles to tense, while the more he tries to fight back these tell-tale reactions and appear outwardly calm, the more violent they will become. Even the voluntary and quite unemotional contemplation of some action will produce electrical discharges from all the muscles which would be involved if it were carried out. A person who thinks of striking a tennis ball will set minute electrical impulses passing along all the nerves and muscles which would be involved in the actual act.

Although man himself cannot detect the smallest of these changes except by means of complicated and very delicate instruments, there is reason to suppose that some animals are able to do so with their unaided senses, and that the very slight muscular tensions and movements which accompany anxiety, the expectation of some momentous event, or a bad temper, may be picked up by a horse and arouse similar sympathetic responses in its own body.

Horses also use touch in all intimate contacts with one another. The young foal, like most young animals, makes use of its mouth and whiskers in its earliest explorations of the world. Friendship and trust are communicated from one horse to another by nibbling along the neck and withers; if a human wants to reassure, congratulate or reward a horse he often copies this by patting it on the neck. When a mare is ready to mate, she will lift up her tail and spread out her hind legs when a stallion touches her under her tail or on the side of her flank; if she is not in a state to mate, however, touches in these places will be answered by kicks and squeals. If any other animal – including man – touches a mare in those same places, her behaviour will be just the same as if the touch had been delivered by a stallion.

Time Sense

Whether horses have an inborn time sense is still an open question. There is no doubt that they are very regular in their habits and expectations, liking to do the same things at about the same times each day. Are these actions really governed by a sense of passing time or by external cues?

As man himself is sadly lacking in the ability to judge time accurately – perhaps it is for this reason that he had to invent clocks – it is unlikely that much insight into the matter will be gained from his introspections. To man, the passage of time seems to be a purely subjective affair, dependent on his expectations and emotions, his occupation and his feelings. When he is busy or when he is hot and feverish, time will pass more quickly than when he is not. An event which is anticipated with pleasure will seem to come more slowly than one that is dreaded, and in retrospect the passing of a few seconds can seem to have taken longer than the hour of which they formed a part. Curiously enough, a person who may be hopeless at judging the passage of a few hours when he is awake may be fairly accurate during sleep, and able to go to bed at night with the perfect assurance that he will wake up the next morning at approximately the desired time.

The difference between the time sense of man and that of some animals indicates that time is not equally important to all species. Is it really important to horses? Most people would insist that it is. As mentioned, horses do appreciate regularity and if free to do as they please will maintain a routine that varies little from day to day. One summer, I kept careful notes of the behaviour of one group of horses which had free access to a barn and a field. Even on days when the flies did not seem particularly bad, the horses tended to retire to the shelter at about 9 a.m. and leave it again only in the evening at about 6 p.m. Their regularity in this respect gave such an impression of time-consciousness that it seemed sensible to admit to this interpretation. Towards the end of the experiment, however, there was a partial eclipse of the sun. For about half an hour in the middle of the day the temperature dropped, the wind died, and darkness seemed about to fall. Man was not apparently the only creature to have the impression of impending night. The chickens began to roost, cows in the neighbourhood lowed for their milkers, and our horses flicked their tails, shook their heads, and walked out into the field for grass. Four hours or ten hours, the interval as measured by clocks seemed to be immaterial to them; it was the external conditions which had prompted them to eat in this case, not the inevitable march of time.

But whether one is justified in arguing from these observations that the times at which stabled horses are fed, watered and exercised is immaterial, is another question.

Inborn Needs and Urges

As well as having their own specialized senses, horses have very special physiological and psychological needs. The horse is built to survive on large, open plains, to gallop fast in order to escape predators, to travel great distances in search of food, and to live in groups or herds. In the natural state, a horse's food is easily available at any time, so, unlike dogs and other hunting species which have to work for their food, a horse never seems to associate food with any special act it has performed. In fact, it never really looks on a titbit as a reward for good behaviour, even though it quickly learns to associate the coming of food with certain sights (such as buckets) or sounds (such as doors being opened). It also quickly learns to associate the presence of good food with certain places or events, so that if a horse originally seems to be afraid of a particular person (such as the vet or blacksmith) or a particular place (such as the inside of a mobile horse-box) feeding it titbits in the presence of these horrors will often allay its fears.

Horses are also slow to learn that if food is present at all, it should be shared equally! They will squabble and fight to take first pick, but those which are pushed away never give up trying to snatch their share. For this reason, taking titbits into a field full of loose horses can be a hazardous task; in their scuffles, the horses are quite likely to kick or knock over their would-be benefactor, and children especially are often hurt in this way.

Being by nature social animals, horses not only have a great need for company, but also have an elaborate system of communicating with one another. A few of their signals are vocal, and we can recognize these without much difficulty. They range from the low, snuffling whicker of friendship, to the high, shrill neigh for help, or the squeal of anger. Most of their signals, however, are made by gesture. The tail and ears are particularly important for this purpose; when the ears are laid back tight and the tail is swished, the horse is indicating that it is angry and is threatening, but when excited, a horse's ears are pricked forward and its tail lifted high over its back. The mouth and the position of the head are also used for conveying signals. A young horse, for instance, will signify its submission to an older one by the 'snapping' posture. This posture is seen when a horse sticks its head out and up, curls back its lips and chatters its teeth. The expression is like the grin seen in many other species, including monkeys, dogs and man.

Even quite old horses will occasionally revert to this gesture if they are introduced to large groups of strangers and want to avoid being attacked. When, for instance, a mare arrives at a new stud and is turned out to graze with the regular inhabitants, she will often greet them with this posture. In general, however, snapping is more usually replaced in older horses by other gestures.

Whether the snapping gesture or, for that matter, any signal, is inborn or learned at an early age from other members of the herd, is a question to which no one really knows the answer. I was able to watch the development of a number of foals which lost their mothers at a very early age and were hand-reared until they were able to fend for themselves. Those which had been reared in total isolation and saw no other horses until they were several months old failed to make the appropriate gesture of submission when they met strangers, and consequently were badly mauled. Those which were raised in groups, however, even if an older animal was not present to show them what to do, snapped regularly at any stranger, equine or human, and had no difficult in being accepted by natural groups. It seems as though the communication signals of a species are probably inborn, but are not practised or released unless the animal properly identifies itself as a member of that species.

In horses, the angle of the mouth and lips are extremely expressive and should always be watched carefully. If the animal is tense or nervous, its jaw will be set hard. Once it relaxes its jaw and begins to make chewing movements (similar to our smacking or licking our lips) one can be sure the horse is relaxing and losing its first fears.

One great difficulty is that in all animals the signs of fear or submission and those of anger or readiness to attack are very similar. Perhaps this is not surprising as the emotions themselves often merge into one another. Just as the grin of friendship in monkeys and man is very similar to the grin of fury – only the shape of the eyes is really different – so, in the horse, the submissive snapping of the foal is very like the threat of attack by an older animal. In these creatures it is probably the angle and activity of the tail which gives a better clue than the shape of the eyes. In submission the tail is kept still whereas in anger it is swished from side to side.

In any group of horses – even a group of two – a dominance hierarchy has to be established and accepted so that all the individuals in the group know what their positions are. At one time it was believed that most animal societies were built on a hierarchical system, the grades of which were often seen to be far more rigid and clearly defined than even the most class-conscious human society. Hens are a classic example. Among all confined communities of these birds it will be found that one is top-ranking and can peck all the others, while one is the lowliest and can be pecked by the rest.

In the majority of animal societies, however, including that of horses, the pattern is seldom so rigid. A major difficulty in assessing an individual's position in the hierarchy is to decide which criteria are to be used in measurement. Threats or gestures of anger would seem the obvious ones, but in fact these might be very misleading. The dominant horse is not always the one which most regularly bullies and threatens the others. In my own time I have had two very dominant mares; in each case, when out in a field with other horses the mare had only to flick an ear or quiver her tail for all her companions to flee. When threats were made, it was usually observed that each individual tended to pick on one or two others for special attention, as if deciding that these were his or her particular rivals and that the others did not count.

Although the positions are established by means of threats (and the occasional attack), animals at liberty seldom do one another any ser]ous damage. The weaker or more lowly individual will usually give way at the critical moment, signalling its submission to the dominant one and then turning on one lower down in rank than itself! A very high-ranking animal does not usually bother to threaten a very low one, but reserves most of its attacks for those nearest to it in the hierarchy, those which constitute the greatest danger to its own particular position.

The tendency for family members to stick together and to form special relationships with one another has been noted by many breeders, but exceptions have also been found. In my own experience, mares react to their offspring in as many different ways as human mothers do. One of the first brood mares I had, a grey three-quarter Thoroughbred, Nuki, was particularly antipathetic to her own daughters. The oldest of these, Nauri, and the second, Nuit, had both inherited many of her dominant characteristics; when they grew to maturity they were as reluctant to play second fiddle as their mother had been. Perhaps it was for this reason that Nuki saw them as her greatest dangers and felt the need to keep them under her control. Her sons and grandsons, however, were very seldom threatened. Although her daughters were not allowed to approach within several yards of her when she was waiting to go through a gate or resting in the shade, she would allow her sons to lean on her without turning a hair.

You may wonder what all this has to do with riding or managing horses, and why any rider – especially one who merely wants to race or jump his horse – should bother to understand how it lives in the wild or how horses communicate with one another. One good reason is that horses react to signals they receive from any other animals, including man, as if they were from an animal of their own species. In fact, to his horse a rider is really just another horse, and his horse will test to see which of the two is going to be boss and give the orders. It is important in any partnership that this is quickly established. Of course it is always possible for one partner to be boss in one situation and the other in another but this arrangement is usually clearly defined between them.

Since man cannot give the same signals that a horse can – having no tail to lash or ears to lay back – how is he to communicate his intentions and desires? One good method is by using the voice (the low, staccato reprimand seems to be accepted as such by all species). Another method is by signalling in much the same way as a horse would, that is to say, by waving something (an arm, a rope, or a stick). The horse will often take this as a threat gesture and that the man means business. Sometimes a very forceful horse will defy this human threat, just as it would defy the threat of one of its own herd; if the threat is accompanied by a painful slap, however, it will soon learn that human threats are to be taken just as seriously as those of its equine companions.

As mentioned above, it is quite possible for a horse to accept that its rider is boss when they are away from home or in strange territory, but for the horse still to believe that it should be boss at home in its own stable. This is especially common when a horse feels that there is something important to fight about, like food. Indeed some horses never seem to learn that man is not a rival for their food and lay back their ears every time a person passes or enters their stable with a bucket.

With the increased physical well-being that results from eating large quantities of oats and becoming very fit, most horses will attempt to rise high in their social hierarchy. This means they will increase the number of threats and challenges they issue to those close to them in the pecking-order. In the case of a working horse this usually means their riders or handlers. Most riders recognize

this when they say their horses are becoming 'fresh'; what their horses are doing is testing out their dominance by acting in ways they know to be forbidden, like shying at familiar objects and bucking when they are supposed to trot or canter. The testing-out can be perfectly good-natured and friendly, but if the rider does not respond with a friendly reprimand there is a grave danger that the horse will take this as a sign of weakness or submission on the rider's part and try something a little less harmless next time. In this way bad habits are quickly established.

Just as it is difficult to distinguish submission from anger, so it is often very difficult to distinguish threats of this sort from genuine fear, for again the two mingle. Sometimes, indeed, an individual himself cannot tell the difference between them, or may feel he has to stand up to and even provoke a fight with the object of his fear, in order to see how strong he is himself. Hence, if a young horse stops when approaching a stream, a noisy vehicle or a brightly coloured obstacle, it is not always easy to tell if this is because of fright or just because it is testing its rider. If it is really frightened, severe punishment could be fatal to its future development, by turning something which was only marginally feared into a source of real terror. If, on the other hand, it was really just being defiant, punishment could prevent an act which started as a simple test of dominance becoming established as a bad habit.

From what has just been said, it is clear that there is another very important factor which determines and regulates behaviour – learning. Horses, like all animals, start learning – that is to say, modifying their innate behaviour patterns in the light of experience – from the moment they are born; but the way they do so and the things that influence them most are not the same as in man. Like man, they do show three different types of learning – perceptual learning, association learning and motor learning – and each of these has a very important effect on their adult behaviour.

Perceptual Learning

The young foal is born with its eyes closed but almost immediately they are opened, so that from the first moment of its life it is able to register everything that it sees. The human child, on the other hand, is unable to recognize another human's face until it is some weeks old. Perceptual learning can proceed in two different ways: differentiation (that is, learning to tell the difference between two things even if they are alike in a variety of ways – the difference, for instance, between a daisy and a buttercup), and generalization (which is learning to recognize in what ways things are alike and can be grouped together overlooking their differences – to recognize flowers because they grow, and have green leaves, or animals because they move and breathe). Man is good at learning by generalization, but finds differentiation more difficult; the horse, while excellent at differentiation, is very poor at generalization. A foal will recognize its home territory after a single day in it, and if anything is changed there, or if it is asked to move away, shows definite concern. If, however, a potentially frightening object such as a white barrel, which it has learned not to fear in one position, is moved to another place, it evokes just as much suspicion as on the first occasion. A familiar shape – even that of a well-known companion – will be treated as completely new if it is altered in any respects. I well remember the absolute panic which was aroused in one group of young horses the first time one of the older ones was turned out with them in a New Zealand rug. The youngsters had been grazing alongside this particular veteran for months before the autumn frosts were considered cold enough for the old Thoroughbred to need protection. When it appeared among them in this altered guise, the young horses treated it as a complete stranger. One of them made repeated threats and mock attacks – alternating these with dashes for safety – until it finally dared to approach near enough to recognize its mistake. Even familiar objects appearing suddenly in the home field or stable for the first time will be treated with intense suspicion, but perhaps the most difficult thing for us to understand is that something can appear different to a horse if the thing itself is not altered at all but the horse's own situation is changed.

A particularly vivid instance of this occurred when I was first schooling Gambit, a horse which went on to become an international show jumper. Gambit, at that time, was sharing a field with his father, Gamesman, whom I was preparing for his first show jumping venture. I had only one jump to use for schooling at that time and it was a homely affair, composed of tin barrels, situated in the field where the two horses were spending their evenings together. Both horses had been schooled to jump these barrels and did so without any fear. In order to make them more impressive and also to accustom Gamesman to the colour, I took a bucket of whitewash up into the field and began to paint the barrels. Both horses were intrigued by my antics, especially Gambit, who did all he could to help or hinder my efforts by licking the wash off as fast as I put it on. The next morning I saddled him and rode him up into the same field, but he behaved as if he had never seen the barrels before. He would not go within twenty yards of them without snorting and shivering with fear, and it was not until I had laid them all down on their sides and made him walk along between them that he finally consented to jump over them. He had jumped them uncoloured without any trouble and he had seen them coloured. But to jump them coloured was something, to him, apparently quite new. One might say this is like altering the angle from which an object is viewed. Although man can be very misled if the visual angle of an object is changed, he would not expect his perception of familiar objects to change each time his situation while viewing them was altered; to see things differently when, for example, going to work, and differently again when visiting friends!

All these instances may give the impression that the horse is incredibly stupid, and indeed, this is often held to be the case. Because man is so good at generalizing and so poor at discriminating, we tend to equate intelligence with generalization, or abstraction. But to survive in its natural habitat, it is clear that discrimination is more valuable to a horse than generalization, so we should be careful in our judgements.

It is very important for a horse to pick out any slight changes in its environment which might betoken the presence of enemies. Things may remain unchanged in many respects but, because of very slight variations, turn from being beneficial to poisonous. This is particularly the case with some plants, which may be nutritious at some times of the year but poisonous at others. A horse which was not alert to these changes would soon be dead.

Clever Hans

An interesting case of a horse's brilliant powers of discrimination was that of Clever Hans, a horse which created a great stir in scientific circles at the beginning of this century. A German of considerable repute, Herr von Osten, claimed to have trained a horse to answer questions, tell the time, be capable of four different methods of arithmetical calculation, and many other feats suggesting that it had powers of reasoning and abstraction little inferior to those of man. The problems could be given either verbally or in writing, and Clever Hans, as the stallion was called, would tap out its replies on a board at his feet, using one foreleg to denote the tens and the other to denote the digits.

The claims of Herr von Osten and the behaviour of Clever Hans aroused such interest that a committee of eminent scientists was established to investigate the matter. They were given every support and co-operation by von Osten himself and in the end they concluded that there was no trickery or faud. Shortly after this, however, a private investigator exploded the secret. He asked the horse questions whose nature was unknown to the men present, bar himself. The investigator discovered that under these conditions the horse was powerless to do even the simplest sums or solve the most elementary problems. Indeed, Hans gave the impression of being far more interested in the questioners than in the question. The investigator therefore turned his attention away from the horse and on to the behaviour of the people in charge of him. Close scrutiny finally revealed the fact that the humans were making slight, almost imperceptible and completely unconscious movements with their heads or bodies each time the horse was due to stop tapping. It became clear that the horse had learned to pick up and interpret these movements and not that he had worked out the problems for himself.

Herr von Osten had attempted to prove that horses were intelligent by showing that they could think in the same way as man, solving the same sort of mathematical and logical problems. When Clever Hans' secret was discovered, Herr von Osten's faith in him was shattered. The gentleman failed to realize that it required a very clever animal indeed to make the minute discriminations shown by Clever Hans in interpreting the nods of the attendants. While the horse may have been unable to solve the problems set him by the examiners it was solving one far more important to its own well-being – the problem of pleasing its owner.

Association Learning

The second type of learning is that of association. This is the recognition of the relationship between signs and events, of what signals demand what acts, and of what questions demand what replies. This sort of learning depends largely on repetition. If A is followed by B on several occasions, one comes to expect B every time A appears. Horses, like other animals, vary greatly from one another in the speed with which they form associations – another aspect of behaviour which is often taken to reflect intelligence. Some animals seem to grasp the importance of a signal at once; others require constant repetition of signal and response before they begin to show signs of realizing that they are related. These differences are particularly noticeable to trainers, who usually relish the quick learners, the 'intelligent' ones – and become impatient with the slow learners.

Quick learning is not, however, an unmitigated blessing. In horses especially it has its disadvantages. Individuals who are quick to learn one thing are usually quick to learn another also – and this can mean bad habits as well as good. A horse which realizes what is expected of it but which does not want to do it will often try various evasive tactics; the quick learners will very soon adopt any evasions that prove successful. The individuals which are slower to learn are often much more reliable in the long run; for habits that do eventually become ingrained are less easily eradicated or modified.

Motor Skills

The third type of learning, that of motor skills, is the most important one to horses, although it is probably the least important to man. The horse depends for its survival on its own physical prowess rather than on the mechanical gimmicks invented by man to support his own rather mediocre physical accomplishments! To refer to a horse's running or jumping ability as a motor skill might at first seem rather odd. In man, whose survival has come from the development of manual dexterity, the term motor skill is usually confined to the things we do with our hands; but the athletic feats of the gymnast, the tennis player, or the figure skater are just as complex, and their acquisition is quite comparable to the learning required of the dressage or racehorse, or the show-jumper.

One tendency very marked in horses is that of repetition. If a horse has done a thing once, it tends to do it again; so if a sign or signal has elicited a certain pattern of behaviour once, it will do so again on all subsequent occasions – unless a very great effort is made to alter it, or unless the horse is simply trying to be difficult. This tendency is not nearly so marked in other animal species; in rats and monkeys, for instance, the very opposite is the case. If a rat or monkey is faced with a T-junction and turns right the first time, it will almost certainly turn left the next, as if exploration is more important than safety. But in the case of horses this is not so at all. If the right-hand turn has not led to any dire results, it will be repeated every time. The horse's repetition tendency is an important thing for trainers to bear in mind, and the importance of ensuring that the first response elicited by a signal is the desired one will be evident. Most experienced horsemen know this, and may, when buying a new horse, prefer to take one completely unhandled rather than risk the danger of taking on a half-trained animal that has already learned bad habits.

In order to ensure that behaviour is shaped in the right way and bad habits are not established, two principles may well be borne in mind. The first of these is to be sure that all signals (which include vocal commands, hand signs or touch aids) are clear and distinguishable from one another. One of the most difficult and unnerving things for any animal is to be unsure of what is expected of it. Horses, as I have already pointed out, are very good at distinguishing minute visual differences from one another; but whether they are equally good at distinguishing sounds and touches, we do not know. This may well be so, and may be why a rider who is tense and anxious can convey his feelings to his horse. Tension in the leg and arm muscles of a rider may change his command signals so much that the horse can be confused. Although the difference might be indistinguishable to another human, they might seem immense to a highly sensitive horse, which in these circumstances would find itself being given signals it had never received before and would not know how to interpret.

The second point to bear in mind is to be absolutely regular with the rewards or punishments which follow your signals. If a horse is patted for jumping a fence well the first time and jabbed in its mouth the second time, it will not know what to do. Once again it will have a sense of uncertainty and insecurity. If this situation is established it may well respond as a human would when he is weary of trying to make sense of contradictory orders and, frustrated, do the first thing that comes to mind – no matter how rash. The horse may merely adopt a defensive strategy and try to gain some comfort from that. The defensive strategies most often taken up by horses are rearing or napping (that is to say, rushing off back to their home field, their stables, or their companions), but individuals have been known to try all sorts of tactics.

It is common at some of the smaller shows to see poor horses and ponies being ridden and even asked to jump by riders who are either so rough or so incompetent themselves that the animals may be certain that, whatever they do, they are going to suffer. If they refuse or knock the fence down, they are going to be beaten; if they jump and do their best they will receive a jab in the mouth and a thump on the loins. It is not surprising that many of them become bad-tempered or nappy: it is only a surprise that so many of them go on, year after year, putting up with it and still doing their best to please.

There are many ways in which a horse can be encouraged to respond instantly and correctly to a signal. The trainer could wait until the horse is already doing what he wants it to do and then give the signal accompanied by a reward. (A vocal 'good boy' or a scratch on the neck are just as effective as titbits.) If the required act and the signal are combined often enough, they will soon be associated with each other in the horse's mind. The trainer should also give reward or encouragement as soon as the horse begins to do what he wants it to do, even if the act is not perfect at first. Once the horse knows what is expected of it, skills can be perfected gradually. Finally, a trainer should never expect more of the horse than it is easily capable of doing at the time. It stands to reason that when a horse is being taught to jump, it will not be asked to clear an enormous coloured wall on the first day. It will be introduced to jumping with very low, unfrightening obstacles which can easily be taken in the horse's stride, and only when absolutely confident over these will it be taken on to larger jumps. The same principle holds for every other sort of training, whether it is introducing a young horse to traffic or getting it to fulfil its potential in a competitive sphere.

One might think – and indeed it is often believed – that the more often and more quickly an act is repeated, the better it will be learned and retained and that if a skill is not practised constantly there is a danger of it being forgotten. To some extent of course this is true; practice does make perfect and long delays do lead to forgetting. A rest of some hours between learning sessions, however, often leads to quicker and more reliable learning than that which is gained from concentrated work. This fact has been demonstrated repeatedly in many different species. A rest immediately after a difficult task has been absorbed is far more beneficial to learning than repeated practice. Much can be gained, therefore, by letting the horse relax – even by turning it out in a field for an hour or two – after a schooling session. A rider may struggle without success for an entire day to teach his animal some simple manoeuvre, refusing to stop until the horse has made a response, however elementary, in the right direction but, in the end, exhausted and exasperated, he is forced to admit defeat. The very next day, perhaps, or even a week later, he may try again and finds to his amazement that the horse responds correctly at the first touch as if it had been doing it for years. It only needed a break from the constant repetition for the learning to be fixed in the horse's mind.

Would the same results have been obtained without the struggle of the previous session? Could the rider have spared both himself and his horse some anguish if he had buried his pride and given in earlier? The answer is almost certainly 'Yes'. Moreover, by stopping before tempers become too frayed, the rider would not only have saved himself much pain, but would have avoided the risk of upsetting his horse. There is always a danger that an animal which loses confidence, instead of absorbing its lesson at however elementary a level, may resort instead to some unwanted defence mechanism.

Emotional State

The speed with which an animal learns, and the excellence with which it will perform at any given moment, are closely dependent on its emotional state. This state is basically dependent on various biochemicals circulating in the bloodstream whose function is to speed up the rate at which impulses pass from one nerve to another, controlling the rate at which all the bodily functions take place. In states of rest or relaxation, many biochemicals are stored in various glands, and only the minimum amount required to keep the body functioning at a normal pace is freely circulating in the blood. If danger threatens, or if for any other reason the individual needs to be aroused (for example, in the mating season), messages will be conveyed through the sense organs to the appropriate glands, and large quantities of their stocks will be set free. The product of each of the different glands throughout the body has a rather different function and effects different activities: one causes the bowels and bladder to contract and so rid the body of waste; another causes the heart to beat fast; a third causes the iris of the eye to contract (hence the narrow eyes of the angry animal). Others make the blood vessels contract so that if the animal is wounded it will not lose too much blood. Still others increase the rate of breathing and so enable the animal to work faster while the sweat glands start moistening the skin to counteract the extra body heat.

All these things can be seen easily and will tell an onlooker that the animal is prepared for action. Some changes take place at times of arousal which are not easily seen but which can be deduced from some of the experiments which have been carried out in recent years. One of these is that the brain functions much more quickly at these times than it normally does. Just exactly how the brain works, we still do not know (nor do we know whether it works in exactly the same way in all the different species of animals), but we do know that in states of arousal it produces more alternative responses and produces these quicker than in states of relaxation. It also tends to retain in memory the events which occurred when it was emotionally aroused, better than those that occurred when it was not.

This state of arousal or emotional tension is excellent as long as it only continues for the duration of the emergency and then subsides, but if it lasts for much longer than it is needed it can be injurious to the animal. During the state of arousal, two processes will be taking place. In the first, the body will be using up great reserves of fat and sugar which may soon be exhausted. In the second, the biochemicals which regulate the activity of the nerves themselves will become depleted, and this loss can only be made good by a period of rest and relaxation. Thus it can be seen that efficiency, both physical and mental, accompanies excitement in an inverted 'U' shape. At first there is a gain of efficiency as the emotional excitement increases, but if the excitement continues to increase beyond a certain point, efficiency begins to drop. This is why an animal which is in a permanent state of anxiety or high excitement tends to lose weight and can very quickly be tipped over the edge into thoughtless panic. Each individual has its own optimum level of arousal for maximum efficiency, and this will depend on its basic emotional state. The phlegmatic, slow, passive character who learns slowly and never bothers to do more than it must, may show a marked improvement if transferred to a new environment; the more highly-strung, suspicious one, who always fears the worst, may be tipped over the edge into blind stupidity by such a move.

This may be one of the reasons why horses often respond in quite different ways to changes in their environment. Take two young horses making their first expeditions to the exciting world of the hunting field or the show ground. It is quite common that the one which was very quiet, obedient and docile at home suddenly becomes almost unmanageable, while the one which at home was jumpy and nervous becomes completely subdued. In these cases, it is not only the initial reaction to the exciting new situation which may vary but also the changes which occur when the situation becomes increasingly familiar. The horse who is usually quiet and whose basic level of arousal is low was stimulated by the excitement but will probably revert to its basic quiet state at the second or third outing. The excitable one, whose basic level of arousal is high, was stunned into unresponsiveness by the extra stimulation, but may become more and more fractious as familiarity decreases its added stimulation load, and frees its muscles for action.

Temperament and Personality
The difference in arousal-level described above may be one of the factors which determine equine temperaments and personalities, but it is obviously not the whole story, for no two very quiet or excitable horses are exactly alike, any more than two quiet or excitable people are. What, then, is the cause of these individual differences?

Two important factors can be deduced from previous sections of this chapter. These are, first, that there are some needs and urges with which the individual is born and which it derives from its parents by genetic means; second, variations may occur in the ways in which these were satisfied in early life.

Many of the differences are associated with – and indeed arise from – the shape and size of the body. The large, heavy Shire horse, for instance, needs a great deal more food than the small pony: the tough northern horse with its thick coat needs less external heat than the thin-skinned Arab.

As well as these obvious differences of size and hair texture, there are even more important differences in types of metabolism. The Thoroughbred, which has been line-bred for speed and excitability, needs a diet much richer in protein than the native pony which has been line-bred for survival on exposed hillsides. The Thoroughbred, which receives its rich food mainly from a human attendant, will almost certainly develop a different attitude to humans than the hill pony which, although it may be hand-fed just as assiduously by a human attendant in its youth, does not have such a basic physical need for rich food, and therefore fails to associate the human with satisfaction.

While there is almost certainly some relationship between gross temperamental types and physical builds, there is less certainty about the relationship between coat colour and temperament. The advocates of the existence of the relationship will swear unequivocally that all chestnuts are 'hot', blacks 'unreliable' or 'vicious', greys 'docile' and so on. Large-scale studies of wild ponies and horses seem to indicate that such a relationship does exist, but these scientific studies do not claim that every chestnut will be hot and all greys docile. What they do show is that a large proportion conform to the stereotypes suggested by their pigmentation. If this is so, the question must be asked, why does pigment affect temperament?

So far no one has produced an entirely satisfactory answer, but one possibility which has been suggested (and still awaits a convincing proof) is that the distribution of blood vessels and peripheral nerves may vary with pigmentation. People in charge of stables know to their cost that horses with white feet and legs tend to give endless trouble. (There is an old horse dealer's saying, 'One white foot, buy; two white feet, try; three white feet, doubt; four white feet, shoot!') The white hooves tend to crack and break; the white stockings are most susceptible to wet. This seems to be because there is a dearth of nerves in the tissue to keep them healthy and combat infection.

If the whole surface-area of a grey horse is equally lacking in nerve cells, the grey horse would doubtless be less sensitive to the touch aids of its rider than a darker horse would be, and any untoward message it might be given due to the rider's tension would fail to reach it. This may well be the origin of the so-called docility of greys, and one reason for their preponderance among children's ponies. The chestnut, on the other hand, usually has very fine, silky hair; this might give the nerve-endings little protection from the rider's touch signals and so make the animals extremely sensitive to slight variations in a rider's aids.

In contrast to their poor sensitivity to touch, grey horses seem to be much more sensitive than darker ones to slight visual stimuli, and can see distant objects, especially in poor illumination. It is the grey which can usually be found standing guard at night and leading the herd in flights from predators.

Another difference which tends to be inherited is that of social dominance. All the offspring of a bossy, dominant mare tend to follow in her footsteps, and although it is unlikely that any of them would be able to challenge their dam for leadership – indeed, she would take great care to keep them in their place – they would, if placed among another group, tend to show the same dominant qualities as their dam. (It has already been mentioned that horses tend to treat their riders or handlers as they do other horses, so a naturally dominant horse will constantly test its rider in the same way as it would test an equine companion. Hence the importance of being alert to this characteristic.) Whether the family characteristics of dominance are carried on by inherited genetic tendencies, or are due to the youngsters copying the sort of behaviour they have seen to be successful, it is difficult to say, but there is a very strong possibly that innate physical constitution plays a part. As already said, social dominance is closely related to physical well-being and the animal which, because of its genetic make-up, turns its food to good physical use is more likely to succeed in the social hierarchy than the one which uses it to cope with its anxieties!

In pointing out, and trying to explain, these differences between temperaments, I am not suggesting that one is better than another. On the contrary, just as it takes all sorts to make a human world, it takes all sorts to ensure the survival of an animal species. If all the members of a herd wanted to lead it, the individuals would quickly destroy each other in their battles for supremacy. If all the individuals concentrated their sensitivity in the skin, there would be none to save the herd from night marauders. Perhaps it is one of nature's built-in security measures that coat colour in horses is one of the most unpredictable features of a mating. Although treatises have been written on the subject and statistics may indicate a high probability that a grey mated to a grey will produce a grey foal, there is still a chance that the results of your own careful selection will prove to be the exception and turn out to be bay or chestnut! If it does, do not be too disappointed. It may not suit you, but it will almost certainly suit someone else: for another of nature's marvellous security measures is that there are just as many differences of temperament among humans as there are among horses and the equine temperament that suits one human may not suit another. For an owner and his horse to be compatible it is very important that their temperaments should mesh, and this is a matter which only they can decide. It is extremely difficult, therefore, for one person, however knowledgeable he or she may be in the equestrian world, to choose a horse for another; although the selected mount might be absolutely right for the rider in all logical respects (i.e. size, shape, ability, experience), if the two do not really feel for one another, the match will be disastrous. On the other hand, countless heart-warming instances can be observed of people who own creatures which other people might think useless, but who are devoted to their charges and are forever making excuses for their shortcomings.

Vices

In contrast to the different individual temperaments described in the last section, some horses develop unpleasant and generally undesirable habits commonly known as vices. These may occur under saddle (bucking, rearing, napping) or in the stable (crib-biting, wind-sucking, weaving).

Bucking may be of two kinds: bronco-bucking, in which the horse puts its head down, humps its back and kicks up its hind legs, or fly-bucking, in which the head is held up and the back hollowed while the legs are kicked up. In rearing, the horse stands on its hind legs and lifts up the front ones. In napping it refuses to leave a place of sanctuary (either its home or the company of other horses) and if pressed to do so will buck, rear or kick. Not all bucking and rearing are of the kind which would qualify as vices. The most well-mannered of horses can occasionally hump its back and kick up its heels when feeling particularly skittish or when letting off steam – perhaps because it has been confined too long without exercise. After its brief display of exuberance it will usually return to its usual pattern of behaviour. (Some well-known show-jumpers and racehorses do tend to indulge in a few light-hearted fly-bucks either just before or just after making a great physical effort. The tendency has obviously become a habit, but does not interfere with the animal's ability to perform its job adequately.) In the same way, horses may well stand on their hind legs for a few seconds without being classed as rearers. These acts should only be considered vices if they are persistently repeated and prevent learning of behaviour which would be more advantageous in a particular situation.

This last statement gives a clue about the origin of vices, for most vices do start as evasion tactics which have possibly been successful in one instance in early life and are then repeated until they become a constant feature of the animal's repertoire. The danger of defensive strategies being adopted in moments of stress and perplexity has already been discussed in the section about how animals learn. Most of the common vices that appear in riding horses begin in this way. Like the tics or compulsions of the human neurotic, they eventually become a kind of mental prison.

Of the stable vices, the commonest are, as mentioned above, crib-biting (in which the horse fixes its teeth on a firm protuberance such as the manger or the top of the door and flexes the muscles of the throat in short, sharp spasms), wind-sucking (the same stance is adopted but without fixing the teeth; at each spasm air is gulped in and swallowed); and weaving, in which the horse stands swaying from one foot to the other, moving its head from side to side. Although these habits are most commonly seen in stabled horses

Icelandic ponies against the harsh mountainous landscape of their native land. For a thousand years the ponies provided the only means of transport, and during that time remained as a breed true to type.

OVERLEAF: Ponies out at grass, though they need less attention than a stabled pony or horse, should still be regularly visited. At certain times (during the winter, or for mares with foals at foot) they will need supplementary feeding.

(and seldom seem to appear spontaneously in horses which have not been stable-kept), they may be carried on outside the stables by animals which have already acquired them.

How the stable vices originate is uncertain. Boredom has often been blamed for their appearance, and indeed a stabled existence is a most unnatural one for an animal that was designed to spend most of its life in action. Unless a horse has plenty of exercise and plenty to occupy its mental resources, its energy will have to be expended somehow and it may well develop unwanted and unnatural methods of letting off steam.

Heredity is another factor which is often blamed, and there is some evidence to support it. This does not mean that all the offspring of a mare or stallion will necessarily develop the same vice as their parents, but two things may be inherited: the first is the level and kind of stress which the individual finds intolerable; the second is the tendency to respond to stress in a particular way.

Stress

Stress-tolerance is a difficult concept for everyone to grasp, because situations which one person might find stressful could leave another unmoved, and vice-versa, but there are some generalizations which can be made. The situations which lead to mental stress can be grouped under three headings: conflict, uncertainty and lack of escape.

In the case of conflict, there is a situation or stimulus which arouses two opposing emotions or desires at the same time; the animal cannot choose between them. If, for instance, it is very hungry, the sight of food will encourage it to make for the food-source as quickly as it can. Supposing, however, it sees something else at the food – possibly a very domineering member of its group, which will certainly kick it if it tries to go too close, it will be in a state of conflict (should it approach or run away?) until either its fear or its hunger predominates and decides the issue for it.

In this sort of situation, and in most of those occurring in a horse's natural environment, conflicts are usually short-lived or can be avoided, but in the unnatural environment of the working horse this is not the case. Being constantly asked to do things which arouse some normal anxiety and fear, and yet punished if it does not do them, the poor horse must spend a good deal of its early life in a state of conflict. Its need for human reassurance to minimize its discomfort will be clear, and yet what might seem paradoxical is that severe punishment for initial reluctance to obey commands can be quite a relief, as punishment forces a decision on the horse, releasing it from the pressure of the conflict.

It is in a case like this that severe punishment is more likely to solve a conflict than mere threats, and if meted out only for unwanted acts, such punishment seldom leads to neurotic or vicious behaviour. Just as a child soon learns to avoid putting its hand in the fire once it has been burned (and does not necessarily develop a phobia for fires because of one such experience), so a horse, if it has

Ponies often seem determined to escape from a perfectly good piece of grazing – perhaps because their curiosity gets the better of them. Strong, safe fencing is essential; ponies are also less likely to stray if they have company.

PREVIOUS PAGE: A group of Exmoor ponies waiting to be sold at auction at Bampton, Devon. While it is possible to pick up a bargain at one of these sales, only those who are really knowledgeable should buy a pony in this way.

been severely punished for doing something, will usually just avoid doing that thing again.

What does worry horses, and soon makes them very neurotic indeed, is being unable to understand whether a situation or a response demanded of them is one which will lead to punishment or reward; this is the second of the stressful situations – uncertainty. I have described in a previous section the importance of making one's riding signals very clear to the horse so that it knows just what is wanted of it the whole time. If this is not done, it may well be put put into a state of conflict and uncertainty; if it cannot tell whether it should stop or go, turn right or turn left, it will not know what to do in order to avoid punishment.

There are situations, however, in which an individual knows that whatever it does, it is going to be punished. These double-bind situations, without possibility of escape, can be the most distressing of all unless the punishment expected is fairly mild and can, therefore, be tolerated. The horse or pony which knows it is going to be jabbed in the mouth if it jumps but hit if it does not is in just such a situation.

You may be wondering what all this has to do with heredity, and especially how it explains stable vices. It is easy, you may think, to see how working situations could produce conflict, uncertainty and the double-bind, but what does this have to do with the animal's behaviour at rest and when away from its work? The answer is that the emotions aroused by the triggering situation will have alerted the body for action, causing all the physical changes to occur within it which have already been described. The muscles will be tense, the heart beating fast, the rate of breathing increased, etc. Unless the body does something to use up this energy, it will be uncomfortable. Not wanting to go forward or backward, right or left, the individual tends to indulge in a 'displacement activity' – that is to say, it just does something to let off steam and release tension; the act it chooses tends to be of a type which brought it comfort in its youth, such as feeding or grooming itself (or in the case of horses, perhaps, escaping by galloping away). It is common to see a cat, thwarted of its goal, sitting down and licking its fur; a dog may scratch itself; a child may put its thumb in its mouth, an adult scratch his head.

These occasional displacement acts would not be considered neurotic; but if the act becomes a compulsive, regular feature of the individual's behaviour, which is repeated over and over again even in the absence of situations arousing the emotional stress, then it becomes a neurotic symptom – or, as it is known in horses, a vice. It is usually in a stable, where the animal cannot get rid of its tension in any other way, that this repetitive displacement act is most likely to be performed.

Heredity, it has been pointed out, plays an important part in determining the type of situation which an individual finds stressful. This is because heredity largely determines the needs of the individual as well as the sensory apparatus with which these needs can be satisfied. Heredity may also play a part in determining the actual act – the vice – which is adopted in displacement. It is known by those who breed horses that the offspring of a mare that crib-bites may become a crib-biter but seldom becomes a weaver, whereas the offspring of a weaving mare seldom becomes a crib-biter. If, as has been suggested, the habits of the mature neurotic are related to those which gave comfort in youth, one would suspect that the crib-biter gained its satisfaction from suckling (it had a great need for food) while the weaver gained its from galloping away (its need for food was less than its need for escape).

Treating Vices
Two of the main purposes of studying the origins of such unwanted acts as vices are firstly so that we can avoid producing them, and secondly so that, if they do occur, we can treat or cure them. Ways of avoiding them have been stressed all through this chapter; what about curing them? There are two rather different – even opposing – methods which may be successful: rest and retraining. The purpose of the rest cure is to allow the individual to overcome its anxiety and generally to relax. During this time it is encouraged to eat as much as possible, put on weight and make up its depleted store of energy-producing substances. While this is happening, the general sense of security and happiness is reinforced by ensuring that everything in the environment is regular and simple so that the animal always knows exactly what to expect at any moment. It is provided with reassuring companions which will provide emotional support. These companions need not be of its own species. Even non-living comforters, such as a cuddly toy in the case of a human child or a piece of soft cloth in the case of a monkey can be a very great comfort to an overwrought animal.

The other method of treating the habit, that of retraining, may be started after a period of rest like the one outlined above, or it may be begun straight away, on the principle that it is just the behaviour which one is trying to alter, not the basic emotional state. (In some cases, this last contention may be right. The basic emotional conflict which gave rise to the habit may have been cleared up a long time ago, but the habit has become so ingrained that it has persisted.) By punishing the individual every time the act is performed and rewarding it every time it is not, the individual can often be encouraged to establish new patterns of behaviour which are more desirable and less crippling than the old. (Sometimes the formation of new habits can be assisted if the animal is first put into a state of mental and physical exhaustion, i.e. brain-washed.)

It is quite easy to see how this method can be successful in the treatment of vices in the working horse, and indeed variations of it are often used very successfully to cure rearing and napping, but there is a much greater problem to be confronted in trying to cure the stable vices. How are you going to punish a horse every time it wind-sucks or weaves? And how are you going to reward it every time it does not? And since the success of training depends on constant and inevitable reinforcement by reward or punishment, the treatment of the stable vices by retraining is seldom very effective.

Before beginning any form of positive treatment, of course, it is necessary to ensure that all possible causes of anxiety, and especially those which triggered off the original trouble, are removed. Here is another major snag; for although one can shield an individual from problems and conflicts for a certain length of time, when it is returned to its usual environment it will face the same sort of situation which led to anxiety in the first place. The individual which may have appeared to make a complete recovery while at rest, more often than not reverts to all its ruminations and rituals when returned to its original environment. The horse which stopped napping when it felt secure will revert to the habit as soon as it feels threatened. This is another argument in favour of retraining rather resting. Advocates of retraining argue that this method will give the individual the strength to overcome any new difficulties it may meet, having overcome the old. Its success in these new situations will, however, still depend on its receiving rewards and punishments at the appropriate times; it will still depend on the presence of a firm, constant master.

In all this talk of vices, and especially in stressing their hereditary natures, the impression may have been given that a horse which produces a vice is a weak, inferior sort of animal which would be totally undesirable. However, it is possible for any horse to develop a vice if it is subjected to enough stress, just as any person could have a mental breakdown if he was subject to sufficient pressure in the sort of situation he personally finds painful. In the second place, the fact that an individual finds one situation stressful and anxiety-provoking does not necessarily mean that he is unable to cope with others. The very opposite is the case. The person or animal which is particularly well-equipped to deal with one type of problem is usually hopeless at others. If a horse shows an unpleasant stable vice (or if it rears or naps on occasions) this should not be taken as proof that the horse is totally valueless. It may well be a particularly brilliant performer, whose main anxiety is that it will not always do as well as it thinks it should.

This chapter has been written in the expectation that those who love and care for horses will be able to gain more pleasure from their equine companions if they know how their minds work. Scientific psychology is a rigorous discipline involving mathematics and a fairly long training, but psychologists do not have the monopoly on observation. Some of the observations made and reported by people who know their animals intimately, even if they know little about any science, may be just as valuable as carefully controlled experiments; so every owner, rider, trainer and groom can add to the knowledge of horse psychology if they take careful note of what they see and tell other people about it.

The
World's Breeds

WORLD FOUNDATION BREEDS

The early horse developed according to the environment in which it lived; the modern horse, in all its enormous variety, can almost certainly be traced to three basic types which emerged as a result of horses inhabiting areas distinctive in terrain and climate. The three prehistoric types were the Steppe, the Forest and the Plateau horses. The first of these has survived virtually unchanged, due possibly to the inaccessibility of its habitat. The Asiatic Wild Horse of Mongolia, *Equus przewalskii przewalskii* Poliakov, was discovered on the Mongolian steppes by Colonel N. M. Przewalski in 1881. This primitive horse is now nearly extinct on the western edges of the Gobi desert where it was first observed by the intrepid Colonel, but it is preserved in zoos.

The Forest horse, heavier and more slow-moving than the Steppe, was the forefather of the 'cold-blood' horse, exemplified by the modern 'heavy' horse breeds of today. The Plateau horse, on the other hand, was almost the exact opposite of the Forest. It was of a finer and lighter build than the Steppe, with longer, more slender limbs and with feet of a form halfway between those of the other two primitive contemporaries, avoiding both the extreme length and narrowness of the Steppe hoof, and the broad, soup-plate proportions of that of the Forest horse.

It is a reasonable assumption that the light horses and ponies of today are the descendants of the Steppe type of horse. The original Steppe type is represented today by the Tarpan, which is still preserved in Poland.

There would probably have been a certain amount of intermingling and thus some variation of the three types but they must, in essence, be regarded as the raw material from which the modern horse and pony has evolved.

The process of evolution and improvement by natural selection has been going on ever since the days of *Eohippus*, the earliest known ancestor of the horse, but the existence of the hundreds of types of horses and ponies which make up the world equine population today is largely due to the influence exerted by man. In many instances environment is still a major factor in the establishment and maintenance of type and character, but since the domestication of the horse some 4000 years ago, human interference by selective breeding, artificial feeding, etc., has played an increasingly large role in the development of the modern horse. Bigger, stronger and faster animals have long been bred with the object of producing a type best suited to a particular purpose, though the establishment of specific breeds, of which there are now more than 200, and the introduction of recorded pedigrees, are relatively recent developments.

A 'breed', as distinct from a 'type', can be defined as a horse or pony which has been bred over a fairly long period of time and which, as a result, consistently produces stock that has clearly fixed characteristics of height, colour, appearance and action. Such horses will be the produce of 'pure-bred' parents whose pedigrees will be recorded in the stud book operated by their governing body, and they, in turn, will be eligible for registration. The Arabian horse is a breed, for instance, as is the Thoroughbred or the Welsh pony. These horses have distinctive and immediately recognizable features and characteristics which are reproduced from one generation to the next. All three are registered in stud books, and it is possible to trace back the breeding of any one for many generations.

Examples of types of horses would be the hunter and (in Great Britain, but not in America) the Palomino. The latter, it is true, has a common coat colour of a golden shade accompanied by a white mane and tail, but these features can be obtained by the mating of parents whose colours may be likely to result in a golden-coated offspring, i.e. a chestnut and a cream will probably give the required colour. Otherwise there is no uniformity of height about the Palomino or any notable characteristic of conformation. Palomino colouring can appear in a small pony or a full-size horse; some may be cobs, or short-legged, stocky individuals, while others may display something of the quality of an Arabian or a Thoroughbred. A hunter, similarly, is often the result of cross-breeding. Many are by Thoroughbred sires out of very ordinary mares of unknown ancestry, themselves the results of a number of cross matches. Some will have a percentage of 'heavy' blood in their veins, while others will have a proportion of native pony blood, such as Connemara, Highland or New Forest.

By modern standards the primitive 'horses' would, in fact, be regarded as ponies because of their height. Today, it is generally recognized that a pony is an animal not exceeding 14·2 hands in height and that anything taller is a horse. An exception is made, however, in the case of the Arab which whatever its height – and many will be just under 14·2 hands – is always known and regarded as a horse. Conversely, polo 'ponies', which since the abolition of a height limit under international rules are almost invariably well over 14·2 hands, are still called 'ponies'.

The Arabian
In any study of the world's breeds one fact emerges with unmistakeable clarity. There is no doubt that the greatest influence, after the primitives, on horse and pony breeds throughout the world, is that exerted by the oldest recognized breed, the epitome of the 'hot-blood' horse – the Arabian. From this enormously prepotent horse is derived the Thoroughbred; few breeds, including some of the 'cold-blood' heavies, have not benefited and been upgraded by an infusion of Arabian blood.

The origin of the Arab as an established and distinctive

specimen, apart from its early development from the primitive warm-blood horses, would be impossible to date with any accuracy. The greatest authority on the breed, the late Lady Wentworth, stated categorically that the Arabian had existed in its pure form as long ago as 5000 BC. Whether or not that is so is open to conjecture, but there is sufficient evidence to show that a hot-blood horse existed in Arabia when Europe was still largely composed of marsh and swampland.

The reasons for the supremacy of this unique horse are due, in broad terms, to three factors: in the first place it is due to its antiquity as a breed of fixed type and character; secondly, to the selective breeding practised in its original environment over a long period; and finally, as a result of both, to the inherent qualities of soundness, stamina, conformation, courage and speed with which the Arab consistently and indelibly stamps its stock. The Arab cross 'nicks' with almost everything and always effects a noticeable improvement in the resultant progeny.

Today, Arab horses are bred all over the world in their pure form, the largest numbers of pure-bred stock being in America; they remain as distinctive as ever. The high-class Arabian is a small horse, the ideal being between 14·2 and 15 hands, although there are pure-breds which exceed this height. The 'dry', fine-drawn head of the Arab is typical, and great store is set on the pronounced, concave 'dish' of the face; the big, widely-spaced eyes; the large, flared nostrils; the tapered muzzle and the shapely ears.

The Arab is no longer revered for its speed; many of its derivatives, in particular, of course, the Thoroughbred, are far more talented in this respect; nor are many pure-breds notably successful as show jumpers or as event horses, although Arabs can and do jump. It remains, however, the supreme riding horse and retains qualities unapproached by any other breed. The greatest achievement of the Arabian, however, is as progenitor of the world's most valuable horse, the Thoroughbred.

The Thoroughbred

To what extent the Arab is responsible for the Thoroughbred is a matter of some controversy, but there is no doubt that the importation of Arabians to Britain in the last years of the seventeenth and the early part of the eighteenth centuries was a major fact in the evolution of the Thoroughbred racehorse.

Racing had been an integral part of the English sporting scene for centuries before the formative period of the Thoroughbred in the hundred years following the Stuart Restoration in 1660. It is, therefore, reasonable to assume that a well-established native stock of 'running horses' already existed, although it seems probable that, well before this time, efforts were made to improve these horses by the importation of Oriental sires and mares.

Nonetheless it is generally accepted that three Oriental sires (known variously as Barb, Turk or Arabian) can be considered to be the founding fathers of the Thoroughbred. These were the Darley and Godolphin Arabians and the Byerley Turk; all modern Thoroughbreds are descended from them in the male line.

The first of Weatherby's General Stud Books did not appear until 1791, but by then a definite pattern had been established, although the word Thoroughbred was not used until 1821 when it appeared in Volume II. It was not until much later that Arabian outcrosses ceased and the Thoroughbred was established as a breed in its own right.

Today the breeding of Thoroughbreds is an industry in every country where racing is carried on, and the world Thoroughbred population is in excess of 400,000. But although the Thoroughbred evolved initially as a British product the breed soon became established in large numbers elsewhere, and in a short time countries like France and America, the latter boasting the largest Thoroughbred population and the most highly capitalized of the world's racing industries, were developing their own type of Thoroughbred horse. These two countries together with Britain and Ireland, all possess ideal soils, climates and general environments for horse-raising, and are the principal centres of Thoroughbred breeding.

To produce so nearly perfect a horse in so short a time is a remarkable accomplishment, and the influence of this horse is by no means confined to the racecourse. By virtue of its size, the symmetry of its proportions, its natural balance and easy action as well as its speed, the Thoroughbred is an ideal riding horse, and when crossed with half-bred mares produces the right stamp of horse for hunting or competitive sports. Smaller Thoroughbreds are integral to the production of riding ponies, and are largely responsible for the supremely elegant children's ponies which are to be seen in large quantities in British show rings.

The Anglo-Arab
A further important product of the Thoroughbred and its progenitor is the Anglo-Arab horse. The Anglo-Arab cannot strictly be considered a 'pure' breed as it is continually in receipt of new Arab or Thoroughbred blood, but in practice it is looked upon as an 'established' breed with defined characteristics. In France, where Anglo-Arab breeding is carried on more extensively than anywhere else, the breed has its own stud book. In Britain the Arab Horse Society also runs an Anglo stud book, but the development of the Anglo-Arab in Britain is not significant when compared with the eminence that the breed has achieved in France.

In theory the combination of the two premier breeds should result in a riding horse that combines the best of both while eliminating their undesirable qualities. Frequently this does happen in practice. The Thoroughbred is far superior to the smaller Arab in speed and jumping ability, but it has disadvantages too. Temperamentally the Thoroughbred can present difficulties. Very often it is too excitable and too impetuous to submit to the disciplines involved in dressage training or show jumping, and it is certainly not as sound or as tough as its Arabian ancestor. The Arab, although full of courage, is almost always an equable, good-tempered horse and transmits to its progeny its intelligence, soundness and stamina, thus countering the disadvantages of the Thoroughbred. The result is, for the most part, an excellent riding horse, not as fast as the Thoroughbred but retaining its size and scope.

The modern French Anglo-Arab is a judicious combination of three elements: Arab, Thoroughbred and Anglo-Arab. The dam may be any of these as long as the progeny possesses 25 per cent Arab blood, which allows for a number of permutations. It is interesting to note that the English Anglo-Arab is eligible for inclusion in the book provided that half this proportion, 12½ per cent, is Arab blood. The best of the French Anglo-Arabs show between the minimum 25 per cent and 45 per cent Arabian blood; it is worth noting that many of the Olympic medals gained by France, as well as her numerous successes in international jumping, have been won by horses of such breeding.

A most important factor in the breeding of the French Anglo-Arab is the racing programme restricted to the breed, which provides a means of selection according to performance. The practice of selection by performance tests is, indeed, widespread on the Continent, but in Britain, where breeding is in the hands of individuals, no such control exists.

The Andalusian Horse

While the debt owed by the modern horse breeds to the Arabian and the Thoroughbred is generally accepted, the contribution of one particular horse, the Andalusian of Spain, is inclined to pass unrecognized. Until the eighteenth century, however, the Andalusian was the first horse of Europe and the acknowledged mount of captains and kings, long before the impact of the Arabian was felt.

Spanish authorities insist that the Andalusian is a native of their country and that the breed owes nothing to outside influences; furthermore they will deny any possibility of the all-pervading Arabian blood which authorities outside Spain frequently associate with the origin of the Andalusian. Certainly there is no historical evidence to prove the presence of Arabian blood in the breed, nor does the Andalusian show any of the pronounced characteristics which are so indelibly stamped by the use of Arab sires. The more probable theory is that the Andalusian evolved from a cross between the light, agile horses of Spain, and the Barb horses of invaders from North Africa. It is likely that the native horses were, in fact, descended from horses of a Barb type that had wandered across from north-west Africa many centuries before when the Iberian Peninsula was still joined to Africa.

From the time of the Roman emperors up to the eighteenth century the Andalusian was regarded as the supreme horse of Europe. Every king and nobleman of that time who had his portrait painted on horseback was depicted sitting proudly upon a long-maned, prancing Andalusian.

In Europe, numerous breeds owe much to this blood and many more owe something. The Lipizzaners of the Spanish Riding School in Vienna are direct descendants: nine stallions and twenty-four mares provided the foundation stock for the stud at Lipizza in 1580. The Frederiksborg of Denmark is another virtually direct descendant: the Royal Frederiksborg Stud founded in 1562 by Frederik II was based on the Spanish Horse. The spotted Knabstrup of the same country is similarly indebted, the foundation mare Flaebehoppen, a Spanish Horse, being crossed with a Frederiksborg stallion. The Kladruber of Czechoslovakia is yet another direct descendant: Andalusian horses imported by the Emperor Maximilian II formed the stud at Kladruby in Bohemia. In the Iberian Peninsula itself the Carthusian monks breed an Andalusian-Carthusian at Jerez de la Frontera as they have done for centuries, and the Altér-Real of neighbouring Portugal also has its origins in this remarkable breed. In Britain the Andalusian has also had an influence, if less clearly marked, on the Cleveland Bay, the Hackney, the Connemara pony and the Welsh Cob.

The *conquistadores* of the sixteenth century took Andalusian horses with them to the New World. This blood, if now much diluted, lives on today in the Quarter Horse, the Appaloosa, the Saddlebred and others. More noticeably of Andalusian descent in both appearance and action are the horses of South America – the Peruvian Paso, the Argentine Criollo and the gaited Paso Fino of Puerto Rico.

The Andalusian, although no longer occupying pride of place in the equine world and possibly irrelevant in the context of competitive sports, is still bred in its native region of Andalusia in the south of the Iberian peninsula. The principal centres are at Seville, Cordoba and Jerez de la Frontera, where the Terry family maintains a notable stud.

NATIONAL BREEDS
Horses of the Camargue

There are still breeds whose origin is shrouded in mystery or at best is a matter of conjecture. France has such a breed in the Camargue, a horse now recognized by the National Stud Services. The Camargue *manades* (herds) live in the harsh, inhospitable land from which they take their name. Positioned between the sea, the Rhône and the ancient town of Aigues-Mortes in the south of France, the Camargue is in every way a forbidding region. In winter it lies covered with a sheet of salt water; salt, in fact, is everywhere, carried over the land by the tearing wind, the *mistral*. In summer, the fierce sun bakes the ground until it cracks. The horse takes its character from the land. The people of the region are very proud of the beautifully desolate swamp-land which is their home, and although the region, the people and the horses – the 'horses of the sea' – are surrounded by legend and romance, the horses are not all that romantic and they are certainly not beautiful. They have large, square, straight heads, short necks and poor, upright shoulders. They do, it is true, have long thick manes and tails, much appreciated no doubt by tourists, but to a horseman their good points are contained in their great depth of girth, good back and short, strong croup. The bone is good and if the feet are large, as befits a swamp dweller, they are, nonetheless, hard and ideally suited to the extremes of their environment. In fact, it is never necessary for the Camargue horse to be shod.

With such an environment the Camargue is naturally hardy and thrives on the poorest food, tough grass and reeds, saltwort and similar plants, which it shares with its compatriots, the massive black Camargue bulls. In height it does not exceed 15 hands, and all are silky white in colour. Poets have been moved to liken the Camargue coat to the foam of the sea. Foals are not, of course, born white. They are either iron grey, black or a mottled brown at birth, and only become white with maturity. The Camargue has a unique and characteristic action typified by a long high-stepping walk and a very free gallop. Obviously it also trots, but in a manner which makes this movement appear stilted and unnatural.

French Riding Breeds

France, of course, in common with the rest of Europe, is rich in horses. Apart from its Thoroughbred and Anglo-Arab population, it has Norman and Anglo-Norman, horses, the latter now being known as the French Saddle Horse with a stud book that is a continuation of the Anglo-Norman one. In fact, the three have close connections, although there is a Norman type which is a draught cob of about 16 hands and quite different from the lighter riding horse. A Norman horse existed in France a thousand years ago and is said to have gone to Britain with William the Conqueror as a war horse. In the seventeenth century the Norman was no more than an ordinary, useful working horse, but the introduction of German horses, Arabs and Barbs, produced a heavyweight riding and coach horse which was later refined by Thoroughbred crosses and some Norfolk Trotter blood to become the Anglo-Norman. The breed has been further improved by the use of the Thoroughbred and is now a very useful riding horse and a successful one in competitive events.

French riding breeds include the French Trotter, the Demi-Sang Trotter, an offshoot of the Anglo-Norman. At an average of 16·2 hands, the French Trotter is larger than other trotting breeds but in France, where trotting is a popular sport, horses trot under saddle as well as in harness and are expected to carry substantial weights. It is a tough horse with strong limbs and good feet but somewhat leggy to the eye of the perfectionist.

British Breeds

Britain, arguably one of the most horse-orientated nations in the world and boasting a greater number of active riders per head of population than any other, is rich in pony breeds and possesses magnificent heavy horses, both of which are discussed separately. It does not, however, have any great variety of riding horse breeds, as British breeders incline always to the quality horse of Thoroughbred or near-Thoroughbred lineage. The Thoroughbred industry is, of course, extensive, and as in other countries there is a significant Arabian population of high quality. The hunter, which is a type not a breed, is bred in large numbers and the best make superb event horses and jumpers. There are, however, two notable British breeds: the Cleveland Bay, and the high-actioned Hackney harness horse, which is unique among the horses of the world. The former has existed in that part of Yorkshire from which it takes its name since mediaeval times. In the past it has been used as a pack-horse, a farm horse, in harness and under saddle as a hunter. Today it is still used in its pure form as a heavyweight hunter and also as a carriage horse. Crossed with the Thoroughbred, it produces a faster, lighter horse for both purposes.

The modern Hackney came into being at about the same time as the Thoroughbred, when Oriental sires were used on the native trotting, as opposed to 'running', mares. These mares were to be found in the counties of eastern England, in parts of Yorkshire and in Lincolnshire and Norfolk. In the eighteenth century the Norfolk Trotter, later to be known as the Norfolk Roadster, was well established and had been much improved by the great foundation sire, Shales the Original, a son of the Thoroughbred, Blaze, by Flying Childers who is a pillar of the British General Stud Book. Before the arrival of the railways and the motor-car, the Hackney was entirely utilitarian, as it could be used in harness and also under saddle, although always at trot. After that the Hackney was almost entirely confined to the show ring, which until the 1920s was dominated by the harness classes. Today the home of the Hackney remains in the show ring, with occasional excursions into coaching and three-day event driving. Such is the popularity of these three sports that the future of the Hackney is well assured.

The Hackney stands between 14·3 and 15.3 hands, and whether at rest or in action is unmistakeable in appearance. The body is strong and compact, the shoulders very powerful, the neck long and somewhat thick, and the head is often a shade large with a convex profile. The legs are short and the feet well-shaped, with a pronounced slope and length to the pastern. But it is the action of the Hackney that is so memorable and unique. This is high and extravagant with enormous thrust and snap from the hocks, and so elastic and free-moving that at trot the horse gives the impression of scarcely touching the ground, each stride having a definite moment of suspension. Allied to this spectacular action is a fire and courage that gives the horse enormous and exciting presence.

Irish Horses

Ireland, which in relation to its size breeds and produces more horses than any other country and must be the most horse-orientated of all, does not, surprisingly, have any specific native breeds beyond the Connemara pony and the Irish Draught, and there is some doubt about whether the latter should be termed a breed. Traditionally, Ireland is the source of hunter breeding: the Irish hunter, with his bone and substance, is among the best bred anywhere, and is in great demand throughout the world. Frequently, hunters are bred out of Irish Draught mares, big roomy sorts with excellent limbs that were developed as farm horses. Unfortunately, the Irish Draught is now waning in numbers in Ireland.

More Continental Breeds

Traditions of horse-breeding are strong in many European countries. The USSR has an almost embarrassing variety of breeds. Poland, a great horse country, relies heavily upon the spirited Arab but has developed bigger, warm-blood horses like the Wielkopolski, a good sort of middleweight hunter when it contains a fair proportion of Thoroughbred blood. The Wielkopolski is the result of improving local stock with Arab, Thoroughbred and Masuren blood. This last breed is in fact the East Prussian horse, renamed by the Poles. The Germans left a number of these horses behind them when they left Poland in 1945 and the Poles, naturally enough, made good use of them. The East Prussian, or Trakehner, is one of Germany's most valuable breeds. They make excellent saddle horses and are good jumpers. They are frequently crossed with Thoroughbreds to produce a horse of more quality. Thoroughbred matings have been increasingly used in the case of the big Hanoverian, formerly a carriage horse and, possibly because of its success as a show jumper, Germany's best known breed. The use of the Thoroughbred has given extra scope and quality to the Hanoverian and resulted in a lighter horse that excels both at show jumping and dressage. Similar to the Hanoverian is the Oldenburg, an even bigger horse which may stand as high as 17·2 hands. The Oldenburg is, or was, primarily a carriage horse and is the result of a most extraordinary amalgam of bloods. The basis of the breed, which has its origins in the seventeenth century, would seem to have been old Friesian types of draught horse to which were added Andalusian, Neapolitan, Barb, Thoroughbred, Cleveland Bay, Hanoverian and Norman blood. Oldest of the German warm-bloods is the Holstein, a somewhat heavy horse bred from the war-horse of the Middle Ages and improved by Oriental and Thoroughbred crosses.

Very similar to the Oldenburg is the East Friesian, which until the division of Germany after the Second World War was, indeed, virtually the same horse. In the last quarter-century, however, this East German breed has been developed on different lines and has become lighter and more refined than the Oldenburg. This process has been assisted by infusions of Arabian blood from both West Germany and Hungary, and more recently by the use of Hanoverian sires, the latter adding substance and strength to the breed.

The breeding of warm-blood horses throughout Europe and Scandinavia has increased significantly in the post-war period, and numbers of saddle-horses, based on the older carriage types and improved by the use of Thoroughbreds and Arabians, have evolved. Sweden has its own quality riding horse in the Swedish half-bred, much in demand for competitive riding, which descends from local mares bred to Oriental, Andalusian and East Friesian stallions 300 years ago and since then carefully brought on by the use of Thoroughbred stallions and a number of horses of the principal German breeds. The Bavarian warm-blood, only recently, in terms of breed history, established as a breed under that name, descends from the old chestnut war-horses of the Rott Valley, the Rottaler, and has been produced again by the infusions of Cleveland, Norman and modern Oldenburg lines.

Hungary, a nation of horsemen from ancient times, and a country well suited climatically and otherwise for the raising of bloodstock, is renowned for its Arabian horses of the Shagya strain, but it has also developed two excellent riding horses in the Nonius and Furioso. The latter breed takes its name from the nineteeth-century Thoroughbred stallion, Furioso, and also owes its existence in part to the Norfolk Roadster, North Star. The Nonius closely resembles the Furioso and was, in fact, the forerunner of the latter, both originating at the Mezohegyes Stud. The Nonius is also bred in Yugoslavia, Romania and Czechoslovakia. This is also the case with the Lipizzaner, probably one of the world's best known breeds because of its association with the Spanish Riding School of Vienna. Although there is a natural tendency to regard the Lipizzaner in the context of Vienna's Winter Riding Hall, performing the airs of *haute école* under the glitter of the chandeliers, the breed is also highly suitable for harness work, and the Hungarians, the world three-day event driving champions, make exclusive use of Lipizzaner teams in this developing sport.

It has already been mentioned that the Lipizzaner descends directly from the Andalusian, or Spanish horse, imported from the Iberian Peninsula in 1580 when that part of the world was within the empire of the Spanish Habsburgs. Until the seventeenth century Andalusian horses were being brought regularly to Lipizza from studs in Granada and Seville, but as the supply of suitable animals decreased, outcrosses were made from blood strains close to the Andalusian and, significantly, from one Arab, the grey Siglavy, born in 1810.

Ever since the stud was established at Lipizza, deliberate efforts were made to breed pure white horses, the colour considered most desirable for the official 'horses of the emperor'. Today, the great majority of Lipizzaners are white, although occasional bays occur, one horse of this colour being kept by tradition at the School. Foals are born black, grey or brown, changing to pure white by the time they reach the age of seven to ten years.

Russian Breeds

In the USSR there are so many horse breeds of both ancient and modern origin that it would be impossible to enumerate them all. In general, the Russian riding horses, often based on the old Streletsk Arab, are small, tough and wiry specimens of considerable quality, while the pony breeds still seem to retain much of the influence of the 'primitives' from which many descend. Not a few of the Russian horses have been developed as breeds in fairly recent times by the judicious mixture of a variety of blood-lines. The Tersky, for instance, a useful grey saddle-horse, emerged as a breed as recently as 1948 and is a mixture of Kabardin, Don, Thoroughbred and Arab blood. The Budyonny, a bigger horse very suitable as a cavalry mount, was instigated by Marshal Budyonny some fifty years ago at the army stud at Rostov. Bred selectively from the original Thoroughbred/Don cross and thereafter subjected to searching performance tests, the Budyonny has emerged as a handy all-round horse with an aptitude for a wide variety of equestrian activities. The Don, forebear of the Budyonny, is the Cossack horse and has always been noted for its remarkable hardiness and ability to thrive on the poorest of natural foodstuffs. The modern Don, taller than the old Cossack pony and of better conformation, is the product of a number of Oriental-type stallions loosed on the steppes in the nineteenth century, and later of Thoroughbred and Orlov stallions, which gave the breed greater

Some horses and ponies try to avoid even putting a foot in a small puddle, but most of them will learn to enjoy splashing in water on a hot day. Sea water is particularly good for their legs, as well as being refreshing.

OVERLEAF: Whatever stage of training a horse or pony has reached, hacking quietly in the countryside will do both it and its rider good; it helps them to relax, and lessons learned in the school can be put into practice in different surroundings.

size and scope. The Orlov is a trotting horse, used extensively in this very popular sport, and there are some 30,000 of them bred at the State studs. The breed began in 1777, when Count Orlov crossed the Arab stallion, Smetanka, with a Dutch mare. The progeny, a colt called Polkan, was put back to another Dutch mare and sired Bars I, considered to be the Orlov foundation sire. Since then, use has been made of Arabs, Thoroughbreds and, in the time that it existed as such, the Norfolk Trotter. The other Russian trotting breed, although it can hardly be said to be sufficiently fixed in type as yet to deserve the title, is the Metis Trotter, a cross between the Orlov and the faster American Standardbred.

Possibly the most ancient of the Russian breeds and one of the most fascinating of all the world's horses, since it is an offshoot of the Turkmene or Turkoman, which is sometimes said to be the ancestor of the Arab, is the golden-coloured Akhal-Teké, a horse of remarkable endurance. Bred on the Turkoman steppes and exposed for centuries to the extremes of heat and cold typical of the central Asian deserts, the Akhal-Teké has extraordinary stamina and a camel-like ability to survive when faced with conditions involving an acute shortage of water.

Horses of the Orient

The Orient, using the term in its most general sense, is naturally an area of great importance to the development of horse breeds, but although it is dominated by the Arab in the minds of most people, that horse is not its sole claim to distinction. Mongolia, for instance, has every right, because of its wild Przewalski, to be considered to be the earliest centre of evolution. Much nearer to Europe, in North Africa, is the home of the Barb horse, an ancient breed whose name continually appears in the history of so many horses. Like that of the Andalusian, the influence of the Barb is overshadowed by the Arabian, with which it is often and wrongly confused. In fact, the Barb has almost as much right to be considered a foundation horse as the Arab; it was used very extensively, both deliberately and otherwise, to improve the light horse breeds and types. Certainly the Andalusian emerged as a result of Barb crosses and its influence, primarily as a result of wars, was very great throughout Europe. Barbs were undoubtedly very plentiful in Britain well before the Thoroughbred was beginning to be established and much of the native 'running' stock would have been up-graded by the use of Barb stallions.

The Barb cannot compare in appearance with the beauty of the Arabian. It is, indeed, a rather plain horse of about 15 hands, with a long, straight face and quarters running away to a low-set tail, but it is a very tough horse, able to live on very little food. It is also courageous and possessed of great stamina.

Elsewhere in the East, where soil and climatic conditions do not favour horse breeding, ponies are the rule rather than the exception. Indonesia has a number of pony breeds, among them the dun

For a number of years the shortage of farriers (blacksmiths who specialize in shoeing horses) was acute in Britain, but now training schemes and other forms of encouragement are increasing their number. It is of prime importance to ensure that horses' feet are properly cared for.

PREVIOUS PAGE: Even if the world of the true show pony may be a long way off, young riders can enjoy competitions. This convincing gypsy and his mount, an obliging Shetland, should do well in their fancy dress competition.

Samba pony, very much a 'primitive' type, which is noted for, of all things, its ability to dance. Owners of Samba ponies decorate them with knee bells and teach them to dance to the rhythm of tom-toms. Another Indonesian pony of more marked Arab characteristics is the Sandalwood, which is used for racing. Java ponies are not attractive and would seem to display all the signs of degeneration, but they are extremely hard-working animals pulling heavily-laden two-wheeled *sados* under the extremes of tropical heat. Timor has its own version of the 'cow-pony', a diminutive fellow of around 12 hands, which is the mount of the local cowboys who, like their American counterparts, use a lasso to catch cattle. Sumatra has the Batak pony, which is now carefully bred and is being improved by the introduction of Arab importations.

It would be impossible to say with certainty just where the Indonesian ponies originated, but since many resemble Mongolians it is possible that they were introduced to Indonesia by the Chinese of ancient times. An interesting point, which lends substance to this theory, is that they are ridden with a bitless bridle which is almost a replica of that used 4000 years ago in Central Asia.

The Mongolian would also seem to be at the root of the Indian breeds, now so intermingled as to be almost unrecognizable. The ponies of Bhutan, Yarkand and Spiti of India's northern states must have originated from the ponies of the armies of Genghis Khan, which were left in depots along the long line of communication between Karakorum and the Pamirs. The Burma pony, of the Shan Hill, and the strong little Manipuri, on which the British first learnt to play polo, must also be descended from the Mongolian.

Arab influence has naturally enough been considerable upon Indian stock and is notable in the curved-eared Kathiawari, now rarely seen in anything approaching pure form, and the hardy Marwari. After the Arab, the most notable importation to India on which much of the present-day stock is based is the Australian Waler, a predominantly Thoroughbred horse developed in Australia and used extensively by Indian cavalry regiments between 1850 and 1930.

More typical of Oriental breeds as such are those of Iran, which are of considerable importance. The area has a large Arab population, and the Persian Arab is notably pure. The Plateau Persian horse, a composite term covering a number of pronounced eastern types, includes the strains of Jaf, Basseri, Darashouri, etc.; and of course the Turkmene, a racing horse of very great antiquity which resembles the Munighi strain of Arab, foremost of the desert racers.

The Turkmene is even today the racehorse of the East. It is not as fast as the Thoroughbred but it has far greater powers of endurance, and there is a school of thought which claims it could have been a part-progenitor of the former, rather than those horses which were thought to be of the Munighi Arabian strain.

North American Breeds

Within a hundred years of the horse's reinstatement in the New World, following the arrival of the sixteenth-century *conquistadores*, the species had spread northwards and bred in sufficient quantities for the Indian tribes of the Western Plains to have become horse peoples. At the same time more horses were being imported into the continent by the European settlers. Horses from England arrived at the Massachusetts Bay Colony in 1629 and, some years before, numbers of Irish horses had been imported into Virginia. As the influx of settlers increased and colonists from more and more European countries were attracted by the opportunities offered by the New World, so the horse population grew in size and variety, the colonists bringing with them their own national breeds and types.

In 1666 the first American racecourse was established at Long Island and this in itself encouraged the importation of English racing stock. A century afterwards horses were imported in large numbers and the Thoroughbred became a major influence in American breeding.

On these foundations, strong and varied in composition, an outstanding horse culture was formed in a period of time that was quite remarkable. It took no more than a few hundred years to establish, and this time, seen in the light of the history of the species, is no more than the twitch of an eyelid.

The original horses, introduced early in the conquest of the Americas, were Spanish. These acted as a base for the later importations, and produced a wealth of equine potential. Some of the early American breeds have now virtually disappeared. The wild Spanish mustang which became the cow-pony from which, in time, the Quarter Horse was bred, has almost gone, only a few being preserved by enthusiasts. Another very early breed, the Narragansett Pacer, is in itself extinct although its influence is to be found in the ancestors of the Standardbred and of the Quarter Horse.

The trotting race is a major American sport which attracts very large audiences; there are some 800 trotting tracks in America, and the sport revolves around the skills of the world's superlative trotter, the American Standardbred. The Standardbred, so called because of the early practice of establishing a speed standard as a requirement for inclusion in the Trotting Register, evolved from a mixture of breeds which included the Narragansett and the Morgan horse, but depended principally on Messenger (1780), a Thoroughbred descendant of the Darley Arabian, the line being through Mambrino, his sire, to Engineer, Sampson, Blaze and Flying Childers, the first among the great racehorses. It was Hambletonian 10 (Ryskyd's Hambletonian), however, who gave the breed its outstanding trotting and pacing abilities. Hambletonian sired 1335 offspring between 1851 and 1875, and 90 per cent of all Standardbreds descend from this one horse.

The Standardbred is not as refined as the Thoroughbred; it is short-legged, longer in the body and often common about the head. On the other hand it has enormously powerful quarters and a very straight action, a necessity if the legs are not to suffer damage at the high speeds these trotters are capable of attaining.

Even more numerous in America is the Quarter Horse. There are 800,000 registered in America and in forty-two other countries. It is arguably the first all-American breed, and because of its vast numbers it is the world's most popular horse. Although the Quarter Horse is considered the supreme cow-pony (it is, incidentally, responsible for the Canadian Cutting Horse), it did not originate, as might be imagined, in the cattle country of the West. Its origins were among the colonial seaboard settlements of the Carolinas and Virginia, where the English colonists crossed Spanish mares with imported horses 'of the blood' – the Thoroughbred as such had yet to be invented. They also reversed the process, mating English mares with Spanish stallions. The resultant stock worked in harness and under saddle but the fame of the Quarter Horse, and its name, is derived from the times when they were raced over short rough tracks hacked out of the undergrowth or even over the length of a village street. The distances were short, seldom more than a quarter of a mile, and so demanded tremendous acceleration from a standing start. As the distance became standardized, the name Quarter Horse was established.

The advent of the Thoroughbred and of longer races on oval tracks temporarily eclipsed the Quarter Horse, who moved with the migration to the West where he quickly adapted to cattle work. The present-day Quarter Horse is an all-round pleasure mount as well as being the star of rodeo contests. He also races, and the recent revival of short-distance racing has resulted in one of the richest prizes, the All-American Futurity Stakes for Quarter Horses, which is worth around $600,000.

The Quarter Horse stands some 15 hands and is compact, almost chunky, with very massive and muscular quarters. The American Quarter Horse Society, founded in 1941 at Fort Worth, is the largest equine registry in the world, employing over 200 people.

Almost as well-known is the Morgan horse, whose origins have an almost fairytale quality. The breed is descended from one exceptional foundation stallion. This horse, originally called Figure, is better known by the name of his second owner, Justin Morgan, who acquired him in payment of a debt in about 1795. Foaled, supposedly, in West Springfield, Massachusetts, he certainly lived his life at Randolph, Vermont, passing through the hands of many owners.

His own breeding is obscure. It is possible he was by a Thoroughbred called True Briton, but it is just as likely, and more probable if the appearance of the Morgan and the statue of Justin Morgan (the horse) at the University of Vermont Morgan Horse Farm is taken into account, that he derived from a Welsh Cob and had a dash of Thoroughbred or Arab blood. Justin Morgan was a work-horse all his life, being used in harness, at the plough, for clearing woodland and so on, and he was forever being matched in weight-pulling contests of extreme severity for a horse that weighed only 363 kg (800 lb) and stood no more than 14 hands. In addition he was unbeaten as a racer both under saddle and in harness, and was a prolific sire of remarkable prepotency.

The modern Morgan is more refined than his illustrious ancestor but is still able to do everything of which Justin Morgan was capable, and to do it very well. The Morgan may vary in height from between 14 to 15·2 hands, but rarely loses type as a result.

The Morgan has a major place as a show horse, but the epitome of the American ring is without doubt the Kentucky Saddler, whose modern name is the American Saddlebred. In the show ring there are three types of Saddlebred: the harness horse, working at the walk and at an animated, showy, park trot; the Three-Gaited Saddler, shown with 'roached' (hogged) mane and an artificially high-set tail, who performs at walk, trot and canter; and the most spectacular of the three, the Five-Gaited Saddler. This horse is shown, in addition to the natural paces, at the slow gait – an elevated four-beat pace in which each leg is fractionally suspended – and at the 'rack'. This is the speeded-up version of the slow gait, and at full speed a Saddlebred will cover a mile in 2 minutes 19 seconds. The original purpose of the Saddlebred was far removed from the glamour of the show ring and very much more utilitarian. The breed was developed by Kentucky planters as a speedy, comfortable horse suitable for riding for long hours but stylish as well as being practical.

The foundation sire of the breed was the Thoroughbred Denmark (1839) and his son Denmark 61 out of a pacing mare. There is also Morgan, early Narragansett and Canadian Pacer elements in the make-up. (The Canadian Pacer was an ambling horse of French origin.) Denmark, with a background of Norfolk Trotter, appears in Hackney pedigrees, and not surprisingly it is the Hackney which the Saddlebred resembles most closely in both appearance and basic movement.

The 'easy-gaited' tradition has vanished in Europe but is still strong in America, where in addition to the Saddlebred there is the Tennessee Walker, claimed to be the most comfortable, and the most 'confidential' (i.e. steady, reliable) horse in the world, and the Missouri Fox Trotter.

Most of the American breeds were instigated as a result of the requirements of the European settler but one, at least, is the creation of the indigenous North American Indian. This is the colourful, spotted Appaloosa horse developed by the Nez Percé tribe who once lived in and around the Palouse valley of Idaho. The breed is a very ancient one and horses of similar markings can be seen in early Chinese and Persian art forms. The ancestors of these horses possibly went into Spain from Central Asia and reached the

Nez Percé, well after the landings of the *conquistadores*, by way of Mexico. The name Appaloosa is a corruption of Palouse or Palousy and the spotted coat, once evident in the Andalusian, is preserved in this distinctive breed of horse. The breed suffered a decline after the breaking up of the Indian tribal lands and between the world wars, but its striking appearance, its all-round ability, its hardiness and tractability has resulted in a renewed popularity within the past thirty years or so

America, apart from its 'wild' ponies on the islands of Chincoteague and Assateague, off the coast of Virginia and Maryland, does not possess a 'native' pony stock. The Chincoteague ponies are indeed little more than stunted horses; lacking in both type and pony character. Nonetheless there is one pony that America can claim as being a home product, even if by European standards it would not be considered sufficiently established to be accorded 'breed' status. The breed, the Pony of the Americas, began only as recently as 1956 when Mr Leslie Boomhower of Mason City, Iowa, crossed a Shetland stallion with an Appaloosa mare and created a miniature of the spotted horse. To qualify for registry in the stud book animals have to fulfil stringent conformational specifications as well as having the

characteristic Appaloosa markings. The height of these ponies is between 11·2 and 13 hands; over 1300 are registered in the stud book.

America itself is a vital, colourful land and has a greater proportion of 'colour breeds' and types than any other country. Palominos are numerous and immensely popular as parade horses and there are the Pintos and the Paints which were so attractive to the colour-loving Indians and to the old cow-punchers. Even the Albino, the snow-white horse with pink skin and often with blue eyes, is bred selectively, although it is not a horse that would find favour in European eyes.

South American Breeds

South America is a vast repository of horses and boasts some very exotic breeds. Possibly the basic horse of the continent is the Criollo, which appears with slight regional differences in the Argentine and Uruguay, and as the Crioulo in Brazil, the Costeno and Morochuco of Peru, the Caballo Chileno of Chile and the Llanero of Venezuela. All of them descend from the original Spanish horses and all are extraordinarily tough and enduring. The Criollo may vary between 13·3 hands and 15 hands, the lack of height being due to the natural selective process of some three centuries during which the horses ran wild on the plains, and to the differences in environment. This compact, not very handsome little horse comes in a wide range of colours, of which a sandy colour and a dun is the most preferred.

Brazil's Mangalarga is a relative of the Criollo though not more than a century old as a breed. It is the result of a cross between Andalusian sires and some of the Portuguese Altér Real stallions and Criollo mares. It is less chunky than the Criollo, but no bigger.

The Peruvian Paso, an exotic mover whose forelegs move extravagantly while the hind legs are driven straight forward from quarters engaged well beneath the body, has been bred selectively for some 300 years and has many of the Criollo characteristics other than those connected with its movement. The foundation is said to be as much as 75 per cent Barb and the remainder Andalusian. Standing between 14 and 15·2 hands, its easy gait can carry its rider over difficult country at some 17·6 kph (11 mph).

Mexico has its own Native Mexican, an all-round saddle horse derived from a mixture of breeds ranging from the Mustang to the Andalusian, Criollo and Arab. It varies very much in type but most are around 15 hands.

Possibly the most arresting of the South American horses is Puerto Rico's Paso Fino, which is also bred in Colombia and Peru. This would seem to be an exact derivative of the sixteenth-century Spanish horse and to have retained the gaits which were once common in Europe and for which the Spanish strains were particularly noted. A strong, small horse of about 14·3 hands, the Paso Fino has three natural, lateral four-beat gaits which are to all intent hereditary. The slow, collected gait is the *paso fino*, in between is the *paso corto* and at full stretch, which can be 25·6 kph (16 mph) and upwards, the gait is called the *paso largo*.

Heavy Horse Breeds

The 'cold-blood' heavy horses are the product of Europe, descendants of the prehistoric Forest Horse. In Britain three stabilized breeds existed by the end of the eighteenth century, although their origins are much older than that. The three British breeds, now enjoying a revival in popularity and interest, were the Clydesdale, the Shire and the Suffolk Punch. In the nineteenth century the British adopted another heavy, the French Percheron horse, a breed which is now centred around the Fen areas of Cambridgeshire.

Up to the turn of the century and well into the present one, the heavies were the sinews of urban road transport as well as playing their important role on the land. The Clydesdale originated in Lanarkshire, Scotland, in the Clyde Valley, the country's best horse-breeding area. Founded by using Flanders stallions on native mares, the Clydesdale is an active draught horse, a good farm worker and because of good feet a suitable horse for town haulage. Not so massive as the Shire or Suffolk, the Clydesdale still stands at 17 hands. The long quarters and a tendency toward 'cow-hocks' gives the impression of weakness behind, but that is certainly not the case. White stripes on the face and pronounced white shanks with heavy feather are characteristic.

The Shire is as British as the bulldog and is claimed to be the purest survivor of the Great Horse. One of the largest horses in the world, the Shire stands some 18 hands and weighs over 1016 kg (1 ton). Founded on the old English Black and, as the name implies, originating in the English 'Shires', particularly in the counties of Leicester, Derby and Stafford, the Shire, whose stepping action is higher and shorter than the Clydesdale, is capable of moving enormous loads. A good Shire can pull 5080 kg (5 tons) and a pair, yoked tandem, have been known to move 18,846 kg (18½ tons).

The Suffolk Punch is the work-horse of East Anglia and as a breed dates back to 1506, although modern Suffolks trace back to one great horse, Crisp's Horse of Offord, foaled in 1760. The Suffolk is always a chestnut, and at 16 hands and a little more is the smallest of the British heavy horses in height. This is due to the shortness of the strong, clean legs upon which its great barrel-like body is supported. Nonetheless the Suffolk weighs upwards of 1016 kg (1 ton). This is an active breed, long-lived and able to maintain condition on minimum rations.

The French Percheron, bred in the Perche region, is a grey or black horse of up to 17 hands. It is descended from Oriental and Norman horses, crossed later with various draught breeds and then once more infused, with a little Arab. The Percheron is probably the most graceful of the heavies and is deservedly popular. France has shown much more interest in the heavies than most countries, and their breeds include among others the Ardennais offshoot, the

Trait du Nord; the old Burgundian heavy, the Auxois; the Poitevin of the enormous feet, whose mares are used to produce mules; the Comtois; the Breton and the Boulonnais. France and Belgium share responsibility for the production of the massive Ardennais.

Elsewhere on the Continent there is Holland's Dutch Draught; Denmark's Jutland, Germany's Rhineland, Schleswig Heavy Draught and the remarkable Pinzgauer Noriker, which is clean-legged and sometimes spotted. In Hungary, where lighter horses are the rule, there is the Murakoz. Belgium has the big Brabant, the old and famous Flanders Horse which had so much influence on the cold-blood breeds of Europe. Sweden has a light draught in the North Swedish Horse and also in the North Swedish Trotter, which is actually raced. The Swedish heavy is the Swedish Ardennes, a product of the Ardennais and North Swedish mares. Finland has an attractive chestnut light draught, the Finnish, which combines both cold- and warm-blood types. Italy has an even more strikingly-coloured Heavy Draught of dark liver chestnut. Alas, as there is little practical use for this last breed it is dying out rapidly, and is now most often bred for the slaughterhouse.

The USSR has three principal heavy cold-bloods: the Vladimir, founded on the Shire and a mixture of Suffolk, Cleveland, Ardennais and Percheron; the Lithuanian, a placid plug of a nondescript chestnut colouring and appalling action and conformation; and the small, 14·2 hands so-called Heavy Draught, which is far more attractive than the other two, though not in the same class as the great heavies of western Europe.

Pony Breeds

Ponies are found throughout the world and there are numbers of distinctive breeds in Europe, but the greatest reservoir of riding ponies is undoubtedly in the British Isles. There seems to be nothing to compare with these mountain and moorland breeds, which have been exported all over the world. In Britain it is accepted that the thousands of child riders learn to ride on ponies, and thus the ponies and their outcrosses are in continual demand. This is not always the case elsewhere, and in many countries of Europe, as well as America, children learn to ride on full-size horses, although in recent years this picture has changed as countries have recognized their deficiency and have begun to import increasing numbers of native ponies. There are, of course, useful and interesting ponies in countries other than Britain, but few, if any, are so suited as children's mounts and even fewer are used for that purpose.

Originally, these British natives were bred on the moorland and mountain areas and it is from these inhospitable environments that they derive, retaining their inherent qualities of soundness, hardiness and pony sagacity. All are easily and economically kept and are able to winter out without ever being stabled. Their great value, apart from their suitability for children, is their potential as breeding stock for all kinds of riding and harness animals. They pass on the good temperament allied to pony character as well as bone, substance and toughness. The most perfect equine specimen of all, the British 'riding pony', which is still looked upon as a type, although in many countries outside Britain it would qualify as a breed in its own right, is a derivative of the native pony, usually Welsh and occasionally Dartmoor, crossed with small Thoroughbreds and with the occasional Arab. The presence of pony blood prevents these ponies from becoming little horses and they retain the most desirable pony characteristics. In no other country are ponies of this supreme quality bred. The bigger native ponies, which will easily carry adults – the Highlands, Welsh Cobs, Connemaras and the Dales and Fells – can all be successfully crossed with Thoroughbred, and sometimes Arab, stock to produce active, short-legged hunters of bone and substance. The second crosses are even better and a number of the best-known event horses have been bred in this way.

The British native pony breeds comprise: the Shetland, originating on the islands of Shetland and Orkney; the Highland, from northern Scotland and the Western Isles; the Dales and Fell, bred on the east and the west of the Pennines respectively; the Welsh ponies and cobs of the Principality; the Exmoor and Dartmoor of the West Country; the New Forest, centred on the forest area of Hampshire; and the Connemara, whose native habitat is on the Irish western seaboard, although the pony is also bred extensively in England and has a separate stud book applicable to the English product.

The smallest is the Shetland, which stands at 96–107 cm (38–42 in) at the wither but is possessed of a strength out of all proportion to his size. Its stout body is supported on short, very strong legs. The pony was bred to work on the island crofts and is able to thrive on the poorest of fare. As a riding pony the modern Shetland, less heavy in the head than the old type bred in the nineteenth century for work in the mines, is limited by virtue of his size to small children, but he is a good child's pony as long as he is treated as a pony and trained accordingly, not regarded as a cuddly teddy-bear.

The Highland is one of the bigger native ponies at between 13·2 and 14 hands and is a breed of great antiquity. Bred for hard work on the crofts, the Highland is still used to cart full-size deer shot on the hills, but his principal use in Scotland is as a very reliable trekking pony.

Although it may be denied in Scotland, to the outside observer it is very clear that there are two discernible types of Highland: the heavier, sometimes almost 'carty' mainland type, and the much lighter Western Isles pony. The latter shows the influence of the Arabian blood which has undoubtedly been introduced in the past and is an excellent riding pony for a child or adult. Both are excellent harness ponies.

As a breed the Highland is most docile and tractable and very attractive in appearance. Colours are varied and include both mouse and golden dun, bay, grey, brown and a chestnut which is often of as deep a shade as a bloodstone and is frequently accompanied by a silver mane and tail. The head is broad with the eyes set wide, the body strong and with good limbs, and the Western Isles type, particularly, has excellent riding shoulders, although the wither is rarely pronounced.

The Dales and the Fell are very much alike to all but the expert, and may indeed share a common ancestry. It seems likely that in view of the proximity of the two, inter-breeding has occurred. Both ponies were originally pack ponies and trotters. The Dales, the heavier of the two, is generally the more suitable for driving. It stands up to 14·1 hands and is usually black or brown with an abundant mane and tail, and it must always carry the characteristic feather on the lower limbs.

The Fell is an excellent and active riding type with a good shoulder. Lighter in the body than the Dales, it is still compact and strong. Colours are bay, brown, black and sometimes grey, and as with the Dales there is a full mane and tail and feather on the legs.

The most numerous and popular of the native breeds are the Welsh. There are four distinct types, each with its own section in the stud book. The smallest and the most beautiful of these ponies and cobs, which inhabited the Welsh hills centuries before the Roman occupation, is the Welsh Mountain Pony, Section A, not exceeding 12 hands. Infusions of Arab and Thoroughbred blood were introduced to improve the ponies in the nineteenth century, and there is evidence of Hackney blood, although of the old-type roadster Hackney which was different from the modern product. Nonetheless the Welsh pony is unmistakeable in character, appearance and type. Hardy, strong and perfectly proportioned, it is full of personality, and while it has fire and courage it is essentially kind and gentle. As a riding pony the Welsh is superb, with a quality head, sharp, pricked ears, glorious eyes and a noticeable dish to the face. The majority of entries in any show class for ponies under 12·2 hands will be Welsh, and they are also excellent in harness.

Section B is a finer, larger version of the Mountain Pony, described as 'of riding type'. It has more scope than the Section A and a longer, lower action, but otherwise retains the same characteristics.

The Welsh Cobs, of which there are two sections, C and D, are, ideally, larger versions of the Mountain Pony. The smaller cob, Section C, up to 13·2 hands is the old, all-purpose farm pony but is a good ride for children and the ideal transition mount between pony and full-size horse. It is described as the Welsh Pony of Cob Type. Section D is the Welsh Cob, which can be as large as 15·2 hands. The cob can trace its lineage to the Welsh pony, but there is also a strain of Hackney blood, and possibly some of the 'old Welsh cart horse', whatever that was. Deeper in the past there was definitely some Andalusian blood.

The great feature of this spirited and magnificently proportioned cob is the trotting action, which is quite unlike that of a Hackney. It is enormously forceful, free and fast but without the exaggerated elevation of the Hackney. The cob is a tremendous harness horse, but without its heavy shoes it also makes an excellent and resourceful hunter in all but the biggest galloping country. It is an ideal choice for the legions of 'weekend' riders.

The oldest of the native breeds is the Exmoor. A strong pony, well able to carry a full-grown man, it has enormous stamina and courage and an independent spirit. In height the breed does not exceed 12·3 hands. It is distinguished by a mealy muzzle; 'toad', slightly hooded, eyes; and an unusual coat and tail. The former is harsh and springy to keep out the worst weather, but in summer it lies close, hard and shiny. The tail is also unusual, a relic of the breed's early origins in far northern regions. It is an 'ice' tail, with an extra fan-like growth at the top. The ponies are bay, brown or dun without any white markings.

The Dartmoor pony, close neighbour of the more rugged Exmoor, is more graceful than the latter and perhaps nearly as old in origin. These were the 'little British horses' driven with their owners, the Walli or Welsh, into the moorlands and forests of Wales, Exmoor and Dartmoor before the advancing Saxons. In the course of improvement other breeds have been concerned with the Dartmoor. These certainly include the Arab, and one particularly effective Welsh cross through the stallion Punchinello in the early part of this century. The Dartmoor does not exceed 12·2 hands. The breed has a small, quality head, strong hocks and back, a very good shoulder and excellent feet. Like all the native ponies it is very sure-footed and a brilliant performer under saddle.

Ponies have run in the New Forest for over a thousand years, but a breed society was not formed until 1891. Up to forty years ago the Foresters had received numerous outcrosses: Arab, Thoroughbred, Welsh, Dartmoor, Exmoor, Highland and even Fell. Not surprisingly there was, until fairly recently, no very recognizable type, and even now, when the type – at least in studs outside the Forest – is pretty well fixed, there is still some variation in size. The Forest pony can be between 12 and 14·2 hands, although the modern variety tends more towards the latter height. Any colour except part colours is acceptable. The modern Forester, a really first-class pony for any child or adult, is increasing in popularity every year, not only in its native country but also overseas, where the breed is much in demand.

The Connemara is a product of Ireland. It is in all probability descended from Galician and Andalusian imports made bfore and during the Roman occupation of Britain. In recent times Arab and Thoroughbred blood has been used to improve the quality. The Connemara is between 13·2 and 14 hands, very strong and with good conformation. The Irish variety is possibly a shade plainer than its English counterpart, but both are tough and are noted for their cleverness and jumping ability.

The Care of the Horse

THE BODY OF THE HORSE

The horse's body is a fine example of nature's ability to relate structure to function, expressed elsewhere in the sharp carnassial teeth of the dog accustomed to tearing at flesh and using its 'bite' for defence, or in the fins of a fish developed for the purpose of propulsion through water. The horse's body is adapted for speed and size. Other animals are as fast as the horse, but not as big, and it is this combination that gives the clue to much of the horse's body structure. It accounts for the highly specialized limbs, in which the number of bones has been reduced to a minimum, so that the horse stands on the tips of four fingers and toes, compared with sixteen in the dog and eight in cattle. The loss of muscle below the 'knee' and 'hock' has accompanied the reduction in the number of bones, for it is these muscles, together with the extra bones, that provide the human or animal ability to grasp and manipulate with the extremity of its limbs. Through the course of evolution, the horse has lost this ability and can move its limbs only either forwards or backwards. This provides it with the optimum method of propulsion. The force is provided by the highly developed muscles attached to the bones of the forearm, thigh and body, the surfaces of bone having been broadened to meet this increased commitment.

Evolution

We know from fossil records how the horse's skeleton has become adapted in the course of some forty million years, from the fox-like creature *Eohippus*, or Dawn Horse, to *Equus caballus,* the modern horse. From these records we can follow not only the elongation and simplification of the extremities of the limbs, but also such changes as the lengthening of the neck and skull, associated with the alteration from browsing habits (i.e. eating soft, succulent fruits above ground level) to grazing habits (i.e. cropping hard, fibrous grass at ground level).

The first fossil record is of the Dawn Horse, but the horse presumably evolved from stock having the mammalian prototype appendages of five fingers and toes, which human beings have retained. The sequence of development of the limb extremities and those which took place in the skull and teeth have been well researched. The teeth mirror the change in feeding habits; the modern horse has front teeth for cropping grass and back teeth with flat surfaces so that the upper and lower molars can grind the hard, fibrous content of its diet.

The horse's body is structured to meet the needs of the equine species; and purposes imposed by man are only incidental. This must be recognized so as to understand the best methods of caring for the horse, in order to gain maximum advantage from its prowess while interfering minimally with its natural functions.

Evolutionary changes help in understanding the horse of today, but it has also to be accepted that the structure of the body of the horse is unalterable, in the sense that within the relatively minor family differences, a horse is a horse; and no amount of artificial or man-inspired influences can change it. It is true that by selection it is possible to breed a miniature Shetland pony or an enormous Thoroughbred or draught horse, but these are still just different breeds of the domestic horse, belonging to the species *Equus caballus*. They all possess sixty-four chromosomes (i.e. inherited material in the cell nuclei). Near relatives such as the zebra, Przewalski's horse and wild ass have different numbers of chromosomes, but are nonetheless identifiable in their body structure as belonging to the Equidae.

Tissues

The horse, in common with other mammalian species, is made up of four basic tissues known as muscle, nerve, connective and epithelium, each with its own special characteristics which contribute to the function of the whole body.

Epithelial Tissue: Epithelial tissue includes the covering and lining of the outside of the body (the skin), and the inner tubes and hollow organs such as the gut, bile duct, bladder and uterus. The glands which produce hormones and other substances are formed of epithelial tissue.

Connective Tissue: Connective tissue is that which contributes special functions such as the bony structures (the skeleton) which support and give form to the body and its softer structures. Blood is a very special form of connective tissue, while more simple forms include tendons, ligaments and sheets of fibrous material which bind or protect various organs or muscles.

Muscular Tissue: Muscular tissue is that which has the property of movement (contraction and relaxation) and is thus responsible for the work performed by the body, as in galloping or, in standing, by resisting the pull of gravity. Body functions are also performed by other types of muscle, such as that in the lining of the gut which produces the peristaltic movement propelling food from one end of the alimentary tract (gut) to the other. The heart too consists mostly of muscle doing the work of a pump.

Nervous Tissue: Nervous tissue has the capacity to transmit messages over long distances, and forms the brain, spinal cord and nerve pathways which control most of the body functions.

The Skeleton and Muscles

The horse's skeleton is composed of approximately 210 individual bones (excluding those of the tail). The skeleton gives support for the muscles, protection for the internal organs, and possesses the necessary mobility of its parts to enable the horse to move at various speeds or to lie down or graze.

Varying degrees of mobility are provided by differing types of joints; for example, that between the femur and tibia, forming the 'stifle', gives great mobility, while those between two vertebrae in the backbone allow restricted movement only. The bones forming all joints are capped with cartilage, which is softer than bone and can make good the effects of wear and tear at the surface. The joint is completed by a capsule which produces synovia (joint oil) to lubricate the joint surfaces, and it is strengthened by ligaments, i.e. fibrous bands connecting the bones on either side of the joint.

The way in which a joint can move is controlled by the shape of the joint surface and the position of the ligaments and other supporting structures which pass over it. The fetlock, for example, can be flexed further than it can be extended; the 'knee' can only be flexed whereas the stifle joint can be moved, to some extent, in several directions.

The skeleton has several examples of nature's way of adapting structure to meet particular requirements or function. The broad flat surface of the scapula or shoulder blade and the transverse processes of the lumbar vertebrae, provide ample space for the attachment of the powerful muscles required to move the fore and hind limbs. The special features of the skull are the relatively elongated face providing space for the teeth and their roots; and the orbits housing the eyes which are placed well above ground level when the horse is grazing. These provide it with a greater area of vision to look out for impending danger.

The parts of the skeleton which have particular practical importance for horse owners are:

1) the splint bones, on either side of the cannon bones, which are remnants of the digits lost during evolution. These bones are bound to the cannon bone by ligaments. It is a fracture of the shaft of this bone, or inflammation of the ligament which binds it to the cannon bone, that causes the painful enlargements known as 'splints'.
2) other small bones which are sometimes troublesome, the sesamoids. These are two small bones forming the back of the fetlock joint, and the navicular bone below the pedal bone.

The Foot: The horse's foot is completely surrounded by a substance similar to a human's finger nail to protect it against having to sustain the wear and tear of carrying one-quarter of the horse's weight in action over any terrain. A horse's foot consists of an outer layer of horn (hoof) inside which is contained the pedal and navicular bones, part of the second phalanx and the deep digital flexor tendon, the end of which is attached to the pedal bone. The foot also contains the digital pad, lateral cartilages, corono-pedal joint, blood vessels and nerves.

The outer layer consists of the walls, sole, bars and frog. The hoof is an inert substance composed largely of keratin which is secreted

In-hand show classes act both as a shop window for breeders and to maintain the quality of the breed. These Connemara ponies, the native breed of Ireland, are being judged at the Royal Dublin Horse Show.

OVERLEAF: An excellent child's pony, and a rider who is happy and confident. Working pony classes provide a chance for the good all-round pony and rider to compete without having to contend with professionally produced show ponies, some of which are hardly suitable mounts for children.

by the coronary corium. The hoof grows at a rate of approximately 0·5 cm (0·2 in) per month and it receives nourishment from the sensitive laminae, leaf-like structures which line the pedal bone and which bind the hoof to the bone as they interlock with comparable leaves from the insensitive laminae of the hoof. The foot as a whole absorbs concussion, and by its continuous growth it is able to replace the surface as this is lost by everyday wear and tear.

Muscles: The muscles that enable the horse to move consist of muscle masses attached to bone at one end and to their respective tendons at the other. For example, the superficial digital flexor of the forelimb is attached to the humerus bone and the posterior aspect of the radius bone. At its lower end it forms the tendon, which runs behind the knee and fetlock joints to become inserted on the lower end of the first and upper end of the second phalanx. Its action is to flex the toe and knee and to extend the elbow joint.

The tendon is encased in a synovial sheath as it runs behind the knee and the fetlock joints. The thin fibrous sheet that composes this produces tendon oil or synovia which has similar lubricating properties to joint oil. Similar sheaths enclose tendons wherever there is likely to be friction between the tendon and bone, or other structures. A bursa is a similar structure except that it does not surround a tendon, but acts more like a cushion between parts that suffer friction.

Most muscles have tendons of varying lengths and not all are as long as those which run below the knee or hock joints. Ligaments, too, vary in length. Most are relatively short, such as those already mentioned which strengthen joints. The check and suspensory ligaments of the forelimb deserve special mention. The check ligament is attached to the ligament at the back of the knee joint and, at its lower end, it joins the deep digital flexor tendon in the region of the back of the cannon bone. It forms part of the stay apparatus which prevents over-extension of the toe. The suspensory ligament is also concerned in this action and is attached above, to the back of the cannon bone and lower row of knee (carpal) bones, and below to the sesamoid bones behind the fetlock joint. From here it sends two branches around the front of the first phalangeal (pastern) bone on each side to join the common digital extensor tendon, through which they are inserted into the front of the second phalangeal and pedal bones. There is a similar arrangement in the hind limb.

Digestive System

The horse's digestive system consists of those organs concerned with digestion, or the turning of complex food material such as hay, grass and grains into simple substances such as carbohydrate, protein (amino acids), fatty acids, etc., which can be used by the body for energy, storage or body building processes. The organs consist of the alimentary tract, which is the tube extending from the mouth to the anus and known also as the gut, intestines or

No matter how young, a rider should be properly prepared for showing a pony. This boy has been taught how to lead his pony in-hand correctly, and is obviously fully in control.

PREVIOUS PAGE: There was a time when all lady riders were expected to ride side-saddle – not only in the show ring but out hunting as well. It is now quite unusual to see ponies being shown side-saddle, but this pair could hardly fail to catch the judge's eye.

alimentary canal, and the accessory organs such as the teeth, tongue, salivary glands, liver and pancreas.

The special characteristics of the horse's mouth are the highly prehensile lips for gathering food, which work in conjunction with the sharp front teeth when cropping grass, and the labile tongue which conveys the food to the back teeth. These have table-like surfaces crossed by ridges that form an ideal grinding surface between the upper and lower jaws.

An adult horse has forty teeth arranged as follows: in each left and right, upper and lower jaw there are three incisors, one canine (present only in colts and geldings), and six cheek teeth (three premolars and three molars). A young horse has temporary teeth, which are replaced by the permanent teeth by the time it is five years old.

Ducts which discharge digestive juices from the parotid mandibular and sublingual salivary glands open into the mouth. The roof of the mouth is formed by the hard palate in front, which continues into the soft palate behind. The soft palate forms part of the pharynx where the air passages and digestive tract cross one another.

As a horse swallows, the food crosses the pharynx and enters the gullet or oesophagus, from where it is conveyed to the stomach and thence to the small intestines, large colon, small colon and rectum.

The alimentary tract, from the stomach to the rectum, together with the pancreas and liver (glands which contribute more digestive juices and bile) are contained in the abdominal cavity. This can be described as a large 'box', the sides of which are the diaphragm in front, the muscles below the spine forming the top, and the muscles of the 'belly', the bottom. The back part of the 'box' is closed by the pelvic outlet through which the rectum, urinary and reproductive tract reach the outside. The abdominal cavity also contains, in the female, the ovaries and the uterus; and in both male and female, the urinary organs, comprising the kidney, ureters and bladder.

The abdominal cavity is lined by the peritoneum and all the organs are suspended by reflections (mesenteries and ligaments) of the peritoneum. A special free fold of the peritoneum is known as the omentum.

The anatomical peculiarities of the horse's digestive system compared with other mammals are:

1) that the greatest volume of the tract is in the hind end, namely the caecum and colon, where the major process of digesting fibre occurs by bacterial fermentation
2) the relatively small stomach
3) the absence of a gall bladder (probably associated with the need for a continual supply of bile in an animal which is a continuous feeder).

The Respiratory System

The respiratory system consists of the air passages of the head (nostrils to pharynx), the pharynx, larynx, trachea or windpipe, bronchi and lungs. The lungs are the two organs in which oxygen and carbon dioxide are exchanged between the blood and air. They are situated in the chest cavity known as the thorax, the walls (ribs and diaphragm) of which can expand or contract, thus allowing the lungs to enlarge or compress. The movements of the chest alternately draw in and expel air into and out of the lungs.

The anatomical features of the equine respiratory system which are of particular interest to horsemen are:

1) the air sinuses of the head and the guttural pouches, which are large blind sacs connecting with the eustachian tubes of the ear and which may be the site of infection or bleeding.
2) the larynx, one side of which may become paralyzed and cause an obstruction to the inflow of air, thus resulting in whistling or roaring.
3) the minute endings of the airways in tubes, known as bronchioles, which connect with the air sacs (alveoli) in the lung. It is these structures which are involved in the condition of 'broken wind'.

The Heart and Vascular System

As in other mammals, the horse's heart consists of four chambers with four sets of valves. Racehorses, as might be expected, have hearts which are rather larger than the average; that of Eclipse weighed about 6·5 kg (14 lb).

Blood is pumped by the heart into arteries which extend to all parts of the body, before returning to the heart in veins. Few people need to know the horse's vascular system in detail, but the following arteries and veins are worthy of note:

1) The jugular vein, which lies on either side of the neck, carries the blood from the head and neck back to the heart. It is easily 'raised' by pressure in the lower part of the neck and may therefore be used for collecting blood samples or in the course of administering intravenous fluid therapy.
2) The aorta is the main artery leaving the heart, and it carries blood to all parts posterior to the chest. It runs along the roof of the chest and abdominal cavity, and in the latter it distributes a branch to the intestines, called the anterior mesenteric artery. It is this branch which may become blocked as a result of the activity of the parasite *Strongylus vulgaris*. This is one of the causes of colic.

Lymphatic System

The lymph system consists of a series of minute channels and venules which carry a relatively colourless fluid, known as lymph, from the extremities and other parts of the body back towards the heart, where they discharge it into the blood-stream. Along these channels are special glands or lymph nodes which filter bacteria and other matter from the lymph stream, thus purifying it. The lymph system is not noticeable except in such diseases as lymphangitis, or when the lymph nodes become enlarged, as in strangles or other infectious conditions.

The Uro-Genital System
The horse, in common with other mammals, has two kidneys, whose function is to filter the blood and form urine. This passes to the bladder through the ureters, and from there the urine passes to the outside through the urethra. The urethra has a common exit from the body with the sexual tract, namely the vagina in the mare and the penis in the stallion. The genital organs of the mare consist of two ovaries and oviducts or fallopian tubes, the uterus, cervix, vagina and vulva.

The ovaries are responsible for producing the female sex cell, i.e. the egg or ovum. A filly is born with many thousands of eggs in her ovaries and no more form during her lifetime. However, during times of sexual activity oestrus fluid follicles develop round one or more eggs and rupture to shed the egg into the fallopian tube. This is known as ovulation. The lining of the follicle bleeds and a 'yellow-body' is formed. The follicle, while it is developing, produces the hormone oestrogen, and the 'yellow-body', the hormone progesterone. If the ovary of a sexually mature filly is cut in half it will contain follicles and 'yellow bodies' in varying stages of development.

A stallion's sexual organs consist of two testes in which the spermatozoa are produced; collecting ducts (including the epididymis) which connect with the urethra after travelling in the spermatic cord with arteries and veins; the accessory glands comprising the prostate, vesicular seminales and bulbo-urethral, and the penis. The penis is housed in the prepuce or 'sheath', and the testes in the scrotum.

The Nervous System
The nervous system is composed of the central nervous system (CNS) and the peripheral nervous system (PNS). The CNS consists of the brain and spinal cord. The PNS comprises the nerve trunks that leave the brain, and others which emerge from the spinal cord, together with those belonging to the special sympathetic nervous system.

The features of the equine nervous system are the relatively highly developed cerebellum, that part responsible for the control of movement; the long course of the spinal cord through the cervical region which makes this part susceptible to injury and to such nervous conditions as 'wobbler' disease; and the routes taken by the nerves running to the extremities of the fore and hind limbs. A knowledge of the latter can be used in the diagnosis of lameness, since they can be 'blocked' at various points by injecting a local anaesthetic around them, so as to desensitize the areas they supply.

The nervous system is something like a telephone exchange, in that it depends on the input and output of messages, to and from the centre. In using this analogy, the brain and spinal cord represent the exchange and its substations, and the nerve trunks are of two sorts, a) sensory, that is carrying messages to the CNS, and b) motor, carrying messages from the CNS to the muscles and other end points, where they produce activity or movement. The sensory nerves depend on endings which are sensitive to pain, pressure, heat, cold, etc., and which, when stimulated, convey these impressions to the brain where they are interpreted by reflex or voluntary action. The special sensory endings are those of smell, sight and hearing, mediated through the nose, eyes and ears.

The Endocrine (Hormonal) System

The endocrine system consists of a number of glands which secrete hormones. A hormone is a substance produced by a gland and transported in blood or lymph streams, to exert an action or cause an effect on another part or parts. For example, the pituitary gland, which is situated below the brain, produces a hormone known as follicle-stimulating hormone (FSH), the action of which is to stimulate follicles to develop in the ovary. Insulin is produced by cells in the pancreatic gland and is responsible for regulating the level of sugar in the blood. Cortisone is secreted by the adrenal cortex and has widespread effects on many metabolic functions of the body. The endocrine glands (and the hormones they produce) are as follows:

a) anterior pituitary – follicle-stimulating hormone (FSH), luteinizing hormone (LH), prolactin, growth, thyroid stimulating hormone
b) posterior pituitary – oxytocin, vasopressin
c) thyroid – thyroxine
d) pancreas – insulin
e) adrenal cortex – cortisone
f) adrenal medulla – adrenalin
g) ovary – oestrogen, progesterone
h) testes – testosterone
i) uterus – prostaglandin

The Skin

The skin is composed of three layers: an outer cellular or epithelial layer which is capable of replacing itself as wear and tear erode the outer surface; a sub-epithelial layer which nourishes the outer layer and in which pain endings and other sensitive structures are found; and the sub-dermal layer which is continuous with the sub-epithelial layer and binds the skin to the underlying bone or muscle. The hair follicles occur in the sub-dermal layer. The skin contains sweat glands and other glands which secrete an oil known as sebum.

THE HORSE'S HEALTH

Good health is something which many people take for granted. In the horse, it is usually regarded as synonymous with normal function, that is the ability to perform the purpose for which the animal is kept. In common terms, a healthy horse is a sound horse; conversely, an unsound horse is one in which usefulness has been diminished, either temporarily or permanently, by some disease or unhealthy condition.

The interrelationship of soundness and disease sums up the horseman's approach to the subject; and it is a practical approach. However, there are certain aspects that lie outside this particular concept. For example, a horse may have a disease, such as a mild infection or a condition of bone, such as a 'splint', yet be able to carry out a useful function.

At this point, there has to be a more strict definition of disease, albeit practical. Disease is any condition where body structure is abnormally altered. This alteration has a cause (etiology), a course of development and recovery (pathogenesis), a likely outcome (prognosis) and a means of treatment or control. These criteria can be applied to all conditions, whence they can be broken down into finer divisions of knowledge such as, is the cause infective, or does the condition have an underlying (predisposing) cause?

Infective Diseases

Infective diseases are those caused by micro-organisms (germs or microbes). There are three main groups of microbes – virus, bacteria and fungus. Each group is subdivided into families, genera and species, just as mammals are classified according to their particular characteristics. Thus within the group of bacteria there are *Streptococci*, *Staphylococci* and *Klebsiella*, according to the characteristics that these microbes display under microscopic, cultural, biochemical, serological and other means of examination which help to distinguish even the most closely related forms.

Microbes can live on the surface of the skin or on the mucous membranes lining the various body cavities such as the mouth, vagina, etc. They can also invade the tissues and live within the various body structures, such as the bones, liver or kidneys. Not all microbes are harmful and some exist within the body in a state of mutual benefit, such as the bacteria in the colon and caecum which digest the cellulose and fibre in a horse's feed. Between those that do cause disease and the host there exists quite a complicated relationship. Each type of microbe has a more or less developed capacity for invading the body and causing damage. This property is known as virulence and is recognized in practice by the severity of the illness it causes, and the ease with which the condition spreads through the horse population. For example, the bacterium *Streptococcus equi* which causes the disease strangles is associated with a feverish condition which spreads rapidly through the inmates of stud or stable. On the other hand its close relative *Streptococcus pyogenes* is more often associated with localized conditions such as infection of the uterus, which are peculiar at any given time to an individual.

Immunity is another factor in the relationship between microbe and host. An individual gathers immunity by the capacity of special cells in the body to produce protective substances (antibodies) which neutralize the invading microbe. The antibody must of course be specific to the microbe, or it will have little or no effect in preventing it from becoming established in the body tissues. For example, there are two strains of influenza virus which are popularly called the Miami and Prague strains. The horse may be immune to the Prague strain, because it has experienced this infection before and is capable, therefore, of producing Prague strain antibodies, but the same individual may be susceptible to the Miami strain because the body has had no previous experience of it. The same difference would exist if the individual had been vaccinated with one, but not the other, strain.

Vaccines illustrate another way in which an individual may develop immunity. In this case the immunity is artificial, but the principle of naturally developing immunity is similar. Protein, in the form of the whole or part of the microbe, enters the body and is recognized by the host tissues as foreign. The protein is known as antigen and is capable of stimulating the production of antibody. The immunity varies with the microbe and the vaccine, which is solid and lasting in some cases and weak or limited in others. In the case of influenza or tetanus (lockjaw), booster doses are required following vaccination, since immunity gradually decreases.

Quite apart from immunity, individuals vary in their response to infection because of predisposing factors, which make the body susceptible. For example, a mare that takes air into the genital tract because of faulty perineal conformation causes the uterus to become more prone to bacterial infection.

The common equine diseases caused by microbes are shown in tables 1, 2 and 3 (see pages 204 and 205).

Parasitic Diseases
Parasites are organisms which live at the expense of another, but which do not necessarily harm it, nor do they usually cause death. They are therefore distinct from microbes, although some parasites do produce severe effects, which may have fatal consequences. An example is the redworm, *Strongylus vulgaris* and *S. edentatus*, the life cycle of which includes a larval phase spent in the blood vessels in the former case and in the peritoneum in the latter.

Parasites may spend part of their development in a free-living state, that is, unassociated with the host. Their parasitic existence may be spent inside (endoparasites), or on the surface (ectoparasites) of the body. The main endo- and ectoparasitic diseases of the horses are shown in tables 4 and 5.

Diseases and Conditions of Bone

Bone disease, as such, is rare in the horse, and is confined mainly to disorders of growth in horses up to the age of two years old. In older horses, it may occur in cases of nutritional imbalance. From

1 BACTERIAL DISEASES

Disease	Chief Symptoms	Cause
Acne*	Small boils and/or weeping sores in skin	Staphylococcus aureus
Brucellosis**	Lameness; poll evil and fistulous withers	Brucella abortus
Glanders**	Nasal catarrh; fever; oedematous swellings; pneumonia	Leofflerella mallei
Leptospinosis**	Fever; jaundice; anaemia	Leptospira pomona
Lockjaw*	Painful spasms	Clostridium tetani
Salmonellosis*	Diarrhoea, usually blood-stained; sudden death	Salmonella typhimurium Salmonella enteritidis
Sleepy foal disease*	Weakness and fever in newborn foal	Actinobacillus equuli
Strangles*	Fever; nasal discharge; abscesses in glands, mainly of head and neck	Streptococcus equi
Tuberculosis**	Wasting; stiffness of the neck	Mycobacterium tuberculosis

* Common diseases   ** Less common diseases

2 DISEASES CAUSED BY VIRUSES

Disease	Chief Symptoms	Virus
Epidemic cough	Cough; fever	Influenza
Sporadic or stable cough	Cough; nasal catarrh; sometimes fever	Rhinovirus Herpesvirus Adenovirus
Pneumonia	Fever; difficult or abnormal breathing (especially in foals)	Adenovirus Herpesvirus
African horse sickness	Pneumonia and enteritis	Reovirus
Warts	Small discrete cornified growths usually around muzzle	Papova virus
Angleberries (sarcoids)	Proliferating growths with tendency to ulcerate and bleed	Papova virus
Spots (coital exanthema)	Small ulcers on vulva of mare and penis of stallion	Equid herpes virus
Equine infectious anaemia	Fever; anaemia; swellings on legs and dependent parts	Unclassified

the horseman's viewpoint, these are conditions of enlargements (sometimes painful) around the fetlock and above the knees or hocks in foals and yearlings caused by inflammation of the growth plate (epiphysitis), or recognizable in older horses as 'big head' in which the bones of the head become softened and distorted.

Most conditions affecting bone in horses, apart from nutritional disturbances, can be traced to trauma or infection. A better understanding is achieved by recognizing that bone is not a static structure, nor can it be regarded in isolation from its relationship

3 DISEASES CAUSED BY FUNGUS AND OTHER MICROBES

Disease	Symptoms	Microbe
Ringworm	Scab covered circular lesions on skin peeling off to reveal ulcer	Fungus: (*Microsporum*) (*Trichophyton*)
Broken wind	Heaves, cough	Various species of fungus
Abortion	Thickened placenta	
Guttural pouch mycosis	Haemorrhage down nose	
Biliary fever (Piroplasmosis, Babesiosis)	Fever; anaemia; jaundice	Protozoa (species of *Piroplasma*)

4 ENDOPARASITIC DISEASES OF THE HORSE

Disease	Symptoms	Parasite
Strongylosis	Diarrhoea; loss of condition; colic; anaemia	*Strongylus vulgaris* *Strongylus edentatus* *Strongylus equinus*
Ascariasis	Diarrhoea in foals; colic; broncho-pneumonia	*Parascaris equorum*
Oxyuriasis	Rubbing tail	*Oxyuris equi*
Tapeworm	None	*Anoplocephala perfoliata*
Bot maggot	Gastritis; perforation of the stomach; rectal haemorrhage	*Gastrophilus intestinalis*

5 ECTOPARASITIC DISEASES OF THE HORSE

Disease	Symptoms	Parasite
Lice	Irritation; rubbing; loss of hair	*Bovicola equi*
Ticks	Irritation; carry disease such as encephalomyelitis	Ixodidae and Argasidae species
Mange	Scabs; intense irritation; loss of hair; thickened skin	*Sarcoptes* and *Psoroptes*
Ear mange	Head shaking; stamping; rubbing	*Chorioptes equi*
Autumn itching	Pimples and scabs on legs	*Trombicula autumnalis* (harvest mites)

with joints or from its attachment to ligaments and muscle (see previous chapter on The Body of the Horse). Bone is lined by a fine membrane, known as periosteum on its outer surface and endosteum on its inner surface. These two membranes mould the shape of the bone by building and breaking down the bony substance, which is nourished by blood vessels and is composed mainly of calcium and phosphorus laid down in a system of canals or spaces surrounded by bone cells.

In practice, we become aware of bony disorders in the form of lumps which may be painful or painless, small or large, and which may or may not cause lameness. These are known as splints, high and low ringbone, osselets, bone spavin, sore or bucked shins, pedal ostitis or, as the veterinarian would say, exostoses, i.e. bony outgrowths. Collectively, they are the result of inflammation of the periosteum and the raising up of the fine membrane from the surface of the bone. The reaction usually spreads to neighbouring tissues, causing a fibrous swelling which precedes the laying down of new bone beneath the periosteal lining. This reaction is seen at its most typical in the development of splints. Here the ligament binding the splint to the cannon bone may become affected, and a fibrous reaction develops which can be seen displacing the skin outwards over the site of reaction. After a time new bone is laid down and the splint becomes calloused, gradually diminishing in size over quite a long period of time.

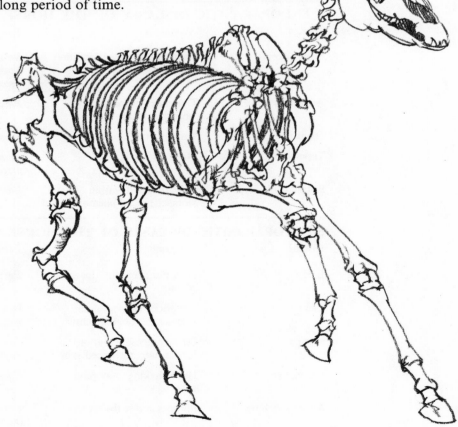

Splints may also be caused by fracture of the slender shaft of the bone, which results in a callus, that is, new bone developed in the fibrous reaction between the severed ends of the shaft. The callus fixes and reunites the fractured part, as also occurs when larger bones are fractured, providing the ends of the bone are immobilized. Sore and bucked shins are often the result of stress fractures of the cannon bone. Resembling nothing more than cracks in china, they are difficult to demonstrate on X-ray. Nonetheless they evoke a reaction of the periosteum and a painful enlargement at the site of fracture.

The periosteum may become damaged when ligaments or joint capsules are torn at the point where they insert into the outer lining of the bone; osselets and sesamoiditis are examples. The reaction takes much the same course, typified by heat, pain and swelling.

Arthritis means inflammation of a joint, and the symptoms are swelling, heat and pain when the joint is moved. Joints are composed of several structures, one or more of which may be damaged, thus giving the symptoms of a sprained joint, but requiring veterinary investigation to determine the exact nature of the condition. For example, a swollen, painful fetlock joint may be caused by a sprain of the joint capsule, of a supporting ligament, or of the articular surfaces of the joint.

The surface of the bones forming a joint is lined by cartilage, which is softer than bone and is able to replace the cells that are lost through wear. Any process which damages the surface, such as infection or trauma, sets up an inflammatory reaction, i.e. arthritis. The swelling of arthritis is caused by an increase in synovial fluid (joint oil) which makes the capsule bulge. A soft swelling is produced and this can be felt at certain points around the joint. The arthritic area on the joint's surface may be likened to an ulcer. It can heal or become progressively deeper until it reaches the bone beneath, which may respond by producing new bone in an effort to repair the damage. However, this new bone is usually too fragile or too profuse to achieve functional repair of the joint. The consequence is seen as bony outgrowths from the joint surface from which small pieces become detached. These pieces lie free in the joint cavity and are commonly described as joint mice.

Fractures: Any bone in the body may be fractured, but those most commonly affected are the pastern, pedal, sesamoid, carpal, cannon and pelvic bones. Fractures may be simple or compound and the broken pieces widely separated or comminuted – that is, protruding through the skin. Treatment of fractures consists of immobilizing the part by bandage or plaster support or by internal fixation.

Diseases of the Alimentary Tract
Colic is the condition most frequently encountered in this category in stud or stabled horses. In this context, it implies pain arising from a disturbance in the alimentary tract. The pain causes the

horse to show certain symptoms such as sweating, pawing the ground, looking round at the flanks, rolling or lying on the ground (flat out, on the brisket or on the back), refusing to eat and passing dungs of abnormal quantity (usually decreased) or quality (hard, mucous-covered, soft, smelly or diarrhoeaic).

The veterinarian distinguishes a number of differing types of colic, according to the symptoms and based on the results of examinations of abdominal sounds (borborygmi) resulting from peristalsis, blood, rectal temperature; palpation of the abdominal contents *per rectum* and examination of peritoneal fluid obtained by needle puncture through the 'belly' muscles may also aid diagnosis.

The chief types of colic are:

1) Simple stoppage (impaction) caused by partially-digested food accumulating in the lumen of the gut. There are certain sites where this is most likely to occur, namely in the pelvic flexure of the large colon, in the caecum and where the last part of the small intestine (ileum) enters the caecum. The quantity of food involved depends on the site of obstruction. In the ileum it is small, but in the colon or caecum large quantities may accumulate.

2) Tympany, caused by gaseous distension of the gut which may be a result of fermentation or over-production of gas by bacteria not normally present in the gut. Tympany may involve enormous quantities of gas or be confined to a small part of the gut, but in either case the wall of the gut is stretched, causing pain.

3) Spasmodic colic implies an over-activity of the gut wall, and this irritability results in painful spasms which are accentuated by local accumulations of gas.

4) Thrombo-arteritic colic follows the blocking of a small or large branch of the arteries which supply blood to the wall of the gut. These arteries travel in the mesenteries by which the gut is suspended in the abdominal cavity. The most common sites affected are the small intestine and the caecum, and the most frequent cause of thrombus is damage caused to blood vessels by the larval forms of the redworm parasite *S. vulgaris*.

The severity of this last form of colic depends partly on the area of wall which is deprived of blood, which in turn depends on the size of the artery in which the clot lodges. However, the sequence of happenings is much the same in all cases, namely the deprived area becomes inflamed and then, if an alternative blood supply cannot be developed from neighbouring blood vessels, the affected part 'dies' in a state similar to gangrene. Inflammation (peritonitis) of the outer lining of the gut causes acute pain and may result in two loops of bowel becoming adherent to one another (adhesions).

Damage of this nature causes an acute obstruction because peristalsis (the movement of the gut which propels the food along the alimentary tract) does not cross the affected part or produces a reflex paralysis of considerable lengths of bowel. The severity and duration of colic depend on the extent of the damage. In some cases it may resolve, but in others it may lead to profound disturbances in fluid and salt content of the blood and culminate in a state of shock and heart failure.

Twisted gut (volvulus) is another example of an acute obstruction. Portions of the intestines become 'tied' in a knot or entangled through tears in the mesentery, with similar consequences to cases of arterial blockage by thrombus. A ruptured gut may be the sequel to any type of colic, but is most frequent following tympany, damage from thrombus or the activity of parasites. The stomach may rupture because of tympany, but the caecum and colon are more prone to the consequences of parasitic damage.

There are specific conditions in which colic is the predominant sign, such as grass sickness. The cause of this disease has not been established, despite intensive research since it was first reported as occurring in an army camp in Scotland at the turn of the century. Current opinion favours the hypothesis that it is caused by a toxin in the grass or other feed, which damages the nerves of the sympathetic system supplying the gut, causing paralysis of the alimentary tract.

Colitis X is the name given to a severe and usually fatal condition, in which the wall of the large colon becomes thickened and haemorrhagic, thought to be caused by a toxin produced by bacteria in the hind gut. Death comes about by shock and gross disturbances in the electrolyte and fluid balance of the body.

Treatment of colic depends on the diagnosis, but it is largely symptomatic. Simple impactions are treated with oily lubricants and salt solutions administered by stomach tube. Pain is controlled by administering suitable drugs, fluid and electrolyte may be transfused into the blood stream to counter unfavourable balance that results from more severe forms of alimentary obstruction. Abdominal surgery is used to correct twists and other anatomical obstructions which cannot be relieved by medical therapy.

Choke: This condition is encountered in horses of all ages, including foals. The most dramatic symptom is the sudden profuse discharge, down both nostrils, of saliva, coloured green or brown according to the nature of the diet at the time. The affected animal usually has an anxious expression and may stand with its head over its water supply, perhaps swilling water through its mouth, but not swallowing. The condition is caused by a dry bolus of food or an object such as a piece of wood becoming lodged in the gullet or oesophagus. Treatment with tranquillizing-type drugs is usually successful.

Diseases of the Liver
The liver has an enormous number of functions. It filters blood carrying the products of digestion from the gut and thereby plays a strategic part in assimilating the protein, carbohydrate and fats of the diet; it detoxicates, or works on toxic substances of food (or of drugs administered by mouth or injection), changing them from

harmful to innocuous compounds. It forms part of the defence mechanism of the body; helps to regulate the protein level in the bloodstream; produces bile which is a means of treating unwanted pigments as well as playing a vital part in the digestive processes of the gut; it acts as a store for sugar in the form of glycogen; and it is a source of enzymes which enter into innumerable metabolic systems forming the basis of life.

Damage of any kind (from infection, toxins, poisons, etc.) may impair one or more of the liver's functions, thereby causing symptoms of disease. Jaundice, for example, may occur because of haemolytic disease in which excess red blood cell pigment is released into the blood stream because of bacterial or viral infection, or because of iso-immune disease (see haemolytic jaundice of the newborn foal), thus flooding the liver, which normally excretes these pigments in the bile. Instead the pigment returns to the bloodstream, albeit in an altered form, and saturates the tissues and membranes, turning visible parts yellow. The liver itself may be damaged by infection or poisons and consequently become unable to deal with normal quantities of pigment reaching it in the bloodstream. This also causes jaundice, but in addition it may interfere with a number of liver functions which may lead to wasting and nervous disorders, as the liver fails in its digestive and detoxicating powers. Equine infectious anaemia and ragwort or metal poisoning are examples. Inflammation of the liver is known as hepatitis.

Diseases of the Genital Organs
The Mare: The genital organs of the mare comprise the ovaries, fallopian tubes, uterus, cervix, vagina, vulva and mammary glands. Primary disease of these organs is comparatively rare, but secondary conditions are common. Tumours of the ovary and uterine infections with *Klebsiella* or *Pseudomonas* species, and coital exanthema (spots) are examples of the first group. Uterine infection with *Streptococci* and other bacteria usually follows predisposing factors such as poor conformation of the vulva and perineum which allows air to enter the genital tract.

Mastitis, i.e. inflammation of the mammary glands, may occur, but without the artificial milking to which cows are subjected it is quite rare. Barren mares seem to be as frequently affected as mares with a foal at foot or those which have recently been weaned. Maiden mares, yearlings, and even foals may be affected. In most cases one half of the udder becomes swollen and painful with symptoms of discomfort, or in severe cases hind limb lameness. Oedematous swellings develop in front of the gland or in an upwards direction between the hind legs.

The Stallion: The stallion's genital organs consist of the testes, epididymis, vas deferens, accessory glands, scrotum and the penis and its sheath. Again primary conditions are rare, consisting of tumours of the testes or infection due to *Klebsiella* species. The stallion may be affected by coital exanthema (spots) which is a venereal infection, and is caused by a herpes virus infection spread at coitus with an infected mare. Small vesicles, which break to reveal small ulcers, develop on the penis. Sexual rest for about ten days is necessary, during which time the ulcers heal. If the stallion is used, the ulcers may coalesce and become exceedingly painful.

The external genitalia are exposed to injury, especially since the coital act is controlled by management, so there is a risk of the stallion being kicked by a mare that is not properly in heat. Haematomas of the penis are the most common injuries, although blows to the scrotum may occur and result in oedematous swellings which necessitate prolonged periods of rest.

Infertility

Infertility implies a relative reduction in the expected efficiency of breeding, and its origins may be traced to the mare or the stallion. The definition depends to some extent on an arbitrary approach; for example, that a mare may be expected to breed every year and to conceive in the selected months of March to June inclusive. Some mares may, for physiological reasons, fail to conceive every year or during the arbitrarily selected breeding season. Such mares are not biologically infertile and their failure can be sought in managerial rather than pathological reasons. There is, of course, no clear dividing line between the reasons for this type of 'infertility' and pathological infertility which may cause a mare to be more difficult to 'get in foal', perhaps for reasons of mild infection of the uterus, or because of being mated with a stallion whose quality of semen is not sufficiently high to ensure conception.

Infertility in the stallion may be temporary (perhaps following injury) or permanent. Symptoms include low libido (e.g. reduced ability to achieve erection, mounting, intromission or ejaculation) or low-quality semen (in terms of low sperm count, motility or increased abnormal forms). Similarly to the mare, the stallion may be infertile in certain circumstances, such as if overworked or mismanaged in other ways, yet fertile if used under optimal conditions. Most stallions should be capable of achieving over 70 per cent of conceptions in a group of forty mares, at a rate of about 2·5 services per mare, per stud season. Less productive rates may be experienced to every level, until the individual is incapable of achieving conception in any mares presented to him, and is therefore defined as sterile. However, for practical purposes, stallions that cannot achieve rates of more than 20 per cent fertility are regarded as completely infertile.

Diseases of Pregnancy

Pregnancy in the mare normally lasts 320 to 360 days. Foals born between 300 and 320 days are described as premature, and are usually small, weak and have difficulty in surviving. Foals born before 300 days are said to have been aborted, and have no chance of survival.

There is now only one common form of epidemic abortion, namely that caused by equid herpes virus 1. This virus primarily infects the respiratory system, and the reason why it causes abortion in relatively few cases is unknown. Abortions occur most often in the seventh to ninth month of pregnancy, but some cases occur later, even up to full term. The abortion is usually spontaneous without premonitory mammary development, and the foetal membranes are expelled with the foal or shortly afterwards. Affected foals born close to full term show signs of septicaemia (i.e. increasing weakness), and die within about four days of birth. In these cases the mare may have normal mammary development and colostrum in the udder.

The most common single non-infective cause of abortion is twins. The mare's placenta covers the whole of the uterine surface and there is, therefore, competition for area of attachment if two foetuses are present. There are three types of situation resulting in twins of equal or disproportionate sizes. In the majority of cases, one twin dies and causes the abortion of both between the seventh and tenth months of pregnancy.

Mycotic (fungal) abortion is most common in about the ninth month. The placenta is grossly thickened with a brownish sticky exudate on its surface. The fungus spreads slowly over the placental surface, gradually destroying more and more placenta and causing the foetus to become under-nourished and emaciated. Abortion occurs because the foetus is weakened or dies, and is therefore expelled from the uterus. However, any factor which can cause such a disturbance may operate beyond the 300th day and be responsible for foals that are born premature or, if born at full term, suffering from conditions recognizable as septicaemia or debility, which reduce their chances of survival outside the maternal uterus.

Diseases of the Newborn Foal

The first four days after birth are termed the neonatal period, for this is the time that the major adjustments, except for feeding, are established to enable the foal to exist independently of the mare. Symptoms of diseases peculiar to this period also become apparent now. As we have already seen, many of these conditions owe their origin to intra-uterine existence.

Neonatal disease can be conveniently divided into four groups, the latter three of which are non-infective:

1) *Group* 1: Infective conditions caused by bacteria or viruses. Symptoms include gradual loss of the suck reflex, developing weakness and inability to hold the suckling position, culminating in eventual coma, convulsions and death.

2) *Group* 2 includes the neonatal maladjustment syndrome (NMS) when gross behavioural disturbances are displayed. These include convulsions, loss of the suck reflex, and inability to recognize and follow the mare. Older terminology describes these cases as 'barkers', 'wanderers' or 'dummies'. The condition is associated

With proper training at home and a good pony, quite young children can enjoy jumping classes at local shows. Some children find jumping becomes almost an obsession, and it is important not to let ponies become bored and stale or to over-face a pony until it starts refusing.

OVERLEAF: Hunter trials and Pony Club events often organize their classes so that competitors go round in pairs, even though they may not necessarily be judged as a pair, as it encourages ponies to jump better. For a proper pairs class, a certain amount of practice is needed to accustom the ponies to jumping at the same pace.

with damage of the brain through haemorrhage or oedema; with profound biochemical and respiratory disturbances and with secondary effects from the deranged behaviour and metabolic status. Meconium colic, which is caused by alimentary disturbances during the passage of the first dung (normally voided within three days of birth) is a relatively simple condition included in Group 2.

3) *Group* 3: Anatomical abnormalities including parrot jaw, cleft palate, ruptured bladder, contracted tendons and a variety of deformities of the head, body or limbs. These conditions may be inherited or developed through disturbances in foetal growth brought about, probably, by virus infection, nutritional errors or the administration of drugs. These causes have been incriminated in many species, but evidence on the subject is still generally lacking, making the cause of equine anatomical defects mostly speculative at present.

4) *Group* 4: Haemolytic jaundice of the newborn foal, also known as iso-immune disease, is an uncommon condition characterized by massive destruction of the foal's red cells by antibodies that it receives from the mare's colostrum. If it is known that the foal is likely to be affected, the condition can be prevented by withholding colostrum during the first twenty-four hours of life. During this time the foal is muzzled and fed colostrum from another mare, followed by artificial milk. The foal may be allowed to suck from its dam after twenty-four hours, as by this time the small intestines have lost the ability to absorb antibody into the foal's bloodstream.

Treatment of neonatal conditions is mostly by symptomatic means. For example, loss of the suck reflex is countered by feeding through a stomach tube; the inability to get up, by help from attendants and general nursing (the inability to get up to suck is dealt with by feeding from a bottle); dehydration, by intravenous fluid therapy and transfusions of whole blood or plasma; and the inability to maintain body temperature, by heating the foaling box. Specific treatment includes antibiotics for infections, surgical repair of a ruptured bladder, and the transfusion of red cells in cases of haemolytic jaundice.

Diseases of the Older Foal and Yearling
Foals up to the time of weaning may suffer from conditions peculiar to this age group, such as infective arthritis (joint ill) and diarrhoea caused by bacteria, rotavirus, fungus or parasites (chiefly *Strongyloides westerii*).

Foals and yearlings are particularly prone to diseases of bone, because during the first eighteen months of life the long bones of the limb are developing rapidly. They are therefore particularly vulnerable to disturbances of growth caused by nutritional imbalance, to infection and from certain actions of management, e.g. over-feeding and under-exercise. Some young horses may have

In spite of the fact that he has lost his hat, and his rather individual jumping style, this competitor has managed to jump 'with' his pony, and has maintained a sensitive contact with the pony's mouth.

an inherited susceptibility to these bone disorders, which include contracted forelegs (straightness of the forelegs and knuckling over), crooked legs and epiphysitis.

Epiphysitis usually occurs when the growth plate at the end of the long bones is due to close. There are various theories concerning the cause of epiphysitis, such as concussion, especially in foals and yearlings which are overweight, or a disturbed calcium phosphorus ratio of the diet, in particular an excess of phosphorus.

Cerebella hypoplasia is a disease, thought to be inherited, which affects Arab and some other breeds. Symptoms include 'nodding' of the head and increasing inco-ordination of the limbs.

Foals are particularly susceptible to viral pneumonia and to infection of the lungs with *Corynebacterium equi*, the cause of summer pneumonia.

Diseases of the Urinary System

The horse is not as prone to urinary disease as many other animals. Horsemen often suspect 'kidney trouble' when a horse has apparent difficulty in staling or is tender in the back region, but these conditions are usually attributable either to certain types of colic or to injuries to the lumbar muscle or spine. Newborn foals may suffer from infection of the kidney with *E. coli* or *Actinobacillus equuli* (BVE) causing multiple minute abscesses and symptoms of 'sleepy foal' disease. Stones and infections in the bladder or urethra are uncommon; when they do occur symptoms include repeated attempts at staling, and passing urine containing protein, pus cells and/or blood.

Diseases of the Nervous System

Areas of the body may be paralyzed or suffer from loss of sensation through injury to nerves. The most common conditions are:

1) Radial paralysis, where there is difficulty in advancing the limb.
2) Facial paralysis, in which the upper lip is pulled to the side opposite from that affected by paralysis.
3) Suprascapula paralysis, in which there is wasting of the shoulder muscles.
4) Laryngeal hemiplegia, manifested by roaring or whistling and caused by impaired function of the recurrent nerve supplying the laryngeal muscles. There is increasing evidence that this condition has an hereditary basis.
5) Wobbler disease, a form of inco-ordination that affects the hind and, sometimes, the forelimbs, caused by compression of the spinal cord as it passes through the neck vertebrae. The condition is incurable and may be caused by injury or by a congenital defect in the vertebral bones.
6) Shivering, a condition of the hind limbs, characterized by shaking movements of the hind limb and tail when the leg is flexed and lowered to the ground. Stringhalt is a nervous disorder in which there is an exaggerated snatching-up movement of the hind limb. Both conditions are regarded as an unsoundness, although horses

affected may still be able to work, but their cause is unknown.

Diseases of the Cardio-Vascular System

Horses do not usually suffer from heart attacks in the same way as humans, that is from a clot (thrombus) blocking the coronary arteries and causing acute illness or sudden death. The most common catastrophe in horses is the rupture of an artery which causes fatal haemorrhage. This may occur in any part of the body, but is most frequently encountered as epistaxis (nose-bleed) resulting from bleeding from the lungs or one of the two guttural pouches; rupture of the aorta as it passes through the chest or abdomen, often as a consequence of parasitic larval activity; and, during foaling, rupture of the arteries supplying the uterus and/or vagina. Recent reports have indicated that horses suffer from obliterative-type lesions in small arteries, causing abnormal changes in the bones of the forelimb, and, in particular, the sesamoid bones of the fetlock and navicular bones of the feet.

Diseases of the Respiratory Tract

Diseases of the respiratory system are referred to as pneumonia, bronchitis, broken wind, cough and roaring or whistling. Coughing may be caused by a large variety of viruses, including those of influenza, herpes and the rhino groups, followed by secondary bacterial infection causing symptoms of nasal catarrh. Coughs may also occur through allergies from mould dust of hay and straw, and the cough may be the only obvious sign of broken wind, which in its best known form results in severe respiratory embarrassment with a marked double expiratory (breathing out) effort, a condition also known as heaves.

Diseases of the Eye

The horse's eye is vulnerable to injury causing ulcers on the cornea which may penetrate to the interior. If this happens, fluid is allowed to escape which can lead to the collapse of the eyeball. Alternatively the ulcers may heal, leaving a scar or corneal cataract. Cataracts of the lens result from trauma or, possibly, from hereditary or infective causes. Periodic ophthalmia (moon blindness) is a condition of recurring attacks in which the pupillary structures become inflamed. The condition is progressive and usually results in loss of sight in the affected eye. The third eyelid is a common site for growth of a malignant tumour.

Diseases of the Skin

Inflammation of the skin is known as dermatitis and horses can suffer from infective, parasitic and allergic types. Ringworm from fungal infection, and acne or spots from *Staphylococcus aureus* infection, are common in stabled horses. Small hard lumps, large weals and eczema may result from allergy-causing substances in feed or bedding, and from midge bites.

THE STABLED HORSE

Ponies of the mountain and moorland breeds or those containing a large proportion of native blood will live out all the year very well, but those of more aristocratic lineage, the Thoroughbred and the various Arab crosses, are not always so well-suited to the rigours of cold and wet weather and do not grow such a thick protective coat. Usually they will need stabling, at least at night, a proceeding involving much extra work, but if they have to live out it may be necessary to provide them with a waterproof New Zealand-type rug – and that, too, involves a lot more work and attention. They will also need larger rations of concentrate foods than the more self-sufficient natives.

Horses, as distinct from ponies, may be expected to be in harder work and for them stabling is frequently a necessity. In days gone by, when hunting was the *raison d'être* for keeping a horse, hunters were put out to grass in May and not brought into the stable until September. The increase in competitive riding has now changed that routine and the majority of horses work throughout the year, being given only a matter of a few weeks when they are entirely at grass. In some ways this arrangement is beneficial since the horse has little or no opportunity to lose his hard condition, whereas the horse out for the whole summer becomes so fat and flabby that an extended period of quiet exercise is necessary to get him into a suitable condition to work at fast paces.

In the case of horses laid off work for the whole summer, management need go no further than the provision of a shelter and regular inspection, with particular attention being paid to the condition of the feet. Usually shoes are removed altogether but it is probably better sense to shoe with 'grass tips', an attenuated form of the shoe proper, to prevent the foot breaking. No additional feeding is necessary beyond that obtained from the grass.

The management of a working horse during the summer will vary according to what is expected of him. A horse used purely for light hacking, for instance, might be stabled during the day and put out at night and would require little or no extra feeding apart from a small concentrate feed and a little hay to keep him occupied during the period spent in his box. For the horse competing regularly, however, a more sophisticated and time-consuming routine has to devised which will be nearer to the programme carried out in the winter months. Clearly such programmes depend very much on individual circumstances and it would be difficult to suggest exercise and feeding routines tailored specifically for the hundred and one compromises which are possible. In general a study of the management of the stabled horse in winter will provide guide-lines for the summer months.

The object of stabling horses, or keeping them under what is called the combined method, where the horse goes out for part of the day in a New Zealand rug to do his own exercising, is so that they may be more easily and effectively conditioned for a particular purpose, such as hunting.

It is possibly appropriate at this point to examine the requirements of the stable before discussing the special needs of the stabled horse in regard to feeding, exercise and grooming.

In every case a loose box is preferable to the old-fashioned stall, which involves the horse being tied up in a comparatively narrow space, facing a blank wall, for the best part of twenty-two hours out of each twenty-four. Nothing could be better calculated to produce a neurotic horse prone to all kinds of stable vices. The bigger the box, within reason, the better; there is less chance of the animal becoming cast – i.e. lying down across a corner and being unable to get up – and it will be more airy. Clearly, more straw will be needed to provide a bed but this should not be a consideration. It is the horse's comfort which counts.

The ideal size of box for a big horse would be 4·25 m by 3·65 m (14 by 12 ft) but most prefabricated boxes do not exceed 3·65 m by 3·65 m (12 by 12 ft) and are seemingly quite acceptable. More important is for the box to be airy, which means that the roof level must not be too low. Up to 3·65 m (12 ft) eaves height is desirable but not always possible, but it should be as high as conditions allow.

Doors, divided into top and bottom sections, the former being fastened back to the outside of the building or even dispensed with altogether, must open outwards, otherwise it can be impossible to get into the box either if straw becomes jammed against the inside or, even worse, if the horse should get cast and be lying across the entrance.

The height of the bottom door needs to be sufficient to discourage any thought of jumping out but low enough to allow the horse to stand with his head out without having to crane his neck. A height of around 1·37 m (4½ ft) is about right, with a width of at least 1·22 m (4 ft). Narrow doorways are an abomination against which horses knock their hips, causing themselves considerable damage even to the extent of bone fractures. Two bolts are necessary on the bottom door, the lower one being of the kick-over type. The latter discourages the horse which kicks its door for the hell of it, and will also frustrate the one who has learnt how to open the top bolt.

Just where boxes should be sited is of great importance. Ideally they should face south and be sited so that the inmates can see as much as possible of what is going on around them. It helps to combat boredom, the bane of the stabled horse and the source of all kinds of mischief. The next three factors to be considered are ventilation, insulation and drainage.

The first of these, ventilation, will be amply catered for if the top door is always left open, but draughts, as much an anathema to the horse as to the human, must be rigidly excluded. They cause aches and pains and contribute materially to colds and chills. Extra ventilation can be obtained from a window of the type that swings inwards from the base so that air enters in an upward stream and not directly on the horse, or by louves, set high in the rear wall, to take away the rising bad air which can accumulate. Windows, of course, as well as light switches, must be protected by a grill of some sort. Fresh air never hurt a horse and it is better in cold weather to give an extra rug and more feed than to shut the top door. This way colds and coughs will be avoided.

Insulation implies the use of materials which keep the building relatively cool in summer and correspondingly warm in winter. Wooden structures for this reason are best lined inside. A material to avoid is corrugated iron sheeting as a roof. It attracts heat and does not keep out cold. The problem of drainage is best overcome by making a slightly sloping concrete floor and an open drain *outside* the stable door.

Equipment within the box is reduced to basic essentials: a ring set in a wall for tying up and receptacles for food and water. A corner manger, made today of plastic, is very satisfactory but a heavy, galvanized tin, moved after each feed, is just as good. It is nice if one can arrange for – and afford – self-filling water bowls, but a bucket, either plastic or rubber, does just as well.

For bedding, wheat straw is used, and also peat moss and sawdust for those animals who delight in eating their beds to the detriment of their wind. Whatever type is used, it needs to be sufficient to encourage a horse to lie down, and the soiled areas must be cleaned out each day with droppings being picked up as a matter of course whenever entry is made into the box.

In the winter a long coat would be a considerable burden to a stabled horse when working hard, causing a tendency to sweat excessively and thus to lose flesh. The coat is therefore removed by clipping, and rugs are used to take the place of the natural protection given by the coat. A balanced diet will be required to build up the body and supply the material required for making muscle, as well as producing the energy for the work the horse has to do. With feeding must be combined two further essential factors, exercise and grooming. The first develops and strengthens the working muscles, hardens the sinews and tendons of the legs and keeps the horse's wind in good order. The second not only helps in the development and toning of the muscles but it cleans the body so that it can work with full efficiency.

A stabled horse, it must be recognized, is kept under artificial conditions and because of the energy demands of work it consumes large quantities of artificial food. The body, as a result, is required to deal with a greater quantity of waste matter. Much of it will be disposed of through excrement and the increased rate of breathing by the lungs, but almost as much is dispersed through the skin. It is necessary, therefore, to keep the skin clean if it is to perform this necessary function.

Although the horse is a remarkably adaptable creature, in one respect, that of feeding, it is we who must conform to its very particular digestive system – the horse cannot conform or adapt itself to suit our convenience. Essentially the artificial diet must be as balanced as the natural one, and furthermore it has to be fed in a way that as nearly as possible resembles the horse's natural method of feeding. The whole digestive system of the horse, which despite its size has a small, and from our viewpoint unfortunately placed stomach, is designed for the consumption of food taken slowly and almost continuously over long periods. It is vital, therefore, that the horse should be fed *little and often*, bearing in mind that its stomach cannot cope with concentrate feeds of more than 4 lb at a time.

Because of the position of the stomach a second rule of feeding emerges, which is that the horse should *never* be worked immediately after a meal. About one hour must be allowed for the digestive process to be completed. The reason is quite simple. The stomach is placed behind the diaphragm, a section of muscle separating it from the chest cavity. This diaphragm is in contact with the lungs in front and with the stomach and liver at the rear. Immediately after a feed the stomach becomes distended and pressure, through the diaphragm, will be exerted on the lungs. This will cause no trouble to a horse at rest, but if it is worked fast in this condition its breathing will be impaired and interference will be caused to the digestive process. At best the horse may develop colic of varying severity; at worst the lungs could choke with blood and a rupture of the stomach occur.

For the stabled horse a balanced diet will comprise foods of three groups – bulk, energy and what may be termed auxiliaries. In combination these must produce five constituents: proteins; fats, starches and sugar; fibrous roughage; salts and vitamins; and, of course, water.

Bulk is provided principally by hay, which is high in its fibrous content as well as containing relatively high percentages of protein, salts, etc. Energy foods containing starches and fats as well as other constituents are, for practical purposes, oats, maize, barley, etc., of which the first is preferred. Nuts and cubes, of course, can also be classified under this heading. Auxiliaries are such items as bran, containing a high percentage of salts, linseed (a fattening food) and the various forms of green food – carrots and other suitable roots. In addition in this group we can include the various feed-additives, designed to repair mineral and vitamin deficiencies: cod liver oil (a conditioner), molasses, glucose and even seaweed concentrates.

The problem, of course, is in feeding the three groups in the right proportions, and in this respect horses are decidedly individual, making it impossible to lay down hard and fast rules. As a guide we can take it that a horse of about 16·2 hands will need a daily intake of food of about 12·7 kg (28 lb). For a horse in regular work and perhaps hunting one day per week the proportion of bulk to the remaining two constituents of the diet would be about half and half.

A horse in lighter work could be given a greater quantity of bulk food and less energy foods, while a horse in fast work, such as racing, would require more energy food and less bulk, although the latter will never fall below one-third of the total intake, since a large amount of energy food cannot be accommodated without its presence.

How much energy food is given relates directly to the amount of energy expended and again varies from one horse to another. In all cases, however, energy foods must be discontinued if work is forced to cease for any reason. A hunter, however, would normally be expected to be in receipt of around 4·5 kg (10 lb) of oats per day, or the equivalent in nuts and cubes, which would be given in a number of feeds and mixed with bran, etc. The hay ration, which is eaten and digested slowly, is usually given in two lots, the bulk as a late feed to keep the horse happy through the night hours.

The rule about watering used to be water before feeding, but modern practice holds that it is better to keep a constant supply of water with the horse, and this is the system most usually followed.

The stabled horse, therefore, demands almost as much attention as a human baby. It will need to be fed five times a day, in addition to at least one hour's grooming and two hours' exercise, and a minimum of a further hour will be spent in making up the bed and cleaning out the stable. A certain amount of labour can be avoided by turning out the horse during the day in a waterproof, New Zealand-type rug; this is a convenient method for those whose time is limited, as it will reduce the period spent at exercise as well as making cleaning out an easier job. If the horse is to be clipped, clipping will usually need to be done twice between October and January, and the mane and tail must be pulled and made tidy. The horse will need to be wormed at the beginning of the season, and to be shod regularly.

All in all it's a far cry from the little paddock and living on grass. Who said that the horse was the servant of man?

KEEPING A PONY AT GRASS

Ponies and paddocks, rather like the 'love and marriage', 'horse and carriage' of the popular song, go together. At any rate that is how it seems to most people, and how beautifully simple it would be if that was the sum total of keeping a pony or a horse. In practice, whilst a paddock is a necessary requirement, the ownership of one of these fascinating but infinitely helpless animals involves a lot more than the provision of an acre or two of scrubby land, producing, at best, a *kind* of herbage in summer and being reduced to an area of glutinous mud in winter. It is true that the 'natural' food of the equine is grass, but it must be available in both the right quantity and quality if it is to provide a means of sustenance all the year round.

Furthermore, the modern horse which, unlike its wild ancestors, works for its living, cannot manage entirely on grass, whatever the quality. Given the same environment as the pre-domestic horse, which was unlimited acreages of grazing including grasses, herbs and shrubs in such variety as to constitute a balanced diet, and constant fresh water; and without having to work at speed and often over obstacles under the weight of a rider, the modern horse would indeed also exist satisfactorily enough. In the spring and summer, when the grass was at its peak nutrient value and when the weather was warm, he would grow fat and sleek; in the cold winds and wet of winter, when food was scarce, he would lose condition and strength, as did his forebears. But the twentieth-century horse, afforded the liberty of a very restricted area in comparison with that enjoyed in his feral state, is expected also to gallop and jump, pursuits which call for an expenditure of energy entailing the feeding of supplementary, energy-producing foods over and above what could be obtained from a piece of grassland. In fact although ponies and paddocks go together, grass and grazing areas, whilst necessary, do not assume such an importance when it comes to managing the larger horse, which will probably spend much of its time in the stable.

Ponies, in Great Britain particularly, but also in many other areas of the world, derive from one or other of the old indigenous breeds. Endowed with stamina and an incredible hardiness these ponies need far less molly-coddling than their larger brothers, whose veins may hold a fairly high percentage of Thoroughbred and Arab blood. Indeed, the pony thrives better if kept out all the year round and is perfectly happy in weather that would reduce many larger horses to shivering misery. Nevertheless, despite his toughness, a pony cannot live on air nor on a tiny, bare paddock. What kind of a paddock is most suitable for an ordinary pony? If it is kept on its own (which is not really a good idea since most of all ponies need the company of their own kind) the paddock needs to be of about three acres of well drained ground. A smaller area will do, but it means that a greater quantity of extra food will have to be given, and there is the danger of a small piece of ground becoming a poached mud patch in winter. Ponies are rarely unsound but they can get mud fever (a painful skin irritation on the legs and belly), cracked heels (when the skin becomes chapped) or thrush (an unpleasant, rotting condition of the feet caused by dirty standings) just as easily as any other equine. The grass must be of fairly good quality, of the sort found in old pasture land, and the ground and hedges free from any of those poisonous plants which are so fatally attractive to horses and ponies. The most common poisonous plants are ragwort, with its yellow flower; most of the buttercup family, which horses will eat if the rest of the grazing is poor; foxglove, monkshood, black briony; and, of course, the most deadly of all, the English yew.

Natural hedges probably make the best fences since, like trees, they afford shelter and act as a wind-break. In their absence the best fencing is wooden post and rails but it is expensive, and a fence almost as good can be made from heavy gauge plain wire stretched tightly between strong posts, with the lower strand not less than 30 cm (1 ft) from the ground. Barbed wire, chicken mesh, old bedsteads and pieces of derelict motor-car are neither suitable nor safe.

If the field offers no natural shelter then one of the open types of field shelter, sited to face away from prevailing winds, is necessary; in any case it is advisable to have one in case the pony has to be kept in for reasons which will be dealt with later. It is quite probable that the pony will not use the shelter in winter, preferring to stand either outside in its lee or under a natural protection. In summer, however, he is likely to go into it more to keep away from the flies.

Finally, the paddock must contain no foreign bodies in the shape of cans, bits of wire, glass, etc., which might cause injury, and most importantly there must be an adequate supply of clean water. A bucket placed by the gate does not constitute an adequate supply and is, anyway, too easily knocked over. Water is best supplied by a field pipe to a trough which has no sharp edges and can be emptied for cleaning, but a galvanized tank serviced by a hose-pipe will do, although it is more difficult to clean. Water, incidentally, is just as essential as solid food – after all, 80 per cent of the horse's body is made up of that commodity. A horse or pony can do without food for as much as thirty days but deprived entirely of water he will die in about a quarter of that time.

Given that such a paddock is available, a prospective pony-owner has a good foundation on which to commence pony-keeping. But that is all it is, a foundation.

In the summer the pony will be quite content with nothing more than grass if he is not doing very much work. On the other hand, such is the perversity of ponies that too much grass is almost as bad as too little. Ponies, particularly the pure native mountain and moorland breeds, were bred originally on the sparsest of grazing and are just not equipped to cope with a large supply of lush, sweet summer grass. Being by nature ever ready to eat that which is offered, they will stuff themselves until they resemble little barrage balloons on legs, and the results can be disastrous. To be grossly overweight is bad for either human or animal, greater strain being placed on the organs and limbs. But an overweight pony, apart from being too fat to exert himself at anything more than a plodding walk, can contract a most painful disease of the feet called laminitis, which is an acute inflammation inside the outer protective casing of the hoof, affecting the sensitive laminae. If, therefore, a pony begins to present too portly a figure one has to be cruel to be kind and deny him access to the luscious grass which he loves but which can be his undoing. Making use of the field shelter, he can be confined there during the day, when the flies are in any case troublesome, and put out at night. If he still continues to put on weight then there must be a general hardening of hearts and his grazing restricted to just a few hours in each day. If he is tubby in the early part of the year he must not be galloped about until he has lost his surplus weight and is in harder condition. Galloping fat ponies is not the way to get them fit; they must be conditioned gradually and exercised at walk and slow trot, otherwise the effort can be too much for their wind and legs.

Perhaps the key to understanding the nutritional needs of the pony and horse is to appreciate that like all living creatures they utilize their food intake to fulfil what may be called the four requirements of life. These are:

1) Maintenance of body temperature (100°–101·5°F, 37·7°–38·6°C).
2) Replacement of natural tissue wastage.
3) Building up and maintenance of body condition.
4) The supplying of energy needed for movement and for the internal processes of digestion, etc.

If food is short and the weather cold the first two requirements will take the lion's share and the last two will get next to nothing. As a result the animal gets thin and loses strength and energy. Even when food is plentiful and all four requirements are satisfied, the animal's condition will suffer if he is made to work hard and expend a lot of energy. The working pony or horse must, therefore, have an input of energy food to match his expenditure of energy if he is not to lose condition.

Energy is produced by foods like beans and peas, oats and to a slightly lesser extent barley. Maize, also, is a heating, energy-giving food. However, these energy foods are not natural ones to the digestive system of the horse, which was designed to cope with grass and similar herbage, and they cannot be digested without bulk and roughage. In the case of the hard-worked pony grass provides this bulk quite adequately. Energy is probably best supplied by oats but unfortunately oats do not really suit ponies, since they frequently become quite unmanageable on even a handful a day, while the mere smell of beans and peas is enough to make them spend half their time bucking, kicking and standing on their hind legs! The answer to the problem is to restrict the grazing to a reasonable level and feed one or another of the proprietary brands of pony nuts and cubes, which are in fact, in some instances, a complete, balanced diet in themselves. A ration of 1·36 kg (3 lb) nuts per day mixed with 0·45 kg (1 lb) bran, which contains a high percentage of essential salts, and a double handful of chaff (a mixture of chopped oat straw and hay) and fed damped, should keep a 13 hands pony sufficiently energetic. Some ponies will of course need more and others less, but this is something that can only be discovered by studying the individual concerned.

By September, in Great Britain, the grass will be losing its goodness and new growth will not occur until the following April. From this point on the pony will require hay, which should be fed throughout the winter months if he is not to lose condition. The feed that kept him sufficiently energetic in the summer will suffice in winter to keep him in condition if he is not doing so much work. Sliced carrots, not chopped ones which might lodge in the gullet, apples, etc., can be added to the concentrate feed to add variety, but *not* household scraps. A pony is not a dog and his system is not designed to digest the remains of the Sunday lunch. Incidentally, if grass is short, the temptation to give the pony a treat by pressing the contents of the lawn-mower box on him is to be resisted. The pony will not refuse the offering but the result can be disastrous and may end in a severe bout of colic due to the cut grass impacting in the stomach. It is wise to give the hay ration in a haynet (a small one in the morning and a larger one in the evening) and to string up the haynet as high as possible, well out of reach of a pawing forefoot. Finally, a block of mineral salt, or even a good, big lump of rock salt, should always be kept in the field to provide those minerals deficient in either pasture or supplementary food.

Should a pony which is being fed and is on reasonable grazing not look well and be generally listless it will not always be because he is not getting enough food – it is far more likely that he has worms, in particular redworms. These parasites are always present in the domestic horse and on the pastures they occupy, the latter being the principal vehicle in their life cycle. Much can be done by managing the grass correctly, resting fields regularly and grazing them with cattle in a rotational system. Horses are bad grazers, being very selective, but cattle are the ideal vacuum cleaner on four legs, and what is more they do not act as a host to the redworm they ingest. However, management of pasture land to the degree required is quite impractical for the majority of one- or two-horse owners, who can often do no more than remove droppings regularly. It is important that this should be done since it is in the droppings that redworm eggs are passed out of the body; they then develop and ultimately regain entry into the system from the pasture, and the whole cycle begins again.

Practically, the main area attack against the redworm must, therefore, be confined to the horse itself. A number of proprietary medicines are available in pellet form but it is probably wiser to consult a veterinary surgeon, who will advise on dosage and frequency after taking an egg count from a sample of dung. Heavy infestation by redworm can result in anaemia, loss of condition to a pronounced degree, and in very severe cases death may ensue.

During September the pony will have begun to grow his winter coat, which provides a virtually waterproof protection against the worst weather when it is fully grown. An important factor in the waterproofing is the formation of a layer of grease next to the skin, and it is therefore quite wrong to set about cleaning and grooming the pony thoroughly during the winter. All that is necessary is a quick brush over with a dandy brush to remove the worst of the mud without interfering with the layer of natural grease.

Possibly the most important factor in managing a pony at grass is supervision. Each and every day, whatever the weather, the pony must be inspected to see that all is well with him and that water is available. In summer leaves, twigs and scum will collect on the drinking trough and must be removed, while in winter there may be ice to clear from the surface.

The last item in the pony's welfare is the care of his feet which, like our nails, grow quite rapidly. It is possible to ride ponies without shoes if they never come off soft going, but in general a working pony needs to be shod if he is not to become foot-sore on hard roads and stony tracks. Once a month his shoes will need to be removed, whether they are worn out or not, the feet trimmed and cut back, and the shoes replaced either with the old set or with a new one. Neglected feet are more prone to becoming diseased and may, indeed, cause quite severe injury if they are allowed to become too long or if the nail clenches rise up and protrude beyond the wall of the hoof. In both the last instances the pony can cut itself with its own feet.

GROOMING AND EQUIPMENT
Stabled horses should be groomed thoroughly every day, not simply to make them look smart, but to keep their coats and their skins in healthy condition. Horses at liberty, although they cannot groom themselves, can do a lot for their coats and skins. They can roll if they feel itchy or are sweaty; they can rub themselves against trees to help them shed their coats in spring and autumn; they can scratch each other when they feel like it, and if they have itchy places under their bellies or between their thighs, they can find handy shrubs or bushes to rub against.

Grooming does not constitute a gentle going-over with a brush. On the contrary, it is a strenuous exercise for the groom, who even in cold weather, should get quite hot in the process.

Grooming kit consists of a dandy brush, body brush, water brush, curry comb, mane comb, hoof pick, hoof oil and brush, stable rubber, small sponges, a rubber curry comb and a sweat scraper.

The dandy brush is used only for removing surface mud and dirt, and never on the horse's more sensitive parts such as the under-belly, between the thighs, and the face. Nor should it be used on the mane or tail as it breaks the hairs, producing a fringe effect on the mane and breaking the flow of the tail. The body brush is the main grease remover, and should be used with firm pressure (which does not mean banging it down on the coat). The grease is removed from the brush constantly by scraping it with the curry comb. This is the curry comb's sole purpose. The water brush is used dampened, for laying the mane after brushing or before plaiting, and also for laying the tail before bandaging or plaiting. The hoof pick's use is obvious and very important. Hoof oil helps to prevent brittleness, especially in light-coloured hooves. The stable rubber is folded into a pad and used to give the horse a final polish, but it can be used also to dry the horse's ears if he comes in wet and cold. The small sponges are for the eyes and nostrils, and for the dock. A rubber curry comb can be helpful when a horse is casting his coat and, used with a circular movement, it will remove a lot of loose hair. The massaging effect is also appreciated by the horse. The sweat scraper has a squeegee action and is used to remove excess sweat or water from the coat.

Grooming, particularly of the body with the body brush, should be done without gloves, so that the sensitive tips of the fingers can be used to feel for any lumps or scratches or irregularities in the skin. Always run your hands down the legs. They should feel cool, almost cold, and the tendons should be firm. If you feel little nodules of mud or dirt work these out gently with the fingers, and then use the brush afterwards. If mud or dirt are left on the legs, they will eventually clog the pores, and may produce a condition known as mud fever. Feel for mud also on the inside of the pasterns, between the coronet and the fetlock joint.

When grooming the head, the headcollar should be undone and buckled round the neck. Care should be taken not to bump the horse's face with the back of the brush, or get it into his eyes. Eyes and nostrils and the dock should be sponged with tepid water. Mares' udders should be kept clean, and with geldings the sheath should be washed periodically. Not everyone realizes this to be a necessity, but if the sheath becomes too clogged with grease and dirt, the animal can eventually find it difficult, even painful, to stale.

Feet should be picked out at least twice a day, during the first grooming and on return from work. Hoof oil should be brushed on, not simply to give a smart appearance but because it is good for the hoof. It should be applied right up to the coronet, which is where the growth of the hoof starts.

A 'wisp' of straw can be made for strapping, a particularly energetic form of grooming which helps to build up the muscle, especially on the neck and quarters, as well as toning up the skin. The stable rubber made into a firm pad can be used to achieve the same result.

Horses change, or 'cast', their coats twice a year at roughly six-month intervals, in spring and autumn. The summer coat is much less dense, and finer, than the winter coat. Few horses except racehorses and those being prepared for showing need rugging in summer, although a cotton day sheet put on after grooming will help keep the coat sleek and clean, and is particularly advantageous when travelling. A horse should also have a sweat rug put on if it is brought in very hot after work or if it has to stand about while it is hot after any kind of long ride or competition. Sweat rugs are made of cotton and are similar to men's string vests.

Winter is a different matter. Horses in work will need to be clipped, as in their heavier winter coats they are likely to sweat unduly every time they go out, and consequently will lose condition.

There are three principal types of clip, known as a full clip, a hunter clip, and a trace clip.

In a full clip, the coat is removed from the entire body. In a hunter clip, the hair is left on the legs as far up as the elbows and the thighs, and on the saddle patch. The theory is that the hair left on the legs offers protection against cold, injury from thorns or other hazards that might cause slight tears and scratches, and wet, muddy conditions that could lead to mud fever and cracked heels. The saddle patch can help prevent a sore or scalded back resulting from a long day's riding.

In a trace clip, the hair is removed from the belly, between the thighs and the forearms, across the chest and up the underside of the neck. It is used mostly on horses or ponies that are kept out, rather than those that are stabled. Sometimes the hair is further clipped off the neck and head, leaving a blanket shape of hair over the back and quarters. This is known as a blanket clip.

Horses that have had a full, or a hunter, clip will need rugging all the time. As the first clipping is usually done in October, they will probably initially need only single rugs, that is a wool-lined jute night rug, and a woollen day rug. Nowadays several patent variations of the traditional forms of rug are available. These are more expensive to buy, but have many advantages. They are much lighter than the old type, but just as warm. The same rug can be worn during the night and day, although it is better to have two, as night rugs invariably get dirty. However, the new rugs are both easy to wash and quick to dry, so a dirty night rug can be washed in the morning, and be dry by the evening.

As the weather gets colder, the horse will need extra warmth, which is provided by putting on one, sometimes even two, soft woollen blankets under the top rug. These must be large, as about a quarter of the blanket should come right over the neck when it is put on, so that it can be folded back over the top rug and caught in place under the roller. Once a horse has started wearing a rug, or rugs, he must continue to do so until the weather gets warmer in spring. If he is wearing underblankets, these can be discarded in succession until finally it is warm enough to discard the top rug as well. If the days are considerably warmer than the nights, as often happens in winter, the horse may not need his underblankets in daytime – this is where common sense must be used. Some horses, like some people, feel the cold more than others. During the winter if a stabled horse is led out for a walk, or turned out for a short time, he should wear a New Zealand rug, which is made of waterproofed canvas, and lined with wool. Alternatively one of the new patented rugs which are also made in waterproof versions can be used. All rugs in use should be aired and shaken out daily. After clipping, the coat will continue to grow, although not so fully as before. Nevertheless, the horse will need a second clip before winter is out, and some horses even need a third. The last clip should be done by the end of January.

Bandages

Tail bandages should be in daily use for stabled horses, and are put on after grooming to lay and smarten the line of the tail. Two other types of bandages are necessary – stable bandages and exercise bandages.

Stable bandages are made of flannel, and are fairly wide. They are used to provide warmth if a horse is chilled or has a cold; to dry off the legs if he comes in wet and muddy so that the mud can be brushed off later; on top of cotton wool or gamgee-tissue soaked in cold water as cold water bandages, and for travelling, when they are put on over dry cotton wool or gamgee. There are nowadays many patent leg protectors available for travelling that are quicker to put on and, unless bandaging is skilfully done, probably more reliable.

Stable bandages should run from the knee down to, and over, the fetlock joint, at which point the bandage should be rolled upwards again, to finish just below the knee. Bandages should never be put on too tightly; it should be possible to insert a finger between the bandage and the leg, both top and bottom. The tapes should not be tied tighter than the bandage itself and they should be tied on the outside of the leg, in a bow, with the ends tucked in.

Exercise bandages are made of stockinette or crepe, and are used to support the tendons and to protect the legs from thorns or prickly undergrowth in rough country. They are put on with cotton wool or gamgee underneath, a small part of which should protrude above and below the bandage itself. It takes a lot of practice to put these on so that they will stay in place during work. It is often better, for example if a horse is going to be asked to go fast across country, perhaps in heavy going, and it is felt he needs extra support, to use special tendon boots. Young horses should wear exercise bandages or boots during lungeing and early schooling, when they can be awkward with their legs. This will prevent unnecessary bumps and bruises. Exercise bandages are also useful for putting on over a poultice, or a liniment which is relieving a sprained tendon. Again, they should never be put on too tightly, or the bandaging will defeat its own ends by stopping the circulation. After taking off any bandage, the leg should be given a brisk rub with the hands. Bandages should be kept clean, which means washing them after use, drying them, and putting them away re-rolled. They should be rolled with the sewn part of the tapes inwards, so that when the bandage is put on the leg, the tapes will be on the outside of the bandage.

Medicine

It is not a good idea to indulge in a lot of amateur doctoring with horses, but basic necessities should be kept in every stable.

DISINFECTANT: The horse has a very sensitive skin, and only the mildest disinfectants should be used to clean out or bathe any cut or injury. Dettol, or similar, is acceptable provided it is used heavily diluted. If there is none to hand when it is wanted, salt and water is an efficient emergency disinfectant. A stronger, domestic disinfectant should be used to keep the stable clean and sweet-smelling.

LINIMENT: There are many excellent brands on the market, some stronger than others. Take your pick, and use according to the manufacturer's instructions for the relief of sprains and strains.

ANTISEPTIC POWDER: Very important, as small cuts and scratches, once clean, heal better if they are kept dry and protected by dusting with antiseptic powder. Use the one recommended by your veterinary surgeon.

ANTISEPTIC OINTMENT: Any good, soft, zinc-based ointment will help to prevent scar tissue forming once a wound has healed. It also encourages the hair to grow again.

KAOLIN POULTICE: This has many uses: put on hot, as a poultice under a bandage, it relieves sprains and strains; put on a cut, or more particularly a puncture wound which is not easy to clean, it will draw out dirt and poison, which will be seen as pus or discoloration when the pad with the kaolin is removed. Being a natural substance and not a drug, kaolin can never do any harm, and in fact often does a great deal of good.

GOLDEN EYE OINTMENT: Horses may get particles of dust, etc., in their eyes; have runny eyes caused by a cold, or scratch an eye against a sharp object. The eye should be bathed with a very weak solution of Dettol and water, and some eye ointment squeezed into the corner to help give relief.

COUGH ELECTUARY: This should be supplied by the veterinary surgeon, but it is a good thing to have it always in stock. Sometimes a cough can be simply the result of eating hay too quickly, but it never hurts to give the horse some electuary straight away.

COLIC DRENCH: In most cases of colic, all but the most experienced people should telephone their vet. It is quite likely, however, that unless he can come at once, he will suggest giving a drench, so it is useful to keep it against such an emergency.

EPSOM SALTS: These are good for horses that may have been on too heating a diet; but all will benefit from a small handful in their weekly bran mash.

SALT AND WATER: This is cooling, refreshing and helps to harden the skin. Sponged over a horse's back, and behind and under the elbows where the girth lies, it will help prevent galls and sores.

WORM DOSING DRUGS: Horses should be wormed regularly. All horses harbour worms, and it is only by regular worming that a dangerous infestation can be prevented. For a horse in healthy condition, dosing every three months should keep him relatively worm-free. Every year, new drugs are discovered and put on the market, all reputed to be more lethal to the worms, and less harmful to the horse. The best solution to this ever-present problem is to ask the veterinary surgeon which he considers most suitable and then, if possible, get him to make up a number of individual doses which can be kept in the stable and given when necessary. New horses coming into a stable should be wormed on arrival.

SCISSORS: A sharp but blunt-ended pair should be kept for cutting away the hair from the edges of wounds or cuts that need dressing.

In addition to all these items it is a good idea to keep some pieces of linen as dressings, or poultice pads, together with some long strips of linen for under-bandaging wounds, a large pack of cotton wool, several packs of gamgee tissue and one or two ordinary crepe bandages. The experienced stable manager will also keep a hypodermic syringe and a supply of needles, but only those who really know what they are doing should attempt to give injections. It is not that this is in itself difficult, but it must be known just where to put the needle, and how to use the syringe skilfully and quickly.

SADDLERY

A distinction should be made between the words 'saddlery' and 'harness', the latter, in particular, being often misused. Saddlery refers to the equipment of the riding horse, while harness is used to describe the accoutrements of the driving horse. To the further confusion of the uninitiated, horsemen will frequently refer to both as 'tack' (i.e. tackle).

In general terms, saddlery is concerned with the saddle and bridle and their accompanying auxiliaries, such as girths, leathers and martingales. It can extend to cover all items made of leather, even if some of those items, e.g. muzzles, headcollars, etc., are applicable to both riding and harness horses. Bandages, rugs and blankets, however, are grouped under the composite term 'horse clothing'.

The early horse peoples managed their horses with the minimum of equipment, concentrating, naturally enough, on methods of control. Initially, control of the horse may have been achieved by a form of noseband encompassing the lower jaws and fitted above the nostrils. Illustrations of Syrian horsemen of the fourteenth century BC show this rudimentary form of bridle quite clearly. There is, however, evidence of a more sophisticated bridle, involving the use of a bit, used at an earlier date. On the tomb of Horenhab of Egypt (dated *c.* 1600 BC) a horseman is depicted on an obviously spirited horse ridden in a snaffle bridle of surprisingly modern design.

As the use of mounted horsemen increased and selective breeding, combined with hand-feeding (i.e. with corn, an energizing foodstuff), produced horses of more quality and spirit, so a greater emphasis was placed on the means of control through the agency of the bridle. By the time the Assyrians had emerged as a major horse people, a bitting arrangement had been devised that gave to the rider a very acceptable degree of control over his mount. Two hundred years later, when the Persians of the sixth century BC had superseded the Assyrians as the leading nation of horsemen, the bridle had become an even more forceful instrument, largely because of a notable change to a heavier type of horse.

These horses would have certainly been corn-fed and they are depicted in various sculptures in a heavily collected posture with the head over-bent, a carriage that would certainly give more control to the rider. The bits used to effect this imposed balance were the familiar phallic-cheeked snaffles combined with a noseband which seems to have been set with knobs or spikes (like the Spanish *careta* still used today), and with the addition of a strap fastened below the bit that is very similar to our modern drop noseband. There were, however, exceptions to the obsessive interest in control. The Numidian cavalry which marched with Hannibal, for instance, managed their small ponies without resort to a bridle of any sort, steering their mounts with a switch applied to the appropriate side of the head. History does not reveal how the halt was effected.

Nonetheless, in general terms the trend continued towards stronger bits, capable of exerting a greater mechanical force and thus allowing the horseman to position and restrain his horse more effectively. From the sixth century BC onwards, bits became increasingly severe, with both Greeks and Persians using mouthpieces that incorporated sharp rollers and spikes. Somewhere around 300 BC the Celts of Gaul produced the curb bit, an instrument that was to develop to monstrous proportions in the centuries that followed.

The curb bit of the armoured knights of the Middle Ages, which existed in only slightly altered form well into the eighteenth century and even later, was made necessary by the sheer size and strength of the heavy horses that were needed to carry a fully armoured man and his weapons, as well as the weight of their own protective armour. To control such an animal, and more particularly to put him in a state of balance which would facilitate the manoeuvres required in battle, or later at the joust and tournament, a mechanical force of some power was needed if the animal's weight was to be placed over the hindquarters and the forehand lightened in consequence.

The use of the bit to place the horse in balance persisted well into the Renaissance period which marked the beginnings of the 'classical art'. The early Masters, like Federico Grisone in Naples and his pupil Pignatelli, did, however, stress the importance of preserving the lightness of the mouth, achieving their object by the use, once more, of the spiked noseband. Even so, from a study of their books (Grisone's *Gli Ordini di Cavalcare* was published in 1550) it is clear that little emphasis was placed on the suppling of the horse and the development of his posture by a progression of exercises, while great store continued to be set on breaking the animal's resistance by forceful means. During this period the prototype of the modern double bridle emerged, with the addition to the curb bit of a thin bradoon, the 'flying trench', which was operated by a second rein. Recognition of the fact that flexion at the poll has to be accompanied by a corresponding relaxation of the lower jaw was marked by the occasional use of metal 'keys' fitted to the centre of the mouthpiece to encourage the horse to play with the bit and create saliva in the mouth. The Greek general Xenophon had, in fact, used the same device on a snaffle bit some 1800 years previously and the modern straight-bar 'mouthing' bit used in the breaking of young horses, and similarly fitted with keys, varies only slightly in detail from that used by the Spartan horseman.

The curb bit, however, with its cheek-pieces often as long as 37 cm (15 in), held its place as the chief weapon in the horseman's armoury until, at the beginning of the seventeenth century, the later classical Masters, like Pluvinel and Newcastle, encouraged the individual study of horses and more patient and gentler methods

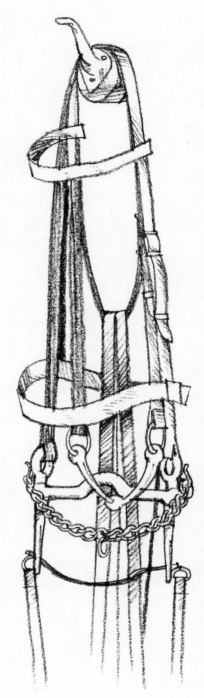

were advocated in their training.

By the following century the art of classical riding had become established, largely through the teachings of the Frenchman François de la Guérinière, who is known as the 'Father of Classical Equitation', and while the curb bit continued as a predominant influence, it ceased to be regarded as an instrument of coercion.

From that point on, the tendency was towards milder bits, but the obsession with the positioning of the head and the control of the horse through the bit continued to occupy the minds of horsemen right up to our own century, despite the increasing frequency and volume of the exhortation 'legs before hands'.

The nineteenth century and the first part of the twentieth produced a huge variety of bits, all of which were acclaimed (at least by their ingenious inventors) as the panacea for all equine ills. However, the passing of the individual craftsmen, forging bits by hand, the considerations of modern commercial practice and methods of mass production, together with an increasing knowledge of equestrian theory, has resulted in the past thirty or forty years in a much simplified range of bitting devices. So much so, in fact, that the modern horseman is restricted, essentially, in his choice to one of five basic groups or families of bits, of which, if his horse has been correctly schooled, he will only rarely need to employ more than two.

These five groups comprise: the snaffle, in its various forms; the double bridle, i.e. curb bit and bradoon (the latter is, in fact, a light version of the ordinary snaffle but changes its name, for no very good reason, when used with a curb bit); the Pelham, a hybrid derived from the curb bit and attempting to produce the same result as the double bridle with the use of a single mouthpiece; the gag snaffle, a gadget borrowed from the harness horse, and finally the bitless bridle, frequently termed a hackamore, which relies solely on pressure exerted on the nose for its effect.

Of these the snaffle is the mildest form of bitting, the most simple and the most common. It is made in a variety of weights, ranging from the pencil-thin to the much more acceptable thick mouthpiece, described by the Irish as 'soft'. The principal division within the group, however, is between those with a jointed mouthpiece and those made without a joint in a 'half-moon' shape known as a mullen mouth, the latter being the milder of the two.

The action of the snaffle depends upon the position of the horse's head and, therefore, upon the stage of training that has been reached. In the young, relatively unschooled horse, carrying his weight on the forehand with a correspondingly low head carriage, the action is upwards against the corners of the lips. In the case of the horse in a more advanced state of training, more weight is carried on the quarters, the forehand is therefore lightened and the head raised to a point where the nose is held a little in advance of the vertical. The snaffle then acts across the lower jaw, lying over the tongue and placing more pressure on the bars of the mouth (i.e. the area of gum between the incisors and the cheek teeth).

The snaffle can become a stronger means of control by variations being made to the mouthpiece. This can, for instance, be twisted or serrated, so as to give a sharper pressure on the mouth, or it can be fitted with rollers, set horizontally within the mouthpiece or round its circumference. The action of the bit can also be altered and/or assisted by the use of auxiliaries such as drop nosebands or martingales.

A drop noseband, the nosepiece resting some 7 cm (3 in) above the nostrils and the rear strap fastening below the bit, fulfils a number of purposes. By closing the mouth it prevents evasions of the bit's actions caused by the horse opening the jaws or attempting to cross them. It helps, also, to maintain a correct position of the head by exerting a downward and backward pressure on the nose, transmitted to it through the action of the rein. The result of a correctly positioned head, allowing the rider's hands to be higher than the mouth, is to give a greater degree of control. A certain, if slight, restriction of the breathing, is involved in the use of the drop noseband – a violent upward movement of the head being countered by a momentary increase of pressure upon the nasal passages.

The use of martingales is also concerned with the maintenance of an acceptable head position. The two principal types are the standing martingale attached to a cavesson (never to a drop) noseband, thus restricting any upward movement of the head, and the 'running' type achieving the same result through pressure on the mouth. The running martingale comprises a bifurcated strap, each end being fitted with a ring through which the rein is passed. Thus pressure is put on the mouth to effect a lowering of the head.

The double bridle, with its curb bit and bradoon, lies at the opposite end of the spectrum in comparison with the snaffle. It is the most sophisticated of the bitting arrangements and within the province of only the educated rider and the educated horse, permitting the former to *suggest* a positioning of the head with a far greater finesse. The snaffle, or bradoon, acts to raise the head, while the curb, when it assumes an angle of about 45 degrees in the mouth, induces a lowering of the nose, flexion of the lower jaw and of the poll. The mouthpiece of the curb is most usually a straight bar made with a central hump, called the port. The purpose of the port is to accommodate the tongue, thus allowing the bearing surfaces of the mouthpiece, on either side of the port, to come into direct contact with the bars. If the mouthpiece was made without a port, the bit would bear more upon the tongue than the bars and would, therefore, be rendered less efficient and direct in its action.

The severity or otherwise of the curb bit depends upon the length of the cheek below the mouthpiece, the longer the cheek the greater being the possible leverage. The length of the cheek *above* the mouthpiece, which incorporates the 'eye' to which the headpiece of the bridle is attached, is, however, of almost equal significance. A long cheek will cause a greater downward pressure on the poll as the 'eye' moves forward in response to the application of the rein, transmitting that pressure through the cheekpiece to the headstrap.

The Pelham bridle is something of a compromise between the extremes represented by the snaffle and the double bridle (the two basic bridles used in the correct schooling of the horse). With one mouthpiece, usually of the half-moon type, and a cheek which incorporates an additional ring for the fixing of a bradoon rein, it attempts to reproduce the effects of the latter. In practice, the snaffle action of the bit will predominate when the bradoon rein is held outside the little finger, and the opposite result will be obtained when the position of the reins is reversed and the curb rein is held in a similar manner.

The 'gag' bridle, on the other hand, is little more than an extension of the snaffle, accentuating the upward, head-raising, action of the latter by its peculiar construction. In the gag, the bit rings are made with two aligned central holes in the ring, through which a cheekpiece of rounded leather is passed, the rein being attached to a ring on the bottom end of the cheekpiece. This arrangement enables the bit to move upwards in the horse's mouth, exerting very considerable pressure on the corners of the lips. In fact, of course, the action produces contradictory pressures, one upwards on the mouth and one downwards on the poll. Nonetheless the gag is held to be a useful aid in controlling an impetuous horse and, perhaps more particularly, for one that approaches his fences rather faster than is considered desirable while holding his head firmly between his knees.

The last of the bridle groups is that which gives control through pressure on the nose alone. This type is often called a 'hackamore', the name deriving from the Spanish *jaquima* – a noseband, used by the *domador* (trainer) in preparing the horse for the 'spade' bit (a curb bit with a solid high port resting on the tongue and sufficiently long to act against the roof of the mouth) which was used by the trainer or 'reiner' of the advanced horse, the *arrendador*. This bitless bridle is part of a sophisticated method of schooling originating in the Iberian Peninsula and passing from there, by means of the sixteenth-century *conquistadores*, to the Americas. There it remains integral in Western riding, but it has also achieved a more general use in recent years. Many riders employing the European system of training use, or more frequently misuse, the bridle, mistakenly supposing it to be a 'kinder' form of control. In fact, in the wrong hands the bridle is a very severe instrument.

The development of the bridle began early in the history of man's association with horses, and in comparative terms it was not long before a satisfactory form of harness evolved. Perhaps surprisingly, the saddle, and more particularly the stirrup, were introduced much later. Most of the pre-Christian horse peoples used coverings and pads, some of the latter being quite elaborate, on the backs of their horses, although Xenophon (430–355 BC), possibly because he was a

Spartan, decried the practice, maintaining that the bare legs of a man wrapped around the sweating coat of his horse gave more security.

The limitations of cavalry operating without the security afforded by a saddle and stirrups would seem to be obvious. Primarily, of course, it prohibited the cavalry soldier from closing with the enemy, but it was not until the fourth century that a saddle constructed on a wood foundation, the 'tree', was in use, and it took almost another hundred years before the stirrup was invented and made possible the cavalry charge against bodies of infantry.

Charles Chenevix Trench, author of *A History of Horsemanship* and a contributor to this book, has this comment to make: 'It is surprising that horsemen took 1500 years to think up something so simple. One is reluctantly driven to the distasteful conclusion that we are not really a very bright set of people.'

It is probable that it was the Sarmatians, a people later absorbed by the Goths, who used a tree and produced a saddle built high at the pommel and cantle to enclose the rider. Credit for the stirrup goes to the Huns of Attila, and a Chinese office writing in AD 477 confirms its use by these Mongolian horsemen.

The same type of enclosing saddle served the mediaeval knight, whose long stirrups were hung well forward so as to allow the rider to brace himself against the cantle. This position prevented his being thrown forward and enabled him to withstand the impact of the charge against infantry without departing unceremoniously over his horse's rump. That saddle exists in recognizable form today as the Western saddle. The *selle royale*, still used at the classical schools of Saumur and Vienna, the home of the Spanish Riding School, and those saddles currently in use in Portugal and Spain, are its direct descendants and little different from the saddles of the late Renaissance period. The only major alteration is in the positioning of the stirrup bars, which are placed further to the rear than in the saddle of the mounted knight. In turn, the modern dressage saddle, although considerably more streamlined in appearance, has its origins in these saddles. Like that of the armoured knight, the dressage saddle is ideally suited to its purpose, fulfilling the rider's requirements in this particular and specialized branch of equitation.

Dressage involves movements demanding a state of collection, the horse moving with the head held high and the greater part of the weight being carried over actively engaged quarters. In order to remain in balance with the horse it is necessary for the rider's body weight to be positioned as nearly as possible over the centre of balance of the horse. In the horse at rest, this can be taken to be at the junction of an imaginary vertical line, drawn from some 15 cm (6 in) behind the withers to the ground, and a horizontal one drawn from the point of the shoulder to the rear. In movement the horse's centre of balance shifts forward, its position being governed by the attitude of the head and neck which act as the balancing agent of the body mass. In the galloping horse, which stretches out its head and neck, the point moves forward. At the opposite extreme, when the horse is in a state of collection, the elevated head carriage and lowered croup cause the centre of balance to move to the rear. The dressage rider, sitting centrally in a relatively dipped seat and with a long leg which can be accommodated by a nearly straight-cut saddle flap, is ideally positioned in relation to that centre of balance. But that seat and that saddle would be of little use to the show-jumping or event rider, who operates at a much faster pace and is concerned with a different balance. In those instances the centre of balance will in general be further forward and on occasions considerably further forward. For a rider to remain in balance he must employ a shorter stirrup leather and use a saddle which, by the position of its bars, over which the weight will be carried, and the advancing shape of its flaps, allows for the shorter leather and assists the rider in maintaining his body forward over the horse's point of balance.

The incentive for the production of such saddles, the modern jumping and general-purpose saddles of today, was provided by an Italian cavalry officer, Federico Caprilli (1868–1908) whose theories resulted in the 'forward system' of riding, often referred to as the 'forward seat'. Up to Caprilli's time the classical influence, directed at the production of the collected horse schooled in indoor arenas, had dominated European equestrian thought, in the vanguard of which were the military schools. Cavalry troopers rode with a 'full' seat (i.e. one firmly implanted in the saddle at all times) and with a long leg, using saddles corresponding to that position.

Caprilli, holding that the role of cavalry was reconaissance, involving crossing at speed a country and the natural obstacles presented by it, thus discarded formal school training. In its place he used the actual type of terrain over which cavalry might operate as a schooling ground, compelling his horses to adjust their own balance and allowing them to do so by giving them complete freedom of the head and neck. He made his riders 'perch' above the saddle with the seat slightly raised, and they used a shortened leather to position themselves forward over the point of balance. The principal was that of non-intervention.

In the intervening period, of course, many saddles were designed that purported to be in accordance with the Caprilli theory. Saddles were built with forward-cut panels and flaps to accommodate the use of the shortened stirrup. Some even incorporated the now familiar 'spring' tree, made by laying two strips of tempered steel on the under-sides of the tree from front to rear to give greater resilience. None, however, found general acceptance – a fact which may be taken to uphold the rightness of Mr Chenevix Trench's comment.

Caprilli's system has not survived in its entirety; competitive riding today is too demanding for that. Instead his system and the classical one have melded. Modern riders practise the dressage on the flat that he discarded, but follow him in sitting forward across country and over fences. Modern saddles, however, are the result of his teachings, even though nearly half a century went by after his death before a thoroughly satisfactory article was made.

The breakthrough came in the post-war years as a result of the work of a Spanish horseman, Count Ilias Toptani, a trainer of the Caprilli persuasion who schooled the South American show-jumping teams. In brief, Toptani increased the depth of the saddle seat, narrowed the waist or 'twist' of the saddle so as not to spread the thighs of the rider, and brought the stirrup bars forward by sloping the head (pommel) of the tree. By so doing he ensured that the rider's weight was positioned forward. The lower body was anchored by the provision of rolls on the panel, supporting the lower thigh just above the knee, and was cut well forward in line with the slope of the head. He used a spring tree to give resilience to the seat and so afford greater comfort to the rider and the horse – the tree 'giving' to the movement of the latter's back.

Toptani's saddle was ideal for jumping but not quite so effective for cross-country riding since it placed the rider rather too far forward. A modification, slightly less exaggerated in shape, coming somewhere between the pure jumping saddle and the dressage saddle, resulted in the now ubiquitous 'general-purpose' saddle. These three are the principal types in use today, outside racing and the show-ring saddle (the latter a scaled down, flatter-seated version of the dressage saddle).

If we reflect that alongside the precision riding developed by the Western horsemen there existed another and opposite form exemplified by the eleventh-century Moors and Mongols, themselves following the style of the earlier Huns in riding short and adopting a very forward position, we may reach another conclusion – that there is very little new in the world.

The Sporting Horse

THE SHOW RING

Showing one animal against others of the same species and breed started some 200 years ago. It sprang from the natural desire of breeders of horses to prove to others that they had used their skill and knowledge to produce an animal that was bigger, better made for the job in life to which it was to be put, and possessed of more strength, stamina, workmanlike qualities and classical conformation than those produced by other breeders. Its movement, quality, symmetrical proportions and general beauty of outline were, and still are, the yardsticks by which it was assessed.

In addition, by producing their products in the show ring, to win over those of their fellow-breeders when judged by experts, they were able to command the top market price for their young stock. Alternatively, other breeders would be attracted to send mares to their stallions. Shows have always been convivial meeting places for those of similar interests and enthusiasms, bound together – albeit in friendly rivalry – by the same concern for good husbandry and the improvement of the breed towards the ideal: the perfect horse. Although this individual has probably yet to be foaled, just as the perfect human being has yet to be born, there is endless fascination in pursuing a quest to achieve it.

Probably the purest form of showing is that of showing the young horse in-hand. Showmanship, which is a considerable art, must always play its part in showing an animal to its best advantage, and a real artist is able to disguise failings of movement, or even lameness, by the way he leads a horse, or runs him out in hand. There are tricks in every trade, and they comprise every professional showman's stock-in-trade, but there is less opportunity for artifice in the classes in which the exhibits are led in-hand than in those where they are ridden. Then an exaggerated throwing of the toe in the trot, or a flashy display at the gallop, can be used to disguise, or to divert the attention from, failings such as faulty action or some other shortcoming.

The aim of the showman is to produce a horse that will 'fill the eye', as the saying goes, and no horse wins many championships without the ultimate blessing of a hard-to-define quality known as *presence*. This is the quality which bestows upon its fortunate possessor the ability to command the attention of whoever beholds it – a quality which not just says, but demands: 'Look at me – I'm the greatest!' A horse may be better made and a better mover than others, but if he lacks presence he will get no further in the world than the man who is denied the benefit of self-confidence.

The hunter classes are the most important of all the classes in the show ring, for they set the standard of the best sort of horse to

breed and therefore wield a wide influence upon breeders and
buyers alike. The youngstock classes, for brood mares and for foals,
yearlings, two-year-olds and three-year-olds, are largely patronized
by people who breed horses for a hobby, or by farmers who breed
them as a lucrative sideline to their serious farm work. The ridden
classes, on the other hand, although they too contain many people
who show horses for the sheer fun of it, are also the happy hunting
ground for the professional showmen who produce horses for other
people – and in so doing, ensure that the standards of training,
riding, production and presentation are maintained at a consistently
high level.

The basic procedure for the led hunter classes never varies. The
youngsters are led into the ring, circle around the judge at a walk
(occasionally at a trot for a short spell, a valuable innovation
borrowed from the Welsh pony classes – movement from the side
being just as important as movement from the back or the front)
until they are called in by the judge or his steward to stand in a
straight line, in preliminary order of merit. The judge then walks
down the line, scrutinizing each animal, before pulling each out in
turn to inspect it again as its leader 'stands it up' (i.e. makes it stand
four-square). Then the judge sees it run out in hand; 'Walk away,
and trot back' is the usual request, but if he is dubious about some
small point – *does* it swing a leg, or throw a foot? – he will ask it to
go again to confirm or allay his earlier suspicions.

Lastly, he has the line of horses circle around him once more
before calling in first his winner and then the lower-placed horses.
In almost every class, he will only have succeeded in pleasing one
person, although there can ever only be one winner! Those less
fortunate will tell themselves and certain selected friends that the
judge is a fool; tell themselves and one or two others, in strictest
confidence, that the judge is a knave; or tell themselves that this is
only one man's opinion, and there is always another day. A fourth
category of exhibitor goes and attacks the judge, but this person is
very rare, and indeed gets increasingly more rare as he has his
entries refused by other shows, for his reputation will quickly get
around. There is an old and true show-ring saying, to the effect
that: 'If you can't take defeat, don't show'.

The ridden hunter classes may have either one or two judges, who
are called upon in England and Ireland (though not in the United
States or Canada) to ride the horses. This they do having seen them
walk, trot, canter and gallop round the ring, whereupon the same
system of calling the horses into a line prevails. If there are two
judges they then start riding, very often from opposite ends; if there
is only one he starts at the top and works his way down. It is
desirable for every horse to be ridden, even if those at the bottom of
the line stand no chance whatsoever of being placed. After all, the
exhibitors have all paid the same entry fee, most have gone to the
same trouble and expense to produce their horses and bring them to
the show, and it is discouraging, to say the least, to be dismissed

with a curt nod. Even if time does not permit the judges to ride every horse (and judges are all too often not given sufficient time to do their job, being constantly hurried along by a steward who is himself being chivvied from higher up, very often because of the demands of the television people, impatient for the show-jumping to begin on time!) the better judges are punctilious about having a final look and a cheery word with the poor man or woman who is unfortunate enough to stand at the very end of the line. A pat on the horse's neck, and an admiring: 'I bet he's a super hunter!' goes a very long way towards mollifying an exhibitor who is about to be sent out of the ring with 'the rubbish'.

The bigger shows will put on classes not only for the conventional three weight divisions – lightweight, middleweight and heavyweight – but also for four-year-olds, novices, small hunters, and ladies' hunters to be ridden side-saddle (and judged, of course, by a lady judge who is proficient in the art of riding side-saddle). Lady judges are among the most long-suffering of all, for they often have to climb up into side-saddles of extreme discomfort which came out of some dank attic and are almost prehistoric in design! Happily, many of these older side-saddles have been sold abroad as antiques to hang on the walls of the home of some tycoon in the New World. Sufficient remain in use, however, to cast a cloud over the most stout-hearted of lady judges.

The winning side-saddle horse does not qualify for the overall show championship, and nor does the four-year-old or the small hunter, but the first and second in the weight classes meet again to compete for the award of the championship and reserve – the final accolade in the life of the show hunter.

Working hunters have to jump a small, comparatively natural course of about six show jumps before being judged for conformation. Jumping performance counts for some 40 per cent of the whole assessment.

Weight-carrying cobs with show quality are, alas, a vanishing breed as the small demand for them makes them uneconomic to breed. The hack classes are quite well filled and the big shows stage classes for novices, and for ladies' hacks to be ridden side-saddle, in addition to the usual classes divided by height (not exceeding 15 hands and not exceeding 15·3 hands).

A hack is an elegant, well-trained animal. In days gone by, they were a common sight in Hyde Park when ridden by ladies and gentlemen for an hour or so on a sunny morning – partly, no doubt, to attract the admiring attention of some member of the opposite sex. Nowadays they are very largely confined to the show ring. A really good hack, of true 'hack' type, is more lightly built and more graceful than a hunter, with a beautiful head and outlook. It is indeed a thing of beauty and, like it, a joy for as long as it lasts. Few modern hacks, however, seem to be schooled with that lightness in hand which, with its free and flowing movement, was so very characteristic of the champions of thirty years ago.

The British show pony, a miniature Thoroughbred, is a remarkable phenomenon which is found nowhere else in the world and is greatly admired in other countries although seldom coveted, except perhaps in the United States. A fair number of British show ponies have been exported to America, but on the Continent the buyers seem to feel, with some justification, that these ponies are altogether too light, too finely-bred and too precious to be suitable for the average child, who will have a great deal more fun riding a native pony, or one only a generation removed from foundation stock.

Even in England, the showing classes today are largely the hunting ground of the professional children on professionally-produced ponies, and few parents want their children to get involved in this sort of rat-race. I was at Windsor Show one day when I heard a professional producer musing to himself: 'There are *five* people riding this pony!' – and so there were! There was the child herself, him, the pony's owner, and the child's mother and grandmother, all calling out instructions to the poor unfortunate jockey every time she came past. Small wonder that child now hates showing and far prefers working pony classes, Pony Club hunter trials and one-day events – *anything*, in fact, which avoids swanning around the show ring looking pretty on a pretty pony which is not capable of doing anything else, and often has to be ridden-in by an adult for an hour or two at the show before it is safe for a child to ride.

It is the working ponies, I am quite convinced, that are the ponies of the future, and these classes, where the ponies are required to jump, are filled to capacity. They keep both child and pony in a happy frame of mind and in their comparatively natural state.

The in-hand riding pony classes are on the whole a great deal more sporting than the ridden show pony classes, with the professional studs well balanced by private breeders who keep the odd mare or two as a hobby. Yet perhaps there is still too much money in these classes, despite the economic situation, for their own good. The dealers are always on the look-out for a top three-year-old to sell on to some deep-pocketed parent and the whole thing starts again, with the pony being sent on to a professional to produce for the show ring. Huge prices are involved and large sums of money change hands.

The native pony classes are far less professional, largely because there is much less money at stake, and the atmosphere is generally far more friendly. This is particularly noticeable among the breeders of Connemara and Welsh ponies, both of whom have a deep love for their protégés. Being sensible, down-to-earth folk, who know ponies, they are also very keen on the performance side. The hardy, sure-footed ponies, reared on the Welsh hills for generations and used as shepherding ponies by the hill farmers, produce offspring that are able to do any job that is required of them, from hunting and jumping to Pony Club events and driving competitions.

The Arab enthusiasts are a law unto themselves, for their breed is a breed apart which has little appeal for the foxhunter or for those who require a horse to enter in three-day events or show-jumping competitions. Most people regard the Arab mainly in the light of an outcross of blood, and many consider that it should ideally be found quite a long way back in the pedigree. But the true Arab lover considers his breed to be a 'pearl beyond price'. As an example, I have a friend who, having acquired an Arab stallion some years ago, sold it to someone in the United States, and was able to build a swimming pool and lay out an extensive shrubbery on the proceeds!

Pride of place at the classic shows, however, and at all the major agricultural meetings such as the Royal, the Bath and West, Peterborough and the Great Yorkshire, and of course at the annual show of the Royal Dublin Society held each August at Ballsbridge, is given to the hunters mentioned earlier. Perhaps Dublin is the most interesting of all, for whereas the English shows tend, towards the end of the showing season, to be simply a different permutation of the same horses, meeting at show after show, all the Dublin horses are new each year. It is the exception, rather than the rule, for a horse to be shown there more than once, for if he is any good he is usually sold. The only reason a horse may appear there for two years is that he is someone's favourite and is not for sale.

There is an endless fascination in watching these horses, the crop of the current season, as they cascade into the ring on the first two days at Ballsbridge – lightweights, middleweights, and finally heavyweights. The last are the richest and rarest, and really what the Irish half-bred breeding industry is all about. Each year they appear to improve in quality, but is this really so or is it simply the inevitable grading-up process, when Thoroughbred sires are used exclusively on the Irish Draught mares? And will Ireland eventually come to the English *impasse*, when almost every horse is practically clean-bred, because of the prevailing shortage of heavyweight foundation stock?

Personally, I doubt it, because even the Irish Horse Board seems to realize that it is imperative to return to the *status quo* by means of the Irish Draught mare, the supreme sheet-anchor of the Irish half-bred breeding industry. Ireland is unique in the world in having this clean-limbed breed on which to draw, and it has been the foundation stock of many famous show-jumpers. Many, indeed sadly most, of the Irish Draught foundation mares were sent to Belgium and eaten during the years immediately following the Second World War. Enough mares and stallions were left, however, to provide a nucleus, which hopefully is being cherished and nurtured, to ensure a foundation stone. Crossed once or twice, or even more often with Thoroughbred stallions, it will assure the retention of a breed sufficiently important for the Italian dealers to continue to maintain stud farms, or at least depots, in Ireland to supply at least their international teams with Olympic-medal

To reach the famous ruins which form part of the tourist attraction of Petra in Jordan, visitors travel on horseback to reach the Sig, the narrow passage leading to the foot of the Nabataean Monastery.

OVERLEAF: The Camarguais horses roam in a semi-wild state through the marshland which is their home. These hardy horses are also invaluable to the *gardiens* who herd the small, black bulls of the district.

winning horses, while other nations turn to the cold-blooded riding horse of Germany.

Britain has no such foundation stock to put to Thoroughbred stallions in the hope of breeding a viable competition horse. The carthorse breeds – Clydesdale, Shire and Suffolk – have all been tried and found wanting. The Cleveland Bay, with its long barrel, can throw up the odd freak of breeding, such as William Barker's North Flight, which was reserve for the 1964 British Olympic show jumping team in Tokyo, but by and large this is not the most successful foundation stock for the top-class international competition horse.

Since the end of the Second World War, no fewer than ten Olympic champions (i.e. the winner of a team or individual gold medal) have been bred in Ireland from Irish Draught foundation stock, while seven have been bred in England. Ireland has to her credit Colonel Harry Llewellyn's Aherlow, Colonel Frank Weldon's Kilbarry, Ted Marsh's Wild Venture, HM The Queen's Countryman III, Captain Martin Whiteley's The Poacher, Major Derek Allhusen's Lochinvar, Italy's Sunbeam (a double gold medallist in Tokyo), King and Royal Love, and Graziano Mancinelli's Ambassador. England's home-bred champions are Wilf White's Nizefela, Colonel Harry Llewellyn's Foxhunter, Mary Gordon-Watson's Cornishman V, Jane Bullen's Our Nobby, Bridget Parker's Cornish Gold, Major Derek Allhusen's Laurieston and Captain Mark Phillips's Great Ovation.

This concentration of success in one small corner of the globe is not simply a fortuitous coincidence – the result of a happy chance. The fact that only West Germany has thirteen champions, all in the field of show-jumping, proves that the powerful German horses are the best performers over really big artificial fences in the world. But it also proves that for going across country, with safety, at speed, jumping whatever fate or the course designer elects to put in the way, there is nothing to touch the Irish hunter, although the English-bred one runs him very close.

Nor is it a coincidence that England and Ireland are the only countries where show classes for hunters exist as they do, without the necessity to bring fences into the ring to find the winner. Conformation is extremely important to any horse. However good a performer, however brave his heart, he will never last unless he has the sound constitution and the correct conformation to stand up to the strains and stresses of work in holding going. For 200 years and more, foxhunting has imposed these strains and stresses, and out of it all has come a tough breed of horse, as well as a number of human beings who understand conformation, fortunately for the continuation of the hunter-type horse.

Luckily there is absolutely no sign that hunter showing is on the decline. It will always be a part, and an important one, of the Irish scene because Irish horses are nearly all for sale, and a horse which has won in the show ring must inevitably command a higher price

In the lush tropical landscape of Fiji horses such as these are frequently used instead of cars to carry visitors to the hilly interior.

than one which has not. But in England, too, showing is enjoying a vastly increased support. Sponsorship, once the prerogative of the show-jumpers, has now been extended to the hunters too, thanks initially to the support of the British and Irish Steam Packet Company, and later to the Waterford Crystal Company – both Irish companies, not slow to realize the value of showing.

There could be said to be a decline in the ranks of the professional nagsmen who abounded in the show ring between the wars, but there are still young men coming on to follow in the footsteps of the Harry Bonners of this world. There is of course a vast number of amateurs who have all the keenness and enthusiasm for acquiring and riding a good horse in the show ring, even if they do not reach quite the same heights of expertise as men whose lives are spent seeking out, schooling and producing the champions.

Judging, too, is going through an interregnum, and for much the same reason. With the cavalry regiments mechanized, and the Army Equitation School at Weedon a thing of the past, young men are forced to look beyond the horse to make a living. The fortunate few to whom this does not apply are denied the opportunity of learning in quite the same school. Their experience cannot extend to riding as many different horses as their predecessors were lucky enough to enjoy, and their knowledge is inevitably more limited. But the realm of the three-day event is a natural recruiting ground for young judges, and so are the ranks of young Masters of Foxhounds, who are very well placed to know what is required of a horse.

One often hears it said, although I do not believe it, that horses are no longer as sound as once they were, and that inherent weaknesses are being bred into English and Irish horses. The myth could have been given credence by the fact that in the old days unsound horses just disappeared from the public eye, and vast numbers were simply put down, or else fell upon hard times. Now, thanks to the ever-increasing stores of veterinary knowledge and experience, palliative measures and techniques are being improved every year. Thus many horses which would once have been regarded as chronically unsound can now be restored to sound working.

All this must be to the ultimate good of the horse, which is surely the most important consideration, even though various governing bodies connected with showing both hunters and hacks have decreed that certain categories of operation render the subject ineligible for the show ring. The rights and wrongs of the matter are endlessly debatable, and I do not propose to enter into them here, save only to regret that this does sometimes lead to horses having their show careers cut short to very little purpose.

Although fashions change in the show ring, as everywhere else, the hunter classes are ultra-conservative; any innovation is rightly regarded with suspicion and frowned upon by the more conservative exhibitors. Such practices as bringing a horse into the show ring with countless tiny plaits up his neck, secured by rubber bands, rather than with the traditional one in front and seven up the crest, neatly sewn in place, are to be deplored.

There is considerable prestige attached to being asked to judge at a leading show, and particularly to being invited to judge in Ireland. The Irish have always asked Englishmen to judge at their major shows, such as Dublin, Cork and Clonmel. This is partly because an English judge should have a good idea what sort of horse would win in England, and therefore will select the type of horse that could probably be sold to an English buyer. It is also felt that an English judge is more likely to be completely impartial, as he probably does not know the horses or many of the exhibitors.

It was the late Nat Galway-Greer, the wizard of Dunboyne, a world-famous and delightful horse dealer who won ten supreme championships at Dublin in the years following the Second World War, who first hit upon the brilliant notion of bringing English riders over to ride his horses at Ballsbridge. There was ostensibly a very good reason for this: the English showmen are a great deal more experienced in showing a horse than their Irish counterparts, and with their meticulous attention to detail they are able to show a horse off to far better advantage. But there was also a more subtle benefit, and this was that the English riders would be known to, and recognized by the English judges, and the horses that they rode would at least be sure to get a second look.

Although some of the other exhibitors were known to resent the presence of the English riders (believing they gave Nat Greer an unfair advantage), the authorities recognized that it gave added interest to the proceedings and raised the standard of the green Irish horses.

There is considerable variety in the standard of horsemanship of the various hunter judges. The criterion is that every horse should go well for a judge, and so certain idiosyncrasies are overlooked as long as this principal requirement is met. Perhaps the worst failing in a judge is bad hands, which must upset any horse unless he happens to have a worse mouth. Once a judge acquires the reputation for being 'mutton-fisted' he will not remain long in ignorance of his failing! There will be several horses produced for him to ride with their curb chains wrapped in chamois leather, lest he hang on to their heads.

There is also the other side of the coin, when exhibitors produce horses in the ring which are quite insufficiently prepared and trained and expect the poor unsuspecting judges to ride them, sometimes at great personal risk. A certain well known major-general, when faced with one of these animals – and a woman's horse, to boot, notorious for being allowed to do whatever it wished – brought it straight back to its owner and declined to ride it any more, thundering: 'Madam, I have not come 200 miles to nag other people's horses!'

The judge who bases his decisions on the form which has prevailed at other shows is either unsure of himself, and thus prefers to play it safe by taking the line of least resistance, or has very little knowledge. The form judge soon becomes known for what he is, and of course he is all at sea at the first shows of the season, before the form book has been 'written'. It is one of the worst breaches of etiquette for any judge to be seen with a catalogue in his hands until he has finished his work in the ring. Of course, judges who are in demand, and are constantly on the circuit, can hardly remain in ignorance of the horses which have been winning at earlier shows, even if they have never actually judged them before. Luckily, there are many judges whose integrity is so well known, and whose reputations are so well established, that they are above criticism.

It must be remembered that judging is bound to be a matter of personal opinion, and few people think absolutely alike about a horse. A big, heavy man is likely to lean towards the big, weight-carrying type of horse that he would choose to ride himself. The slim, lightweight judge, on the other hand, prefers a Thoroughbred type.

Dublin's green horses, too, are great levellers, for riding green Irish horses is a peculiar art, especially where they have done most of their work in a snaffle and are but newly introduced to a double bridle.

In an age when every hunter is so much infused with Thoroughbred blood, Harry Bonner has said that years ago the back row of a hunter class was more impressive than the front row is today. Apart from the fact that the stamp of horse is often not so good as it used to be, he feels that the standard of production has suffered even more. It is impossible, he is sure, to spend too long in riding and making before the actual nagging begins. Most people indulge in far too much of the latter, plus an inordinate reliance on tack and similar contrivances which are sometimes wrongly regarded as a short-cut to success. Declining standards are also manifested by the spectacle of horses – particularly young horses – being forced beyond their natural paces. 'They learn to cut their corners and become ring-crafty quickly enough, without actually showing them the way.'

Looking at photographs of some of the great hunter champions of the past, with their abundance of bone and their great depth, one must concede that such specimens are becoming increasingly rare today. Bad hocks, weak hind legs and long cannon bones were not so prevalent in the old days, perhaps because the stallions of the time were bigger and stronger, with more bone and more substance.

The stallions that are shown at the National Stallion Show of the Hunter's Improvement and National Light Horse Breeding Society at Newmarket each March, for the award of the Society's premiums, are judged by a hunting man and a racehorse trainer, working together. This is an unusual alliance, as the hunting man requires qualities in a horse that will enable it to stay all day, while the racing man – particularly the flat race trainer – looks for the type of horse that will stay for no more than 1·5 km (1 mile) or so at top speed. Strangely enough, they usually seem to see eye to eye.

The really knowledgeable judge of every horse and pony looks for good limbs, a well-sloped shoulder going obliquely back into the body, depth in the girth and the loin, a nice front with generous outlook, and strong quarters and second thighs – in this order. Conversely, bad limbs, shortage of bone, bad walkers, straight shoulders, a shelly, shallow body, and weak hind legs are an anathema to all.

Many of the horses which are bred behind the Iron Curtain have many of these faults, which leads one to suppose that breeding is not as selective as it might be on the State studs, or else that the priorities are different in parts of the world where foxhunting is not endemic. It may also be that whatever the breed, if all the emphasis is placed upon performance, rather than at least half of it being on conformation, there must inevitably be a decline.

Thus the show ring is of very real value to any breed of horse or pony, and while there are still people who care about a breed, as there always will be, there will be shows at which breeders and owners can exhibit their stock in competition with others. A champion obviously commands a higher price than the run-of-the-mill horse or pony, and great sums of money lie between the successful show horse and his full brother who has never proved himself in the show ring.

In discussing the show ring it is inevitable that much emphasis will be placed on the well-established British and Irish pattern, which has provided the standard for shows held in other English-speaking countries, particularly in Australia and South Africa. Indeed, both these countries frequently invite British judges to officiate at their major shows and the classes held approximate, with local variations, very closely to those held in Britain.

America, while deriving its tradition from the same source, has developed its own classes and established a system of judging that inclines strongly towards performance in the ring and, in many instances, takes particular account of style.

SHOW JUMPING

Although men have been riding horses for more than 3000 years, persuading them to jump over obstacles is a comparatively new idea. Show jumping, which has grown out of this, is thus also a fairly recent innovation compared with other equestrian activities. Only in the second half of the eighteenth century did jumping on horses begin to achieve some recognition, and then it was slow to gain ground. The first mention of it being included in any cavalry manual belongs to the French, in 1788, and although the British foxhunter thinks of his predecessors going across country from time immemorial, it was the Enclosure Acts of the eighteenth century, bringing about the considerable increase in the number of hedges and fences to enclose fields, that set them jumping.

It was something like another hundred years before jumping, as opposed to steeplechasing, was officially recorded, and then it sprang up in various parts of the world within a very short period. Ireland, in which country steeplechasing had its infancy, was again a front runner in show jumping, and at the Royal Dublin Society's annual show in 1865 there were competitions for 'wide' and 'high' leaps. There were competitions in Russia at about the same time, and in Paris in 1866, although here the competitors paraded at the show and then went out into the country to jump over mainly natural fences. Nine years later the famous French Cavalry School at Saumur included an exhibition of jumping in their display of *haute école*.

In England jumping was primarily a part of agricultural shows, and was first officially recorded at the five-day show at the Agricultural Hall, Islington, London, in 1876. Horses entered for the show classes were also eligible for the leaping, which was decided solely on style, and judged by Masters of Foxhounds. Even when a few rules concerning jumping ability were introduced, style was still an important factor. It enabled the judges to arrive at the most diplomatic result for it would never have done for the local squire to be beaten by one of his tenants!

In the United States the National Horse Show was started at Madison Square Garden, New York, in 1883. The 'Garden' has been moved twice since then but the show goes on as strongly as ever. By the turn of the century, the 'new' sport was very firmly established internationally; Germany held shows in towns all over the country and in the second of the modern Olympic Games, at Paris in 1900, three jumping competitions were included, a high jump, a long jump and prize jumping. The following year, in Turin, saw the first recorded official international show jumping, with German army officers invited to pit their skill against their Italian counterparts: a milestone in the establishment of the sport.

In London the first International Horse Show (forerunner of the Royal International) was held at Olympia in 1907, as a result of a meeting held at The Hague two years earlier. The Earl of Lonsdale directed the International Horse Show, the board and directors of which comprised men from many European countries and the United States. High and wide jumps were included in the programme, and the prize money was quite considerable. Two Belgian riders – Haegemann and Van Langendonck – had won at the Paris Games, and the same country, and Holland, dominated that first International. Tommy Glencross, who was to play an important part in the development of show jumping in Britain, won a high jump competition.

In 1906 the Swedish Count Clarence von Rosen had put a proposition to the Congress of the International Olympic Committee that equestrian sports should be included on a permanent basis in the Games – there had been none at all in St Louis in 1904 – and although the suggestion was not greeted with abundant enthusiasm, Baron Pierre de Coubertin, the founder of the modern Games, asked von Rosen to present more detailed proposals to the 1907 Congress. These were for three events – dressage, an equestrian pentathlon and a game called *jeu de rose*.

The British members of the IOC agreed that these should be included in the 1908 Games, which were to be held in London, and the committee of the International Horse Show consented to organize them, provided there was a minimum of twenty-four entries from six different countries. In fact there were eighty-eight entries from eight countries, which perhaps proved too much for the International Show, itself still in its infancy. At the last minute the equestrian events were dropped from the Olympic programme. Von Rosen did not lose heart, however. The next Olympics were to be held in Stockholm, and in 1909 a committee, with himself as secretary-general and Prince Carl of Sweden as president, produced three events for the 1912 Games. These were dressage, a three-day event, otherwise known as the Military, and show jumping.

International jumping was increasing. In 1909 the first Lucerne show was held, with Italians, Germans, French and Belgians in opposition to the Swiss. That same year the National Horse Show in New York introduced international jumping. A team of five British army officers, captained by Major J. G. Beresford, took part, and won one of the events. Four years later, a military team competition, a forerunner of the Nations Cup, was held at the show.

Team jumping was held at the London International for the first time in 1909, when the French won the inaugural King Edward VII Cup. Before the show, in common with almost all others, was suspended for the First World War, and before the Russian revolution, the Tsarist cavalry came to London to complete a glorious hat-trick of wins of the Cup, in 1912–14, under the leadership of Captain Paul Rodzianko. He and his compatriots took the King Edward VII Cup, which they had then won outright, back to Russia in 1914, and it was never seen again.

The 1912 Olympic show jumping was run under a complicated set of rules. Ten marks were given for each fence, with deductions for faults; for example, a first refusal cost two marks, a second, or fall of horse and rider, four, a third, or fall of rider only, six. Clearly it was considered more ignominious to fall off a horse than to cause him to fall too. There were marks for hitting a fence with hind or forelegs, for landing on or within the demarcation line of a spread fence, and altogether so many complications that judging must have been far from easy.

In the 1912 Games each country was allowed to enter six competitors for the individual jumping, and four, with the best three scores counting, for the team. Eight countries – Belgium, Chile, France, Germany, Britain, Norway, Russia and Sweden – entered a total of thirty-one riders in the individual, which was won by Captain Cariou of France, also the winner of a bronze in the three-day event. Sweden won the team gold medal from France and Germany, followed, in order, by the United States, Russia and Belgium. The next year Germany founded its own Olympic Equestrian Committee, but of course the war brought the sport to a standstill in Europe. In the United States in 1917 what was to become known as the American Horse Shows Association was founded, with representatives of fifty shows at its inaugural meeting. The AHSA was to be the official representative body for the United States in international affairs.

The effects of the system of training of the famous Italian, Federico Caprilli, was given dramatic emphasis at the first post-war Olympics, held at Antwerp in 1920, when two Italians schooled under his methods, Lt Tommaso Lequio and Major Valerio, won the gold and silver medals. The Italian team took the bronze, behind Sweden and Belgium. No British riders took part in the 1920 Games because of a cattle-disease ban, but the London International was reopened that same year.

Although equestrian sports were now a recognized part of the Olympic movement, they had no ruling body of their own. But Baron de Coubertin, looking ahead, had encouraged the creation of world federations for each sport, so that they could standardize their rules and bring an overall uniformity and control into sports. Commandant Georges Hector, of France, drew up statutes for the Fédération Equestre Internationale, which were adopted at a Congress in Paris in November 1921. Thus Sweden and France were the prime movers in the establishment of the FEI; the other six founder-members were Belgium, Denmark, Italy, Japan, Norway and the United States. Germany became affiliated to the International Federation in the year of its creation, and Switzerland joined in 1922.

Canada began to take an active interest when the Toronto Winter Fair started in 1922, and the first Canadian Nations Cup was held five years later. Show jumping was by no means confined to the northern half of the American continent. The first international show in Buenos Aires was held in 1910, with riders from Italy, Spain and France as well as other South American countries. Two Chilean riders had also competed in London and the Olympics in 1912.

Britain's fairly chaotic show jumping situation was gradually sorted out after the foundation of the British Show Jumping Association in 1923. Lord Lonsdale accepted the position of president of the Association, with Colonel V. D. S. Williams, father of television commentator Dorian Williams, as secretary. A mixture of military men and the top civilian riders helped to form the Association, which by improving both judging and the courses they jumped began to produce British riders and horses of international standard.

A record entry of 99 riders on 110 horses from 17 countries at the first Olympic events to be held under FEI rules, at Paris in 1924, showed that the sport was continuing to grow in popularity. Sweden again won the team event, but Lecquio, the individual winner four years earlier, was now beaten by the Swiss, Alphons Gemuseus.

Britain joined the FEI the following year and in 1926 the Royal Dublin Society, having helped to get the sport off the starting block some sixty years earlier, introduced international jumping.

Although successes for United States show jumpers are no rarity nowadays, their rider Fred Bontecou was something of an exception when he won the coveted King George V Gold Cup at the London International in 1926.

Jack Talbot-Ponsonby, the first man to win the King George V Cup three times, and later to become one of Britain's finest course builders, had the first of his three victories in the 1930 show, at which Mike Ansell also had his first taste of international success. Both went with the successful British army team to New York the following year, helping to foster in Ansell an enthusiasm for the sport which grew and in turn helped Britain develop into a world power in show jumping.

Olympic equestrian events were held outside Europe for the first time when the Games went to Los Angeles, but they were hardly a success. Only six countries and a total of thirty-four riders competed. International travel for horses in those days was a long, arduous and expensive business, and only France, Holland, Sweden and Japan sent horses to take on the United States and Mexico. France and Holland did not enter show jumpers, and no country had three finishers in the show jumping, so there were no team awards. Baron Takeichi Nishi won the gold for Japan, beating the American Harry Chamberlin, one of the most brilliant horsemen his country has ever produced.

The Berlin Games in 1936 proved a showcase for German superiority, and their riders won both the individual and the team gold medals at show jumping, dressage and the three-day event.

During the war, while a prisoner, the now legendary figure of British and international show jumping, Mike Ansell, started to work on his master-plan for bringing the sport in his home country up to the top international level. It was fortunate that Ansell, who had been partially blinded and was to end up completely without his sight, should have found himself in the same prisoner-of-war camp as two other show jumping enthusiasts and old team mates of his, Nat Kindersley and Bede Cameron. From the ideas they tossed around grew the dream which, as soon as he was repatriated in 1944, Ansell started to make into a reality. In December of that year he was invited to become chairman of the British Show Jumping Association, a post he held for more than two decades.

He chose for his committee men of like mind, intent on making show jumping into the exciting, crowd-pulling sport it has become. They had a lot to do. In those days there was virtually no limit to the time a rider could take to complete his round, circling as often he wished to make his approach to a fence exactly right, unclipping his martingale as he came to the water jump. On each fence was a slat, a thin lath of wood which, if knocked off, cost half a fault. Thus accuracy was essential, no matter how long it might take. The courses were uninteresting, normally consisting of a few uprights along each side of the ring, before turning in to a water jump or big spread in the middle.

Gradually these impediments to a slick show were weeded out. A grading system, on prize money won, was introduced, so that horses would compete against others of roughly similar ability and experience. Then Ansell and his men looked for a venue at which to put their new-look show jumping to the public test. They chose the White City, London, and so began what was to be a long and successful association. The first show included the National Championship, won with that story-book touch which Ansell so often seemed to conjure out of thin air, by a repatriated Nat Kindersley. The following year, two shows were held at the White City, and the Victory Championship went to Colonel Harry Llewellyn, who in the jump-off beat the eighteen-year-old Douglas Bunn – two men who were to have incalculable influence on British show jumping over the next few decades.

The National Show in New York restarted in 1945; the FEI reopened its shop in 1946, and throughout Europe, in common with other sports, show jumping was restarted. For the first time civilian riders took the international stage, including one of the greatest of all, the Frenchman Pierre Jonqueres d'Oriola, a mercurial man whose career has been a succession of ups and downs. The ups started with the 1946 Grand Prix in Zurich and took in two Olympic individual gold medals – a feat no other rider has achieved – in 1952 and 1964. The International was reborn, at the White City, when d'Oriola won the King George V Cup. For the first time the show was televised, so beginning the build-up of a massive audience which, in turn, has had a considerable effect on the growth of the sport.

The Olympic Games restarted in 1948, when they were held in England. The Royal International Committee, under Mike Ansell, was given the job of preparing a combined team and individual competition for the show jumping, which was to be the last competitive event before the closing ceremony in the vast Wembley Stadium. Getting the course built in time was a herculean task, for weeks of rain had left the ground a quagmire and work could only start after the soccer final had finished the night before. All the fences had to be manhandled onto the ground and the water jump dug by hand because of the state of the ground. Fifteen teams of three started, and the individual gold was won by the Mexican Humberto Mariles on the one-eyed Arete. His team, too, emerged triumphant, beating Spain, with the British gaining their first Olympic show jumping medal, the team bronze.

The following week, the British team captain, Harry Llewellyn, and Foxhunter won the first of their three King George V Gold Cups – Foxhunter is the only horse so far to have won this classic three times. And four years later in Helsinki, Foxhunter's final clear round clinched the team gold medal for Britain. Wilf White and Nizefela might well have taken the individual gold too, but

for a belated decision by only one of the two judges that he had gone in the water. In the end there was a five-sided jump-off for the medals, won by d'Oriola, with Chile's Oscar Christi winning the individual silver and ensuring that his team also finished second.

That year was notable also for the first of the official FEI championships for Juniors – those between fourteen and eighteen years – in which there were only two teams. The Italians, including Graziano Mancinelli, beat Belgium. Gradually the International Federation introduced other championships, for seniors also, beginning with the Men's World Championship, held for the first time in Paris in 1953. It was won by the popular Spaniard Francisco 'Paco' Goyoaga, an achievement made more remarkable by the fact he was riding a horse who had, or so it seemed beforehand, lost his enthusiasm for the game. They beat Germany's Thiedemann by just half a point. D'Oriola was third, followed by Piero d'Inzeo, an auspicious cast indeed to the new championship.

Initially the world championships were held every year, and two years later Hans Gunter Winkler won the first of two successive world titles on Halla. This horse was arguably the greatest show jumping mare of all time, on whom Winkler also won the individual Olympic gold at Stockholm in 1956, when she practically had to carry him round the second course after he had badly hurt a muscle. Winkler was also in the winning team, a feat he repeated in Rome, Tokyo and Munich, to give him five golds, more than any other rider in Olympic history.

Raimondo d'Inzeo, the more successful of the two Italian brothers, won the next two world titles – after going down to Winkler and Halla in a jump-off in 1955. By this time, the world championships had settled down to a four-year cycle, interspersed with the European championships, which are now held every other year. Winkler won the first of the Continental titles, in 1957, and Thiedemann the second. There was often a challenger from outside Europe for the title, and in 1966 Nelson Pessoa, the Brazilian who spends his summers in Europe, won from Frank Chapot of the United States, with Hugo Arrambide of Argentina third. Soon after this the FEI decreed that the European championship should be confined to the riders that its title suggested, a sensible enough move, for it makes the world championship relatively more important.

A European championship for women was also introduced in 1957, when it was won by Pat Smythe, who is conceivably the greatest woman rider the sport has produced. Britain dominated this title over the years (until it was amalgamated with the men's title in 1975), but no one more so than Pat, who achieved a hat-trick in 1961–1963 on Flanagan. When women were first admitted to Olympic show jumping in 1956, Pat Smythe and Flanagan were in the team at Stockholm, together with Wilf White and Peter Robeson, and they took the bronze behind Germany and Italy, proving that women could participate successfully.

Pat Smythe and Flanagan were back in the British squad four years later in Rome, together with another of their sex, Dawn Wofford, *née* Palethorpe. The brilliant young David Broome joined them in the individual on Sunsalve, a horse he had ridden to victory in the King's Cup within two weeks of first trying him, and now took the bronze. It was Italy's day, however, and Raimondo d'Inzeo took the gold and his brother, Piero, the silver. Their team could finish only third behind Germany, in which Winkler and Thiedemann were joined by another destined for the highest honours, Alwin Schockemöhle, who having been reserve for both the show jumping and three-day event teams four years earlier, was making his debut.

Alwin, after winning this team gold, went through an aggravating series of individual near-misses for major titles, three times second and twice third for the European, and fourth for the world championship in 1970 behind David Broome. He finally broke his duck in 1975 in the first running of the European Amateur Championship (until then professionals and amateurs alike were eligible for all FEI titles), and then went on to take the Olympic gold in Montreal. He did not have a horse good enough to make his country's team in Tokyo, where Winkler was joined by Herman Schridde and Kurt Jarasinski, who collectively proved good enough to complete a German hat-trick of team golds. D'Oriola helped his team take the silver, but for himself it had to be the gold, riding a horse who had only made his international debut that same season.

With d'Oriola in the French team at the Tokyo Games was a girl, only eighteen years old, whose brillance was on a par with his, Janou Lefèbvre (now Janou Tissot). She went on to take another team silver in Mexico, and holds two of the only three women's world championships to be held. The first of these was in 1965 at Hickstead, the ground that Douglas Bunn had founded in Sussex five years earlier. With its exciting permanent obstacles and gradually improved facilities, it has had a profound effect on show jumping in England, introducing the sort of course that had previously only been found on the Continent. Kathy Kusner, the American girl, with two victories in the Dublin Grand Prix to her credit, was confidently expected to take this first world title, but could finish only second to Marion Coakes (now Marion Mould) and her brilliant pony Stroller. This pair had just become the youngest rider and the smallest horse to win the Queen Elizabeth Cup.

Hickstead was to prove the happiest of hunting grounds for Marion and Stroller, where they also won the British Jumping Derby two years later. They also won the silver medal in Mexico in 1968 behind Bill Steinkraus, who climaxed a brilliant career by giving the United States their first ever individual show jumping gold. The course for the team competition was generally condemned as one of the worst ever for an Olympic Games, primarily because of the awkward placing of fences, which produced some astronomical scores. It was finally won by the Canadians with 102¾ faults. By contrast Germany won in Tokyo with 68½ – itself a record – and in Munich with 32 faults. The course in Munich was a much more sensible one, although still demanding enough. The Montreal course had to be reduced in size because of the torrential rain which nearly prevented the competition being run in the main Olympic stadium at all.

It was in 1975 that all equestrian competitions became open for men and women. This made sense, for in the Olympic Games the competitions were mixed, and the women, though numerically outnumbered, repeatedly showed their merit by taking a large percentage of the medals. It was in that same year, also, that changes to the various championships separated amateurs from professionals. Thus the European championship, won by Alwin Schockemöhle, was for amateurs only, as a result of which, after some arguing, no British riders took part. The British federation was the only one which had taken Prince Philip's strictures to 'put their house in order' seriously, creaming off the top score or so of their riders into professional status and putting the country at a great disadvantage in Olympic competition. The World Professional Championship, which should have been held in 1975, did not take place because the FEI refused to allow the sponsors to append their name to it. It seems likely that the fluid situation will resolve itself again, into 'Open' competitions everywhere, save in the Olympic Games, over which the FEI does not have the final say. One day they too may be open, but that is surely a long way off.

Although Schockemöhle's victory in the 1975 amateur championship was a fairly bloodless one, with his compatriots also filling the minor places, he undoubtedly gave a superlative performance to win the gold medal in Montreal. The individual was held in the stadium at Bromont, some 70 km (43 miles) from Montreal, on a dirt surface which rode deep after a lot of rain. Over two big courses there was only one clear round each time, both from Schockemöhle. His horse was thus the first ever to win an Olympic gold with two clears.

Because of the unexpected rainfall before and during the Games, on ground which had not been drained because it was afterwards to have an artificial surface, there were doubts until the very last minute whether or not it would be possible to hold the team jumping there. Luckily the weather relented sufficiently just in time; the course was reduced in size, the final fence, which should have been a treble, became a double, and the competition went on. At halfway, the French and German teams were level in the lead, the pendulum slightly tipped in favour of the consistent French quartet; a clear by Schockemöhle would have clinched another team gold for Germany, but his horse hit two fences. Thus France achieved its first show jumping team gold in Olympic history.

THE THREE-DAY EVENT

The term 'three-day event' is very inadequate for an exciting, exhilarating sport which calls on the full range of a horse's ability and his rider's skill. Though the name implies some form of threefold competition, it divulges nothing of the qualities to be tested.

The three-day event was designed originally as a trial for military chargers, and was in fact known as the Military. The requirements of a charger were that he should be fit to cover sometimes long distances at a good average speed, travel over open country jumping whatever obstacles stood in his path, and be bold enough to tackle any unknown hazards at which his rider put him. For his part, the rider had to be able to produce a really fit horse and keep him that way, to know just how much he could ask of his mount and judge exactly the right pace, or combination of paces, to reach his target safely and quickly – but without exhausting his horse, because a new day would bring fresh demands.

The hard core of the Military, therefore, was an endurance test at working pace, with a section across country negotiating natural obstacles, and generally some form of steeplechase course to be ridden at speed. Later, a dressage test was added to demonstrate the charger's physical development, his mastery of the basic paces and obedience to his rider's unspoken commands. Finally there was a simple show jumping test, representing the everyday life to which a charger must be fit to return, even after an exceptionally demanding exercise.

The arts of military equitation have long been practised and admired on the continent of Europe, and for many years this was strictly a continental sport. France's military academy of equitation at Saumur still maintains the highest cavalry tradition, while the Spanish Riding School in Vienna is famous to this day for its cultivation of classical equitation, using the white Lipizzaner stallions it has used for generations.

The British – possibly because their native horses were the small, stocky, hardy, mountain and moorland breeds – had no such tradition of high-school equitation. With their temperate climate they could ride out of doors throughout the year, and hunting was their national equestrian sport. When they did import Arabian horses to found the fleeter, more refined Thoroughbred strain, it was for the headier delights of racing, both on the flat and over fences.

For most sports, international competition got under way with the foundation of the modern Olympic movement by Baron de Coubertin in 1896, but equestrian events were not introduced to the Games until 1912, in Stockholm, largely at the instigation of Count von Rosen, Master of the Horse to the King of Sweden. He realized their tremendous value – that of the Military in particular – in stimulating interest and improving standards of equitation and horsemastership, and he saw the Olympic Games as a means of spreading this improvement beyond army circles to all horsemen.

Entries for the Olympic equestrian events were exclusively from the military at first, but gradually civilians took part too. The three-day event became known as the *concours complet*, or complete competition.

The form of the *concours complet* was fairly fluid at first, but between the wars it settled down into more or less the form in which we know it now. The competitors, following each other in succession, must undertake three different tests on three separate days. These are:

1) Dressage – a set programme of some twenty movements of medium difficulty, performed at the walk, trot or canter, in an arena 60 × 20 m (approx. $65\frac{1}{2}$ × $21\frac{3}{4}$ yds) in area. Marks are awarded by a panel of three judges, who assess fluency and accuracy of performance, balance, impulsion, rhythm and suppleness in the horse, as well as the rider's seat and application of the aids (or directions).

2) Speed and endurance – a four-phase test consisting of phases A and C, held over roads and tracks totalling 10–20 km (6–12 miles) to be ridden at the trot or slow canter; phase B, a steeplechase course roughly 2–4 km (1–2·5 miles) long with 8–12 fences, to be ridden at the gallop; phase D, a cross-country course, 5–8 km 3–5 miles), with 20 to 32 fixed obstacles, to be ridden at the gallop. Penalties are incurred for falls or refusals at the obstacles for exceeding the minimum time allowed for each phase.

3) Show jumping – a course of 700–900 m (750–1000 yds) with 10 to 12 obstacles. Penalties are incurred for fall or refusals at the obstacles and for exceeding the time allowed.

Horses are submitted to a veterinary inspection before the start of the competition, another during the speed and endurance test and a final one before the show-jumping test on the last day. The same horse and rider have to complete all three tests, and the competitor with the lowest total penalties is the winner. In a team competition there may be three team members or four, and it is the three best final scores that count for the team's final placing.

The scale of marks weights the value of the three tests in the ratio of three for dressage, twelve for speed and endurance, and one for show jumping. The rules lay down the speeds and distances, and the dimensions, of the obstacles; the course and conditions should be so planned as to conform as closely as is practicable to this ratio.

Although this is the basic task confronting a three-day event competitor, it is really only the beginning. No two events are alike; the essence of the competition is the cross-country phase, and thus the natural countryside in which it is set, which can of course vary enormously. Besides the type of terrain, there are always variations

The British heavy horses are still popular with the public even though they are now rare on the land. This pair of Shires, Hengist and Horsa, is taking part in the Regent's Park Parade.

OVERLEAF: The showy elegance of the Arab makes it ideally suited to ceremonial occasions. Not surprisingly, the horses of the Moroccan Garde Royale are all Arabs; they are kept in sumptuous stables at the royal stud.

in the state of the going, the altitude, the climate, the weather – and that is all quite apart from the obstacles. The permutations are endless and the horse must be fit and bold to cope with them all, as he gallops and jumps over a course he has never seen before.

The rider has the advantage of being allowed to walk the course the day before, to assess the problems it poses and decide how to tackle them in the light of his horse's particular capabilities. He must work out the speed, the line of approach to an obstacle, and the angle and exact point at which to jump it (there is often a choice, with one alternative perhaps easier but more time-consuming than another). He must not be tempted to ride the steeplechase faster than necessary, or he will take too much out of his horse too early in the day, and he must keep up a good steady pace on the cross-country, ensuring that the horse takes the jumps in its stride without any waste of time, if he is to escape penalty. The horse may be tiring by then and it will take all the rider's strength and skill to get him safely round without undue effort.

Both horse and rider must be supremely fit, with steady nerves and considerable courage, and the greater the experience they can muster – preferably in partnership – and the greater their mutual understanding and confidence, the better.

There is a notable absence of personal rivalry among competitors. For them the challenge lies in the course rather than the other contestants, and it is with the course that each one must settle his own account. Furthermore, victory for the team is, in general, much more highly prized than individual success.

The roads and tracks for phases A and C, which constitute the endurance element, are perfectly straightforward. So is the steeplechase course for phase B, although the definition of a steeplechase fence may vary in different countries.

The crux comes in phase D, the cross-country. For this the track may be flat or steep, and the obstacles are fixed, solid in appearance and built of the strongest materials. The stronger and more solid the obstacle, the more inviting and reassuring it will appear to the horse, and therefore the safer it will be to jump. Also, each obstacle must be able to withstand the assault of wind and weather, so that it is the same for the hundredth competitor as it was for the first.

The course builder must contrive to test the rider's judgement and nerve, and the horse's scope, courage and obedience, but without making any unnatural demands or springing any unfair surprises. His course must produce a worthy winner but must not destroy the losers, and it is undoubtedly a job which calls for special skill and great experience. Like any other craft that is exposed to constant comparison and critical inspection, course building in general is improving all the time and the international standard is now very high indeed.

Certain obstacles have become bywords in the sport and will be found in more or less the same form on many courses. The Coffin, at Badminton, is one of these: it comprises a narrow trough at the

In the industrial countries of the world the heavy horse is making something of a comeback, and is particularly popular in the show ring. True working horses are still vital to the agricultural life of many areas.

PREVIOUS PAGE: The exceptionally hardy Don horse of the steppes, mount of the Cossacks since the eighteenth century, is still both ridden and driven today, and excels at long-distance races. This team is harnessed to a racing *tachanka*.

bottom of a wide ditch, with a post-and-rails on both banks, before and after. The Trout Hatchery at Burghley is another – a pool approached downhill, with a tree trunk or rails to be jumped on the way in or out, or both. The Normandy Bank, which is a jump up on to a flat bank with a rail on the edge of the drop on the far side, was unknown before the European championships in Normandy in 1969. The Helsinki Steps – rails forming the outline of steps dropping down a hillside – first appeared in the 1952 Olympic Games, while the Trakehner – a tall post-and-rails set in the bottom of a ditch – is familiar in Germany. An Irish Bank – a high bank which is too big to fly at a single leap, so that the horse has to touch down fleetingly on the top – can be very disconcerting to a horse which has never met one before. As can be seen, every country has its own style of obstacles and the more distinctive ones are sure to find a place, sooner or later, in the repertoire of other course builders.

The first Olympic three-day event, at Stockholm in 1912, started with speed and endurance tests, followed by the show jumping. The dressage came last. Sweden won both the team and individual gold medals, as she did again at Antwerp in 1920, when the dressage was replaced by a second endurance test.

For the 1924 Games in Paris the three-day event took shape as the competition we know today, with dressage first, speed and endurance second and show jumping last. Holland managed to break Sweden's grip and won both team and individual competitions.

A record number of twenty nations took part at Amsterdam in 1928, including Japan, Argentina and the United States. Once again, Holland won both titles, the individual gold medal going to Lt C. P. de Mortanges on Marcroix, who together set up a record, never yet broken, by winning again in Los Angeles in 1932. On that occasion only six nations were represented, probably because of the enormous cost to European countries of transporting their teams halfway round the world. The United States took the gold in the team event.

At Berlin in 1936, the cross-country course was a particularly stiff one and the fourth obstacle, a pond, with sloping bed and swollen with rain, caused havoc among the competitors. Germany won both team and individual gold medals. For the London Games, in 1948, the recently-formed British Horse Society was charged with the organization of the three-day event at Aldershot – the first time Great Britain had ever held such an event. The United States won the team competition, and Captain Chevallier of France the individual, but this was a turning-point for Britain in the history of the sport.

Despite the complete absence of three-day event background, Britain had got along well enough so far, recruiting and training army teams for each Games as they came along. But in 1948 the Duke of Beaufort, then Master of the Horse, came to the conclusion that this was a sport at which British horses and riders ought to excel. He was determined that in the next Games, at Helsinki in 1952, Britain would put up a team which was not only properly trained, but had gained some experience at the game before being thrown into the international arena.

The park of the Duke of Beaufort's home at Badminton, in Gloucestershire, covered some of the finest open country in England, and as Vice-Patron of the British Horse Society, he invited the B.H.S. to hold a national three-day event there in the spring of 1949. It was to be called the 'Olympic Horse Trials'. The event attracted a great deal of interest and quickly became popular, so much so in fact that it turned into a highly successful annual fixture and soon gained a reputation as the foremost three-day event in the world. As a result, Britain was to become a leading Olympic contender, with more international honours in three-day events to her credit than any other country, and regarded as an authority on both course design and organization in general.

But back in 1952, a small band of British riders and horses who had shown up well in national events were sent for several months of concentrated training under the direction of Captain Tony Collings (winner of the second Badminton) at his riding establishment at Porlock, in Somerset. Two years later, Captain Collings was tragically killed when one of the early Comets, in which he was travelling on a lecturing and judging tour, crashed into the Mediterranean. In his lifetime, however, he had a tremendous influence on eventing in Great Britain and must take his place among the sport's founders.

The British team at Helsinki (Reg Hindley, Bertie Hill and Laurence Rook) put up a very good show, but Laurence Rook's horse unfortunately put his foot in a hole towards the end of the cross-country course and his rider was concussed in the fall. Rook remounted and completed the course, but passed the wrong side of the finishing post and was eliminated. In those days each country was allowed to enter only three competitors, so this put the whole team out of the running. Sweden regained both team and individual titles, their gold medallist being Baron Hans von Blixen-Finecke.

The suggestion was then put forward that a European championship should be held in non-Olympic years and Badminton was asked to be the first to hold it, in 1953. Sadly, Badminton's April date proved too early in the year for most European countries to produce really fit horses, and only Switzerland and Ireland, apart from the hosts, were able to raise a team, so the championship was abandoned.

That autumn, the B.H.S. started up an autumn three-day event at Harewood, in Yorkshire, by permission of the Princess Royal. Vivien Machin-Goodall won, to become the first lady winner of a three-day event.

In 1954, Switzerland volunteered to hold the championships, and put on an event of high standard at Basle. Britain's Bertie Hill was the winner and British riders filled four out of the next six places, so they took the team championship as well. Among them were the first lady riders to compete in an official international championship – Margaret Hough, who finished sixth, and Diana Mason, riding for the team, who finished seventh.

This was a red-letter year for Britain on several counts: their new-found success, proof that girls could hold their own in what had been regarded hitherto as too tough a game for them, and the emergence as a team of three riders, Bertie Hill, Frank Weldon and Laurence Rook, who apart from their outstanding record of success were all to play a leading part in the three-day event world. Hill was to produce some superb horses and train many of the leading riders of future generations; Weldon was to captain the British team when he gave up competing and became a world authority on cross-country courses when he subsequently took over the direction of Badminton, and Rook was to become chairman of the sport's governing body in Britain and the technical delegate of the Fédération Equestre Internationale at many official championships and Olympic Games.

In 1955, the European championships were held at Windsor, by invitation of Her Majesty the Queen. Britain successfully defended its title with the same team, and Weldon carried off the individual championship. In seventeenth place was a youngster from Lancashire who had won the Pony Club championships, Sheila Willcox on High And Mighty.

In the Olympic Games at Stockholm in 1956 Britain's hopes were high and they were represented by three very experienced and successful riders, mounted on proven, high-quality horses. They didn't have it all their own way (Bertie Hill's Countryman slipped in the heavy rain and got hung up on a trakehner fence, but was salvaged and went on to finish the course), but they established a clear lead which they retained to the end. So Britain won her first team gold medal, while Frank Weldon took the individual bronze. Sweden's Kastenman won the individual gold medal.

In 1957, Britain won the European Championship at Copenhagen, where Sheila Willcox on High And Mighty became the first lady champion. She made history again in 1958, with her third successive victory at Badminton.

In 1959 Harewood was the setting for the European championships, in which the USSR entered for the first time. Britain's star had waned, and Germany won the team championship and Switzerland's Hans Schwarzenbach the individual, on a horse he had purchased from Frank Weldon. In the interim, Weldon had suffered the tragic loss of his great horse Kilbarry, who had broken his neck in falling at an innocent-looking fence in a one-day event at home.

In 1960, Australia sent a posse of horses and riders to train for six months in Britain before tackling the Olympic Games in Rome. They joined the circuit of national horse trials, as they had done in

1956, but this time with marked success. Bill Roycroft won at Badminton, and the team went on to capture the gold medal in Rome (Bill Roycroft was taken to hospital with a broken collar-bone after the cross-country, but defied doctors' orders in order to ride in the show jumping next day). Australia's Laurie Morgan won the individual gold medal and his compatriot, Neal Lavis, took the silver. The others went home to Australia afterwards, but Morgan returned to England, to ride in the Grand National and win at Badminton the following spring.

A new three-day event was started up at Burghley, home of the Marquess of Exeter, in 1961, to take the place of the Harewood event, which had closed down. It was won by Anneli Drummond-Hay on Merely-A-Monarch, the great horse with which she went on to win at Badminton in 1962 and then to become a successful international show jumper. In 1962, Burghley was the scene of the European championships, which were won by the USSR, the individual champion being Britain's James Templer.

At the 1964 Olympics the only 'first' scored by the British horses was that of flying over the North Pole on the newly-opened route to Tokyo! Richard Meade, fresh from winning at Burghley, had led at the end of the speed and endurance test – only to jump a disastrous

round on the final day. Italy won both team and individual titles.

It was fitting that the USSR should win the European team championship at Moscow in 1965, while Poland's Marian Barbierecki on Volt won the individual, gaining this country's sole victory in the history of the sport.

The first world championships were scheduled for Burghley in 1966, but an outbreak of African horse sickness prevented the movement of horses throughout Europe. Nevertheless, Ireland, the USSR and the United States overcame the veterinary ban by flying their horses direct to England, and a gallant band from Argentina made the mammoth journey by sea, their horses regaining health and vigour during a month's enforced quarantine. It proved worthwhile, as Argentine's Tokyo silver medallist, Carlos Moratorio, put up a performance worthy of the first world champion. Ireland, always a dashing and joyous participant in three-day events, achieved the team title at last, with its superb team of Eddie Boylan, Tom Brennan, Penny Moreton and Virginia Freeman-Jackson.

Ireland's first international event was the European championships, held at Punchestown in 1967. The organization was good and the hospitality generous, but the Argentinian technical delegate had thought it best to add an apron of gorse to the front of each steeplechase fence, with disastrous effect. Ireland's Eddie Boylan won the individual title with Durlas Eile, on which he had won Badminton two years earlier, and Britain carred away the team title.

Britain's star was in the ascendant once more, and by 1968 she was again in a position to send a team of experienced, successful riders on top-quality horses to the Olympic Games. The course, at unprecedented altitude in Mexico, was not a difficult one and was approved as such by Britain's technical delegate Laurence Rook. Halfway through the speed and endurance test the rain start to fall heavily, turning the course into a quagmire and the water jumps into torrents. Derek Allhusen on Lochinvar was safely round, but Jane Bullen's Our Nobby (the little horse that had won at Badminton in the spring) slipped and fell twice. It was left to Ben Jones on The Poacher and Richard Meade on Cornishman V to perform epic feats of valour to bring the team out on top. They took the gold medal and Allhusen the individual silver, behind France's J. Guyon on Pitou.

Reunited with his owner, Mary Gordon-Watson, Cornishman won the European individual championship at Haras-du-Pin the following year and Britain the team title, with what amounted to her 'second eleven', although it included Ben Jones on The Poacher. These two great horses (which both have the distinction of contributing to the British team's victory in five successful international championships or Olympic Games) figured in the team again in 1970, for the world championships at Punchestown, The Poacher ridden this time by Richard Meade.

An insubstantial fence constructed on the brink of a sharp drop caused a lot of trouble at Punchestown and collected much criticism, but the British team survived to win the team championship and Mary Gordon-Watson, on Cornishman, the individual.

Nobody was surprised when Britain won the European championships at Burghley the following summer, but the individual title went to something of an outsider, HRH Princess Anne on Doublet. This brilliant horse she was later to lose in most distressing circumstances, the horse breaking a hind leg during gentle exercise at home. Despite her success at Burghley, Princess Anne was considered insufficiently experienced for the Olympic Games at Munich in 1972. The British team took the gold medal on this occasion, and Richard Meade at last, after many years' sterling service in the team, won a well-deserved (and Britain's first) individual gold.

This moment of triumph marked the end of Britain's second cycle of international success. Germany won the team, and Russia the individual European title at Kiev in 1973, and the United States took the world championships by storm at Burghley in 1974. America's Bruce Davidson, on Irish Cap, won the individual title. Things perked up a bit for Britain at Luhmuhlen in 1975, when Lucinda Prior-Palmer won on Be Fair and Princess Anne was second on Goodwill, but the team championship slipped from the grasp of the first all-girl team, leaving the USSR to collect the laurels.

Both these leading ladies were in the British team for the Montreal Olympics in 1976, but Be Fair slipped a ligament on completing the speed and endurance test, Princess Anne was concussed in a fall (though she remounted and completed the event most creditably) and Hugh Thomas's horse broke down. Only Richard Meade, riding an inexperienced horse and competing now in his fourth Olympic Games, was able to finish well up the line, in fourth place. The much-fancied United States team, on the crest of the international wave, took a richly-deserved team gold medal, and also the individual gold and silver by Tad Coffin and Mike Plumb respectively.

For Britain then, three-day eventing started with a bang in 1949. Badminton started off a succession of preparatory one-day events and these have grown steadily in number, efficiency and popularity ever since. Controlled by the B.H.S.'s Combined Training Committee, the sport has taken firm root, with a packed programme of annual fixtures and a registry of hundreds of competitors, most of whom take part simply for fun, with no aspirations to ride for their country.

Popular though these events are with competitors, however, it is difficult for them to make enough money to be really self-sufficient, and commercial sponsors have provided invaluable support. Badminton and Burghley both have their sponsors, and the prize money they contribute at least helps the winners to meet the high cost of keeping a horse for these competitions. In 1969, the BHS had the good fortune to find a sponsor for its official horse trials in the Midland Bank, a partnership which has played an important part in consolidating the sport in Britain.

Britain is not the only country to have experienced a postwar boom in three-day eventing. Ireland's progress has been similar, as Irish competitors have ridden at Badminton from the start. Interest spread to Australia and then to New Zealand, which received great stimulus from Australia's gold medals in 1960.

The United States has had a very consistent Olympic record right from the start, and the programme of national fixtures there has grown enormously in the last couple of decades. Canada is a keen participant too. Mexico and Argentina have always had a strong equestrian tradition, and these four countries have been the mainstay of the Pan-American three-day event, held at regular intervals since 1955. Japan, too, has adopted the sport, though it has less opportunity than most for international competition.

In Europe, the three-day event tradition has continued to grow, notably in Sweden, Holland, Germany, Switzerland, Italy and France. There have been ups and downs (in Sweden, for instance, three-day events disappeared altogether for almost a decade, following a fatal accident), but the general development has been maintained. Eastern European countries have followed suit – particularly the USSR, Poland, Bulgaria and Romania.

Most countries have at least one international three-day event a year in addition to their domestic programme. These competitions, relieved of the importance and solemnity of an official championship, are extremely friendly, enjoyable affairs and do much to foster international goodwill. But the large-scale development of three-day events as a whole has had another result – one which would have gladdened the heart of Count von Rosen – and that is a steady improvement in the standard of fitness and training of the horses taking part and the general state of preparation among competitors.

Of course there is still plenty of room for improvement, but it must be a source of considerable satisfaction that, by continual comparison with the best horses and most successful riders over the best-built courses in all countries, and constant striving for success, standards are being set which are improving the lot of horses the world over. Horses are no longer a necessity of life to most people. but a source of pleasure. It is fitting that they should reap the benefit of a sport in which they play such a vital and gallant rôle.

THE HUNTING HORSE

The hunting horse is a type, not a breed, and there is no record of the first use of the horse as a means of transport in pursuing hounds. It is something that happened in the mists of pre-recorded history.

We must define hunting as the pursuit of a wild animal in its own environment by man employing a pack of hounds. The link between horse and hound is vital, since the speed and activity of the hound has always been the major influence in producing the hunting horse.

The ancient Chinese, Egyptian and Greek civilizations did much of their hunting on foot, although they used horses extensively in the chase as well as on the battlefield. The great horse master, Xenophon, born in 430 BC in Athens, made it clear in his classic book on equitation that basically the same priorities in stamina, fitness and obedience were required in the hunting horse then, as are still sought by the hunting fraternity of today.

The Roman writer Oppian, in the third century AD, described the points he would look for in buying a hunter-charger as follows: 'He must have size and substance and well-knit limbs; a small head carried high, with a neck arching like the plume on a helmet; forehead broad, thick curly forelock; eye clear and fiery, broad chest; and back with a double chine; a good full tail; muscular thighs; fine, clean legs, pastern sloping, hoof rising high, close grained and strong. These are the qualities prominent in Tuscan, Armenian, Achaean, and the famous Cappadocian horses; and such are the horses for hunting wild beasts or for use as chargers in war.'

Oppian referred to the need in hunting for 'an active horse accustomed to leap over stone fences and dykes', but for many centuries – certainly throughout medieval times – the hunting horse was not required to possess the jumping ability expected from the modern top-class quality hunter.

To be relevant, it is inevitable that any discussion of the hunting horse must be centred almost exclusively on Britain and Ireland. In both these countries organized hunting (providing the pattern for that practised in America, South Africa, Australia, New Zealand, India and elsewhere) has been a major equestrian activity for some 300 years and has exerted, in consequence, a corresponding influence on horse-breeding. Indeed, before the growth of competitive riding to its present level, an extension belonging only to the last quarter of a century, hunting was the principal horse sport and today it is still the one attracting the largest number of participants. As a result, established hunter breeding industries exist in Britain and Ireland but are not found in other countries where less emphasis is given to the sport.

Stag, boar and fallow buck were the main quarry for hounds in

Europe for centuries, and continued to be so long after William the Conqueror brought discipline to the chase. To pursue these, the hunting horse needed stamina for the long days in the great royal hunting grounds, of which the New Forest in Hampshire is the last surviving example, but there was little requirement for a horse capable of jumping vertical obstacles at speed in the hunting field until the latter half of the seventeenth century at last saw the fox becoming a more popular quarry.

The clearance of the great forests coupled with changes in farming methods, especially the enclosure of fields in the early eighteenth century, increased the emphasis on hunting the fox in the open, rather than pursuing the deer in the woodland. The great grazing grounds of Leicestershire allowed hounds to run fast in the open country, and the fox proved a worthy quarry in such a setting. In the late eighteenth century William Childe came to the Quorn country from Shropshire and is credited with introducing the art of riding 'to hounds' as opposed to 'after hounds'.

Now the hunting horse was required to gallop and jump fences and take ditches in his stride. He had to clear without hesitation the new 'oxer fence' – a hedge with a rail in front designed to keep young beef cattle from damaging the hedge. A double oxer, a hedge with timber rails standing on both sides, was a formidable obstacle indeed, and is still encountered in some areas in the hunting field, as well as in a more sophisticated form in show jumping courses.

As foxhunting gained strength, the hunting man in Leicestershire required far more quality in his horse and it became essential to use Thoroughbred sires in producing hunters. Not everyone approved of the trend. Hugo Meynell, Master of the Quorn, complained that after the young 'bloods' emulated 'Flying' Childe's methods 'he had not enjoyed a day's happiness'.

The rate at which Childe and his friends crossed country in pursuit of hounds was to be far exceeded in the nineteenth century, when huntsmen of the Leicestershire packs developed the art of providing 'the quick thing'. This was a very fast burst across grass and fences with the mounted field riding as close to hounds as their nerves, and their horses' ability, would allow.

In the early days of the nineteenth century the conditioning of hunters frequently fell far short of the new demands imposed by the increasingly popular sport of foxhunting. Charles James Apperley, who was the most celebrated hunting correspondent of the period, writing under the *nom de plume* Nimrod, advised: 'Do not trespass too far on the willing powers of your horses. Rather than insist upon their coming home, when showing signs of distress, let them remain at some village for the night, leaving a whipper-in in attendance. Hundreds of good hunters have been destroyed by the neglect of this mere act of humanity towards exhausted nature in a noble and willing animal'.

The practice was growing of taking out two hunters for a day's sport, particularly in the grass countries of Leicestershire, Rutland

and Northamptonshire. Frequently the hunting man would also use a 'covert hack' as well, riding this horse to the first covert to be drawn by hounds. There he would change to his first hunter, which would have been taken on ahead by the groom so as to be fit and fresh for the first run of the day.

The growing demands for suitable horses were immense, and provided impetus for enormous growth in all the ancillary activities such as growing corn and hay, horse doctoring and dealing, and making saddlery.

Nimrod had grand ideas, but he was a good reporter, and he estimated that a Master hunting hounds would need fourteen hunters to ride himself, and a further twelve for the use of whippers-in. Labour was cheap, but the price of really top-class hunters could be extremely high, as can be realized by translating several thousand guineas in the last century into today's money values.

Already Ireland was recognized as a source of superb hunters. The mild climate and abundant grass produced horses of bone and substance; as Nimrod said, 'It is owing to the practice of the young horses of Ireland scampering across the country in their colthood, that they are such good fencers as we find them, unless it be at timber, at which they have no practice.'

Ireland's importance as a producer of hunters is as strong now as then, but today the English hunting man finds it increasingly difficult to compete with buyers from continental Europe, the United States and even South Africa, who pay high prices for Irish horses as potential show jumpers and eventers.

At the top of the sport in the nineteenth century such colourful characters as Squire Osbaldeston and Thomas Assheton Smith were performing extraordinary feats of endurance and courage with their hunters. Yet the bottom of the hunter market was often appalling, both in the lack of quality of horses available, and in the difficulty of finding a sound one. Robert Surtees wrote amusingly, yet scathingly, of the tricks employed by horse dealers who found a new market of 'mugs' in the influx of newly-rich, middle class merchants and businessmen benefiting from the Industrial Revolution and seeking to gain status in the hunting field. This was obviously a gullible and readily exploited market.

The new demand for riding horses in the hunting field was such that nearly £7 million was spent abroad on importing horses into Britain in the ten years up to 1882. In 1885 the Hunters' Improvement and National Light Horse Breeding Society was founded to encourage breeding in Britain, and it continues to perform an invaluable service today. The Society distributes thousands of pounds each year in the form of premiums, or subsidies, to the owners of about sixty stallions selected at the Society's annual stallion show, held each spring at Newmarket.

The owner of each stallion awarded a premium receives a grant, and in addition there are a number of 'super premiums' receiving extra awards. Through these subsidies the stallions are made available to non-Thoroughbred brood mares at reduced fees. Fees for Thoroughbred mares are made by arrangement with the owner of the stallion concerned. The stallions, selected from regions throughout the country, are regularly and rigorously checked to ensure that they remain sound and therefore fit for their work.

It is impossible, however, to consider the hunting horse in isolation, for it was from the hunting field that steeplechasing, show jumping and horse trials evolved. The HIS scheme has therefore produced distinguished winners in National Hunt racing as well as other types of equestrian sports, and its basic influence on the quality of horses in the hunting field has doubtless been immensely beneficial.

The HIS summer show for mares and youngstock, held at Shrewsbury, is a wonderful shop window, displaying much that is best in modern hunter breeding. Ireland's great exhibition of hunters is in August at the famous Dublin Horse Show. This event is as much a fair as a show, for nearly every exhibited animal is available for buyers, who come from all over the world. In England the great county shows, and the Royal International and Horse of the Year Shows at Wembley in London, provide the stage for the show hunter classes. Despite increasing costs and much lower prize money than is available in show jumping, these classes are keenly contested.

Judging the ridden hunter classes in the main ring at say, the Royal at Stoneleigh, requires considerable aplomb as well as skill and experience from the judges. Their own performance in the saddle as they ride and assess each entry in the ring is as keenly noted as the quality of the animals on show. The judges who officiate at the wealth of in-hand and ridden classes throughout the summer season shows provide an immense service in helping to maintain standards. But the greatest boon of all to the hunter type is that it is still a genuine working horse for which attested performance is the priority. It is never just a question of 'how does he look?'; the more important query in the mind of a hunter judge is 'how does he move?'. Many a good-looking horse never gets into the front row of a hunter class because he does not gallop well.

The recent growth and popularity of the working hunter classes places the emphasis even more firmly on performance, and here the hunters are required to jump as well as work on the flat in front of the judges.

It is, however, the continuance of more than 245 packs of foxhounds in Britain and Ireland, plus nearly sixty harrier packs, and half a dozen each of staghounds and draghounds, that ensures more work and demand than ever before for the hunting horse. Foxhunting, in particular, has seen an immense boom in the postwar years and there are over thirty more packs of foxhounds in existence in England and Wales now than at the turn of the century. Hunts are better supported and more people are following hounds on horseback than ever before, in spite of the fact that the quality of cross-country riding available to the hunting field has deteriorated considerably in many areas. This is mainly attributable to modern farming's increasing reliance on arable land instead of grass, and the enormous increase of barbed wire in the traditional beef, dairying and sheep farming areas has been another blow to the mounted field.

The biggest problem in terms of the hunting horse in recent years has been in finding a suitable mount for the heavyweight man. He requires a seven-eighths bred horse with quality and substance; not only is this the hardest to come by, it is also the most expensive to purchase and maintain. Such a horse can fetch several thousand pounds nowadays as an untried youngster if it has real potential for show jumping or horse trials.

In the English and Irish hunting field clean-bred horses are still in a minority, but those people who are of the right weight, and possess the skill to ride Thoroughbreds out hunting, claim that no better hunter exists. The threequarter-bred and half-bred hunter is still heavily relied upon for adults in the United Kingdom and Ireland. The real weight-carrying cob is sadly a much rarer sight in the hunting field nowadays than at one time, but there is a considerable increase in middleweight riding horses which generally contain a large proportion of Thoroughbred blood. These are suitable mounts for many of the lady riders who nowadays often form the majority of the mounted followers in the hunting field, especially on weekdays.

The native pony breeds have had considerable influence on horses used in the English hunting field. Their inherent hardiness, toughness and agility are all traits required when following hounds in the extremely varied countries where hunting still flourishes. Galloping on the moors of the West Country and the north, traversing hilly tracks in Wales and the Border countries, scrambling over banks, or negotiating stone walls, all call for physical and mental qualities which can be well supplied by horses containing Welsh pony or cob blood.

The Connemara is another highly favoured foundation stock for producing excellent hunters, and the native ponies themselves have successfully introduced many an aspiring Nimrod to the hunting field in his youth. The modern riding pony containing Thoroughbred blood may perform brilliantly in the hunting field, but the native pony's sensible temperament, sure-footedness and instinctive knowledge of his own environment still make him the best choice for a child's first pony to be ridden after hounds. Indeed they are not exclusively for children – in Wales, and the West Country particularly, you will see many an adult enjoying his hunting on a pony. The Exmoor shepherd, on his sturdy little mount, his legs dangling by its sides, will see more of the sport than most followers when the Devon and Somerset Staghounds are running.

In France, where deer, hare and wild boar are still hunted, there are in general far fewer obstacles to be jumped in the hunting field than in the majority of English hunting countries. A blood horse, or nearly clean-bred horse, would be appropriate to follow staghounds, when the speed of the quarry and the stronger scent associated with deer decree many long, fast points throughout the day.

Foxhunting enjoys popularity as a sport in the United States, and the Thoroughbred horse is used far more widely in following hounds than in Britain. In Virginia and Maryland, particularly favoured for the sport, there is still plenty of grass, and the horses are mainly faced with timber fences, some of which are imposing in height and solidity. Americans who visit Britain usually find the hedges and ditches of the vale countries and High Leicestershire a most novel challenge.

Australians and New Zealanders often use Thoroughbreds in the hunting field, but again the nature of the terrain is a major factor. In New Zealand there are no foxes, and it is the harrier packs that are well supported. Visitors are frequently surprised and impressed by the ease with which New Zealand hunters habitually jump formidable barbed wire fences, five or six strands high.

Teaching horses to jump wire is a somewhat increasing trend in the English hunting field, but wire is still shunned by many riders. In Ireland the wide ditches of Co. Meath, and the banks and walls of such famous hunting countries as Limerick, Tipperary and Kilkenny, offer a special challenge to the hunting horse and his intrepid rider.

It is still considered advisable to buy Irish horses young if they are to hunt in England or elsewhere. The experienced Irish hunter tends to take his fences slowly, often from a trot or a walk. He will usually jump on to an obstacle rather than over it, which works brilliantly over Irish country, but woe betide the horse who takes off slowly and attempts to bank an English thorn hedge with a wide ditch on the landing side! Properly cut and laid hedges are rarer nowadays, and the modern hedge-cutting machine makes a hedge an even broader and more difficult obstacle for the hunter. The Blackmore Vale in Dorset, the Berkeley country in Gloucestershire, parts of Buckinghamshire and Northamptonshire, and some areas of Leicestershire, are among the countries offering the stiffest fences still tackled by the modern hunter.

The hunting horse is a miracle of evolution and survival; he is much in demand, and still performs a tough job in an extraordinary diversity of environments. And because he remains a true working animal, he has avoided the destructive fads and fancies which have ruined so many breeds of pet dogs.

THOROUGHBRED RACING

Europe

The 'founding fathers' of the Thoroughbred racehorse were three Eastern stallions imported into England: the Darley Arabian, the Byerley Turk and the Godolphin Barb. Every Thoroughbred in the world today is descended in direct male line from one of them.

The blaze-faced, prick-eared Darley Arabian was purchased in 1704 in Aleppo for James Darley by his merchant son. He had been bred by the renowned Anazeh horsemen living on the edge of the Syrian desert, and is said to have been splendidly conformed and to have had three white stockings. He became the paternal great-great-grandsire of the famous Eclipse.

The Byerley Turk was originally a cavalry charger; acquired by Captain Robert Byerley when fighting against the Turks in Hungary, he carried Byerley (then a colonel in charge of the Sixth Dragoon Guards under King William of Orange) into action in the Battle of the Boyne in 1690. When they returned to England, the Byerley Turk first went to stud in Co. Durham and then was sent to Yorkshire. He achieved lasting fame as the paternal grandsire of Herod.

The Godolphin Barb, which was bred in Morocco and given by the ruler of that country to King Louis XIV of France, was brought to England from Paris by Edward Coke. Legend has it that Coke discovered the stallion in the shafts of a cart in the streets of the French capital! When Coke died in 1733 he left the horse to a friend who in turn sold it to Lord Godolphin, who had inherited all of Coke's mares. The Godolphin Barb was the paternal grandsire of Matchem, the famous sire of winners of more than £150,000.

However, while the Darley Arabian, the Byerley Turk and the Godolphin Barb are the only male lines which have lasted until today in direct descent from sire to son, a number of other imported stallions have played important parts in the development of the Thoroughbred. Two of the best-remembered are the grey Alcock Arabian and the Leedes Arabian. Another famous horse was the Darcy White Turk, the sire of Hautboy, whose name appears all of nine times in the pedigree of Eclipse, while the Darley Arabian's name is listed only once.

Racing as an organized sport really got under way in England with the restoration of the Stuart monarchy in 1660. Charles II was a devotee of racing and a very accomplished race-rider himself. James I and Charles I had used the Suffolk village of Newmarket as a hunting box, but Charles II made it into the centre of racing. He would go to Newmarket for weeks at a time to see racing and to take part in races on the famous heath.

Queen Anne started racing at Ascot in 1711, and while she was on the throne nine Arabian, eight Barb and seven Turkoman stallions were imported. Playing a role of fundamental importance in the development of racing at this time was Tregonwell Frampton, known as 'the father of the English Turf'. He had been made Superviser of the Royal Racehorses at Newmarket by William of Orange, and he was paid £1000 a year to provide ten racehorses and ten lads to ride them. In those early days before the founding of the Jockey Club, Tregonwell Frampton's word on racing matters carried almost the weight of law.

The Jockey Club was founded twenty years after Frampton died, and the Duke of Cumberland, second son of George II, was the first member of the royal family to be elected to it. The Duke was commander of the army that defeated Bonnie Prince Charlie's Highlanders at the Battle of Culloden, and he was also one of the first great Thoroughbred breeders of history, for his stud produced both Herod and Eclipse.

Herod was foaled in 1758 and was one of the fastest racehorses of his time. At stud he sired the winners of more than £200,000, including Highflyer, a racehorse that was never beaten and was later purchased by Richard Tattersall, founder of the famous firm of bloodstock auctioneers of that name. Highflyer was a very successful sire, and when he died Tattersall had engraved on the stone above the horse's grave, 'Here lieth the perfect and beautiful symmetry of the much-lamented Highflyer, by whom and by his wonderful offspring the celebrated Tattersall acquired a noble fortune, but was not ashamed to admit it'.

In 1750 the Duke of Cumberland acquired a brown yearling colt called Marske, whose dam was a grand-daughter of the Darley Arabian. At stud Marske was at first not popular, and his chances of siring good stock were extremely restricted because of the poor quality of the mares to which he was put. However, eventually he was mated with a good mare named Spiletta, a grand-daughter of the Godolphin Barb, and she produced one of the greatest racehorses of all time. This was Eclipse, foaled on 1 April 1764, a day that was notable for an eclipse of the sun.

Eclipse first raced in May 1769, nearly four years after the death of his breeder. He won this first contest easily, and during the next two years he competed twenty-six times and was never beaten. When he went to stud Eclipse was also enormously successful – he sired 344 winners of more than £158,000 in stakes.

During the period that Herod and Eclipse were making history on the racecourse, important changes were occurring on the Turf, many of them detailed in the various Racing Calendars published by John Pound, William Fawconer, William Tutin and Newcastle solicitor James Weatherby. It was the Calendar produced by Weatherby, however, which won the day and became established as the authentic record of the English Turf.

Until the last thirty years of the eighteenth century horses were not usually raced until they were four or five years old. The inauguration of the July Stakes at Newmarket for two-year-olds in 1785 was therefore a momentous step, and races for youngsters of this age soon proliferated. One important proviso that was often included in the conditions for races for 2-year-olds at that time was that animals sired by Eclipse and Highflyer should carry an extra 1·4 kg (3 lb)!

The most far-reaching single event influencing the future of the English Turf was the founding of the Jockey Club, which came to wield tremendous power over the conduct of racing throughout the country. The Jockey Club originally met at a Pall Mall inn called the Star and Garter, and later the members gathered at The Corner, Hyde Park, where public relations-minded horse auctioneer Richard Tattersall put a room and a skilled chef at their disposal. The Jockey Club moved to its own premises in Newmarket in the 1750s.

Sir Charles Bunbury was the leading member of the Jockey Club during its early days. He was its President for more than forty years, during which time he was the owner of Diomed, the colt that won the first Derby; Eleanor, the first filly to win the Derby and the Oaks; and Smolensko, the first colt to win the Derby and the Two Thousand Guineas. In a stern age, Sir Charles Bunbury was remarkable in that he never allowed his jockeys or stable lads to use a whip on his horses because he believed that treatment of this kind would make them unruly and even vicious.

In 1779 Edward Stanley, the 12th Earl of Derby, and some friends organized a race at Epsom for three-year-old fillies. They named it after Lord Derby's Epsom home 'The Oaks', and it was so successful that the following summer they inaugurated a race for three-year-old colts, and called it the Derby.

The winner of the first Derby at Epsom was Sir Charles Bunbury's Diomed, a muscular chesnut which stood at Bunbury's stud for sixteen years following his notable victory. But he was not a success as a stallion in England, and at the advanced age of twenty he was sold for a low sum to an American breeder. In America he lived on until he was thirty, and also founded the first great line of American racehorses.

The Derby and the Oaks were in fact the second and third Classic races to be established. Earlier, in 1776, the St Leger had been organized at Doncaster for the first time by Colonel Anthony St Leger. The pattern of Britain's five Classic races was completed when the Two Thousand Guineas and the One Thousand Guineas were run for the first time at Newmarket in 1809 and 1814 respectively.

Meanwhile, the very active Jockey Club was taking great strides in making its authority felt in what had been a fairly anarchic and undoubtedly rather villainous racing world. Lord George Bentinck, often called 'the Napoleon of the Turf', followed Sir Charles Bunbury as formidable leader of the Club. Bentinck's father, the Duke of Portland, had won for the Jockey Club the legal right to warn undesirables off Newmarket Heath, and his son was active in introducing further innovations. He began the practice of parading the runners in the paddock before a race, along with that of numbering the horses. And it was Lord George Bentinck who began the system of starting races with a flag.

Following on Bentinck came another tremendously able 'Dictator of the Turf', Vice-Admiral the Hon. Henry James Rous, who virtually ran racing affairs from the middle of the nineteenth century until his death in 1877. Rous was the ultimate authority on the rules of racing, and in 1850 he published *The Laws and Practice of Horse Racing,* which detailed the history of the development of the Thoroughbred, the rules of racing, and his explanation and interpretation of them and the duties of the racecourse officials, along with actual details of a number of complicated racing cases.

In 1855 Admiral Rous became handicapper to the Jockey Club and was responsible for drawing up the 'Scale of Weight for Age'. His investigations and observations led him to declare that the Thoroughbred had made tremendous improvements as a breed during the previous century, and that the best racehorses of 1750 would have been beaten by the worst runners of 1850. Englishmen could indeed feel proud of the horse that their country had created.

But there was an unpleasant surprise in store for patriotic English racegoers – a decade after Rous had become handicapper the French horse Gladiateur won the English Triple Crown of Two Thousand Guineas, Derby and St Leger. This outstanding horse, which was owned by the son of one of Napoleon's generals, was promptly nicknamed the 'Avenger of Waterloo'!

Racing had started in France, which was to become one of the foremost racing countries in the world, when the French Jockey Club was founded in 1833 by an Englishman living in Paris, Lord Henry Seymour. He was encouraged by Ferdinand Philippe, Duc d'Orléans, the heir to the French throne. In 1837 the French equivalent of England's Derby, known as the Prix du Jockey Club, was run for the first time at the exquisite racecourse of Chantilly. Two decades later racing was started at Longchamp in the Bois de Boulogne – and just inside the entrance gates to the racecourse was placed a statue of the famous Gladiateur.

Twenty years after Gladiateur had stunned English racing enthusiasts with this sudden sweeping success, one of the greatest Thoroughbreds of all time appeared upon the English racing scene. This was St Simon, by Galopin from St Angela, and bred by Prince Batthyany. The striking colt was bought at the age of two years by the Duke of Portland for 1600 guineas after the Prince dropped dead at Newmarket just before the race for the Two Thousand Guineas. St Simon had not been entered for either the Derby or the St Leger, and he was not allowed to run in the Two Thousand Guineas of 1884 because his nomination had become void on the death of Prince Batthyany. But St Simon was to prove his great worth as a racehorse anyway.

He ran in ten races, including the Epsom Cup, Goodwood Cup and Ascot Gold Cup, and won them all effortlessly. His trainer, Matthew Dawson, who won the Derby with Thormanby, Kingcraft, Silvio, Melton, Ladas and Sir Visto, said of St Simon, 'I have trained only one smashing good horse in my life – St Simon'. Dawson went on to say that 'The extraordinary thing was that St Simon was as good at a furlong as he was at three miles, as distance never seemed to worry him.'

At stud St Simon was a phenomenal success: he headed the list of sires of winners in England for seven consecutive years, 1890 to 1896 inclusive, and again in 1900 and 1901. Ten of his sons and daughters won seventeen English Classics, and in 1900 his progeny won all five of the Classics – Diamond Jubilee won the Triple Crown of Two Thousand Guineas, Derby and St Leger, Winifreda won the One Thousand Guineas and La Roche took the Oaks. During a total of twenty-two years as a stallion, St Simon sired the winners of 571 races and £553,158.

Meanwhile, breeding theories were proliferating. The basic maxim right from the start had been 'breed the best to the best', and by and large this tenet has guided the development of the racehorse ever since. But there was plenty of room for imaginative schemes of all kinds. One of the most famous was formulated by the Australian Bruce Lowe, who towards the end of the nineteenth century listed forty-three tap-root mares of the breed in numerical order, based on

the number of direct descendants of each mare, through the female line, which had won the Derby, the Oaks and the St Leger up to that time. The number one was given to the family whose foundation mare had given rise to the most winners of these three English Classics among her descendants in female line when the system was compiled. Lowe then allotted the number two to the female family with the second-largest aggregate of winners of the three Classics, and so on down the line.

Modern knowledge of genetics has, however, shown how basically unsound Lowe's theory in fact was, and it hardly ever plays a part nowadays when breeders are working out the matings of their animals.

There were many other theories which captured the interest of Thoroughbred breeders at one time or another. Among them, Friedrich Becker's Theory of Female Influence postulated the conclusion that the factors being handed on in straight male line descent, when intensified by inbreeding, cause the sire line to degenerate, and Colonel J. Vuillier's System of Dosages was based on the analysis of a horse's pedigree to the twelfth generation, by which time all of 4096 ancestors had come under scrutiny! From his work Colonel Vuillier concluded that certain sires were desirable in a balanced 'mixture' in a pedigree to produce a top-class racehorse.

One of the most notable breeders and owners of the twentieth century in Europe, the Aga Khan, was so impressed by Vuillier's theory that he employed the Colonel as his manager and adviser, and certainly the Aga Khan had great success. He bought his first yearling in 1921, and three years later came up with his first Classic winner, Diophon, which captured the Two Thousand Guineas. Altogether, his famous racing colours of green with chocolate hoops were carried to victory in no less than thirty-six European Classics, including five English Derbys, six St Legers and six Irish Derbys.

The Epsom Derby of 1933, however, fell to the extremely popular English-bred Hyperion, measuring just 15·1½ hands on the day that he won the premier Classic by four lengths. Hyperion, by Gainsborough out of Selene, was bred and owned by the then Lord Derby, and ran in thirteen races, winning nine of them and being placed three times in a career that lasted three years. At two years he was fast enough to win the New Stakes at Royal Ascot, and the same year that he took the Derby he also won the St Leger.

Hyperion went on to become one of the most successful sires of this century. He was the leading sire of winners in England six times, and sired the winners of eleven English Classic races, including Derby winner Owen Tudor. Another of Hyperion's famous sons was Aureole, which won the King George VI and Queen Elizabeth Stakes and the Coronation Cup, was placed second in the Derby, and was leading sire in England in 1960 and 1961. Among Aureole's successful sons are Derby winner St Paddy, also a sire of note, and Saint Crespin III, winner of the Prix de l'Arc de Triomphe and another successful sire. Hyperion's great influence as a sire was, in fact, felt in just about every racing country in the world, with America no exception. There he sired the stallions Alibhai, Khaled and Heliopolis.

This century has also seen the incredible successes of the Italian breeder Federico Tesio, hailed by many as a genius. He bred two of the greatest racehorses and sires both of this century and of all time, Nearco and Ribot, as well as a host of other outstanding animals.

Nearco, by Pharos out of Nogara, was the unbeaten winner of fourteen races from five furlongs to a mile (1 to 1·6 km), including the testing Grand Prix de Paris. Tesio himself summed up the splendour of the horse he bred, trained and later sold to an English stud by writing, 'Beautifully balanced, of perfect size and great quality. Won all his fourteen races as soon as he was asked. Not a true stayer, though he won up to 3000 metres. He won these longer races by his superb class and brilliant speed.'

Nearco was twice leading sire of winners in England, and was in the list of the top ten sires for fifteen consecutive years, from 1942 to 1956 inclusive. He was the sire of two Derby winners, and another two Derby winners were from mares by Nearco. Interestingly, he carried four crosses of the fabulous St Simon in the first five generations of his pedigree. The Italian-bred, English-based stallion also had a profound influence on breeding in the United States; his son Nasrullah was leading sire in England once and in America five times, and is the world's leading sire of Stakes Winners, with 101 of them to his credit. Nasrullah's son Bold Ruler, sire of the 'super horse' and 1973 American Triple Crown-winner Secretariat, is the second leading sire of Stakes Winners. Significantly enough, too, the recent American-bred Epsom Derby winners Sir Ivor, Nijinsky, Mill Reef and Roberto are all male-line descendants of the truly great Nearco.

Federico Tesio's other phenomenal home-bred horse was Ribot, which won all sixteen of his races, including the Prix de l'Arc de Triomphe twice and the King George VI and Queen Elizabeth Stakes. The average winning margin in Ribot's races was six lengths, and when he was retired to stud at the age of four he had won more prize money in Europe than any other single Thoroughbred up to that time.

At stud Ribot had an equally brilliant career: he was leading sire in England in 1963, 1967 and 1968, and in the top five on the lists of leading sires in the USA, France and Italy. More than fifty of his progeny have won high-class races, and they include such famous animals as Ragusa, Ribocco, Ribero, Molvedo, Tom Rolfe, Graustark, Arts and Letters, Long Look and Romulus.

During recent years Europe has seen some outstanding racehorses; the beautiful Brigadier Gerard was hailed as one of the best horses bred and raced in England in this century, and he won seventeen races from eighteen starts, including the Two Thousand Guineas and the King George VI and Queen Elizabeth Stakes; Grundy in 1975 won the Epsom Derby, the Irish Sweeps Derby, the

King George VI and Queen Elizabeth Stakes, and the Irish Two
Thousand Guineas; and, during the last few years, the American-
bred fillies Dahlia and Allez France have added an extra element of
lustre and excitement to the European racing scene. Other recent
notable performers have been Mill Reef, Nijinsky and Sir Ivor.

America

During the last decade, American Thoroughbred breeding has risen
to the top of the international tree, and today the best American
bloodstock is the most sought-after in the world. Sir Ivor, Nijinsky,
Mill Reef, Roberto, Dahlia, Allez France, San San, Pistol Packer –
these are just some of the Thoroughbred stars that have come to
Europe from American pastures to win the biggest races that the
Old World has to offer.

Why have American racehorses had such resounding success
abroad in recent years? American breeders lay a great emphasis on
speed in the Thoroughbred, they have purchased the best foreign
bloodstock whenever possible, and they rigorously apply the
so-called 'racecourse test', meaning that American horses are raced
much more often and harder than their counterparts in Europe, and
therefore are asked to prove their soundness and toughness to a
much greater degree.

Sheer speed has been and still is the great American racing
passion. Of the races staged for three-year-olds and over in North
America, 56 per cent are held over distances of 6 furlongs (1·2 km)
or less, and 80 per cent are run over a mile (1·6 km) or less. But
speed is the inverse of stamina, and American breeders found that
their racehorses were badly lacking in staying power. They therefore
went to the British Isles, France, Italy and South America looking
for breeding stock that would rectify this deficiency.

The result today is that there is hardly an American-bred horse of
standing which does not contain some imported blood 'close up' in
its pedigree. During the 1970 racing season in North America, for
instance, 97·3 per cent of American-bred winners of stakes worth
$10,000 or more had imported ancestors within the first three
generations of their pedigree. And 73·2 per cent had imported blood
in the first two generations of their family tree. This obviously
means that the best so-called American-bred racehorses are not
'American' in the fullest sense of the word – foaled in America, they
are the product of a recent judicious mixing of American and
foreign bloodlines. The result is the combination of the scintillating
speed that thrills American racegoers plus enough stamina to
capture Europe's Classics.

For instance, Never Bend, the sire of the famous American-bred
Mill Reef, now standing as a stallion at Britain's National Stud,
never won a race of more than nine furlongs (1·8 km). And before
the appearance of his Prix de l'Arc de Triomphe-winning son, Never
Bend had not sired an animal which had won a race over more than
a mile and a quarter (2 km).

Even more surprising, Traffic, the sire of Rheffic, the 1971 winner of the French Derby (1½ miles or 2·4 km), himself never won a race of more than six and a half furlongs (1·3 km).

Another contrast between American and European racehorses is the number of times that they compete. Four of the greatest European-bred sires, for example, were St Simon, which raced ten times for ten victories, Hyperion, which ran in thirteen races, Nearco, which was unbeaten in fourteen races, and Ribot, which won all sixteen of his races.

The great American sire Bold Ruler, on the other hand, started all of thirty-three times for twenty-three victories, and was unplaced only four times in all these races. Bold Ruler's son Bold Commander, which sired the 1970 Kentucky Derby winner Dust Commander, ran in forty-one races between the ages of two and four for seven wins and eleven places.

But the racing record of the famous Stymie makes these numbers of starts almost pale into magnificance – before he finally went to stud at the age of six, Stymie had competed in all of 131 races!

The overseas successes of the best American-bred racehorses are directly reflected in terms of demand and prices paid at the select yearlings sales in the United States. At the 1975 Keeneland sale of select yearlings, for instance, foreign buyers, mainly Europeans, spent nearly $4,850,000 – more than 26 per cent of the sale gross.

Horse-racing was introduced to America, as was the Thoroughbred itself, by the first British colonists of the Maryland-Virginia 'tidewater country' in the early part of the seventeenth century. America's first horse races were staged in the short main streets of the burgeoning towns – later the race fans chopped narrow quarter-mile-long (400-metre) straight raceways in the woods and held their racing there. Towards the middle and end of the seventeenth century the rich planters of the South began to import some fine racehorses from England, and it was not long before racetracks suitable for them were being constructed. Nevertheless, the first formal racecourse was laid out in the North, at Long Island, New York, and was called Newmarket, in honour of Britain's racing centre.

By the time of the American War of Independence there was considerable breeding and racing of horses, and the racing Establishment boasted George Washington and Thomas Jefferson among its members. Once the war was over, racing soon got back into its stride. Between 1784 and 1798 four stallions were imported from England which had considerable success in America and founded highly successful lines. These sires were Medley, a neat, good-looking son of the famous Gimcrack; Shark, by Marske, the latter being the sire of the mighty Eclipse; Messenger, by Mambrino, the foundation stallion of the American Standardbred breed and a successful sire of gallopers as well; and Diomed, mentioned in the section on European racing, which had won the very first running of the Derby at Epsom, and which, after a long, undistinguished stud career in England, was to found an enduring line in America. One of his famous sons was Sir Archy, the greatest racehorse and sire that had been foaled in America up to that time.

American breeders still, however, resorted to England for new importations and brought in some excellent sires. One of the most successful was Glencoe, purchased in 1838 and for eight years the leading sire of winners in America. One of his most notable get was the filly Peytona, who won more races than any member of her sex to that time.

Early on, the gentlemanly South with its big houses, leisured life and tradition of fine horseflesh was the centre of racing and breeding, with Virginia and Maryland leading the way. However, the increasing wealth of the North, particularly New York, led to a growing interest in racing there, and this in turn sparked North-South rivalry in the racing of Thoroughbreds.

The first big clash came in 1823 when William Ransom Johnson, a Southerner, pitted Sir Archy's son Sir Henry against the Northern racer American Eclipse, which belonged to the New Yorker Cornelius van Ranst. American Eclipse won this contest, but in 1836 Johnson got his own back by racing his John Bascombe against the New Yorker's Post Boy. Six years later, though, Johnson got an unpleasant shock when his highly fancied Boston travelled north to be beaten by the New Jersey-bred mare Fashion.

Fashion, too, was defeated in turn, by Peytona in 1845, the last of

the great North-South contests before the more serious conflict
between North and South began. In the years preceding the
American Civil War, racing had become strongly established at
racetracks in New York, Baltimore, Chicago, Cincinnati, New
Orleans, Charleston and St Louis.

The holocaust of the Civil War meant the end of the old
Thoroughbred stud farms of the tidewater country, and Kentucky,
which had missed out on much of the wartime devastation and
where some of the old Virginia horse breeders had resettled, became
increasingly important. Racing, too, had suffered from the
hostilities, but as soon as the war finished the sport sprang back to
life with renewed vigour. In 1864, while the Civil War was still in
progress, Old Saratoga staged its first meeting, and in the decade
after the end of the conflict the major racetracks of Pimlico, at
Baltimore, the Fair Grounds at New Orleans, and Churchill Downs
at Louisville, were inaugurated. All these racetracks are still
functioning today, and Churchill Downs is now the home of the
world-famous Kentucky Derby.

Meanwhile, due to the intense pressure of certain religious groups
which disapproved of racing and betting, horse racing disappeared
from many of the Southern states where it had formerly flourished.

Some time after the end of the Civil War, the Americans
introduced the now-universal crouching jockey's seat, at first
derided in England as the 'monkey on a stick' seat. Its effectiveness
did not take long to be proved, however, with the outstanding
American jockeys Tod Sloan and Danny Maher as two of the
leaders in this race-riding revolution.

About this time, a number of coloured riders joined the top ranks
of American jockeys, the most successful being Isaac 'Ike' Murphy,
who won 44 per cent of the races in which he rode. But like
England's gifted Fred Archer, he did not live to enjoy the fruits of
the considerable sums he had earned, for he died at the early age of
thirty-seven, soon after he had retired from race-riding.

In the years following the end of the Civil War many of the most
important American races were first staged. In fact the war was still
being fought when The Travers, the oldest stakes event in North
America, was first held in 1864. The American Triple Crown races
came into being not long after: the Belmont in 1867, the Preakness
in 1873, and the Kentucky Derby in 1875.

Naturally, this upsurge in the popularity of racing meant that a
number of really outstanding Thoroughbreds were seen in action:
Ruthless, a very fast filly, won the first Belmont Stakes; Norfolk
was an unbeaten star; and Longfellow took part in some stirring
renewals of the old North-South racetrack clashes.

It was during this period, too, that some of the great lines of
American Thoroughbreds were firmly established by stallions of the
calibre of Hanover, Domino and Ben Brush.

By the close of the nineteenth century racing was flourishing in
the United States as never before. Many called it a 'golden age' for

American racing. But there was another side to it – of fixed races, doped runners, horses racing under names other than their own. The eventual result of these ever-increasing abuses, and the publicity they attracted when discovered, was a great public outcry against the whole sport. Much repressive anti-racing legislation was enacted, and by 1911 only two States, Maryland and Kentucky, still had horse racing. Many racehorse owners had to ship their animals to Canada or abroad, and American racing was in a perilous state.

Nevertheless, in 1908 in Kentucky the answer to American racing's plight had already been found. It was the brainchild of Matt Winn, who was then running Churchill Downs at Louisville, the home of the Kentucky Derby. The staging of the 1908 Derby had been threatened when a law was passed forbidding the continuation of trackside bookmaking – but Winn had a solution. He installed totalisator machines, brought over from France, which enabled the betting public to establish its own odds according to the various amounts bet on each horse in a race. Winn had, in fact, already tried out the machines on the Churchill Downs public without success, but now that there were no 'bookies' the pari-mutuel machines found instant public favour. The 1908 Kentucky Derby was saved – and so was racing in the United States.

The pari-mutuel machines provided the States with a straightforward way of taxing revenue from racing. When the bookmakers were operating trackside, it had been difficult to levy taxes on racing income, but with the machines giving a complete record of betting, it was obvious to the tax-gatherers that a regular percentage could be deducted from each betting pool in return for licensing racing – thus producing substantial revenues. Not only that, the machines made it more difficult for gamblers to pull off big coups, which had played an important part in bringing the sport of racing into such public disrepute.

As a result of the introduction of the pari-mutuels and the keen-eyed vigilance of the state racing commissions which were formed to police the sport, racing made a big comeback at major centres. Once again America was able to watch the racetrack exploits of such performers as the Triple Crown winners Sir Barton, Gallant Fox, Omaha, War Admiral, Whirlaway, Count Fleet, Assault and Citation. There was Regret, the only filly ever to capture the Kentucky Derby, and Zev, which beat Epsom Derby winner Papyrus in a much-heralded match race at Belmont Park. So many names of so many outstanding horses – Bold Ruler, Swaps, Nashua, Round Table, Native Dancer, Stymie, Tom Fool, Buckpasser, Damascus, Dr Fager, Kelso. . . .

But of them all – and there have been some truly great ones – two horses, both of a burnished chestnut colour, stand clear. They are Man o'War, fondly nicknamed 'Big Red', and Secretariat.

Man o'War was foaled in 1917 at a stud farm near Lexington, Kentucky. He was by Fair Play out of Mahubah, by Rock Sand, which had won England's Triple Crown in 1903. Sold as a yearling at Saratoga for $5000, Man o'War had a tremendously successful two-year-old season: out of ten starts he won nine races. In the race which he failed to win – by only half a length – the Sanford Memorial, his admirers claimed that his rider had him facing the wrong way at the start!

At the end of Man o'War's two-year-old season, the *Daily Racing Form* handicapper placed him at the top of the American two-year-olds of 1919 with a weight of 16·6 kg (136 lb) – 7·2 kg (16 lb) above the second animal on the handicap, Blazes. He grew into a massively splendid three-year-old, standing 16·2 hands high and weighing around 521·6 kg (1150 lb). He had a broad chest and a great amount of heart room.

Incredibly enough, Man o'War did not race in the Kentucky Derby, because his owner, Samuel D. Riddle, thought that the race asked too much of a three-year-old at the beginning of May. So the colt's first race at the age of three was in the Preakness, and he took this Classic easily by one and a half lengths. He went on to win the Withers Stakes of 1 mile (1·6 km) in New York in record time, and in the Belmont Stakes he passed the winning post twenty lengths ahead of the only other animal that had remained in the race.

After winning his next race, the Stuyvesant Handicap, Man o'War took part in what many regard as his most famous race: the Dwyer Stakes of nine furlongs, in which 'Big Red' faced John P. Grier, carrying 8·1 kg (18 lb) less. The two colts raced neck and neck until they turned into the stretch, when John P. Grier's jockey urged on his much smaller mount to surge past the huge Man o'War. As John P. Grier sprinted ahead, Man o'War's rider, Clarence Kummer, started to use his whip on the big chestnut, which lengthened out his stride in immediate response. Locked together again, the two colts flashed past the mile post in 1 minute 36 seconds, two-fifths of a second ahead of the track record. But the smaller horse had reached its peak, and Man o'War went on to win the race by a length and a half in the new American record time of 1 minute 49½ seconds.

During his almost unbelievable three-year-old career, Man o'War raced eleven times for eleven victories including, as well as those mentioned above, the Miller Stakes, the Travers, the Lawrence Realization, the Jockey Club Gold Cup and the Potomac Handicap.

Finally, in 1920, Man o'War ran in a match race against Sir Barton, the best three-year-old colt of the previous year, which had won the Kentucky Derby, the Preakness, the Belmont and the Withers. The match race was staged over ten furlongs at Windsor, in Ontario, Canada, and Man o'War won by seven lengths, breaking the track record by 6⅖ seconds. At the end of 1920, Man o'War's earnings had reached $249,465, a new American record.

At stud Man o'War also did very well, although many authorities think that because he was virtually a private stallion he did not cover nearly as many good mares as he would have done if he had been at public stud, and so his potential as a sire was never fully exploited. Nevertheless, he was America's leading sire for 1926, and was among the ten top broodmare sires for all of twenty-two years. He sired the 1937 Triple Crown winner, War Admiral, which in turn was leading American sire in 1945.

Among Man o'War's other distinguished progeny were War Relic, Clyde Van Dusen, Bateau, American Flag, Florence Nightingale, Crusader, Edith Cavell, Mars, Annapolis, Battleship and Scapa Flow.

The great Secretariat was foaled more than fifty years after Man o'War, in 1970, at the 2600-acre (1052-hectare) Meadow Stud near Doswell, Virginia. He was a splendid-looking foal from the moment of birth, and his breeding was superlative: by the great Bold Ruler out of Something Royal, a mare which had already produced Sir Gaylord, a top racehorse and highly successful sire (he sired the 1968 Epsom Derby winner, Sir Ivor).

Towards the end of his yearling year Secretariat went to veteran trainer Lucien Laurin to prepare for his future on the racetrack. In his first start, at two, the tall chestnut colt was heavily bumped into by another runner at the start of a maiden race, took time to get into his stride, and finished in fourth place.

But next time out Secretariat won a maiden race by six lengths, and then picked up an allowance race at Saratoga. His next contest was the Sanford, in which he defeated another good horse, Linda's Chief. Trainer Laurin's hopes were high, and they were justified as Secretariat swept all before him – the Hopeful by five lengths, the Futurity by two, the Laurel Futurity by eight and the Garden State by three and a half. He also won the Champagne Stakes by two lengths, but had bumped another horse during his drive to victory and was disqualified.

His final tally for his sparkling two-year-old season was seven wins and $456,404 from nine starts.

At three Secretariat quite simply became a legend. He won his first two races, then surprisingly finished only third in the Wood Memorial, held two weeks before the Kentucky Derby.

In the Derby he started slowly and was in last position for the first part of the race. Then he started to move forward – and kept going relentlessly until only Sham was left in front of him as they turned into the home stretch. Secretariat's rider Ron Turcotte flicked down his whip, and the giant chestnut flew past Sham into the lead and on to victory and a new Kentucky Derby record. In the second leg of the American Triple Crown, the Preakness, Secretariat soon took command and stayed in front to win by two and a half lengths. This time Turcotte never had to move his whip. Then the Belmont, the last of the Triple Crown races, and, at a mile and a half (1·6 km), the longest. The race was one to remember forever – Secretariat ran the first ten furlongs in an even faster time than he had galloped the record-breaking Kentucky Derby! At the finishing line he was an incredible thirty-one lengths clear, and he smashed the record for the Belmont by $2\frac{3}{5}$ seconds.

HARNESS RACING

In many parts of the world the phrase 'going to the races' – generally understood as meaning flat racing, steeplechasing or point-to-pointing – refers to 'trotting' races, for the sport of harness racing has grown in stature during the second half of the twentieth century, and in some countries equals flat racing in popularity.

Harness racing as we know it today originated and developed among the colonists of North America, although that does not mean there was no interest in trotting horses before that time, or in other countries. On the contrary, in England 'ambling palfreys' were popular as far back as Chaucer's day, and later there were many celebrated trotting matches involving horses such as the Norfolk Roadster, forerunner of the present-day Hackney.

Among the animals taken to North America by the early settlers were horses of Dutch extraction which showed a natural inclination to pace. Such horses were both ridden and driven, the type becoming known as the Narragansett pacer, taking its name from the local tribe of Indians. Initially, the increasingly popular sport of racing was centred around the Thoroughbred, but in 1788 America imported a horse which was to become the founding father of one of the world's most illustrious trotting breeds – the American Standardbred.

Ironically the horse was an English Thoroughbred and one which did not, himself, race at the trot. His name was Messenger, and he was a son of Mambrino, thus tracing back to the Darley Arabian. Messenger was mated to a great variety of mares, including descendants of the Narragansett pacers, and sired over 600 foals. His descendants showed a marked aptitude for fast trotting – one, Lady Suffolk, became the first horse to trot a mile (1600 m) in harness in $2\frac{1}{2}$ minutes – and infusions of Morgan and Clay blood (Clay horses were descendants of a Barb imported into the United States in 1820) further improved the trotting strain.

Hambletonian, the horse which was to have the most profound influence on the Standardbred, was foaled in 1849, and he inherited Messenger blood from both his sire and his dam. The latter, the Charles Kent Mare, was by Bellfounder who also counted among his ancestors the Norfolk Trotter, Old Shales. Hambletonian became a prolific sire of trotters, producing an incredible 1300 foals. Four of his sons, George Wilkes (sired in 1856), Dictator (1863), Happy Medium (1863) and Electioneer (1869), founded the male lines responsible for 99 per cent of trotters and pacers in the United States today, and it was Hambletonian's success that led to Messenger being designated the founder of the Standardbred.

The term Standardbred was not introduced until 1879, when the

National Association of Trotting Horse Breeders drew up a set of qualifications for the admission of horses into the American Trotting Register (first published in 1871). The original 'standard' was based on speed – the ability of a horse to cover a mile (1600 m) in 2½ minutes. Subsequently, this time was reduced to take into account the huge improvements achieved by harness racehorses, and today admission is based on breeding, not on performance.

The major breakthrough in harness racing performances came with the introduction of the purpose-built, lightweight sulky, a vehicle which was to enable horses to achieve much faster speeds. The racing sulky is actually an adaptation of a vehicle used in pre-American Revolution times for crossing particularly rough terrain unsuited to more conventional vehicles. It was a solid affair, with heavy wooden wheels, and was designed to carry one person, who rested his feet on the strong crossbars. High, two-wheeled sulkies were introduced into harness racing in the mid-nineteenth century and the sport began to take on a more organized air with the provision of racetracks – no doubt to the delight of pedestrians, who went in fear of their lives when impromptu races took place on the roads! The combination of racetracks and lighter vehicles, plus the continuing improvement of the breed, began to produce improvements in speeds. In 1892 came the advent of the low bike-wheel sulky with bent axles, shock absorbers and low-slung seat (for less wind resistance). The sub-two-minute mile was now in sight. In 1906 the great Dan Patch, pacing behind a galloping pacemaker, covered the mile (1600 m) in 1 minute 55 seconds, an improvement of 35 seconds over the original 'standard'.

Pacers are marginally faster than trotters, but both now achieve speeds approaching those of galloping Thoroughbreds. In the early days of harness racing, pacers were considered inferior to trotters, hence the title of the governing body of the sport in the United States – the United States Trotting Association. Since this body was founded in 1939, however, the pacer has come into his own and is now as popular as the trotter in many parts of the world, including the United States and Australasia. In Europe, however, the trotter is preferred, for many people still find the pace an 'unnatural' gait, objecting to the hobbles the horses wear. Some horses, however, show a natural tendency to pace at an early age and the hobbles are used to encourage, rather than to force, the gait. Once the horses are established in their preferred gait it is often the trotter who is the more inclined to break (that is, into a gallop). If this happens during a race, the driver must pull over to the outside of the track and get his horse back into trot before rejoining the field.

Harness racing in the United States today is an immensely popular and lucrative business, but it has not been a story of unbroken success. There was a time at the beginning of this century when the internal combustion engine was threatening to win men over entirely from the horse, and harness racing suffered a good deal through the enthusiasm shown for the motor-car. In addition, reports of scandalous goings-on within the sport – including the inevitable 'stipping' of horses by unscrupulous trainers or drivers in return for bribes from desperate punters – damaged it in the eyes of the public, and for a time it fell into disrepute.

It was the exploits of one horse that did much to re-awaken public interest. In the 1930s a Standardbred called Greyhound, one of the great trotters of all time, fired the imagination with his many outstanding performances. Among them was a new world trotting record of 1 minute 55¾ seconds for the mile (1600 m) – a record which remained unbeaten for thirty-one years. Public interest continued to grow, albeit slowly, until in 1940 New York's Roosevelt Raceway broke fresh ground by introducing night racing. This was the beginning of an upward trend which has continued ever since. Night racing was found to attract people who would like to go to the races but could not because of daytime jobs. It also avoided clashes with flat race meetings, thus allowing those with an interest in both sports to go flat racing in the afternoon and harness racing in the evening. In 1946, the Roosevelt Raceway made another significant contribution to the sport by introducing the first successful mobile starting gate. Time-wasting false starts were henceforward eliminated and the gate ensured an even start every time – always pleasing to the punter.

In the early days of the sport, harness races were usually run in heats, which demanded a good deal of stamina on the part of the horses. Nowadays, although a few races are still run on the old lines, it is more usual for them to follow the conventional flat racing pattern of one horse – one race. Consequently in breeding, the accent tends to be on speed, rather than on endurance and stamina.

Raceways usually consist of an 800 m (½ mile) oval track, wide enough to take about eight horses abreast. Fields must necessarily be smaller than in flat racing, owing to the degree of manoeuvrability required by each horse and sulky. Handicapping can be operated by placing the best horses on the outside of the field, the horse with the inside berth, of course, having the advantage of a slightly shorter distance to be covered. The average distance of races is 1600 m (1 mile). The sport is big business in the United States, and the government's revenue from betting is considerable. Top races, such as the $200,000 Roosevelt International Trot, attract entries from all over the world, and American-trained horses likewise compete in the top international races in Europe, such as France's Prix d'Amérique.

The American Standardbred has been exported to many parts of the world and has been used both to found new, and to upgrade old, trotting families. One of its notable successes has been in New Zealand and Australia, countries which were without horses until the first English settlers arrived in 1788. New Zealand has proved to be the ideal horse-raising country. Its equable climate, coupled with perfect grazing land, enables horses to be raised in entirely natural conditions, the foals running unrestricted with their dams until weaning time. Such conditions usually ensure that mares have a good milk supply and the foals are thus given an excellent start to life, developing good bone and sound constitutions.

New Zealand horses are well known for their stamina, and Thoroughbred flat racers have won many of Australia's top long-distance races, while New Zealand-bred jumpers are now doing well in National Hunt races in England. Not surprisingly, New Zealand has also produced a world-class strain of trotters. It began by importing American Standardbreds and crossing them with its own carefully selected hack mares. The New Zealand Standardbred resulted, and as the breed became established it began to be exported to Australia, where interest in harness racing soon spread. In more recent times, the New Zealand breeding industry has enjoyed something of a boom and horses have been exported both to the United States (thus completing the cycle) and to Europe. It was a New Zealand-bred horse, the mighty Cardigan Bay, which raced successfully at home and in the United States and which became the first harness horse to break the coveted million-dollar barrier in stakes money. Cardigan Bay paced the mile (1600 m) in under two minutes on several occasions.

In Europe, harness racing is popular in a number of countries and particularly in France, where a breed known as the French Trotter has been developed. The breed traces back to the beginning of the nineteenth century when Thoroughbreds, half-breds and Norfolk Roadsters were imported from England and crossed with Norman mares. The first important influences on the breed were Young Rattler, a Thoroughbred foaled in 1811, and another English Thoroughbred, The Heir of Linne, who was used for upgrading purposes some thirty years later. These two sires predominate in the pedigrees of the old Anglo-Norman trotters, and some 90 per cent of modern French Trotters trace back to five of their descendants: Conquerant, Lavater, Normand, Phaeton and Fuchsia. The French Trotter has not, however, escaped the influence of the American Standardbred, which has undoubtedly helped the French breed to achieve its present world class.

The first trotting races in France were held in Paris in 1806 and interest spread to the provinces in the following two or three decades. The first raceway appeared at Cherbourg in 1836 and the sport at once took on a more organized air. In 1864 the Société pour l'Amélioration du Cheval Français de Demi-Sang was founded (this title was changed to the Société d'Encouragement à l'Elevage du Cheval Français in 1949). It held its first race meetings at Caen, but later acquired a track at Vincennes. Around the turn of the century another society, Le Trotting Club de Paris, organized races at Neuilly-Levallois but these died out in 1901, and since the First World War the premier Parisian raceways have been those of Vincennes and Enghien. At Enghien, trotting races are held in

Horses are still herded in parts of America as they have always been. The word rodeo originally meant 'roundup', though its meaning has altered and is now used for the sporting contests which used to accompany the roundup itself.

OVERLEAF: The routine of the long cattle drives of the United States has hardly changed over the years. Cowboys and their mounts quietly guide the herds over all kinds of terrain, from open grassland to hilly woodland.

ARTHUR DAILEY
1971

conjunction with steeplechases, in the same way that many British racecourses cater for both flat racing and steeplechasing.

France is of particular interest in the world of trotting in that it is the last great stronghold of ridden races. At some meetings, ridden and driven races alternate on the race card and the rules permit horses to compete both in harness and under saddle. The most important international races are held at Vincennes, a unique raceway 2000 m (10 furlongs) round, and incorporating a downhill stretch at the start and an uphill finish. This is unusual in harness racing, which normally takes place on level ground. The most important races to be staged here are the Prix d'Amérique for driven horses (run over 2600 m (13 furlongs) in early January), and the premier race for ridden horses, the Prix de Cornulier, run over the same distance a week earlier. Although horses may compete in both races, it is as unusual for a trotter to excel in harness and under saddle as it is for an English Thoroughbred racehorse to be equally brilliant over steeplechase fences and hurdles. Winning both races is a feat which may be compared with Britain's elusive Cheltenham Gold Cup/Champion Hurdle double, and only four horses have succeeded in doing so. These are Venutar, Tidalium Pelo, Masina and, most recently, Bellino II. Other famous names in the annals of French trotting history include Uranie, three times winner of the Prix d'Amérique between the wars; Roquepine, who equalled this record in the sixties; and Une de Mai who, although she never managed to win the premier French race, was twice world champion in the United States.

As the French Trotter may be required to race under saddle, it tends to be a more upstanding, robust sort of horse than the American Standardbred, and the breeding policy has ensured that stamina has not been sacrificed to speed. The harness horse is marginally faster than the ridden horse, the difference being in the region of 4 seconds over a distance of 1 km (0·6 miles).

Trotting takes place throughout the year in France, but in Italy the chief races are held in the spring. Naples and Milan are the main centres. The sport is also popular in Germany, particularly in Hamburg, Munich and Berlin, the leading German race being the Grosser Preis von Hamburg. Holland, Denmark, Austria and Romania all have raceways, while in Belgium ridden, as well as driven, races are still held. Outside France harness racing in Europe probably has its biggest following in Scandinavia and the Soviet Union. In fact, prior to the advent of the American Standardbred, the USSR could boast the best trotting horse in the world – the Orlov Trotter. Trotting was very popular in Russia in pre-revolutionary times, and the Orlov was developed with racing in mind. The name comes from Count Orlov, a Russian nobleman who lived from 1737 to 1808 and who, apart from his military and political activities (he is said to have been the murderer of Tsar Peter III), became interested in breeding horses. He combined English Thoroughbred, Arab, Dutch, Danish and Mecklenburg

A sheep farmer with his wagon droving sheep in New South Wales; sheep as well as cattle are important to the Australian economy.

PREVIOUS PAGE: Cattle in the Australian outback need to be herded in the same way as their counterparts in North America, and horses are very much part of the everyday scene on the stations.

blood to produce the Orlov Trotter. At the beginning of this
century, Count Orlov's stud was acquired by the state and named
the Khrenovsky National Stud, and in 1975 the Orlov Trotter's
birthplace celebrated its 200th anniversary. The Orlov's supremacy
may have been toppled by the Standardbred, but trotting still
flourishes in the USSR and some admixtures of American blood
have helped to improve the Orlov's performances. The leading races
take place in Moscow's famous Hippodrome.

In Britain the story is somewhat different. The Thoroughbred has
long dominated racing, and although there are a few harness
raceways the sport has never become popular in a big way. It is
difficult to assess the reasons for this. From the public's point of
view perhaps there has always been sufficient racing to cater for
them; certainly British steeplechasing occupies a unique position in
the world and no other country has a sport which can compare with
Britain's varied and well-organized 'Winter Game'. In other
countries, where Thoroughbreds are raced chiefly on the flat,
harness racing acts as a nice foil, but it may be that National Hunt
racing renders such a foil unnecessary in Britain. British racing is
also run on rather different lines from that of other countries.
Instead of being centralized, as it is, for instance, in the United
States and France, racing takes place on some 60 widely spread
courses in England and Scotland alone, and many of these have
facilities for both flat and National Hunt racing. Racing enthusiasts
in most parts of the country thus have easy access to a number of
courses.

However that may be, the Englishman's enthusiasm for the old
Yorkshire and Norfolk trotting horses certainly dwindled, and today
harness racing attracts only a relatively small following, being
confined mainly to the Midlands and north of England and to north
Wales. The governing body is the National Harness Racing Club of
Great Britain, and the sport has its headquarters at the Chasewater
Raceway in Staffordshire, a splendid modern course based on its
American counterparts, with an 'all-weather' track, floodlights, and
comfortable stands. The Chasewater track is an exception, however,
and most British harness race meetings cannot boast such good
facilities. The horses that compete are mainly American and
Continental imports, although some trotters are being bred in
Britain, notably at Lord Langford's stud in North Wales.

Lord Langford, who was a leading light in the sixties in bringing
a degree of organization and uniformity to the sport in this country,
used a New Zealand-bred foundation mare at his stud. The
performances of British horses do not as yet compare with those of
American or French horses, and it would probably take a
considerable expansion in the sport to produce the necessary
improvement. It seems unlikely that such an expansion will take
place in the near future; but it is equally unlikely that the
immensely keen trotting enthusiasts will allow the sport to die out
completely in Great Britain.

DRIVING – THE FOURTH DISCIPLINE

In 1966 HRH The Prince Philip, Duke of Edinburgh, President of the International Equestrian Federation, visited the Aachen Horse Show where he saw driving competitions for teams and pairs of horses. This first gave him the idea of formulating standardized international rules for driving.

In 1969 he asked Col. Sir Michael Ansell, the British representative of the FEI Bureau, to draft rules. After an almost all-night session at his home in Somerset, described in his book *Soldier On*, a first draft was produced by Col. Sir Mike with the aid of Mr Frank Haydon and his secretary. A series of meetings was held on the Continent during the summer of 1969 to which representatives were invited from any country with an interest in establishing international driving competitions. The first of these meetings was at Aachen, chaired by Col. Sir Mike with M. Menten de Horne and M. Michels from the headquarters of the FEI in Brussels, and representatives from Germany, Switzerland, Poland, Holland and Hungary.

Later meetings were held in Berne and Brussels, and among those present were Dr Lehrner from the Piber Stud in Austria, Mr Bernard Mills from Great Britain, American enthusiast Mr Philip B. Hofmann, and the Canadian, Mr Jack Pemberton. The draft was discussed at length at these gatherings before being presented to the FEI Bureau for approval in December 1969. The rules were ratified by the Bureau and brought into use in 1970.

Great Britain took the next step, when the Committee of the Royal Windsor Horse Show decided to hold a national competition for teams and pairs, using the new rules. Nine competitors took part, six teams and three pairs, including Col. John Miller with a team owned by the Queen. The next move was the staging of an international event for four-in-hands at Lucerne in conjunction with CHIO (Concours Hippiques International Officiel) in May 1970. This was organized by Herr Jakob Ruckstuhl of Switzerland – who had been in at the planning meetings the previous year – and Col. Sir Mike was the technical delegate. Of eighteen entries received, only two were absent and six European nations were represented.

In 1971, the Hungarians offered to hold the first European championships at Budapest. In 1972 – Olympic year – it was decided to stage the first world championships in Germany, although driving was not an Olympic sport – and the town of Munster was chosen as the venue. Since then there have been European and world driving championships in alternate years. 1973 saw the second European championships at Windsor, England, and in 1974 the second world championships were held at Frauenfeld,

Switzerland. Poland was host for the 1975 championships and in 1976 world championships took place in Holland. Apart from these major international fixtures, competitions have been held in Great Britain, Germany, Holland, Switzerland, Poland, Hungary and elsewhere in Europe, as well as more recently in the United States.

The Rules

The first rules were based on those laid down for the three-day event, and they have gradually been developed and amended to suit the needs of a driving event. However, like ridden eventing, the competition is divided into three sections, although the first is subdivided further – into presentation and dressage, known as competition A; competition B, the cross-country marathon; and competition C, obstacle driving.

The purpose of 'presentation' is to judge the turnout, cleanliness, general condition and impression of the horses, driver and grooms, and harness and vehicle. Teams are judged at the halt, and a maximum of fifty marks is awarded by each judge. Marks are added together and divided by the number of judges and then taken away from the maximum to give a score in penalties.

A similar system is used in scoring the dressage, which has a maximum of 150 marks. As in ridden dressage, the aims are to judge the freedom, regularity, harmony, impulsion, suppleness, lightness, and ease of movement of the horses, but in addition they are judged as a team, not individually. The whip is also judged on his style of driving, accuracy and his command of his team. The dressage arena is 100 × 40 m, with the standard lettering used in an international ridden dressage arena. Three tests are currently recognized for international competition – Elementary, Intermediate and Advanced, but other tests are produced by various countries for use nationally.

The tests include halt, walk, trot (working, collected and extended) and the rein back, and involve changes of direction, loops, circles and serpentines. Particular attention is paid to the execution of transitions. The canter is not used; indeed the only time canter or gallop is seen during the entire competition is at given points on the marathon and perhaps in the obstacle driving.

Ideally the marathon should be the most severe of the three tests in a combined event. For this reason the marathon rules have perhaps changed the most since the early days of the competition. Formerly there were four sections, namely A, trot, B, walk, C, fast trot and D, trot. Section C, although still limited to trotting, was performed at a higher speed and there were no hazards. The scoring system allowed for bonus points to be awarded for the trot sections, with a quarter bonus point for each period of 15 seconds less than the set time for sections A and D, and one bonus for each period of 15 seconds less in the fast trotting section C, up to a maximum of five minutes.

As experience was gained the rules were changed to make the

marathon more testing. It was lengthened to include a second walk section after the fast trot section, so that there were now five in all. Artificial and natural obstacles were introduced, including water crossings, narrow awkward turnings such as gateways, or a weaving track through a group of trees. Artificial obstacles may be built from timber fencing or straw bales, for example, to make a serpentine, tight circle or series of sharp turns. Natural inclines are incorporated, if possible, to make the obstacle more testing. In section C a number of obstacles now have to be included, each with its own penalty zone. Within the zones pace is not stipulated and competitors may either 'spring' their horses – that is, put them into canter or gallop – or alternatively they may walk if the difficulty of the obstacle makes this wise. Additional penalties are awarded for such things as putting down the whip, grooms or passengers dismounting, leaving the zone before completing the obstacle, disconnecting one or more traces in order to continue or, indeed, turning over a vehicle! The driver may well decide to drive out of the penalty zone in order to get an easier or better approach to a tricky part of the obstacle, and for this he will not be eliminated, although fairly heavy penalties are awarded.

The bonus points system has also been dropped and a maximum and minimum time is set for each trot section. Penalties are given for being either too early or too late in the section – the latter being twice as severe as those for being early. The 'free' time – that between the time allowed and the minimum – is two minutes for sections A and E but only one minute for the fast section. These rules have meant that accurate judgement of timing is essential. It is not enough simply to drive clear round the obstacles, although with today's sophisticated courses this is difficult enough. Indeed, it is interesting to note how few clear rounds there have been in recent championship events compared with the earlier ones, despite the natural improvement of the competitors.

The marathon course may be anything from 24 to 32 km (14 to 20 miles) long; the championship courses are even longer – up to 42 km (25 miles). It is impossible for the jury to see every part of all competitors' performances, and a referee therefore travels on each carriage to watch for any transgressions, awarding penalties accordingly. For example, competitors are penalized for doing other than the pace laid down for each section – except in the penalty zones. In addition the referee must report back any deviations from the course. Because it is difficult to ensure that all referees judge to exactly the same standard, they are briefed very carefully before the event, and are also responsible to the jury, which is at liberty to uphold or adjust the penalties awarded by the referee.

Obstacle judges, too, are responsible to the jury. Their responsibility lies only within the penalty zone of their obstacle, and in any cases of doubt the jury has the final word.

Penalties for the marathon are added to those for presentation and dressage, and the results so far determine the order of start for the third and final section, the obstacle driving. In a combined competition, such as a championship or three-day event, the obstacle driving is judged as a fault competition. Here again, because of the analogy with ridden horse trials, the scoring system was transposed and four penalties were awarded for a knock down, three for the first disobedience, six for the second and elimination at the third. Results of some early competitions showed that these penalties did not necessarily give a fair overall result. A competitor knocking down four obstacles would only add sixteen penalties to his total, making the relative value of the competition too generous. The necessary amendments were therefore made and ten penalties are now awarded for each knock down.

The obstacle driving takes place in an arena and competitors are asked to drive a course of some sixteen to twenty varying obstacles marked by pairs of cones, which are placed only fractionally wider apart than the track width of the competing vehicle. Accurate driving is essential; a fault can mean the difference between first place and no place at all in the final reckoning. There is a time allowed of 200 m per minute to add to the whip's difficulties, and this in itself is not easily achieved unless the course is designed to allow for a flowing round. The course may include circles, figures-of-eight, L-shaped bends, a bridge and perhaps a watersplash, which is always popular with spectators, particularly if there is a run-off against the clock. Although this does not count towards the final placings in the combined competition, there is often a special award for each competition and in the obstacle driving this is decided by running off those with clear rounds against the clock.

Under the original rules, points were awarded for the placing in each of the three competitions, instead of adding together the penalties gained as is the system now. There was a system of relative values, and competitions were scored in the ratio of dressage $\times 2$, marathon $\times 3$ and obstacle driving $\times 2$. This was later changed, and presentation was also scored separately, giving a ratio 1:3:4:2. Thus the winner of presentation would score one point, the winner of dressage three, while second in the marathon would gain eight and third in the obstacle driving, six. Points for each competition were added and the winner would be the competitor with the lowest score.

Happily this complicated method of obtaining a result has since been replaced by a system in which penalties only are involved in the scoring of each competition, and these are totalled to give a result.

The rules published by the FEI are laid down for teams of four horses, but within these rules provision is made for competitions for singles, pairs and also tandems. Britain is one of the countries which has introduced competitions for these other categories, and for ponies under 14·2 hands. At Windsor in 1976 the first international competition for pairs of horses was held, as well as the well-established team competition. Where categories are introduced other than horse teams, certain adaptations have to be made to the published rules.

The Championships

After the success of the competitions held at Lucerne, Windsor and Arnhem in 1970, the Hungarians offered to hold European championships at Budapest in 1971. Sixteen teams from seven nations were present at the event, which was held in August as part of the Hungarian EXPO – the World Exhibition of Hunting. Although there was no separate presentation phase in the competition rules at this time, there was a special directive to all competitors to wear the traditional national dress – or uniform – and harness of their own countries. This led to the pageantry and high standard of presentation which is prevalent today.

HRH The Prince Philip was a visitor to the event in Budapest, and was escorted on horseback during the competitions by Melinda Fulop, champion of dressage in Hungary. Her brother, Sandor Fulop, Imre Abonyi and Joseph Papp were the three entrants from the host nation and finished in the first three places, to take the team and individual titles. West Germany sent Franz Lage, W. Sirrenberg and Fred Freund, and took second place in the team event while Great Britain, represented by Col. John Miller and Douglas Nicholson, was third. Then, as now, the team championship was decided by adding the scores of the best two competitors from each nation. Results of this first major international event gave promise of the strength of competition to come from these nations in the future.

1972 saw the continued expansion of this new equestrian sport, and Germany offered to hold world championships at Munster in May.

Following shortly after the British annual competition at Windsor, Munster had nineteen entries for the championships. Among the entries was Mr Philip Hofmann of the United States, who went on from England to compete. Sadly, however, Mr Hofmann, whose participation would have truly justified the title 'world' for the event – all other competitors being from Europe as in the past – was unable to compete owing to some difficulty at the border, which caused his horses to be forbidden entry into the country.

Together with the British teams, the Hungarian, Polish and Yugoslav teams travelled on from Windsor, and they were joined in Germany by teams from Switzerland, the Netherlands and the host country. In addition there were two more teams each from Poland and Hungary to join those who had visited Britain, so that there were six nations competing for the team title, with three competitors each. Yugoslavia also had one individual competitor – Bozo Prpic.

The Munster event was the final occasion when the original complicated points system was used to obtain a result; indeed, after 1972 there were many rule changes which brought the competition to something like it is today. The obstacle driving course for the final day's competition was so twisted and long that not one driver achieved a perfect round. The best performance was by Georg Baur of Germany, and he was the only one to finish this phase with a score in single figures. The weather was so bad on this final day that the competition had to be held up more than once.

Fortunately conditions for the previous day's marathon were much better, although there was a high wind. The marathon was completed without fault by five competitors; Dubey from Switzerland, who thereby maintained his lead after two days; Miller and Nicholson from Great Britain; Abonyi from Hungary – the reigning European champion; and the German competitor, Lage. It was this marathon event that first illustrated the need for very accurate timing, unlike previous competitions, when a rather happy-go-lucky attitude had prevailed. The bonus points system had been abandoned and now it was necessary to be most careful about timing, as penalties were awarded for being too fast as well as for being too slow.

In addition to the world championship event, there was a Grand Prix event with thirty-eight competitors taking part, thirty-two of whom were from Germany. This was run on the general lines of the FEI Rules for Driving, but the marathon was shorter and there was an additional phase – a timed walk competition. Winner of the Grand Prix was Germany's Emil-Bernhard Jung, who has since been to many international events at home and abroad.

Once again, Prince Philip was present at the championships and on the final day of the show there was a grand parade with at least eighty equipages taking part. Prince Philip rode beside the winner, Auguste Dubey, through the town, after presenting him with the winner's sash at the stadium. The Idee Kaffee trophy, an ornate gold model of a coach and horses, was presented to the triumphant British team by the show organizer, Herr Eric Greiss.

Great Britain was given the opportunity of organizing the second European driving championships in 1973. It was decided to hold the event in conjunction with the Royal Windsor Horse Show in May, where an international four-in-hand driving competition had been staged for the last three years. The Windsor organizers made use of their wide experience to produce a smooth-running competition in which twenty-four competitors took part. There were five national teams from Germany, Hungary, the Netherlands, Switzerland and Great Britain. Poland, like Yugoslavia, sent only one competitor on this occasion. Besides the three team members there were seven individuals from the home nation, making a total of ten British teams, a clear indication of the fast-growing popularity of the sport in Britain.

The presentation and dressage phase took place on the first day of the competition; at the end of the day world champion Auguste Dubey stood equal first with Col. Miller with only twenty-four penalties, having gained only nineteen penalties in the dressage test out of a possible 140. An excellent marathon course had been designed in Windsor Great Park by Windsor's regular course builder, Col. Charles Adderley, and no competitor completed it without penalty. Dubey came first in the marathon with twenty-two penalties to add to his overnight score, putting him in a very strong position to win his second title. Second was his team-mate, Robert Doudin, so in addition Switzerland looked set to take the team title.

Finishing third in the marathon, Britain's Douglas Nicholson looked likely to finish in the third medal position, and this was indeed the case after the obstacle driving on the final day. Switzerland predictably took the team gold, with West Germany in the silver medal position. Prince Philip finished second in the obstacle driving after a timed run-off among those who had gone clear in the first round. This was his first appearance in an international event, and in fact only his second full competition ever. This royal participation in the sport has played a large part on putting it on the map.

With international driving now firmly established in the calendar, the fourth major international – the second world driving championships – were planned to take place in Frauenfeld, Switzerland in August 1974. The change from the spring to the end of the summer for this fixture was welcomed, as in previous years it had been necessary to select a team to go to the championships before the season was truly under way.

The Swiss organizing committee, under Herr Heinrich Jung, put a
lot of thought and time into the planning of this event, which was
held on the racecourse at Frauenfeld in northern Switzerland, near
Lake Konstanz. There were a record thirty-five entries, and for the
first time in a championship event Denmark, Sweden and the
United States were represented. Czechoslovakia also returned to the
fray.

Mr Philip Hofmann, whose hopes were thwarted two years
previously in Munster, came to Frauenfeld, having spent the season
in England competing at all the national events in that country. Mr
Benny Olsen from Denmark and Col. Bengt Blomquist from
Sweden had also started the season by appearing at Windsor, where
Olsen finished a very creditable fifth.

Auguste Dubey was defending his individual world title, and the
British their team crown. However, Dubey was dogged with bad
luck; losing the services of two of his horses and wishing to
conserve his dressage specialist for the higher events, he started the
marathon with a scratch team of reserve horses. Nevertheless, he
managed to finish the competition in the top half of the field.

By now the points system of scoring had been replaced by a
straightforward penalty system and the multiplication factor had
been completely abandoned. Nevertheless, there were still some
problems, particularly on the marathon. The rules, as they then
stood, forbade any reining back within the penalty zones and eleven
out of thirteen eliminations were caused because of this rule. Since
then the rule has been changed and now allows freedom of movement and pace in the penalty zone, permitting the whip to exercise
his skill in a coachman-like way.

The terrain was used to effect by the course designer to produce a
marathon course that was truly world championship class, with a
rise of 250 m (800 ft) during the first third of the route. The tough
fast trotting section, put at the end of the course, included three
serpentines or similar, with two mountain streams used as water
crossings.

British competitor Jack Collinson misjudged one of the tree
obstacles and broke a wheel. Not despairing, his quick-witted
groom jumped down and broke the spokes away from the hub and
axle so that they could continue on three wheels. They completed a
further 4 km (2½ miles), including a water hazard, to finish the
course.

Among those eliminated was joint overnight leader, Abonyi,
while his fellow-countryman Fulop completed an immaculate clear
round. The third phase had a considerable effect on the final results
on this occasion, none of the leading six getting a clear round.
Fulop managed to maintain his lead, while twenty-year-old
Christian Iseli, an individual competitor for Switzerland, moved up
to second place from fourth, and Britain's George Bowman went up
from sixth into the bronze medal position. Although Sir John
Miller dropped seven places in the final reckoning his score,

together with Bowman's, was enough to secure Great Britain its second world team championship.

The third European driving championships were held at the Polish seaside resort of Sopot, between Gdynia and Gdansk on the Baltic coast. In 1973 a small national competition had been staged at Sopot, so here again the organization for the championships was very smooth. Poland has always been one of the countries to the fore in driving, Czeslaw Matlawski being a member of the FEI Driving Commission and one of those who attended the formulative meetings in 1969. The highest placed Polish competitor in this event was Tadeusz Czerminski, a member of the Polish Driving Commission driving a team from the Rzeczena Stud. Zygmunt Szymoniak, another Polish competitor, had already represented his country abroad on numerous occasions. These two came equal fourth and sixth in the championships, and it was only the might of neighbouring Hungary which robbed them of their first gold medal. Once again the first three places were filled by Hungarians.

The marathon course was unlike any previous championship course. Not only did competitors have to contend with regular motor traffic on the town sections, but they also had the distractions of the holiday-makers on the beach. The first part of the route took them from the racecourse, through part of the town to the beach, and thence along the sandy shoreline, into the sea and under the town pier.

Eng. A. Orlos, the course designer, took competitors along the main thoroughfare towards Danzig in order to get them to the mountainous woodland above Sopot for the fast section. His obstacles, almost all using trees, were very long and twisty, longer in fact than the rules permit in some cases, but were allowed to remain so by the technical delegate whose duty it is to pass the course. The gradients within the penalty zones were steep, tackled more easily by the shorter-coupled horses such as the Lipizzaners and Hungarians, than by the bigger breeds like the Oldenburgs.

Because it held both the European and world individual titles, Hungary had the right to stage the championships in 1976, but she opted not to do so. Instead Holland put in a bid to the FEI and became the venue for the third world driving championships. They were held at the royal palace of Het Loo at Apeldoorn, organized by the Dutch Equestrian Federation, and opened by Princess Margriet of the Netherlands. Three new nations took part – namely France, Denmark and Belgium. Hungary continued supreme, taking the team and individual gold, with Germany in second place (their highest placing in major international competition to date).

Permission was given for the fast section to come at the end of the marathon, and although it was very tough and longer than ever before, nine of the thirty-three competitors finished with less than 20 penalties. Two clear rounds were achieved, by Emil-Bernhard Jung (Germany) the eventual silver medallist, and George Bowman of Great Britain, who had acquitted himself so well in Switzerland two years before. Imre Abonyi, that master of the art of cross-country driving, was given one penalty on the course, but his clear round on the third day was enough to make him once again the winner by two points from Jung and Poland's Waliszewski, who took the bronze.

Development

Even before the introduction of international rules, driving for pleasure had been growing in popularity over the previous fifty years on both sides of the Atlantic. Driving competitions were held in Europe, the best known probably being the Aachen Show and the Hamburg Driving Derby in Germany. The Hamburg Derby consisted of a series of competitions for teams and pairs (the pairs being put together to form teams) and points were awarded for each contest. Teams from other nations competed, but the competitions were under German rules. The organizing committee of the Aachen Show are now considering bringing their competitions within the FEI rules, although at present probably without a marathon because of the lack of facilities for a course.

Although Germany has never won a major championship, she has a wealth of expert whips and has been represented abroad by eight or more different people. She is undoubtedly one of the leading driving nations, having the famous names of von Achenbach, founder of the elegant style of driving in use so widely today, and Max Pape, the great present-day master of the Achenbach school.

Supreme in four-in-hand driving at the present time, the Hungarians, too, are represented by many outstanding drivers. Like most of the Eastern European nations, their competing teams come from the State studs. Hungary holds a series of national competitions for teams each year, including those at Melykut and Apajpusztas, and the national championship is decided on a cumulative points system. Hungarians were invited, along with Czechoslovakian and East German competitors, to the Polish event at Ksiaz following the European championships at Sopot in 1975.

Poland, whose equestrian prowess is famed, plans to expand its driving activities still further. Competitions have been held in Poland since 1969 for pairs and teams, and the standards have improved over the years as the FEI rules have developed. It holds national championships at Plekrity, one of the State studs, and most of the drivers use horses from the State studs or stallion depots. At Sopot a major equestrian centre is planned with a driving section. Visitors will be able to drive for pleasure there, and it is hoped also to revive the art of coach-building and repairs at Pniewy, near Poznan.

The role of Switzerland in competitive driving has already been seen. In 1970 the very first international event under the new rules was held at Lucerne, and Switzerland has not only staged the world championships, but has also produced a past European and world champion in Auguste Dubey. More recently, Belgium, France and

Spain have begun to take an active part in the new sport.

In the United States and Canada driving's development has gone forward with a bound in the competitive field. These countries have long been strongholds of showing, but the recent formation of the American Driving Society, affiliated to the Carriage Association of America, has been a great step forward. The first combined driving competition within the scope of the FEI rules was held at the Shone Driving Establishment, Millbrook, New York in 1974. The following year a second event made its debut at Myopia, Hamilton, Massachusetts and since then others have followed. The organizers of these competitions have adapted the rules for singles and pairs, and have introduced a novice element into their classification for the encouragement of beginners. Judges for the American events come from both America and Canada and there is no doubt that three-day event driving will progress rapidly in these countries.

In Britain the sport has perhaps progressed more rapidly than anywhere else. Following its close association with the formation of the rules in 1969, it has sent representatives to every major international since then. In 1972 the British Horse Society Combined Driving Group was formed to control and promote the sport. The committee which launched combined driving – as it is known in Britain – realized the great potential of the sport for a much wider competing element. Finance alone would limit the development of the sport to only a small number of four-in-hands, so the committee organized competitions for single horses and ponies, pairs of horses and ponies and horse and pony teams. Latterly classes for tandems have also been introduced – at the request of competitors – and entries are quickly increasing.

In its first year the Combined Driving Group held three competitions for singles, pairs and teams at Lowther Castle, Cumberland, at Eaton Hall, Cheshire and at Cirencester Park, Gloucestershire. In addition, the Windsor international for teams of horses was already well-established. Since that first year, membership of the Combined Driving Group has quadrupled and there is every indication that it will continue to grow.

The committee of the British Group has evolved a set of rules for national competitions which are complementary to the FEI rules. These have been devised to make the competition more meaningful for singles, pairs and tandems. Different speeds are set for ponies for certain phases so that it is possible for them to compete on equal terms with the horses within their own classification, although at the major British events there are separate classes for all classifications.

As a spectator sport, driving has quickly caught the imagination of the equestrian public. For maximum enjoyment, spectators should walk the cross-country – at least the fast section – to see the skill of the competitors negotiating the various artificial and natural obstacles put in their way. For many, there can be no greater thrill than to see a well-driven four-in-hand going clear through the most awkward of cross-country obstacles.

POLO

Polo, a stick and ball game played on horseback by opposing teams of four a side, is a very ancient game which originated in the Orient well over 2000 years ago. The earliest references to it are made in conjunction with Alexander the Great and Darius, King of Persia, from which country the game is believed to have originated, although it was certainly played in one form or another throughout the East, from China and Mongolia to Japan.

The Moslem invaders from the north-west and the Chinese from the north-east took the game into India. In the middle of the last century, English planters discovered it in Assam and brought it back to England. In Assam it was played on the local Manipuri ponies, some of them barely 12 hands, and called *kangjai*. In Persia it was known as *chaugan* (a mallet – by which name the polo stick is known in the United States today) and its present name is a derivative of the Tibetan word *pulu*, meaning a root, from which the wooden polo ball is made.

It did not take the British very long to organize the sport in typical English military fashion. Silchar, capital of the Cachar district, was soon to become the birthplace of modern polo, and the Silchar Club is the oldest polo club in the world. It was founded in 1859, and the rules drawn up then are those on which the present rules are based. Teams originally had nine riders, but this was later reduced to seven and eventually to four as the ponies became bigger and faster. In 1876 the height limit in India was set at 13·2 hands, and in England at 14 hands. Twenty years later it was increased to 14·2 hands, and in 1919 the height limit was abolished. Nowadays, the average height is about 15·1 hands.

In 1869 the game was introduced into England by some army officers from the 9th Lancers, 19th Hussars, 1st Life Guards and Royal Horse Guards. They played polo, with eight aside, on Hounslow Heath near London, and those who watched dubbed it 'hockey on horseback'. It immediately caught on and the Hurlingham Club became the headquarters of English polo, issuing the first English rules in 1875. At about the same time the Indian Polo Association was formed. It framed its own rules until the Second World War.

1878 saw the first Inter-Regimental Tournament, and in 1893 the National Pony Society was founded, with the purpose of promoting the breeding of polo ponies. The game soon spread across to other parts of the world, particularly the British Empire, the United States and Argentina. In the last-mentioned country it was an immediate success, as it still is today. Indeed, Argentina became the biggest breeder and exporter of polo ponies, owing to the scale on which horse breeding is carried out there on the estancias, the number of natural horsemen available for schooling ponies on a low wage, and the toughness of the native breed, which enabled ponies to be produced extremely economically. A number of English dealers have had contacts and connections in Argentina for many years; others went out there to live, so as to exploit a lucrative market, and make frequent shipments back to England.

Polo was introduced into the United States in 1876 by James Gordon Bennett, who brought Western horses east to be trained for the game. The 'golden age' of United States polo was during the 1920s and 1930s when Tommy Hitchcock, Cecil Smith and others competed in national and international matches and tournaments. Now polo is mainly played on a club level under the aegis of the United States Polo Association.

International polo matches started in 1886 with teams from Britain and the United States competing for the Westchester Cup. Between the wars, skilled teams from India – where most of the polo was still conducted on a regimental basis – were frequent visitors to England. Teams also came from Australia, but it was from the United States that the most successful players came, at least until Argentina overtook them. After 1945 the Argentinians reigned supreme and were unbeaten in the Cup of the Americas, the only international championship which remained in existence. Argentina by then had some 3000 active players, to 1000 Americans and about 500 British.

After the war, Hurlingham, Ranelagh and Roehampton were no longer the headquarters of the game and it nearly became moribund. But there was a renaissance in 1950, largely thanks to the efforts of Lord Cowdray, who was a pre-war player as the Hon. John Pearson, along with a handful of other pre-war players. The patronage of HRH Prince Philip, Duke of Edinburgh – whose uncle, Admiral of the Fleet Earl Mountbatten, was a distinguished writer on the game under the pen-name of Marco – was another strong contributory factor in the general upsurge of interest.

The late Sir Humphrey de Trafford's small Thoroughbred, Rosewater, is generally considered to be the foundation of the modern polo pony which is bred in England. He was used on numerous pony mares who had been selected for their performance on the polo ground. His three most famous sons were: Sandiway, out of Cuddington; Lord Polo, out of Lady Florence; and Hurlingham, out of Esmeralda.

The performance of any polo pony is the acid test of quality, for in this very fast game he must be able to gallop flat out, stop in his own length, 'turn on a sixpence', swing round in a pirouette, and start off from a standstill at top speed in any direction. When 'riding off' other ponies he must do two-track work at a gallop, and flying changes of leg must be second nature to him. Courage is a prime essential, and so are a long neck, good shoulders, a short, strong back, depth of girth, exceptionally strong quarters and hocks that are well let down.

The quick stop and the turn at 180 degrees are the most important of all manoeuvres on the polo ground. It is also essential that the pony, ridden as he is with only one hand, should have been taught to neck rein. The mouth is unavoidably subjected to considerable strain from the hasty checks and turns. Likewise, the legs also come under great stress, for which reason supporting bandages are very necessary.

A polo ground may not exceed 274 m (300 yds) in length and the goals, 7·3 m (8 yds) wide, must not be less than 227 m (250 yds) apart. The goal posts are at least 3 m (10 ft) high. The ball is made of willow or bamboo root, is not more than 8 cm ($3\frac{1}{4}$ ins) in diameter and weighs 120–130 gms ($4\frac{1}{4}$–$4\frac{1}{2}$ oz). The polo stick (mallet) is a cane of some 120–137 cm (48–54 ins) in length with a head set at right-angles. This forms the hitting surface, and is 21–23 cm ($8\frac{1}{2}$–$9\frac{1}{2}$ ins) long. The stick is made of sycamore, ash or bamboo and the whippiness of the cane varies; a more whippy cane allows length of drive with a minimum of effort, but it is less easy to manoeuvre in close work. A stiffer cane is more accurate but requires more strength, and more accurate timing. The grip can be bound in leather, rubber, lampwick or towelling, and a wrist sling prevents the stick from being dropped.

The aim of the game, of course, is to get the ball into the opposing side's goal, to which purpose, because polo is essentially a team game, the four players – the forwards, numbers 1 and 2; the centre-half, number 3 and the back, number 4 – connive and manoeuvre to attack the enemy's goal. Not all top-class polo players are outstanding horsemen, although basic horsemanship, good balance and a secure seat are all necessary attributes. More important still, however, is a good natural eye for a moving ball, while courage and judgement, plus a sense of timing, are equally essential.

Players are taught how to strike the ball on a dummy horse in a polo pit. The strokes are: offside forward, offside backhand, offside under the neck of the pony, nearside forward, nearside backhand, nearside under the neck, and offside and nearside back shots under the tail. Other strokes which may be used to good effect are the push, an offside stroke to anticipate the action of an incoming player, and the lateral, that is underneath the pony's body and between his legs. For a forward shot, the ball is struck when it is in front of the withers, and a rear shot is taken when it is about level with the quarters.

The novice, having mastered the strokes and proved able to hit the ball with accuracy in the pit, progresses to mounted work and then to slow chukkas in practice games. The game itself is played in chukkas of $7\frac{1}{2}$ minutes each. There may be four, six, seven or eight chukkas, although now there are usually between four and six. There are three minutes between chukkas, and a five-minute break at half time. Every time a goal is scored the teams change ends.

Barrel racing is one of the spectacular sports to be seen at Western rodeos in both the United States and Australia. Horses need to be fit and agile to compete successfully.

OVERLEAF: A ladies' trotting race on one of America's dirt tracks. The horses often wear protective boots to prevent overreach injuries being caused by the powerful stride of their hind legs.

The number 3 player is the one who initiates attacks and covers number 4 in defence. Thus it is essential that he is well mounted, and is a long and accurate hitter. Numbers 1 and 2 follow up the attacking moves made by number 3, and in defence mark the opposing numbers 3 and 4. Number 4 defends his side's half of the territory, and is at the same time ready to support number 3.

Most games are played on a handicap basis, with all players rated at their value in goals or minus-goals, from minus-two to ten. In handicap tournaments the total individual handicaps are added together and then one is subtracted from the other, in order to assess the number of goals start given to the team with the lower handicap.

The rules are principally concerned with safety, and thus are mainly concerned to clarify right of possession of the ball. They lay down penalties for infringing this right and causing danger – for example by crossing the line of the ball in front of a player who has right of way, riding into a player at a dangerous angle, zig-zagging across a rider at full gallop, intimidation or sandwiching a player between two opponents. Penalties vary according to the offence and its gravity, while a deliberate foul to save a goal incurs the award of a penalty goal. Dangerous fouling carries 27 or 36 m (30 or 40 yd) free hits at an open, undefended goal. The game is stopped if a pony falls or is lame, if a player is injured, if there is a potentially dangerous accident to the pony's gear, if a player loses his helmet, and finally, if the ball goes out of play.

Polo is not a poor man's game, for ponies are expensive and at least three ponies are needed to play in a match. A pony can only play two chukkas, and there must be a reserve in case of injury or lameness. But although the old days of mounted cavalry being able to use troop horses and enthusiastic young officers being mounted through the regiment have gone, there are numerous polo clubs which enable the young man to play the game. Most have a pool of club ponies, which they hire out for a specified fee per chukka. A certain number of young players come up through the Pony Club, which encourages the game increasingly, and this has led to a number of girls becoming active players.

The governing body of polo in England is the Hurlingham Polo Association, but sadly the international effort is curtailed by lack of funds. Argentina and the United States head the world league from Australia, Mexico and other South American countries. Polo is also played regularly in Ireland, India and Pakistan, France, Germany, Italy, New Zealand, Rhodesia, South Africa, Kenya, Nigeria, Ghana, Malaysia and Jamaica.

The centres in England now are Cirencester, Cowdray Park and Windsor. There are some 49 polo clubs in existence in the United Kingdom, with some 400 players, and there are another 100 or so players within the British army in West Germany. Sponsorship has been of great benefit to English polo, as it has to all other equestrian sports, and so has the interest shown by the Prince of

Coloured horses have always been popular in America since the days of the Indians, who soon discovered that their patchy colouring provided good camouflage. The name Pinto is derived from the Spanish word *pintado*, meaning 'painted'.

PREVIOUS PAGE: Harness racing is very popular in the United States. Pacers move with their legs in lateral (as opposed to the usual diagonal) pairs; the hobbles worn by this horse act as a reminder not to break stride during a race.

Wales, who has followed in the footsteps of his father as a keen and gifted player.

A shortage of well-schooled ponies can only be regarded as inevitable in view of the current shortage of high-class trainers of horses. Apparently it takes two years to train a polo pony from the time of his initial breaking until he can play fast chukkas. In Argentina ponies are nearly all worked on the estancias before starting their specialized training, but their trainers still like to give them a further two years, to avoid a high wastage rate caused by unsoundness or problems of temperament. Some English racehorses have begun playing fast polo in just one season, but they have usually had a season or two in training and are physically mature.

The late John Board, a great expert on polo, said that there are three games of polo – Indian, English and American. He thought the Indian game the most attractive, the English the most difficult and the American infinitely best! He attributed the fact that England last won the Westchester Cup as long ago as 1921 to the fact that the Americans have adopted the forward position, ride a couple of holes shorter, keep well forward on their feet and seldom get left behind. In addition their balanced forward position enables them to hit more accurately and get enormous length on the ball. He once saw Raymond Guest hit a ball, on a drizzly day and against a light breeze, which would have travelled at least 155 m (170 yds) had it not struck a pony.

The Indian is a natural horseman and a formidable opponent, particularly as he is usually superbly mounted on first-class ponies. These are the stock of English and Argentine Thoroughbreds, imported by the English, as well as some top-class Australian stock. There is also a theory that the native athlete can see a ball, whether cricket or polo, a full metre sooner than the white man.

A variation of polo known as polocrosse, which was played in Japan a thousand years earlier and is now popular in Australia, had a brief vogue in England, particularly in the West Country. The clumsy instrument with which the ball is scooped up and thrown made the vogue a short one, however, much to the relief of those who were dedicated to the revival of polo in post-war England and resented this distraction to potential followers.

**ENDURANCE AND LONG
DISTANCE RIDING**
Endurance riding and its related
equestrian endeavours, competitive
trail and long distance riding, are
comparatively recent additions to the
great variety of sports in which man
and horse participate together. Great
effort and courage is required from
the horse in this instance, as well as
application and dedication from
the rider. As its name suggests it is a supreme test, for great
distances are covered over all types of terrain, in sometimes
diabolical climatic conditions. At the finish of a 120 km (75 mile) or
160 km (100 mile) ride, both parties must be in a fit state to turn
around and go again – truly a feat of endurance.

Although the youngest of the equestrian sports, endurance riding
has a large international following. In its present form it began little
more than twenty years ago in the United States, where it flourished
for a decade before catching on in Australia. More recently, Great
Britain, South Africa, New Zealand and West Germany have
become similarly involved.

Among its enthusiasts may be found the widest range of riders
mounted on the greatest variety of horses and ponies imaginable.
Indeed it is one of the sport's main attractions that no specific type
of horse is needed in order to participate and complete the course
successfully. In endurance rides in America, I have come across the
typical American breeds such as Appaloosa, Morgan, Quarter
Horse, Moyle, Standardbred, Saddlebred and Walking Horse, as
well as the Arabian, Thoroughbred, Connemara and Welsh. In
Britain the range of breeds is not so great, but the Arabian and
Thoroughbred and their crosses are a popular choice, as are
hunters and a variety of cobby types. Larger native breeds are used,
some crossed with Arabian or Thoroughbred, as well as many
imported breeds. On Germany's 160 km (100 mile) ride from
Hamburg to Hanover, representatives of such national breeds as
Hanoverians, Trakheners, Westphalians, Holsteiners, German
Trotters and Brandenburgs will be seen, as well as such
non-German breeds as Norwegian Fjords, Welsh Cobs, Arabs,
Lipizzaners, Hungarian Half bloods, Haflingers and Icelandic
ponies.

From just these three participating countries it can be seen that
the scope for the type of horse used is very wide indeed, although
those people who really become involved generally find the lean,
athletic type of horse is the most suitable and successful. Arabs and
Arabian crosses are notable for enjoying markedly greater success
overall than any other breed. Horses are required to be five years of
age or older before they can compete; there is no maximum or
minimum age for riders and young children often compete,

accompanied by an adult.

The collective term 'long distance riding' covers the sport's three major aspects. In its lower echelons it offers an introduction to newcomers by participating in shorter-distanced pleasure rides, of between 23 km (15 miles) and 46 km (30 miles). These are ideal for novice riders and/or horses, and being non-competitive provide an opportunity to learn to travel quietly and competently over a variety of terrain. Young horses become used to travelling in company, so that when a rider wants to turn to competitive riding his mount will have achieved a fair amount of mental and physical stability on the trail, and will thus be able to cope with the stresses engendered by competition.

Competitive trail rides are the next step. These are judged rides in which there is a speed bracket, which varies slightly between different countries. The prime judging factor, however, is overall fitness of horses before, during, and after the competition. All CTRs have winning and placed horses, the criteria used being perfect time score and a veterinary assessment encompassing many aspects that indicate fitness. The major stress factors are those relating to pulse and respiration and the speed of recovery to normal after heavy exertion. If a fit young horse has settled into the routine of travelling smoothly and efficiently and is unflustered by extraneous activity, he will register better recovery than one who is alarmed by all the unusual happenings of the ride.

CTRs range in distance from the lower limit of 40 km (25 miles) to the upward limit of 96 km (60 miles) in one day in Britain. America stages a great number, ranging from 40 km (25 miles) in one day up to 160 km (100 miles) run over three days. Germany has many rides run along similar, although not identical lines, with awards going to horses in the best condition and also to those completing the course in fit condition and approximating to ideal timing.

The top rung of the long distance riding ladder is endurance riding, with courses ranging in Britain from 80 km (50 miles) to 160 km (100 miles) in one day, and in America from 40 km (25 miles) up to 163 km (102 miles). There is a strong move in America now to have a lower limit of 80 km (50 miles) to stop over-stressing horses at too high a speed, the feeling being that rides of this distance and above induce greater caution in competitors. Germany has rides of 80 km (50 miles) up to 160 km (100 miles); New Zealand has a lower limit of 72 km (45 miles) and a present upper limit of 120 km (75 miles), while Australia has the famous Quilty 160 km (100 mile) ride and a number of shorter 80 km (50 mile) rides. South Africa has a series of 80 km (50 mile) rides and a major 220 km (130 mile) ride each year.

An endurance ride winner is the fastest fit horse over the distance, and the times turned in on some of the endurance rides are a tribute to the stamina and courage of the horses taking part. Some of the 160 km (100 mile) rides held over really tough terrain are repeatedly won in riding times of under twelve hours. The 80 km (50 miles) rides consistently show winning times around the five-hour mark.

The leading country in this sport is undoubtedly still the United States, whose inauguration began in 1955 with the first running of the Tevis Cup. This 160 km (100 mile) ride was originally run from Lake Tahoe to Auburn, California over the Sierra Nevada and was mapped out along the old Western States Trail that carried hordes of hopeful miners during the California Gold Rush, as well as the equally acquisitive pioneers heading for the Nevada Silver Lode.

Since then, endurance riding has gripped the enthusiasm of thousands of American horsemen so that this ride has blossomed into a fistful of similar distanced rides run nationwide, with more than 150 shorter, but demanding, events filling each year's long distance calendar. Associations exist solely to help run the sport's many aspects. Many of these are regional, as would be expected when such enormous territories are covered, but two in particular can be termed national. The American Endurance Rides Conference controls the endurance side and the North American Trail Ride Conference governs competitive trail riding. Other regional bodies are the Pacific Northwest Endurance System; the Midwest Endurance System; the East Coast Trail Ride Association, which caters for both endurance and competitive trail rides, and the Eastern States Competitive Trail Ride Association. The Rocky Mountain Trail Ride System operates over Montana and Idaho, and there are many locally based groups that run unofficial rides prior to joining in to the system best suited to their activity and locale.

Many of the breed associations are realizing that distance riding is the ideal testing ground for their horses, and many breeders are using the sport to prove their stock. The undoubted leader in this is the Appaloosa Horse Club Registry. There is also a considerable amount of veterinary research being done in America on distance rides in an effort to determine what really makes a horse successful. From the results it is apparent that the lighter type of horse is more to the fore, and winners and placed horses consistently weigh about 430 kg (960 lbs) or less.

A real cross-country endurance test, run in the 1976 Bicentennial year, was the Great American Horse Race from New York to Sacramento, California. For the 4800 km (3000 miles) plus course each entrant was allowed two mounts – one led while the other was ridden. It began over the Memorial Day weekend in May and the scheduled finish was Labour Day in September, thus keeping horses *en route* for a little over three months. Veterinary supervision was drawn from top veterinarians on the Tevis and other endurance rides. The winner, from a hundred entries, was Verl Norton riding a mule!

Three notable endurance riders in the United States are Dr Richard Barsaleau, DVM, also one of the nation's leading endurance judges, and as a regular and successful competitor in the

Tevis and other endurance rides he sees both sides of the coin; Appaloosa breeder Sharon Saare, a very experienced and constantly successful competitor who rides a variety of horses; and Jan Worthington, who has the outstanding record in the eastern states of having won every three-day 160 km (100 mile) ride at some time with her crossbred Appaloosa/Arabian mare, Blanc Seurat.

Other countries have drawn heavily on the tried and proved format used in the United States for both endurance and competitive trail rides, with Australia being one of the first to tackle a 160 km (100 mile) ride in one day patterned on the Tevis Cup. This was the Tom Quilty Endurance Ride, first run in 1966 and won in its inaugural year by Gabriel Stecher on his pure-bred Arab stallion, Shalawi, in a time of 11 hours 24 minutes. The achievement was even more remarkable as he rode the whole distance bareback. Staged annually ever since, the winning time has become increasingly faster with winners now coming in not much over the ten-hour mark. The ride was named after Tom Quilty, a famous horseman who was persuaded by Reg Williams, the Editor of Australia's premier equestrian magazine *Hoofs and Horns*, to sponsor the ride. It is run in climatic conditions where temperatures and humidity soar, and over a tough course in the Blue Mountains of New South Wales.

Since 1966, the Australian endurance scene has grown, with new rides constantly being included and also with a National Association being formed to guide the sport along the right lines. As with all endurance ride systems, the help of veterinary surgeons is essential and the Australians have been able to call on the experience of a team from the Sydney Veterinary School at Camden.

New Zealand also has a very thriving, although young, endurance riding structure and almost all the rides are in the endurance category. Only one or two are run along competitive trail ride lines. Until recently there have been eight major established endurance rides, five in South Island and three in North Island, but there are definite plans to include more in the annual calendar. Rules are drawn from the Tevis and Quilty rides, and the varied terrain includes many steeply climbing sections. Weather conditions often turn the ground in some areas into bogland overnight, making an additional hazard. The longest ride is the Rocklands 80 km (50 miles) and 120 km (75 miles), run in January each year. Winning times for 80 km (50 mile) rides range around the five-hour mark with some competitors finishing in an appreciably shorter time. Leading combinations in New Zealand over the past few years are Alastair Fleming riding Joe Pittam's Waimeha Whirlwind, a pure Arab gelding; Pat Hansen and Silver King, a pure Arab stallion; and Jocelyn Allen on Royal Blue, an Anglo-Arab gelding. An up-and-coming partnership is Laurie Bethune and Flicka, a part-bred Arab palomino mare; Phil Proctor and Fella are noticeable for breaking Arab dominance, Fella being a bay gelding of mixed

Standardbred and hack blood.

Plans for New Zealand's future are to work towards the 160 km (100 mile) ride in one day. As in other countries where the sport has not long emerged as a major horse activity, many riders are joined in a dedicated group which keeps enthusiasm growing by active participation.

Currently in Britain there are two bodies involved with long distance riding. One is under the aegis of the British Horse Society, which operates a section for long distance riding. It runs a series of local Golden Horseshoe Qualifying Rides of 64 km (40 miles) and a final competition of 120 km (75 miles) run over two days on Exmoor, in Somerset. There are also plans for expanding the scope of rides.

The other body is the Endurance Horse and Pony Society (EHPS), a national body whose sole concern is the management of rides and the dissemination of ideas and practical information gained from veterinary research and actual ride data. The EHPS was founded in 1973 and has a network of rides throughout the country, the endurance rides following the Tevis Cup format, the competitive trail rides being run along very similar lines to those used by the North American Trail Ride Conference. In 1975 the EHPS ran its first 160 km (100 mile) ride in the New Forest in Hampshire, with a team of veterinary surgeons headed by the Society's veterinary advisors, Messrs R. G. Orton, MRCVS, John Hartley-Sampson, BVSC, MRCVS, and Peter Hall-Patch, BVSC, MRCVS. The winner of this, in a riding time of 12 hours and 1 minute was Nizzolan, a pure-bred Arab stallion. Winner of the best condition prize was Miss Margaret Montgomerie's black gelding Tarquin, also placed third in the ride. It was this pair who journeyed to Hamburg in 1976 to tackle the German 160 km (100 mile) ride. As a result of this EHPS ride, veterinary research into haemotology pertaining to endurance horses has been started, and other areas of research are under way.

Similar to the American judging procedure, the EHPS also has a points system where horses accumulating points throughout the year campaign for High Points Trophies. The overall trophies are the Manar Trophy for the Leading Senior Horse of the Year, and the Zarpa Trophy for the Leading Junior Rider.

The South African Long Distance Riding Association has been operative since 1972 and was initiated by McFee Morgan, an Arab horse breeder in the Transvaal. Another Arab horse breeder from the Transvaal, Dick de Voss, joined him as secretary, and the group owes a lot to its veterinary adviser and founder member, Professor Sandy Littlejohn. Active participation is reported to be growing, with indications that the sport is soon to enjoy a tremendous upsurge. The South African National Championships are held over a three-day 220 km (130 mile) ride held at Fauresmith in the Orange Free State. This ride is sponsored jointly, with trophies donated by the Farmers Weekly Trail at Fauresmith for the winner, and the Arabian Horse Society for the leading Arab. The ride is run over varied terrain and rules are drawn from the Tevis Cup. Although run over three days, it is judged on endurance lines.

Prior to the championships, there are four 80 km (50 mile) pre-rides from which the committees decide the horses capable of tackling the longer course at Fauresmith. The pre-rides are held in Natal, Orange Free State, Transvaal and Cape Province. Minimum weights of 73 kg (160 lbs) are mandatory except in the junior division, where riders up to 16 years of age ride at catch weight. Juniors must be accompanied by an adult rider. Results from the past three years indicate again that the ability of the Arab is prominent, and indeed most horses used in South African distance riding are of Arab blood. In 1974, Anglo-Arabs filled five out of ten of the highest places in the National Championships, and in following years, the winners have consistently been pure-bred Arabs.

South African distance horses are generally of the lean, athletic type that is becoming universally known for its ability to endure as it is not hampered by excess bone and flesh. It is indicative of the success of this type that throughout the endurance riding world, horses which are repeatedly successful fall into this category. Endurance riding is certainly one of the equine spheres where athletic ability and lean fitness are definitely a major plus.

West Germany is one of the European countries with a major involvement in the sport, and a national body was formed in November 1976 to assist the running of distance riding. Distance riders in Germany have long been well catered for in a variety of rides, but until the formation of the national body there had been no standard guidelines for the management of rides. Each organizer thus had to learn by trial and error. It says a lot for their ingenuity that the sport has flourished in the way it has. It is apparent that the majority of Germany's enthusiasts wish for cohesion among organizers, so competitors will know what to expect throughout the whole country. Regular correspondence has been held with the EHPS of Great Britain in efforts to achieve an international set of rulings with only slight national and regional differences – itself a definite help in the furthering of endurance riding.

Most current German rides fall into the endurance category and range from 80 km (50 miles) to 160 km (100 miles) in length. Several shorter rides are held throughout the year, but the major rides at present are the Laichingen 100 km (60 mile) ride held near Ulm in southern Germany over demanding territory, and the Hamburg to Hanover 160 km (100 mile) ride held each autumn.

Conditions on the Hamburg to Hanover ride as I experienced rides held in other countries. Basically it was an endurance ride with the fastest horse pronounced the winner (except in a tie when the fastest horse pronounced the winner (except in a tie when the horse's condition was the deciding factor); it also had a series of penalty points and bonus points. Deviating from the course incurred penalties for so doing, as well as loss of time. Other penalties could be incurred for overtaking unless prior permission from leaders had been given and also for failure to negotiate hazards at first try. A curious feature of the ride was an 11 km (7 mile) section that had to be ridden in a specific time, riders not knowing how long or where the 'time trial' was to take place until they arrived at the venue. Penalties were incurred if horses went outside the time limits, a one-minute leeway being allowed. The ride itself was well vetted and there were no casualties, and the awards for the first four places were filled by completely different types of horse, namely an Irish heavyweight gelding, an Arabian stallion, a 16-year-old mare of mixed Hackney type (judging from her action) and a Trakhener gelding. A 13 hands Norwegian pony with a ten-year-old rider won the class for *klein Pferde* (small horses), proving that ponies and young children can readily tackle rides of this distance.

One other country in Europe that is showing signs of joining the endurance merry-go-round is Denmark. Discussions have been held with the EHPS Committee and advice sought on the founding of a long distance group. It would seem to be from among the Arab breeders and enthusiasts in Denmark that the beginnings of organized distance riding are likely to come. At present all long distance riding is on a purely informal friendly basis, the way it started in all other countries.

It can be seen from this overall picture that endurance riding is a major growth sport internationally. There is furthermore a tremendous rapport between interested and involved countries as evidenced by competitors who travel abroad to compete. The Germans have sent a team to Britain, and in 1976 the EHPS reciprocated. Sharon Saare of the Appaloosa Horse Club of America has competed in British rides. The interflow between Australia and America for the Quilty and Tevis Cups is now commonplace; Switzerland sends horses to the German rides, and South Africa has hosted overseas riders as well as sending representatives to compete elsewhere.

Each country has its own minor differences in rules and regulations, but it is reassuring that the basic structure is similar so that riders travelling from one country to another know what to expect. This also gives a universal basis on which to work towards gathering information and relevant statistics from rides so that research and veterinary knowledge of the stresses involved can be furthered. This of course can only be generally beneficial, especially to the courageous horses that constantly give of their best throughout even the toughest of endurance rides.

WESTERN SPORTS

The event that to most people is synonymous with Western sports is that of the rodeo. The roots of rodeo lie in the work and leisure activities of nineteenth-century cowboys in the American West. In the decades preceding the Civil War of 1860–1865, great numbers of Americans went to the south-western region of the United States to work on ranches. Later, such post-war industrialization as railroading opened lands west of the Mississippi River and huge ranches were carved out from Texas to Montana.

Ranch life was demanding and hard. Herds of cattle had to be brought each spring from winter pastures, so that calves could be branded and altered into steers. Then the herd had to be tended until the autumn trail drives to the railroad depots. Each cowboy required a string of horses for this work, and no one could afford the time for the niceties and refinements of training. Green horses would be roped, saddles thrown on their backs, cowboys would climb aboard, and the education process went on until the animals – or the riders' bones – were broken.

One of the few respites from this existence came at the end of annual trail drives, when everybody got together in the saloons and gambling halls. Conversations soon turned to prowess with lariat or horse, and proof of alleged expertise would be demanded. The town's main street or stockyard became the scene of these impromptu riding and roping contests, with part or all of the year's wages bet on the outcome. Competitions of this sort quickly caught on. Called a 'rodeo' (from the Spanish word for 'round-up'), a more formal event was staged in Wyoming and another in Kansas during the 1870s. In 1883 the town of Pecos in Texas offered prize money for a steer-roping contest, and five years later, when a Denver, Colorado rodeo charged admission to spectators, rodeoing became a fully fledged business.

Two of the five 'classic' or standard events staged at rodeos today have their origins in actual ranch work. Calf-roping is one, and it demands dexterity with a lasso as well as a well-trained horse. The idea is to rope, then tie a calf, as if to prepare it for branding. A calf is given several seconds' head start down the arena, before horse and rider gallop in headlong pursuit. Then the cowboy tosses his lasso over the animal's head, and almost in one motion he secures the other end of the rope around his saddle horn, throws himself from the saddle and runs towards the calf. The horse has been trained to step back to keep the rope taut. The calf is thus restrained, and becomes fair game for the approaching cowboy, who flips it onto its side and ties three of its four legs together with a short length of rope (called a piggin' string) which he has been holding in his teeth. Time is the deciding factor, although a cowboy will be automatically disqualified from the competition if the calf slips out of the tie within five seconds.

The other event is saddle bronc riding which evokes memories of the method used by cowboys to 'break' their mounts for riding. The saddle in this instance is a modified stock saddle, smaller and without a horn, while the rein is merely a rope attached to the horse's halter. A bucking strap is tightened around the animal's flank to encourage its action. Horses and the order of going are selected by lottery. Before the ride begins, the cowboy lowers himself into the starting chute and onto the back of the horse he has drawn. When he has securely wrapped the rope around one hand, he signals for the gate to be opened, at which point the horse bucks wildly out into the ring. The rider is required to place his spurs on the horse's shoulders at the start and to use them on the first jump out of the chute. The actual ride, which must last ten seconds, calls for extraordinary balance and timing to achieve maximum scores.

Scoring for bronc riding follows a recognized procedure. Two judges each award from zero to 25 points for the rider's performance and the same range of points for the horse's, which explains the reason why cowboys hope to draw difficult mounts. The aggregate is the rider's score for that round. Disqualification results from a rider changing hands on the rein, touching the horse with his free hand, or being thrown before the ten-second buzzer sounds.

The three remaining 'classic' events that form part of every rodeo arose out of Westerners' bragging, along such lines as 'I'm so tough I can ride a bronc bareback, stay aboard a brahma bull, or wrestle a steer to the ground'. Naturally enough, from this sprang the contests of bareback bronc riding, bull riding, and steer wrestling, which is also known as bull-dogging.

Although bareback bronc riding certainly requires brute strength, the rider can use only one hand to hold the grip, which is attached to a strap around the horse's girth. Rules and scoring are similar to saddle bronc competition, except that eight, not ten, seconds is the time limit. Bull riding is particularly perilous, since a bull will chase and gore an unseated cowboy. Riders are permitted to use both hands on the girth grip, and again they must try to last until the eight-second buzzer sounds. Steer wrestling or bull-dogging begins when a steer is released from a pen and made to run the length of the arena. The cowboy gallops after it, with another rider (called a hazer) racing on the other side to keep the animal running straight. When the cowboy draws level with the steer's head, he flings himself from the saddle, and grabs the animal's horns as he plants his boots in the dirt to get a firm grip. His arms tightly wrapped in a deadlock on the animal, the cowboy then wrestles the steer onto its side. The deciding factor in this event is time.

Barrel racing is an event for cowgirls. Three large oil drums are placed to form a triangular course, around which horse and rider gallop in a cloverleaf pattern. The fastest time of all contestants wins.

Larger rodeos feature other events beside the five standard ones. One popular competition is for cutting horses, trained to separate a calf or steer from a herd, then to interpose itself to prevent the animal from returning to the group. Another is team roping, which involves two cowboys. One of them lassoes a calf around the head while his partner ropes the animal's hind legs. Colourful and wild affairs are the chuck wagon races, which are reminiscent of something out of *Ben Hur*. Teams of four or six horses pull Connestoga wagons around a track at a madcap speed.

A rodeo is also a great display of pageantry, from the opening grand entry of all participants to the crowning of a rodeo queen and her court of attendants. Exhibitions put on for general amusement and as part of the day's proceedings may include trick riding, fancy roping, or a musical ride. One group of rodeo employees whose function may appear to be primarily entertainment, although they actually fulfil a vital purpose, are the clowns. They divert the bulls and wild broncs from fallen riders. More than a few cowboys owe their lives to the quick reflexes and courage of rodeo clowns. Equally essential to the contestants are the mounted pick-up men, who help bronc and bull riders to dismount at the conclusion of their rounds.

Dedication, as well as ability, is a prerequisite for professional rodeo cowboys. The 'suicide circuit', as the tour is wryly known, goes on all year and involves travelling around very great distances. Unlike most other athletes, rodeo riders pay their own way throughout, and that includes entry fees, room and board, and stabling fees for their horses. As may be imagined, injuries are commonplace, yet still everyone will strive for the 'pot of gold' at the end of this rainbow. It contains prize money, which will help realize a profit for the season, but more important it means the gain of the title of All-Around Champion. Based on the amount of prize money won over the year, the championship also opens the door to additional income from sponsoring clothing manufacturers, free beer, and other products which are somehow equestrian-related. Among the best known all-around champions are Casey Tibbs, Jim Shoulders, and Larry Mahan. In 1974, Tom Ferguson set the all-time money mark of $120,000. A year later he tied with Leo Camarillo for the title, each having won exactly $90,240.

There are more than a thousand rodeos held annually in the United States and Canada. The 'big leagues' include the Cheyenne Frontier Days in Wyoming, Pendleton Round Up in Oregon, Denver Stock Show in Colorado, and the Oklahoma City All-American Finals. Small cities and towns have their own fixtures, many of which are sponsored by civic or charitable organizations. On a younger, but certainly not small, scale, university and high school students throughout the West engage in the sport as part of intercollegiate, varsity, and club athletics.

Less dangerous and spectacular perhaps than rodeos, but equally enjoyable in their way, are the four sections of Western-style riding found at horse shows around the United States. These four sections comprise stock seat equitation classes, stock horse classes, trail horse classes and pleasure horse classes. Riders wear the traditional and colourful gear of broad-brimmed hats, high-heeled boots, and chaps or Western pants. In some instances, a rain slicker is worn or secured to the saddle. Horses are shown in stock saddles and bridles, with curb bits and split reins. The technique of Western riding requires that riders hold the reins in only one hand, and sit with their legs hanging straight and slightly forward to the stirrups. They must not rise (post) to the jog trot.

Contestants in stock seat equitation classes are judged on their riding skills, although the performance of their horses contributes immeasurably to the final scores. Riders and their mounts are asked to walk, jog, and lope (the Western term for canter) in both directions, and the horses should be in perfect balance at all times, working off their haunches. Some classes involve a variety of tests, such as figures-of-eight at the jog and/or lope, riding without stirrups, flying changes of lead at the lope, 360 degree turns, and the impressive sliding stops.

The stock horse section demonstrates the kind of qualities and techniques needed for ranch work. Each entry goes through the Western equivalent of a dressage test, which comprises figures-of-eight at the jog and lope, turns on the forehand and haunches, and halts. Particular qualities of stock horses are good manners, handiness, response to light rein contact, and the ability to work at reasonable speed while remaining completely under the rider's control. Hesitations, anticipations and disobediences are deemed faults.

Trail horses are asked to negotiate obstacles which might be found on a cross-country ride. A course set up around the arena would probably include a gate (which has to be opened, passed through, and then closed), logs, a ditch, a bridge, an expanse of water (simulating a stream to be forded), and bales of straw through which the horse is made to back. Performance and manners are the criteria for judging.

Pleasure horse classes place great emphasis on suitability and manners to be a good Western hack. Horses are shown at the walk, jog, and lope on a reasonably loose rein. In some classes, conformation and also equipment may be taken into account.

In addition, certain breeds, such as Appaloosas, Arabians, Morgans, Palominos, Pintos, and Quarter Horses, are eligible to be shown in Western sections of their divisions.

AUSTRALIAN RIDING

Horses have made an enormous contribution to life in Australia. With unflagging energy and unfailing loyalty, they helped map out the vast areas of arid deserts, grassy plains and rugged mountains, and could well be described as pioneers in their own right. Although not indigenous to the country they settled happily and remain today in high esteem.

Governor Phillip brought the first horses to Australia in 1788 when he arrived with the First Fleet. Landing at the Cape of Good Hope to take on supplies, he took aboard a stallion, three mares and two yearling fillies. Unfortunately, on landing, all but the stallion and one mare escaped the lax eye of their convict groom, and fled into the bushland. More horses were imported over the next ten years from the same source, along with some English Thoroughbreds and Arabs from India and Persia, and although these first imports were not first-class breeding stock, they progressively improved with each successive generation.

By 1798, there were 117 horses in the new colony, 73 of them mares. The first serious step to improve the stock came with the importation of the English-bred horse Rockingham. By the early 1820s there were 5000 horses, although Rockingham cannot be credited with siring all of them! During the 1899–1902 Boer War, 16,375 horses were gathered from all over Australia to mount the regiments.

It was from the mixed breeding lines of the early imports that the famous Australian Waler was founded. Standing between 15 and 16 hands, he was of 'dense bone' and capable of carrying up to 108 kg (17 stone) all day. The Waler proved himself to be a courageous mount and is on record as having out-lasted and out-paced the camel in the desert campaigns.

During the First World War, Australian horses, by now famous for their courage and stamina, were exported to India and Europe. In fact more than 121,324 went to war. But the end of the war and the decline of the cavalry saw the end of the Waler. Now he is virtually extinct and no longer recorded in the stud books. If the early explorers were grateful for this tough colonial horse, which proved himself indispensable to them, the fact is not recorded.

Robert O'Hara Burke travelled across the continent and half way back again on his horse Billy before starvation made him shoot it. The diaries record that the 'flesh was healthy and tender, without a trace of fat'. It seems that the meat from his old friend did not stick in Burke's throat as one might have imagined.

As the colony became more settled and mail and coach routes were established, the bandit or bushranger made his appearance. Often excellent horsemen from Ireland, these escaped convicts or 'easy-living men' were fearless riders. The price on their heads made them particular about their mounts and they stole only the best – well-blooded horses in fact, which continue to prove their worth today as stock-horses.

In a country with an ever-expanding beef and wool industry, horses play a major part. Motor bikes, trucks, even light aircraft and hovercraft have failed to prove as efficient in the management of stock. Now larger properties carry several hundred head of horses which are bred (usually from the property's Thoroughbred stallion), born, work and die on the same station. They often run virtually wild in large paddocks, so that the overseas visitor travelling in the outback may, on seeing a large mob, assume they are 'brumbies' or wild, unowned horses. This is seldom the case and closer inspection would show the property's brand mark.

The wild brumbies are still to be found in the desert or mountain areas, however, especially in the Northern Territory. Graziers resent sharing their grasslands, so wild horses in the Territory are classified as vermin and shot, or fenced off from water so they perish. The same fate awaits the wild donkeys who roam the grassy plains in mobs of a hundred or so, although the popularity of this little animal has reached the city and many are finding good homes or being used as foundation stock by newly-formed donkey studs.

Years ago professional horsebreakers travelled from station to station, breaking in mobs of horses at the rate of dozens a day. Today the property's animals are broken by the stockmen as part of the station routine. The horses are mustered and brought to the station's yards, from where mares with foals at foot are returned to the paddocks, yearlings are branded and also returned, while those required for breaking are retained. Today most stockmen use the 'Jeffery' method of breaking which relies on gaining the horse's confidence, and in nearly all cases this method succeeds. The horse is driven by himself into a small yard and caught with a loop of rope or greenhide carried on the end of a long pole. Once secured around the neck, he is gently encouraged to move closer to the breaker. Then he is tied up, handled, and the bridle and saddle put on him. This part of his breaking usually takes about three hours, after which he is turned loose in the yard to get the 'feel' of the saddle. Caught again, he will be mounted. Some are led around the yards from a reliable breaking horse; others are required to walk around with the rider neck-reining them as they approach the corners of the yard. They are then taken to a larger yard and walked around that for some time longer. The whole operation clearly requires a good deal of patience.

The stock saddle has a high pommel and knee pads and is fastened by canvas girths that are laced to rings or buckled in the conventional manner. The stockman rides in a loose, completely 'fluid' manner. His hands are featherlight on the long reins, his legs hang almost straight and slightly forward in long stirrups.

After a period of work – maybe many months – the horses are turned out, or 'spelled' and a new lot brought in for work.

In every mob of horses there is nearly always the 'rogue' that doesn't take kindly to working with or for man. He is the sort that will buck with real determination until the day he dies. These were the 'unrideables' that were talked about round bush fires in drovers' camps years ago, and men who had succeeded in riding them became legends, held in high esteem. The challenge to prove themselves as horsemen was great among the drovers and bets were wagered as to whether, and for how long, a man could ride a particular outlaw horse. This was the early beginning of rodeos – a real Australian sporting event that carries big prizes and attracts the toughest riders in the country. The sport is now organized and controlled by the Australian Rough Riders Association.

Saddle bronc riding is one of the foundation events of the sport, and one that requires skill, balance, timing and experience. As in the similar event in American rodeos, the contestant literally climbs aboard the horse, which is confined between high wooden rails with a gate at either end. As the horse bucks and plunges in this 'chute', mounting can be a hazard in itself! Once mounted, the rider takes the rope of the headcollar in one hand and positions his legs forward onto the horse's shoulder points. The gate is opened and he leaves the chute for his ten-second ride, throughout which he must leave one hand free of all equipment, the horse and his own body. Staying on is not the only judging criteria, though. Two judges, one either side, note how well he rides the bucks, how wide the sweep of his spurs and with what style the horse bucks.

The standard saddle for these events has two girths, one positioned further back than usual to prevent it being bucked over the horse's head. A headcollar with a rope from the central dee is the only means the rider has to guide his mount – if indeed there is any guiding to be done!

Bareback riding is another crowd pleaser at rodeos. In this instance the horse is unhaltered and wears only a surcingle to which is attached a leather loop for the rider to hold. Again it is a one-handed ride, lasting this time for eight seconds and judged on the competitor's style and the horse's ability to shift him.

Another event which has been handed down from the everyday work of the stockman is calf roping, and here a clever, fast horse that can anticipate his rider's needs is invaluable. A rope is attached to the saddle horn and on a given signal the rider sets out after a calf which is released from the chutes. He ropes the calf around its neck, and exactly at the moment the rope touches the beast's neck, the horse skids to a halt on its haunches, thus pulling the rope taut. The competitor ties the calf's legs as quickly as possible and remounts. The fastest time wins.

Perfectly trained horses are used for steer wrestling, too. A steer is let loose from the chutes and the rider gallops alongside it waiting for an opportune moment to leap from his horse and grab it by the

A relatively informal race meeting in Australia's Northern Territory. As in America, most races in Australia are run over dirt tracks rather than the green turf found at European meetings.

OVERLEAF: Sydney's Royal Easter Show is one of the most important events in the Australian equestrian calendar. This highly successful champion pony is being paraded after the judging has been completed.

horns, unbalance it and bring it to the ground. The whole process usually only takes between 2½–11 seconds, and is ridden at a speed of 50–65 km (30–40 mph).

The horses used for rodeo work are sometimes supplied by local farmers who have unrideable stock, or they may be the property of one person who travels the rodeo circuit with them. The horses that appear regularly have quite a reputation and are often promoted as 'killers'. Animal protection societies have for some years been trying to have all rodeos stopped on the grounds of cruelty to horses and cattle, but such is their popularity that all attempts have so far been unsuccessful.

No such move has been made against camp-drafting events, which are often staged at rodeos, major shows and as competitive attractions in their own right. This stockman's sport carries high prizes and has led to some specialized breeding of horses. Good drafting horses seldom change hands for under four figures. The ideal horse stands about 15 hands (any larger and they find it difficult to execute the acute turns necessary) and is up to carrying a fairly large man while pushing a beast around at the same time. He has to be fast, and for this reason many good drafters have Thoroughbred blood in them, although recent years have seen Quarter Horse lines introduced with success. Camp-drafting takes place in natural bush surroundings, and the rider selects a beast from the mob or camp, and drives it to another spot known as the yards. In competition camp-drafting, a course is marked out by pegs or oil drums, and the number of cattle in the herd kept small. The fewer false moves made along the route, the faster the course is completed, and the higher the score. A good horse never takes his eye off the chosen beast, and any guiding becomes unnecessary. He will lean into the beast with his shoulder at the most frightening angles to prevent it from turning. Executed at great speeds, camp-drafting is a thrilling spectator sport.

Camp-drafting is not restricted only to adults. Pony Club members learn the rudiments during novelty races staged at their rallies through such competitions as bending in and out of oil drums at a gallop. Of course some country members get first-hand experience at their home farms, but the Pony Club in Australia has given all young riders an opportunity to learn this and other techniques.

In the past, horsemanship skills were handed down from one generation to the next. For country children there were always ponies to ride and adults to learn from, but new generations growing up in the cities and suburbs had parents who themselves had no knowledge of horses. To them the Pony Club has been a boon, and the interest it has fostered is evident at the suburban rallies where sometimes more than 200 children attend. Formed in the 1950s, the Pony Club in Australia follows the same instructional lines as its parent body in England. Regular working rallies make up a major part of the meetings which are staged at

The Grand Parade at the Sydney Royal Easter Show. All types of ridden and harness horses are catered for at the show, as well as the livestock which can be seen at the far side of the ring.

local show grounds, racecourses or individual's properties. All branches – from the tiny country branch with a membership of maybe fifty to the larger inner-suburban ones – hold courses.

Camps are run during the holidays and the climate and open spaces make Australian children luckier than many others. Informal barbecue meals under the shade of gum trees and sing-songs or horsey quizzes and competitions around the camp fire at night add to the fun.

Each state runs its own affairs, but is governed by the Australian Pony Club Council. Inter-state competitions are stages of the biggest event in the annual calendar – the Pony Club Championships.

In recent years the Inter-Pacific Exchange Scheme has been in operation. Every two years, members visit a 'host' country and as guests are supplied with mounts and equipment, and taken on various tours. Countries participating in the Exchange Scheme are America, Canada, New Zealand and Australia. It has been said that, per capita, Australia has the most enthusiastic members in the world and the interest and enthusiasm is certainly very evident at horse shows held around the country.

Every town, however, small, holds an annual show and some of the larger townships may stage more than one. Novelty races, jumping and riding events and displays by the local branch of the Pony Club are usually featured at these 'family affairs', but it is at each state's Royal Show that the country really comes to the city.

Amid an atmosphere bustling with fair-ground sideshows and stalls, country life is well exhibited. The latest in agricultural equipment is on view; sheep shearing competitions, butter-making demonstrations and wood-chopping races are held; while cattle, sheep, poultry, pigs, caged birds, cats, dogs, goats and even fashions are judged, sold, viewed and (in the case of butter) tasted during the show. Grand parades of the winning animals are held each day.

Horses remain one of the favourite exhibits among all the competition. The permanent stables are crowded with admirers and the evening jumping competitions, or displays of tent pegging by the mounted police branches, are great crowd pleasers. The jumping events are keenly contested, for it is from the 'Royals' that future Olympic riders will be picked. At Sydney's Royal Easter show, a regular three-day event is staged, which is closely watched by the Olympic selectors. The hack, hunter and other ridden classes attract so many entries that judges never ride – it would take too long. The breed classes, with the heavy horse breeds, Arabs, British native breeds, palominos, harness and Australian ponies, take hours to judge and the number of entries goes up every year.

Most states hold their Royal Show in such high regard that a public holiday is declared during its running, to give workers and school children a chance to attend. It is interesting to note that, unlike many Australian public holidays, show day is actually spent at the show, instead of on the beach, or at home. It demonstrates how interested city dwellers are in all things from and of the country.

For those competitors following the circuit of shows, Easter and the Sydney Royal marks the beginning of the season. The Brisbane (Queensland) Exhibition follows in August, with Melbourne, Adelaide and Perth in September and Tasmania in October. The enormous distances between each state capital make showing an expensive hobby, but the prestige attached to winning a Royal championship makes many competitors travel the circuit. Obviously a hack that has won five or six state championships in one season is a very valuable animal.

One of the highest awards in the Australian show ring, and one contested by riders from all states, is the Garryowen event staged at the Melbourne show. This riding event is for lady riders over eighteen years of age and the winner receives the Perpetual Garryowen Trophy. The cup was named after a top hack who died in a fire more than thirty-eight years ago. The horse's mistress, Violet Murrell, died too trying to save him from the flames. The winner of the event also receives a sash (sashes are used instead of rosettes in Australia) with a portrait of Mrs Murrell on a brooch.

Nine Olympic Games passed before Australia competed with an equestrian team. In 1956, when the Games were held in Melbourne, they felt morally obliged to enter even though the equestrian events took place in Stockholm. Their first three-day event team consisted of Ern Barker, Bert Jacobs, John Winchester, Brian Crago and Wyatt Thomson, and they finished a very creditable fourth. The Stockholm adventure fired the Australians' enthusiasm and thenceforth three-day events became regular events in the country. In Rome, four years later, the team really triumphed, with Bill Roycroft making his heroic effort in the final phase and jumping a clear round even though he had a broken collar bone. As well as winning the team gold, Laurie Morgan won the individual gold. Australia was well and truly on the equestrian map. The 1964 Tokyo games saw Australia's first show jumping team and Bill Roycroft's son Barry was included, while 'Dad' was once again in the three-day event team. The Mexico Games saw another Roycroft enter the ranks of Olympic horsemen when Wayne joined the team. Clarke was to follow years later, and all the time Bill rode for his country.

The performances by the Australians, and in particular the veteran Roycroft, demonstrate the great talent of Australian riders and the ability of their horses. In the cross-country phase both are in their element, and recent years have seen much improvement in the dressage, which is now an integral part of all major shows. It has developed quickly from beginners' classes to Prix St George standards.

If it was Bill Roycroft who put Australia on the international eventing map, that big red galloper, Phar Lap, can claim the country's racing fame. Although he has been dead for more than forty years, the nation remembers him with great affection, perhaps heightened by his mysterious death in the United States in 1932. Phar Lap died after a racing career of only three years in which he amassed more stake money than any other Australian horse before him, winning 37 times from 51 starts. Such was the affection of his fans that his body was flown back to Australia, dissected and divided. His heart is now in the capital, Canberra, his skin in Melbourne and his skeleton in New Zealand – the country where he was bred.

The first race to be run in Australia was in 1810 at Sydney, and the sport soon proved popular. The first Melbourne Cup – probably Australia's most famous race – was staged at Flemington, near Melbourne, in 1861. It was won by Archer, a big horse who galloped along with his tongue lolling out, his long stride earning him the nickname 'the Bull'. He won it the following year too, a record only repeated twice (at the time of going to print) – by Rain Lover in 1968/1969, and Think Big in 1974/1975. Thousands of eager racing enthusiasts from all parts of the country flock to Flemington each year for this popular race, which is traditionally held on the first Tuesday in November.

However, such is the nation's interest in the sport of racing that even the small bush track (which also serves as an airstrip) can attract a mighty crowd. Many false starts may be made and the horses lost from view in the dust, but the enjoyment among the heat and the flies is as real as the pleasure for those on the well-kept lawns of Randwick racecourse in Sydney or that in Flemington.

A few years after the introduction of racing, fox hunting took on a popularity. Englishmen, bored with chasing kangaroo and dingo, imported a few foxes to brighten up their sport. In Tasmania natural, indigenous, quarry is still hunted, although the hunts do not last long. The largest hunting fraternity now is in Adelaide, South Australia, which has eleven hunt clubs. The Adelaide Hunt Club Cup is run in July each year for $1700, the highest stake in the country for a Hunt Cup.

The oldest hunt in Australia, the Melbourne Hunt Club, meets on Saturdays and only hunts the fox. It gathers a relatively small field, usually about sixty. The season is from May to September, and during these months the aim is to kill the fox, for from those few early imports the bushy-tailed predator has multiplied. Hare and fox are hunted by another old-established club, while some use a drag, in which case hunts usually last no more than three to four hours and are over strategically placed jumps. As in Great Britain, there are a few demonstrations every year to have foxhunting banned.

The introduction of polo came not long after racing and hunting, but it was only after the end of the First World War that the game really went ahead. In 1925 the Australasian Gold Cup was introduced and was competed for between the different Australian states and New Zealand. Because station-bred ponies are readily adapted to polo, the game is much played in the country areas, and Queensland has produced a number of top-class players. All matches are well attended by spectators during the season. Polocrosse is also popular and is played by Pony Club and riding club members.

Australia's links with the horse are as strong today as they were at the birth of the nation, and there exists a deep love and respect for the animal. Office workers on their way to work will stop and pat the police horse on point duty; the gambler will talk affectionately of 'his horse', even though he might lose; and school children are still held spellbound by the skill and daring of 'Clancy' and the 'Man From Snowy River', who chased the 'colt from old Regret'. To Australians, the horse is part of their heritage.

PONY CLUBS AND RIDING CLUBS

To the uninitiated the words 'Pony Club' can conjure up a vision of a crowd of little girls with 'jockey caps' tilted snootily over their noses, tittuping their ponies around a Colonel Blimpish figure as he bellows out the quasi-military commands of out-dated riding instruction. The truth is somewhat different.

The Pony Club stands for many different things to many different people. It can be a heaven-sent answer to the prayers of completely un-horseminded parents with pony-mad children. It can provide the solution to the apparently devilish pony that plays up and takes off at the mere sight of another of its own species. It has proved itself many times over to be an excellent nursery for the future top-class performer, often at international level. But above all the Pony Club still provides an enormous amount of fun and interest for thousands of young people under twenty-one living in many different countries.

Up to the First World War horses and ponies were everywhere still very much part of everyday life, and most of the families who possessed them had as a matter of course ingrained, inherited horse-sense. Then came the stringencies of the war years, and afterwards the machine age rapidly took over, until owning a horse or pony was a rare luxury and several generations grew up mostly without any basic horse knowledge or interest. This state of affairs did not necessarily stop children from wanting to ride, but it did provide their parents with good reason for not doing anything about it. And too often where they complied and a pony joined the family, sheer lack of knowledge resulted in a frightened child put off riding for ever, or a spoilt pony being sold downhill through no fault of its own, or even cases of unintentional cruelty. Now, largely owing to the good work of the Pony Club all over the world, such instances are relatively rare, and the pleasures of riding and the real needs of horses and ponies are yearly becoming better known.

The Pony Club in Britain began in 1929, when an offshoot of what was then the British Institute of the Horse was welded into an association to encourage children to ride, to enjoy the sports and pastimes connected with horses and ponies, and to learn how to look after their own animals. From the very beginning the idea was popular. By 1934 there were 8000 members, and the numbers increased rapidly until the outbreak of the Second World War closed all branches for the next six years. It was an act of faith to start up again in 1945, as a revival of widespread general interest in riding and ponies appeared remote at a time when the attention of both young and old was fixed on machines and television, and the actuality of space travel was only round the corner. But it turned out that children still wanted to be involved with living creatures, that learning to care for ponies did interest them, and that the lure of the countryside remained irresistible. The present and still growing total Pony Club membership of 80,000 proves the point.

The backbone of the Pony Club has always been the working rally. These meetings are usually held in the Easter and summer school holidays, but in Canada some of the branches reverse the order, and if a heated indoor school is available they confine their Club activities to the cold winter months. But whether a rally is being held under the cloudless skies of an Australian summer, or at 6.30 a.m. in the already steamy heat of Singapore, or in the steady downpour of what should be a flaming August day in England, the programme is much the same.

The chief business at a rally is instruction in riding and jumping at different levels, and in the care of pony and 'tack'. The members are divided into groups, or 'rides', according to their ability, and the child who rides her rough pony well will go into a more senior ride than the perfectly accoutred child with a show pony, who is less able. Even the most nervous novice is sure to find others of the same standard, and the bottom ride often contains quite young children – although here the help of an active teenager on foot, with a leading rein to act as handbrake, can be very useful.

Nowadays a big effort is made to keep all instruction in line and up to date, but the teaching is flexible and suited to the particular needs of different clubs. In Canada, for instance, there are several that cater exclusively for the members who prefer to ride Western, in the relaxed style of the cowboy, rather than in the more conventional 'English' position, and the lower grades of the Pony Club tests are modified accordingly. A rally is not all work, and time is given to having fun and to the joy of 'just riding' when children play mounted games and go for the occasional country ride, at the same time learning the country lore which is part of the curriculum.

Pony Club officials, of whom the majority offer their services for free, do the coaching and examining for the various Pony Club tests and train aspirants to a team for one of the inter-branch competitions. They are also always willing to advise on such matters as the most suitable bit for a particular pony, or to point out tactfully why a saddle like the 'Pony Club Approved' is likely to do more for the rider's position than Dad's pre-war ex-hunting saddle. They will do their best to find a remedy for the foibles of a problem pony, but reserve the right to turn away any animal that seems to present a real danger to its own or other rides, or any mares in foal, the occasional one that comes complete with foal 'at foot', and any too infirm, too young or too aged for the job.

Obviously to have his own pony is every member's ambition, but it is not a requisite for joining the Pony Club. Many of the ponies attending rallies are hired for the occasion, and in towns, where restricted space sometimes necessitates instructing rides in turn, the same pony often copes with two riders. Most Clubs also include a few dismounted rallies during the year, used for demonstrating such important items as feeding or shoeing, or for paying a visit to some place of interest like a racing stables or hunt kennels.

The Pony Club does its best to cater for most riding tastes. The athletic horse vaulting is very popular with boy members in the United States, and is an American Pony Club speciality; polo lessons and matches are also very well attended and organized by many branches. In Britain there is a senior and junior annual polo tournament, and an almost exclusively masculine sport is the pentathlon championships, which include tests in running, fencing, shooting and swimming as well as in riding.

Eventing, the prevalent name for horse trials, is an increasingly popular sport in many countries, and at Pony Club level helps to further the exciting scheme for members to exchange visits, not only to other branches at home but also overseas. Horse trials consist of three phases: dressage, cross-country, and show jumping and there are inter-branch team competitions as well as international competitions. The Inter-Territorial Horse Trials, put on by the thriving South African Pony Clubs, usually include teams from Britain and Rhodesia, and British members have competed in Denmark. In 1965 a team had the luck to be the first from Britain to take part in one of the International Pony Club Exchange visits, held that year in America. And although transport, even for inter-branch and inter-regional competitions, is often a problem in a country as large as Canada, a Canadian team is always included in the annual Inter-Pacific Exchange with New Zealand, Australia, Japan, Britain and the USA.

As well as the horse trials, several Clubs have given the show jumping enthusiasts an annual inter-branch team competition of their own as well as the horse trials. In 1957 Prince Philip presented a special challenge cup, which is named after him, to the British Pony Club, and inaugurated a competition for those members up to sixteen years old who ride the well-trained but non-special type of pony. Every year since then, teams from all over the British Isles have competed for the Pony Club Mounted Games Championship, and the winners of the area competitions ride off against each other in the thrilling finals which are part of the Horse of the Year Show in the autumn.

Some people consider that nowadays the Pony Club tends to concentrate on training the lucky few who 'make' the teams for the various competitions, at the expense of the less expert majority. In a few cases this may be true, but this is a competitive age, and the ambition to get into a team acts as a powerful and worthwhile incentive. Also, most branches hold their own gymkhana, hunter trials or even horse trials, geared to suit most riding standards and types of pony; and trail riding, open to all, is quickly becoming as favourite a pastime elsewhere as it is with the American and Canadian Clubs.

A camp is often the highlight of the Pony Club year, although few branches can aspire to anything as wonderful as the safaris, sometimes 13,000 feet up to the snowline on Mount Kenya, enjoyed by the lucky members of the Molo Hunt and Kipkabus Pony Clubs. Nor are the facilities of iced water and air conditioning, with comparable comforts for the ponies, which are supplied by the Singapore Turf Club for their local Pony Club, usual components of camp life. But equal fun is usually had by all, whether in tents, with ponies tethered army fashion, or in the lofts and stabling attached to some historic castle.

Branch and Club interests vary from region to region as well as in different countries, and are often determined by local conditions. A well-to-do district often means a bigger percentage of better-class ponies, with the emphasis on eventing. Built-up areas can mean confining the Club's activities within the four walls of a covered school. Difficult riding terrain, such as that of Malta, may mean that there is adequate space within some venue like that of the Marsa, the island's general sports arena, but little change of scene. The interests of the Irish Pony Clubs reflect the traditional enthusiasm for hunting in Ireland, as do those in Cyprus, where the members quickly pass their 'C' Test in order to qualify for hunting with the Dhekelia draghounds. Danish children are so afraid of losing any time that could possibly be spent in actual riding that their Pony Club instructors find it difficult to instil horsemastership as well as horsemanship.

When the Pony Club was first formed in Britain practically all children rode ponies, and though nowadays a number of members take to horses at quite an early age because of the increasingly high standard of the competitions, the British Isles remain basically pony-minded and the Club is certainly not mis-named. In America the opposite is true; it is only comparatively recently that Americans have given thought to ponies at all, and the Pony Clubs are not in the least height or type conscious. The majority ride horses as a matter of course.

As in the United States and Canada, it has been customary in Australia to pass down the ex-racehorse or stock horse to the children. A number do ride the utility types over 14 hands and under 15 hands known as Galloways, and in the western states particularly the younger members often have strains of those active, if plain, little ponies whose ancestors were imported from Timor during the nineteenth century. But it was, and in many cases still is, a common sight to see the largest component of an Australian Pony Club rally made up of quite small children perched on enormous horses. However, with the many studs of imported pony breeds, and those of the registered 'Australian Ponies' that derive from early importations of riding types, an increasing number of children are using the smaller animals, and the trend is being fostered by the big variety of showing classes for ponies of different breeds and abilities.

Australia is such an enormous country that the Pony Clubs differ as much in interests as in saddlery and riding clothes. Around cities such as Melbourne the Clubs are very smart and the emphasis is on eventing and kindred sports. The standard in dressage and jumping is good, and the Inter-Branch Horse Trials Championships have grown to a large two-day affair, with up to fifty teams competing.

Up-country the rallies provide enjoyable meetings for both parents and children living in scattered communities. At those gatherings the tack often consists of scaled-down stock saddles with sacks for saddle-cloths, and though members wear the obligatory hard riding-cap, for the rest of their riding attire jeans predominate, with a wonderfully colourful assortment of jackets. The effect may not be as technically correct as that of some Pony Clubs, but the spirit is every bit as keen and the enjoyment as great. So long as safety, and comfort for the pony, are not contravened, no one minds if the bridle is tied up with string, if it is done so adequately. No child is made to feel inferior, and those owning the most primitive tack can often be awarded good points for keeping it clean and supple.

Many Clubs ride on expeditions into the Australian Alps, or go from property to property spending a night at each, their ponies often accommodated and hay fed in the sheepyards. On summer camps the boys usually sleep in the station woolshed, the girls in the shearers' huts; the shearers' kitchen makes the perfect mess room, and somewhere to swim, be it river, hole, dam or pool, is an essential for after-work hours.

All members are gymkhana-minded, and some Clubs play polo . . . at all levels. Most children do well at some aspect of this game, and when a Shetland, taking advantage of its rider's two-handed grip of the polo stick, dropped its head to have a snack, the language of its youthful owner would have done justice to any ten-goal player!

In October 1944 a momentous meeting at Hawkes Bay, in New Zealand's North Island, resulted in the formation of the Heretaunga Pony Club. This was the first of its kind in the Islands, and provided the prototype for the New Zealand Pony Clubs Association, which now has around eighty branches with an approximate membership of 8000. There was never any lack of membership material, since petrol was still rationed and many country children rode their ponies to school as a matter of course, and in the towns there were numberless children clamouring to ride who did not have the facilities to do so. An initial problem of the Pony Club was, however, to introduce and establish more modern methods of riding, which were very different from those that had prevailed before. It was plain that dressage would be of small interest to the young Maori who rode miles to a rally bareback, controlling his mount with a single rope attached to part of a halter. On the other hand the children who found it easier to win gymkhana races once they had learned to control their ponies largely with seat and legs, instead of by yanking at the bit, quickly came to appreciate the value of what they were being taught. They continued to attend rallies in increasing numbers, and the whole project was helped along by the co-operation of New Zealand's numerous and influential hunt clubs.

The Pony Club is going from strength to strength in New Zealand, and now many members are helping with a very worthwhile project for aiding disabled children by lending them their most suitable ponies to ride. This idea is gaining ground all over the world and bringing great pleasure, and proved therapeutic benefit, to many of the mentally and physically handicapped.

Riding Clubs

In many ways a riding club is the adult equivalent of the Pony Club, and there are numerous riding and saddle clubs in almost every country. In Britain 'the Riding Clubs' usually refers to the association of nearly three hundred clubs that includes dressage groups, clubs at universities, the saddle clubs of the three services, and clubs in Jersey, Guernsey, the Isle of Man, Isle of Wight and a few overseas – all of which affiliated to the British Horse Society.

The first of the committees formed to administer this association was constituted in 1952, and headquarters now operate from the National Equestrian Centre at Kenilworth, in Warwickshire. They keep in touch with all the various clubs spread throughout England, Scotland and Wales, through nineteen liaison committees, which have the additional function of promoting co-operation between the clubs in a particular area. Some of the clubs have junior members who may take the Pony Club tests if they wish by special arrangement, though they are barred from any of the official riding clubs' competitions until the age of seventeen.

In the early years riding clubs had the reputation of being an association for 'weekend riders' only. It is perfectly correct that the membership consists largely of those who work for their living and therefore have to restrict their riding activities, but the slightly derogatory implication that the clubs were composed only of complete novices is far from true. Nowadays the association prides itself on having a membership that includes every kind of rider, from the complete beginner to the most professional, and welcomes anyone who can ride, at whatever level, so long as they are genuinely interested in horses and equitation. The clubs also aim to give encouragement and assistance to their members, with the wider targets of improving the overall standard in riding and horsemanship, and of developing public riding facilities.

Since the majority of the members have full-time jobs, many of the instructional classes and practice rides are arranged for one or two evenings a week, usually at some suitable and conveniently placed riding school. Other activities and most of the competitions take place at weekends. Many members hire horses for club events, and some riding schools will co-operate with reduced fees for a regular arrangement. Those who have their own animal often keep it at grass, because they have neither the time for daily exercising nor, possibly, the money to keep it stabled. With the use of common sense and knowledgeable horsemastership it is of course possible to keep a horse at grass fit enough not only for ordinary riding club activities but also for the competitions, but the fact remains that for various reasons ponies are better adapted than horses to living out.

Whether one rides a horse or a pony is of no consequence until it comes to the annual competitions for the championships, when animals of 14·2 hands and under are excluded, which is a pity. Apart from considerations of convenience and cost, there are many riders who would like to have a go at their riding club competitions, but who cannot do so unless they sell the much loved and well schooled pony of their youth in order to buy a more expensive horse of unknown potential. Obviously the fences in a competition including jumping will be constructed with the horses' scope and stride in mind, but a good pony is usually capable of coping, and does not have to be an out-of-this-world performer like the incomparable Stroller to do so.

Many of the riding club competitions are the same as those of the Pony Club, but at a different standard. There are championships for dressage, show jumping and the riding club horse trials, all run off first at area level. The finals of the dressage, horse trials and the novice dressage-cum-riding test known as the Prix Caprilli, all take place each autumn at a special riding clubs' weekend held at the National Equestrian Centre.

As well as the competitions there are various riding club tests to be acquired, and a special series of awards devised especially for riders whose riding time and area is particularly restricted. The scheme is non-competitive, but the awards become progressively more difficult, and they test ability in horsemanship combined with a knowledge of farming, forestry and lore of the countryside.

All the riding clubs' competitions and championships carry some reservations about the previous successes and experience of both riders and horses, and animals under five are barred, except in the Prix Caprilli where four-year-olds are eligible. In the official events each horse or pony must either belong to the member, or to the club concerned, or to a riding school where it has been regularly ridden by members of the club for at least three months.

Pony Clubs and riding clubs did much after both world wars to encourage and aid the transition of horses from being a necessary part of everyday life to becoming a general source of pleasure to a great many people. Not only did they fill the gap in a modern generation's knowledge of horse care and riding, they also provoked increasingly wide interest in a competitive age by the institution of competitions, events, horse trials, trekking and tests. Riding is now everywhere on the increase and Pony Clubs' and riding clubs' memberships and the number of shows grow larger each year.

Great Equestrian Competitions

Racing – France

Prix de l'Arc de Triomphe

YEAR	HORSE	OWNER	TRAINER	JOCKEY
1960	Puissant Chef	n.a.	n.a.	M Garcia
1961	Molvedo	n.a.	n.a.	E Camici
1962	Soltikoff	n.a.	n.a.	M Delpalmas
1963	Exbury	n.a.	n.a.	J Deforge
1964	Prince Royal II	n.a.	n.a.	R Poincelet
1965	Sea Bird II	J Ternynck	E Pollet	T P Glennon
1966	Bon Mot	M F W Burmann	W Head	F Head
1967	Topyo	Mme L Volterra	C Bartholomew	W Pyers
1968	Vaguely Noble	N Bunker Hunt	M Zilber	W Williamson
1969	Levmoss	S McGrath	S McGrath	W Williamson
1970	Sassafras	M Plesch	F Mathet	Y Saint-Martin
1971	Mill Reef	P Mellon	I Balding	G Lewis
1972	San San	Comtesse Margit Batthyany	A Penna	F Head
1973	Rheingold	H R K Zeisel	B Hills	L Piggott
1974	Allez France	D Wildenstein	A Penna	Y Saint-Martin
1975	Star Appeal	W Zeitelhack	T Grieper	G Starkey
1976	Ivanjica	J Wertheimer	A Head	F Head
1977	Alleged	R Sangster	V O'Brien	L Piggott

First staged in 1920, the Prix de l'Arc de Triomphe has become the most prestigious event in the international racing calendar – as well as the richest. It is run annually on the first Sunday in October over a distance of 2·4 km (1½ miles) at the Longchamp course outside Paris.

Prix du Jockey Club

YEAR	HORSE	OWNER	TRAINER	JOCKEY
1960	Charlottesville	HH Aga Khan	n.a.	n.a.
1961	Right Royal	Mme J Couturies	n.a.	n.a.
1962	Val de Loir	Marquise du Vivier	n.a.	n.a.
1963	Sanctus	M Ternyncks	n.a.	n.a.
1964	Le Fabuleux	Mme G Weisweiller	n.a.	n.a.
1965	Reliance	M Dupre	n.a.	n.a.
1966	Nelcius	M Duboscq	M Clement	Y Saint-Martin
1967	Astec	Baron de la Rochette	W Head	F Head
1968	Tapalque	M Plesch	F Mathet	Y Saint-Martin
1969	Goodly	M Lehmann	W Head	F Head
1970	Sassafras	M Plesch	F Mathet	Y Saint-Martin
1971	Rheffic	Mme F Dupre	F Mathet	W Pyers
1972	Hard to Beat	M Kashiyama	R Carver	L Piggott
1973	Roi Lear	Mme P Wertheimer	A Head	F Head
1974	Caracolero	Mme F Berger	F Bootin	P Paquet
1975	Val de L'Orne	M Wertheimer	A Head	F Head
1976	Youth	N Bunker Hunt	M Zilber	F Head
1977	Crystal Palace	G de Rothschild	F Mathet	G Dubroeucq

The Prix du Jockey Club was founded in 1836 and runs annually at Chantilly over a course of 2·4 km (1½ miles).

Racing – United Kingdom

One Thousand Guineas

YEAR	HORSE	OWNER	TRAINER	JOCKEY
1960	Never Too Late	Mrs H Jackson	E Pollet	R Poincelet
1961	Sweet Solera	Mrs S Castello	R Day	W Rickaby
1962	Abermaid	R O'Ferrall	H Wragg	W Williamson
1963	Hula Dancer	Mrs P Widener	E Pollet	R Poincelet
1964	Pouparler	Beatrice, Lady Granard	P Prendergast	G Bougoure
1965	Night Off	Maj L Holliday	W Wharton	W Williamson
1966	Glad Rags	Mrs J Mills	M O'Brien	P Cook
1967	Fleet	R Boucher	C Murless	G Moore
1968	Caergwrle	Mrs N Murless	C Murless	A Barclay
1969	Full Dress II	R Moller	H Wragg	R Hutchinson
1970	Humble Duty	Jean, Lady Ashcombe	P Walwyn	L Piggott
1971	Altesse Royale	F Hue-Williams	C Murless	Y Saint-Martin
1972	Waterloo	Mrs R Stanley	J Watts	E Hide
1973	Mysterious	G Pope jnr	C Murless	G Lewis
1974	Highclere	HM The Queen	W Hern	J Mercer
1975	Nocturnal Spree	Mrs D O'Kelly	H Murless	J Roe
1976	Flying Water	D Wildenstein	A Penna	Y Saint-Martin
1977	Mrs McArdy	Mrs E Kettlewell	M Easterby	E Hide

Established in 1809, the One Thousand Guineas is the second of the five English Classics. It is run over a distance of 1·6 km (1 mile).

Two Thousand Guineas

YEAR	HORSE	OWNER	TRAINER	JOCKEY
1960	Martial	R Webster	P Prendergast	R Hutchinson
1961	Rockavon	T Yuill	G Boyd	N Stirk
1962	Privy Councillor	Maj G Glover	T Waugh	W Rickaby
1963	Only For Life	Miss M Sheriffe	J Tree	J Lindley
1964	Baldric II	Mrs H Jackson	E Fellows	W Pyers
1965	Niksar	W Harvey	W Nightingale	D Keith
1966	Kashmir II	P Butler	C Bartholomew	J Lindley
1967	Royal Palace	H Joel	N Murless	G Moore
1968	Sir Ivor	R Guest	V O'Brien	L Piggott
1969	Right Tack	J Brown	J Sutcliffe	G Lewis
1970	Nijinsky	C Engelhard	V O'Brien	L Piggott
1971	Brigadier Gerard	J Hislop	W Hern	J Mercer
1972	High Top	Sir J Thorn	B van Cutsem	W Carson
1973	Mon Fils	Mrs B Davis	R Hannon	F Durr
1974	Nonoalco	Mrs M Berger	F Boutin	Y Saint-Martin
1975	Bolkonski	C d'Alessio	H Cecil	G Dettori
1976	Wollow	C d'Alessio	H Cecil	G Dettori
1977	Nebbiolo	N Schibbye	K Prendergast	G Curran

The Two Thousand Guineas is both the first classic race of the season and the first leg of the Triple Crown title. Held at the Newmarket Spring Meeting, it is run over 1·6 km (1 mile).

The Derby

YEAR	HORSE	OWNER	TRAINER	JOCKEY
1960	St Paddy	Sir V Sassoon	N Murless	L Piggott
1961	Psidium	Mrs A Plesch	H Wragg	R Poincelet
1962	Larkspur	R Guest	V O'Brien	N Sellwood
1963	Relko	F Dupré	F Mathet	Y Saint-Martin
1964	Santa Claus	J Ismay	J Rogers	A Breasley
1965	Sea Bird II	J Ternynck	E Pollet	T Glennon
1966	Charlottown	Lady Z Wernher	G Smyth	A Breasley
1967	Royal Palace	H Joel	N Murless	G Moore
1968	Sir Ivor	R Guest	V O'Brien	L Piggott
1969	Blakeney	A Budgett	A Budgett	E Johnson
1970	Nijinsky	C Engelhard	V O'Brien	L Piggott
1971	Mill Reef	P Mellon	I Balding	G Lewis
1972	Roberto	J Galbraith	V O'Brien	L Piggott
1973	Morston	A Budgett	A Budgett	E Hide
1974	Snow Knight	Mrs N Phillips	P Nelson	B Taylor
1975	Grundy	Dr C Vittadini	P Walwyn	P Eddery
1976	Empery	N Bunker Hunt	M Zilber	L Piggott
1977	The Minstrel	R Sangster	V O'Brien	L Piggott

The major event of the English flat season, the Derby is held annually in June at Epsom. Instituted in 1780, reputedly after a party held to celebrate the running of the Oaks at which the Earl of Derby was present, the race is run over 2·4 km (1½ miles). The Derby is a supreme test of stamina and although open to both colts and fillies of three years old, it is generally run by colts. The Derby forms part of the Triple Crown, a title awarded to any horse that in one year wins the Derby, the St Leger and the 2,000 Guineas.

The Oaks

YEAR	HORSE	OWNER	TRAINER	JOCKEY
1960	Never Too Late	Mrs H Jackson	E Pollet	R Poincelet
1961	Sweet Solera	Mrs S Castello	R Day	W Rickaby
1962	Monade	M Goulandris	J Lieux	Y Saint-Martin
1963	Noblesse	Mrs J Olin	P Prendergast	G Bougoure
1964	Homeward Bound	Sir F Robinson	J Oxley	G Starkey
1965	Long Look	J Brady	M O'Brien	J Purtell
1966	Valoris	C Clore	M O'Brien	L Piggott
1967	Pia	Countess Margit Batthyany	W Elsey	E Hide
1968	La Lagune	M Berlin	F Boutin	G Thiboeuf
1969	Sleeping Partner	Lord Rosebery	D Smith	J Gorton
1970	Lupe	Mrs S Joel	C Murless	A Barclay
1971	Altesse Royale	F Hue-Williams	C Murless	G Lewis
1972	Ginevra	C St George	H Price	A Murray
1973	Mysterious	G Pope jnr	C Murless	G Lewis
1974	Polygamy	L Freedman	P Walwyn	P Eddery
1975	Juliette Marney	J Morrison	A Tree	L Piggott
1976	Pawneese	D Wildenstein	A Penna	Y Saint-Martin
1977	Dunfermline	HM The Queen	W Hern	W Carson

Named after the 12th Earl of Derby's home and first won, in 1779, by his filly Bridget, the Oaks is the leading event of the year for three-year-old fillies and is the penultimate Classic. It is traditionally held at the same Summer Meeting at Epsom as the Derby over a distance of 2·4 km (1½ miles).

For the cross-country course at an international three-day event, horse and rider must be prepared for anything. Here Bruce Davidson and his mount emerge through the spray at the Munich Olympic Games.

Polo ponies need determination and courage, agility and obedience, in order to achieve the various tactical manoeuvres demanded of them, such as 'riding off' an opponent's pony at a gallop.

OPPOSITE: Mary Chapot on White Lightning, an internationally successful American show jumping combination.

St Leger

YEAR	HORSE	OWNER	TRAINER	JOCKEY
1960	St Paddy	Sir V Sassoon	N Murless	L Piggott
1961	Aurelius	Mrs V Lilley	N Murless	L Piggott
1962	Hethersett	Maj J Holliday	W Hern	W Carr
1963	Ragusa	J Mullion	P Prendergast	G Bougoure
1964	Indiana	C Engelhard	J Watts	J Lindley
1965	Provoke	J Astor	W Hern	J Mercer
1966	Sodium	R Sigtia	G Todd	F Durr
1967	Ribocco	C Engelhard	R Houghton	L Piggott
1968	Ribero	C Engelhard	R Houghton	L Piggott
1969	Intermezzo	G Oldham	H Wragg	R Hutchinson
1970	Nijinsky	C Engelhard	V O'Brien	L Piggott
1971	Athens Wood	Mrs J Rogerson	H Thomson-Jones	L Piggott
1972	Boucher	O Phipps	V O'Brien	L Piggott
1973	Peleid	Col W Behrens	B Elsey	F Durr
1974	Bustino	Lady Beaverbrook	W Hern	J Mercer
1975	Bruni	C St George	R Price	A Murray
1976	Crow	D Wildenstein	A Penna	Y Saint-Martin
1977	Dunfermline	HM The Queen	W Hern	W Carson

First run in 1776, the St Leger is the oldest and the longest of the five British Classic races. It is held at the Doncaster course in Yorkshire and is run over 2·9 km (1 mile 6½ furlongs). The St Leger takes place annually in September and forms the last leg of the Triple Crown title.

Grand National

YEAR	HORSE	OWNER	TRAINER	JOCKEY
1960	Merryman II	Miss W Wallace	N Crump	G Scott
1961	Nicolaus Silver	C Vaughan	F Rimell	H Beasley
1962	Kilmore	N Cohen	H Price	F Winter
1963	Ayala	P Raymond	K Piggott	P Buckley
1964	Team Spirit	J Goodman	F Walwyn	G Robinson
1965	Jay Trump	Mrs N Stephenson	F Winter	Mr C Smith
1966	Anglo	S Levy	F Winter	T Norman
1967	Foinavon	C Watkins	J Kempton	J Buckingham
1968	Red Alligator	J Manners	D Smith	B Fletcher
1969	Highland Wedding	T McKoy	G Balding	E Harty
1970	Gay Trip	A Chambers	F Rimell	P Taaffe
1971	Specify	F Pontin	J Sutcliffe	J Cooke
1972	Well To Do	Capt T Forster	T Forster	G Thorner
1973	Red Rum	N le Mare	D McCain	B Fletcher
1974	Red Rum	N le Mare	D McCain	B Fletcher
1975	L'Escargot	R Guest	D Moore	T Carberry
1976	Rag Trade	P Raymond	F Rimell	J Burke
1977	Red Rum	N le Mare	D McCain	T Stack

The most famous steeplechase in the world, the Grand National was first run in 1837. It is held annually in late March or early April at Aintree racecourse, Liverpool. The distance of 7·2 km (4½ miles) with 30 fences requires stamina and jumping ability. The course is a combination of hedges, ditches, drops and water jumps and includes the daunting Becher's Brook, a 1·47 m (4 ft 10 in) fence with a drop of 1·83 m (6 ft), and the famous Canal Turn.

Racing – United States

Preakness Stakes

YEAR	HORSE	OWNER	TRAINER	JOCKEY
1960	Bally Ache	Turfland	H Pitt	R Ussery
1961	Carry Back	Mrs K Price	J Price	J Sellers
1962	Greek Money	Brandywine Stables	V Raines	J Rotz
1963	Candy Spots	R Ellsworth	M Tenney	W Shoemaker
1964	Northern Dancer	Winfields Farm	H Luro	W Hartack
1965	Tom Rolfe	Powhatan	F Whiteley jnr	R Turcotte
1966	Kauai King	M Ford	H Forrest	D Brumfield
1967	Damascus	E Bancroft	F Whiteley jnr	W Shoemaker
1968	Forward Pass	Calumet Farm	H Forrest	I Valenzuela
1969	Majestic Prince	F McMahon	J Longden	W Hartack
1970	Personality	E Jacobs	J Jacobs	E Belmonte
1971	Canonero II	E Caibett	J Arias	G Avila
1972	Bee Bee Bee	W Farish 3rd	D Carroll	E Nelson
1973	Secretariat	Meadow Stable	L Lauren	R Turcotte
1974	Little Current	Darby Dan Farm	L Rondinello	M Rivera
1975	Master Derby	Golden Chance Farms Inc	W E Adams	D G McHargue
1976	Elocutionist	E C Cashmam	P T Adwell	J Lively
1977	Seattle Slew	Mrs K L Taylor	B Turner	J Cruguet

The Preakness Stakes were first held in 1873 and now take place annually in the middle of May. The race, held over a distance of 1·9 km (9½ furlongs) at the Pimlico course, Maryland, constitutes one third of the Triple Crown.

Belmont Stakes

YEAR	HORSE	OWNER	TRAINER	JOCKEY
1960	Celtic Ash	J O'Connell	T Barry	W Hartack
1961	Sherluck	J Sher	H Young	B Baeza
1962	Jaipur	G Widener	B Mulholland	W Shoemaker
1963	Chateaugay	J Galbreath	J Conway	B Baeza
1964	Quadrangle	P Mellon	J Burch	M Ycaza
1965	Hail to All	Mrs B Cohen	E Yowell	J Sellers
1966	Amberoid	R Webster	L Lauren	W Boland
1967	Damascus	Mrs E Bancroft	F Whiteley jnr	W Shoemaker
1968	Stage Door Johnny	Greentree Stable	J Gaver	H Gustines
1969	Arts and Letters	P Mellon	E Burch	B Baeza
1970	High Echelon	Mrs E Jacobs	J Jacobs	J Rotz
1971	Pass Catcher	October House Farm	E Yowell	W Blum
1972	Riva Ridge	Meadow Stable	L Lauren	R Turcotte
1973	Secretariat	Meadow Stable	L Lauren	R Turcotte
1974	Little Current	Darby Dan Farm	L Rondinello	M Rivera
1975	Avatar	A A Seeligson jnr	A T Doyle	W Shoemaker
1976	Tell Me All	Hobeau Farm	H Jerkens	J Ruane
1977	Seattle Slew	Mrs K L Taylor	B Turner	J Cruguet

First held in 1867, the Belmont Stakes are regarded by some as the most important of the Triple Crown races. The race is run over a distance of 2·4 km (1½ miles) at its now permanent home at Belmont Park, New York.

Kentucky Derby

YEAR	HORSE	OWNER	TRAINER	JOCKEY
1960	Venetian Way	Sunny Blue Farm	V Sovinski	W Hartack
1961	Carry Back	Mrs K Price	J Price	J Sellers
1962	Decidedly	El Peco Ranch	H Luro	W Hartack
1963	Chateaugay	Darby Dan Farm	J Conway	B Baeza
1964	Northern Dancer	Winfields Farm	H Luro	W Hartack
1965	Lucky Debonair	Mrs A Rice	F Catrone	W Shoemaker
1966	Kauai King	Ford Stable	H Forrest	D Brumfield
1967	Proud Clarion	Darby Dan Farm	L Gentry	R Ussery
1968	Dancer's Image	P Fuller	L Cavalaris	R Ussery
1969	Majestic Prince	F McMahon	J Longden	W Hartack
1970	Dust Commander	R Lehmann	D Combs	M Manganello
1971	Canonero II	E Caibett	J Arias	G Avita
1972	Riva Ridge	Meadow Stable	L Lauren	R Turcotte
1973	Secretariat	Meadow Stable	L Lauren	R Turcotte
1974	Cannonade	J Olin	W Stephens	A Cordero
1975	Foolish Pleasure	J L Greer	L Jolley	J Vasquez
1976	Bold Forbes	E R Tizol	L S Barrera	A Cordero
1977	Seattle Slew	Mrs K L Taylor	B Turner	J Cruguet

Founded in 1875, the Kentucky Derby has become the greatest of the American classic races, and forms part of the Triple Crown title awarded to any horse which wins this race together with the Preakness Stakes and the Belmont Stakes in one year. Held on the first Saturday in May over the course at Churchill Downs, Louisville, Kentucky, it is run over a distance of 2 km ($1\frac{1}{4}$ miles) and is open to three-year-olds.

Racing – South Africa

Durban July Handicap

YEAR	HORSE	OWNER	TRAINER	JOCKEY
1960	Left Wing	Birch Bros	n.a.	n.a.
1961	Kerason	Gp Capt Dalzell	n.a.	n.a.
1962	Diza	F Lambert	J H Gorton	A Roberts
1963	Colorado King	P S Louw	S Laird	n.a.
1964	Numeral	C W Engelhard	n.a.	n.a.
1965	King Willow	Mr & Mrs H Oppenheimer	J Breval	I Bailey
1966	Java Head	B Levin	S Laird	H Cawcutt
1967	Sea Cottage	S Laird	S Laird	R Sivewright
1968	Chimboraa	Mr & Mrs Burstein	B A Cherry	D Payne
1969	Naval Escort	D & C V Saunders	A Reid	F W Rickaby
1970	Court Day	M Livanos	R T Knight	n.a.
1971	Mazarin	Mr & Mrs T Tenderini	S C Laird	R Sivewright
1972	In Full Flight	N Ferguson	n.a.	n.a.
1973	Yataghan	J M Scrimmel	S C Laird	B Hayden
1974	Ribovilla	Mr & Mrs G Mosenthal	G Azzie	M Schoeman
1975	Principal Boy*	n.a.	n.a.	n.a.
1976	Jamaican Music	Dr C A Crobin	R Rixon	B Abercrombie
1977	Lightning Shot	C H & G Els, Mr J W Sloane	D G Rich	D Mustard

The most important and richest race in South Africa, the Durban July Handicap, is run over 2·1 km (10½ furlongs), at Turffentein outside Johannesburg.

*Gatecrasher came in first but was disqualified and put back to third place.

Racing – Australia

Melbourne Cup

YEAR	HORSE	OWNER	TRAINER	JOCKEY
1960	Hi Jinx	T Knowles & K Sly	T H Knowles	W A Wmith
1961	Lord Fury	Mr & Mrs N Cohen	F B Lewis	R Selkrig
1962	Even Stevens	J Wattie	A McGregor	L Coles
1963	Gatun Gatun	M P Reid	H G Hearney	J Johnson
1964	Polo Prince	Mr & Mrs W L Day	J P Carter	R W Taylor
1965	Light Fingers	W J Broderick	J B Cummings	R Higgins
1966	Galilee	Mr & Mrs M L Bailey	J B Cummings	J Miller
1967	Red Handed	F Clarke, Condon, A Tyson	J B Cummings	R Higgins
1968	Rain Lover	C A Reid	M L Robins	J Johnson
1969	Rain Lover	C A Reid	M L Robins	J Johnson
1970	Baghdad Note	E C S Falconer	R Heasley	E J Didham
1971	Silver Knight	Sir Walter Norwood	E Temperton	R B Marsh
1972	Piping Lane	R W Trinder	G M Hanlon	J Letts
1973	Gala Supreme	J P Curtain	R J Hutchins	R Reys
1974	Think Big	R J O'Sullivan & C N Tan	J B Cummings	H White
1975	Think Big	R J O'Sullivan, C N Tan & Tunku Abdul Rahman	J B Cummings	H White
1976	Van Der Hum	L H & R A Robinson, E L G Abel	L H Robinson	R J Skelton
1977	Gold and Black	Mr & Mrs J Harris, Mr & Mrs H B Gage	J B Cummings	J Duggan

A two-mile handicap run at Flemington Racecourse in Melbourne, which attracts the attention of the whole nation. It is run on the first Tuesday in November. It was first run in 1861.

Three-day Event

World Three-day Event Championships

YEAR	TEAM	INDIVIDUAL	HORSE	COUNTRY
1966	1 Ireland	1 Capt C Moratorio	Chalan	Argentina
	2 Argentina	2 R Meade	Barberry	Gt Britain
	All other teams eliminated	3 V Freeman-Mason	Sam Weller	Ireland
1970	1 Gt Britain	1 M Gordon-Watson	Cornishman V	Gt Britain
	2 France	2 R Meade	The Poacher	Gt Britain
	All other teams eliminated	3 J Wofford	Kilkenny	USA
1974	1 USA	1 B Davidson	Irish Cap	USA
	2 Gt Britain	2 M Plumb	Good Mixture	USA
	3 W Germany	3 H Thomas	Playamar	Gt Britain

European Three-day Event Championships

YEAR	TEAM	INDIVIDUAL	HORSE	COUNTRY
1962	1 USSR	1 Capt J Templer	M'Lord Connolly	Gt Britain
	2 Ireland	2 G Gasumov	Granj	USSR
	3 Gt Britain	3 J Wykeham-Musgrave	Ryebrooks	Gt Britain
1965	1 USSR	1 M Babierecki	Volt	Poland
	2 Ireland	2 L Baklyshkin	Ruon	USSR
	3 Gt Britain	3 H Karsten	Condora	W Germany
1967	1 Gt Britain	1 Maj E Boylan	Durlas Eile	Ireland
	2 Ireland	2 M Whiteley	The Poacher	Gt Britain
	3 France	3 Maj D Allhusen	Lochinvar	Gt Britain
1969	1 Gt Britain	1 M Gordon-Watson	Cornishman V	Gt Britain
	2 USSR	2 R Walker	Pasha	Gt Britain
	3 W Germany	3 B Messman	Windspiel	W Germany
1971	1 Gt Britain	1 HRH Princess Anne	Doublet	Gt Britain
	2 USSR	2 D West	Baccarat	Gt Britain
	3 Ireland	3 S Stevens	Classic Chips	Gt Britain
1973	1 W Germany	1 A Evdokimov	Jeger	USSR
	2 USSR	2 H Blöcker	Albrandt	W Germany
	3 Gt Britain	3 H Karsten	Sioux	W Germany
1975	1 USSR	1 L Prior-Palmer	Be Fair	Gt Britain
	2 Gt Britain	2 HRH Princess Anne	Goodwill	Gt Britain
	3 W Germany	3 P Gornuschko	Gusar	USSR
1977	1 Gt Britain	1 L Prior-Palmer	George	Gt Britain
	2 W Germany	2 K Schultz	Madrigal	W Germany
	3 Ireland	3 H Karsten	Sioux	W Germany

Three-day events, also known as horse trials and combined training events, date from the days of the great military academies. The idea originated as a means of testing an officer and his charger in every aspect of equitation. This event is an arduous competition for horse and rider which is completed over three consecutive days. It demonstrates the skills of the rider and his mount in every discipline of the art. The first day consists of a demonstration of obedience in the form of an advanced dressage test, followed on the second day by a test of speed and endurance over road-and-tracks, steeplechasing and cross-country. The final day is devoted to show jumping. The scores are tallied in penalties and the horse and rider with the lowest score for the three days is the winner.

374 **GREAT EQUESTRIAN COMPETITIONS**

Badminton Horse Trials

YEAR	RIDER	HORSE	COUNTRY
1960	W Roycroft	Our Solo	Australia
1961	L Morgan	Salad Days	Australia
1962	A Drummond-Hay	Merely-A-Monarch	Gt Britain
1963	(cancelled owing to bad weather)		
1964	Capt J R Templer	M'Lord Connolly	Gt Britain
1965	Maj E A Boylan	Durlas Eile	Ireland
1966	(cancelled owing to bad weather)		
1967	C Ross-Taylor	Jonathan	Gt Britain
1968	J Bullen	Our Nobby	Gt Britain
1969	R Walker	Pasha	Gt Britain
1970	R Meade	The Poacher	Gt Britain
1971	Lt M Phillips	Great Ovation	Gt Britain
1972	Lt M Phillips	Great Ovation	Gt Britain
1973	L Prior-Palmer	Be Fair	Gt Britain
1974	Capt M Phillips	Columbus	Gt Britain
1975	cancelled		
1976	L Prior-Palmer	Wideawake	Gt Britain
1977	L Prior-Palmer	George	Gt Britain

The Badminton Horse Trials is a three-day event competition which takes place annually in April, weather permitting. They were first held in 1949 at the invitation of the Duke of Beaufort in the grounds of his estate at Badminton House, Gloucestershire. In common with other three-day events, the first day is devoted to dressage, the second to tests of speed and endurance and the third to show jumping. The Badminton Horse Trials is a severe test to both horse and rider and since its inception has become a classic international event.

Show Jumping

Men's World Championship

YEAR	RIDER	HORSE	COUNTRY
1960	1 Capt R d'Inzeo	Gowran Girl	Italy
	2 C Delia	Duipil	Argentina
	3 D Broome	Sunsalve	Gt Britain
1966	1 P d'Oriola	Pomone B	France
	2 A de Bohorques	Quizas	Spain
	3 Capt R d'Inzeo	Bowjak	Italy
1970	1 D Broome	Beethoven	Gt Britain
	2 G Mancinelli	Fidux	Italy
	3 H Smith	Mattie Brown	Gt Britain
1974	1 H Steenken	Simona	W Germany
	2 E Macken	Pele	Ireland
	3 { F Chapot	Main Spring	USA
	{ H Simon	Lavendel	Austria

Women's World Championship

YEAR	RIDER	HORSE	COUNTRY
1965	1 M Coakes	Stroller	Gt Britain
	2 K Kusner	Untouchable	USA
	3 A Westwood	The Maverick	Gt Britain
1970	1 J Lefebvre	Rocket	France
	2 M Mould	Stroller	Gt Britain
	3 A Drummond-Hay	Merely-A-Monarch	Gt Britain
1974	1 J Tissot	Rocket	France
	2 M McEvoy	Mr Muskie	USA
	3 B Kerr	Magnor	Canada

Competition discontinued

Presidents' Cup

YEAR	COUNTRY	YEAR	COUNTRY	YEAR	COUNTRY
1965	1 Gt Britain	1969	1 W Germany	1974	1 Gt Britain
	2 W Germany		2 Gt Britain		2 W Germany
	3 Italy		3 Italy		3 France
1966	1 USA	1970	1 Gt Britain	1975	1 W Germany
	2 Spain		2 W Germany		2 Gt Britain
	3 France		3 Italy		3 { Italy
1967	1 Gt Britain	1971	1 W Germany		{ Belgium
	2 W Germany		2 Gt Britain	1976	1 W Germany
	3 Italy		3 Italy		2 France
1968	1 USA	1972	1 Gt Britain		3 { Ireland
	2 Gt Britain		2 W Germany		{ Italy
	3 { Italy		3 Italy	1977	1 Gt Britain
	{ W Germany	1973	1 Gt Britain		2 W Germany
			2 W Germany		3 Ireland
			3 Switzerland		

Regarded by many as a 'circus art' during the early years of this century, show jumping really only became accepted as an equestrian sport after 1945, and with the help of television and other media is now one of the most popular spectator sports in any sphere.

Courses, fences and competitors have far advanced. Many international events offer high prize money, and with the introduction of sponsorship can be highly lucrative for owners and riders.

Each horse must be registered with its national show jumping association and all are graded according to their ability and prize winnings. The judging of competitions is by calculating faults incurred at each fence – there are no penalties for style, or lack of it.

An international show jumping championship instituted in 1965. A trophy is awarded annually to the national team gaining the most points in Prix des Nations events (Nations Cups) over a twelve-month period between 1 December and 30 November. Nations Cups are held only at official international horse shows.

Men's European Championship

YEAR	RIDER	HORSE	COUNTRY
1961	1 D Broome	Sunsalve	Gt Britain
	2 Capt P d'Inzeo	Pioneer	Italy
	3 H Winkler	Romanus	W Germany
1962	1 C Barker	Mister Softee	Gt Britain
	2 { H Winkler	Romanus	W Germany
	Capt P d'Inzeo	The Rock	Italy
1963	1 G Mancinelli	Rockette	Italy
	2 A Shockemöhle	Freiherr	W Germany
	3 H Smith	O'Malley	Gt Britain
1964	No competition		
1965	1 H Schridde	Dozent II	W Germany
	2 A Queipo de Llano	Infernal	Spain
	3 A Schockemöhle	Exakt	W Germany
1966	1 N Pessoa	Gran Geste	Brazil
	2 F Chapot	San Lucas	USA
	3 H Arrambide	Chimbote	Argentina
1967	1 D Broome	Mister Softee	Gt Britain
	2 H Smith	Harvester	Gt Britain
	3 A Schockemöhle	Donald Rex	W Germany
1968	No competition		
1969	1 D Broome	Mister Softee	Gt Britain
	2 A Schockemöhle	Donald Rex	W Germany
	3 H Winkler	Enigk	W Germany
1970	No competition		
1971	1 H Steenken	Simona	W Germany
	2 H Smith	Evan Jones	Gt Britain
	3 P Weier	Wulf	Switzerland
1972	No competition		
1973	1 P McMahon	Pennwood Forge Mill	Gt Britain
	2 A Schockemöhle	The Robber	W Germany
	3 H Parot	Tic	France
1974	No competition		
1975	1 A Schockemöhle	Warwick	W Germany
	2 H Steenken	Erle	W Germany
	3 S Sonksen	Kwept	W Germany
1976	No competition		
1977	1 J Heins	Severn Valley	Netherlands
	2 E Macken	Kerrygold	Ireland
	3 T Ebben	Jumbo Design	Netherlands

The European championships were first held in 1957. To begin with competitors from outside Europe were allowed to compete, but eligibility is now confined to European riders. The competition consists of three jumping rounds, with the points from each round accumulating to decide the winner.

Women's European Championship

YEAR	RIDER	HORSE	COUNTRY
1960	1 S Cohen	Clare Castle	Gt Britain
	2 W Wofford	Hollandia	Gt Britain
	3 A Clement	Nico	W Germany
1961	1 P Smythe	Flanagan	Gt Britain
	2 I Jansen	Icare	Holland
	3 C Cancre	Ocean	France
1962	1 P Smythe	Flanagan	Gt Britain
	2 H Kohler	Cremona	W Germany
	3 P de Goyoaga	Kif Kif	Spain
1963	1 P Smythe	Flanagan	Gt Britain
	2 A Givaudan	Huipil	Brazil
	3 A Drummond-Hay	Merely-A-Monarch	Gt Britain
1966	1 J Lefebvre	Kenavo	France
	2 M Bachmann	Sandro	Switzerland
	3 L Novo	Oxo Bob	Italy
1967	1 K Kusner	Untouchable	USA
	2 L Novo	Predestine	Italy
	3 M Bachmann	Erbach	Switzerland
1968	1 A Drummond-Hay	Merely-A-Monarch	Gt Britain
	2 G Serventi	Gay Monarch	Italy
	3 { M Coakes	Stroller	Gt Britain
	{ J Lefebvre	Rocket	France
1969	1 I Kellet	Morning Light	Ireland
	2 A Drummond-Hay	Xanthos	Gt Britain
	3 A Westwood	The Maverick	Gt Britain
1971	1 A Moore	Psalm	Gt Britain
	2 M Dawes	The Maverick	Gt Britain
	3 M Leiten-Berger	Limbarra de Porto Conte	Austria
1973	1 A Moore	Psalm	Gt Britain
	2 C Bradley	True Lass	Gt Britain
	3 P Weier	Erbach	Switzerland
1974	No competition		
1975	Combined with Men's European Championship		

The European championships for women were first introduced in 1957, and remained as an independent competition until 1975, when they were amalgamated with the men's event.

Dressage

World Championships

YEAR	TEAM	INDIVIDUAL	HORSE	COUNTRY
1966	1 W Germany	1 J Neckermann	Mariano	W Germany
	2 Switzerland	2 R Klimke	Dux	W Germany
	3 USSR	3 H Boldt	Remus	W Germany
1970	1 USSR	1 E Petouchkova	Pepel	USSR
	2 W Germany	2 L Linsenhoff	Piaff	W Germany
	3 E Germany	3 I Kisimov	Ikor	USSR
1974	1 W Germany	1 R Klimke	Mehmed	W Germany
	2 USSR	2 L Linsenhoff	Piaff	W Germany
	3 Switzerland	3 E Petouchkova	Pepel	USSR

European Championships

YEAR	TEAM	INDIVIDUAL	HORSE	COUNTRY
1963	1 Gt Britain	1 H Chammartin	Wolfdietrich	Switzerland
	2 Romania	2 H Boldt	Remus	W Germany
		3 H Chammartin	Woermann	Switzerland
1965	1 W Germany	1 H Chammartin	Wolfdietrich	Switzerland
	2 Switzerland	2 H Boldt	Remus	W Germany
	3 USSR	3 R Klimke	Arcadius	W Germany
1967	1 W Germany	1 R Klimke	Dux	W Germany
	2 USSR	2 I Kisimov	Ikor	USSR
	3 Switzerland	3 H Boldt	Remus	W Germany
1969	1 W Germany	1 L Linsenhoff	Piaff	W Germany
	2 E Germany	2 I Kisimov	Ikor	USSR
	3 USSR	3 J Neckermann	Mariano	W Germany
1971	1 W Germany	1 L Linsenhoff	Piaff	W Germany
	2 USSR	2 J Neckermann	Van Eick	W Germany
	3 Sweden	3 I Kisimov	Ikor	USSR
1973	1 W Germany	1 R Klimke	Mehmed	W Germany
	2 USSR	2 E Petouchkova	Pepel	USSR
	3 Switzerland	3 I Kalita	Tarif	USSR
1975	1 W Germany	1 C Stuckelberger	Granat	Switzerland
	2 USSR	2 H Boldt	Woycek	W Germany
	3 Switzerland	3 K Schluter	Liostro	W Germany

European Championships in this discipline are held every other year while the World event takes place every four years between Olympic Games. The most successful nation has undoubtedly been West Germany since the war, although the Russian horses and riders with their lighter touch in performance were in favour for a while in the early seventies. The Americans are slowly rising through the ranks, mainly because they have secured the heavy German-type horses whose movements seem to appeal to the top judges at the moment.

One of the world's supreme exponents of the art of dressage, Liselotte Linsenhoff competes with Piaff at the World Championships. Piaff displays the essential lightness and grace of a highly-trained horse.

Driving

World Championships

YEAR	TEAM	INDIVIDUAL	COUNTRY
1972	1 Gt Britain	1 A Dubey	Switzerland
	2 Switzerland	2 Sir John Miller	Gt Britain
	3 W Germany	3 D Nicholson	Gt Britain
1974	1 Gt Britain	1 S Fulop	Hungary
	2 Switzerland	2 C Iseli	Switzerland
	3 Poland	3 G Bowman	Gt Britain
1976	1 Hungary	1 I Abonyi	Hungary
	2 W Germany	2 E Jung	W Germany
	3 Poland	3 Z Waliszewski	Poland

European Championships

YEAR	TEAM	INDIVIDUAL	COUNTRY
1971	1 Hungary	1 I Abonyi	Hungary
	2 Germany	2 S Fulop	Hungary
	3 Gt Britain	3 J Papp	Hungary
1973	1 Switzerland	1 A Dubey	Switzerland
	2 W Germany	2 R Doudin	Switzerland
	3 Gt Britain	3 D Nicholson	Gt Britain
1975	1 Hungary	1 I Abonyi	Hungary
	2 Poland	2 G Bardos	Hungary
	3 W Germany	3 A Miuty	Hungary
1977	1 Hungary	1 G Bardos	Hungary
	2 Poland	2 T Velstra	Holland
	3 W Germany	3 E Jung	W Germany

The European Championships were first held in 1971 while the World event first took place in 1972. They consist of three phases, similar to the ridden three-day event: dressage, cross-country, and obstacle driving for a team of four horses. The horses and vehicles are also closely inspected for condition and turnout and marks are awarded accordingly for this extra phase. The sport has grown rapidly in the six years of its international existence, due in no small way to the participation and encouragement of HRH the Duke of Edinburgh, who has represented Great Britain on several occasions with a team of Cleveland Bay horses belonging to HM The Queen. Another of Her Majesty's teams was driven by Crown Equerry, Col. Sir John Miller.

Olympic Games

Dressage

YEAR	TEAM	INDIVIDUAL	HORSE	COUNTRY
1960	No team awards	1 S Filatov	Absent	USSR
		2 G Fischer	Wald	Switzerland
		3 J Neckermann	Asbach	Germany*
1964	1 Germany*	1 H Chammartin	Woermann	Switzerland
	2 Switzerland	2 H Boldt	Remus	Germany*
	3 USSR	3 S Filatov	Absent	USSR
1968	1 W Germany	1 I Kisimov	Ikhov	USSR
	2 USSR	2 J Neckermann	Mariano	W Germany
	3 Switzerland	3 R Klimke	Dux	W Germany
1972	1 USSR	1 L Linsenhoff	Piaff	W Germany
	2 W Germany	2 E Petushkova	Pepel	USSR
	3 Sweden	3 J Neckermann	Venetia	W Germany
1976	W Germany	1 C Stuckelberger	Granat	Switzerland
	2 Switzerland	2 H Boldt	Woycek	W Germany
	3 USA	3 Dr R Klimke	Mehmed	W Germany

Equestrian events were first included in the 1912 Olympic Games held at Stockholm, mostly due to the efforts of Count Clarence von Rosen, Master of the Horse to the King of Sweden. There are now three disciplines for competition: dressage, three-day event and show jumping. In dressage, the team and individual competitions are judged as two separate events, with the top twelve competitors from the team section going forward to the individual ride-off. The

Three-day Event

YEAR	TEAM	INDIVIDUAL	HORSE	COUNTRY
1960	1 Australia	1 L Morgan	Salad Days	Australia
	2 Switzerland	2 N Lavis	Mirrabooka	Australia
	3 France	3 A Buhler	Gay Spark	Switzerland
1964	1 Italy	1 M Checcoli	Surbean	Italy
	2 USA	2 C Moratorio	Chalan	Argentina
	3 Germany*	3 F Ligges	Don Kosak	Germany*
1968	1 Gt Britain	1 J-J Guyon	Pitou	France
	2 USA	2 Maj D Allhusen	Lochinvar	Gt Britain
	3 Australia	3 M Page	Foster	USA
1972	1 Gt Britain	1 R Meade	Laurieston	Gt Britain
	2 USA	2 A Argenton	Woodland	Italy
	3 W Germany	3 J Jonsson	Sarajevo	Sweden
1976	1 USA	1 T Coffin	Bally Cor	USA
	2 W Germany	2 M Plumb	Better and Better	USA
	3 Australia	3 K Schultz	Madrigal	W Germany

Show Jumping

YEAR	TEAM	INDIVIDUAL	HORSE	COUNTRY
1960	1 Germany*	1 Capt R d'Inzeo	Possillipo	Italy
	2 USA	2 Capt P d'Inzeo	The Rock	Italy
	3 Italy	3 D Broome	Sunsalve	Gt Britain
1964	1 Germany*	1 P d'Oriola	Lutteur	France
	2 France	2 H Shridde	Dozent	Germany*
	3 Italy	3 P Robeson	Firecrest	Gt Britain
1968	1 Canada	1 W Steinkraus	Snowbound	USA
	2 France	2 M Coakes	Stroller	Gt Britain
	3 W Germany	3 D Broome	Mister Softee	Gt Britain
1972	1 W Germany	1 G Mancinelli	Ambassador	Italy
	2 USA	2 A Moore	Psalm	Gt Britain
	3 Italy	3 N Shapiro	Sloopy	USA
1976	1 France	1 A Schockemöhle	Warwick Rex	W Germany
	2 W Germany	2 M Vaillancourt	Branch County	Canada
	3 Belgium	3 F Mathy	Gai Luron	Belgium

*Prior to 1968 West and East Germany sent a joint team to the Olympic Games

three-day event has three phases: dressage test, speed and endurance and show jumping. In this event, the team and individual winners are decided simultaneously to avoid over-exerting the horses. In the show jumping, an individual event is now held separately preceding the Prix des Nations, which is traditionally held as the final event of the Olympic Games. Countries may nominate different horses and riders for each event, that is three to jump individually and then, if necessary, another four to take part in the team competition. Of the four members of the team competition, the score of the best three competitors is to count over two rounds. No prize money is given and there are no individual awards.

The Language of Horsemanship

Above the bit An evasion of the bit when the horse raises its head to avoid the action of the bit in its mouth, thereby reducing any effective control the rider has over the horse. This habit is remedied through schooling, by encouraging the horse to lower the head and to accept the bit.

Account for To kill a fox.

Acey deucey Riding with one stirrup leather longer than the other, a style sometimes adopted by jockeys in the US to help them keep their balance on sharp bends.

Acting Master A person appointed temporarily to organize a hunt, either for a day or for a longer period pending the appointment of a permanent Master.

Action The manner in which a horse moves. Good action is to plant all four feet freely and with equal weight on each foot at every pace; bad action is moving unevenly or with an unlevel gait; 'tied in' action describes a horse which cannot extend its limbs to move freely.

Against the clock In show jumping a competition or jump-off decided by time, the winner being the competitor with the least number of faults in the fastest time.

Aged A term used for any horse or pony over eight years. Age up to eight years can be judged accurately by inspecting the teeth, but after this age it becomes increasingly difficult to judge with certainty.

Aids The signals, through hands, legs, seat and voice, whereby the rider communicates his wishes to the horse. See also Artificial aids.

Airs above the ground A form of *haute école* where the horse is elevated off the ground in some form of leap or jump. This is performed only by the most advanced horses, such as the stallions of the Spanish Riding School.

Albino A colour-type of horse rather than a breed. The true albino has white hair, pink skin and blue-tinted eyes, as it lacks any true pigmentation. The albino horse is recognized in America as a colour type.

All on A hunting term normally used by the whipper-in to let the huntsman know all hounds are up with the pack.

All-round cow horse A horse which is skilled at carrying out all the duties required of it by a cowboy.

Also-ran Any unplaced horse in a race.

Alter To castrate a horse or colt, thus rendering it sterile.

Amble A slow gait in two-time in which the horse's hind and foreleg on the same side are moved forward together.

Ante-post betting The placing of bets on a race at an agreed price prior to the day of the race.

Anvil (a) A heavy iron block with a smooth flat face, usually of steel, on which horse-shoes are shaped. (b) (Western US) a horse, particularly one which is shod, which strikes the forefeet with the hind feet.

Appointment card A card sent out to interested parties by the hunt secretary informing them of the time, date and place of forthcoming meets.

Apprentice A youth who is being trained as a jockey and serves an indentured apprenticeship of five to seven years.

Apron A covering made of strong horse-hide worn by farriers to protect the front of the body while a horse is being shod.

Arena The area in which a horse show or show-jumping competition is held.

Artificial aids Items such as whips, spurs and martingales which are used by the rider to help convey instructions to the horse.

As hounds ran The distance covered in a hunt by hounds.

Automatic timing An electrical apparatus used for show-jumping events. The horse breaks an electronic ray as it goes through the start, triggering off the mechanism which starts the clock. As it goes through the finish it breaks a similar device which stops the clock.

Autorisation spéciale A pink card issued to a rider by his national equestrian

federation permitting him to compete in an international dressage, show jumping or combined training event.

Autumn double The Cesarewitch Stakes and the Cambridgeshire Stakes – two racing events held annually at Newmarket, England in the autumn.

Azoturia Often known as 'Monday morning disease', because it affects horses which have been left standing in on a Sunday. It is a blood disorder that causes the muscles to atrophy and seize up if too much heating food is given without enough exercise.

Back (a) The mounting of a horse for the first time in its training. (b) To place a bet on a horse.

Backer A person who places a bet on a horse.

Back hander A polo stroke in which the player travelling forwards hits the ball backwards in the opposite direction.

Back jockey The stop skirt of a Western saddle.

Badge of honour An award presented by the FEI to riders competing in Prix des Nations competitions with points given as follows: bronze–5, silver–25, gold–50. Competing in an Olympic Games is counted as competing in five Prix des Nations.

Bag fox A fox that is caught and kept and then released for the purpose of hunting. This practice is not approved by the hunting fraternity.

Ballotade An air above the ground in which the horse half rears, then jumps forward, drawing the hind legs up below the quarters, before landing on all four legs.

Bandages A form of support and protection against cold and injury. They are used on a working horse, usually on the legs but also to protect the tail while travelling or to keep it in a tidy state while the horse is in the stable.

Bang Method of cutting the tail squarely with scissors.

Bareme Any of the three tables of rules set by the FEI under which show jumping competitions are judged.

Barrage A jump-off.

Bareback riding Riding a horse without a saddle or blanket on its back.

Barrel The part of the horse's body between the forearms and the loins.

Barrier (a) The point at which a race starts. (b) In a rodeo arena the barrier behind which the roper or steer wrestler's horse waits until the stock is far enough out of the chute.

Bars There are various different 'bars' related to the horse and its equipment: the bars of the mouth are the sensitive areas of the horse's lower jaw where the bit lies; the bars of the foot divide the sole from the frog; the bars of a saddle are the metal parts to which the stirrup leathers are attached; the bars of the bit are the cheek pieces on a curb bit.

Bay (a) A dark skinned horse with a dark brown to a bright reddish- or yellowish-brown coat, with a black mane and tail and normally black markings on the legs. (b) the noise made by a hound.

Bayo coyote A dun horse with a black dorsal stripe.

Beaning Disguising an unsoundness in a horse.

Bedding The form of bedding used in a stable can vary from straw to wood chips, sawdust or even peat. This provides a soft surface upon which the horse can lie in the stable without injury to itself. Bedding must be changed regularly to ensure a healthy horse.

Bed down To put down a bed for a horse in a stable or loose box.

Bell As rung in show-jumping competitions to signal competitors to start, restart or stop, or to indicate elimination.

Betting (a) The quotation of the wager prices of horses in a certain race. (b) To place a bet on a horse.

Bit A device, normally made of metal or rubber, attached to the bridle and placed in the horse's mouth so as to regulate the position of the horse's head and to help control the pace and direction of the horse.

Bitless bridle Any of a variety of bridles used without bits, pressure being exerted on the nose and the curb groove instead of the mouth.

Black A horse with a black coat, mane and tail with no other colour present, except possibly white markings on the face and/or legs.

Black saddler A saddler who specializes in making items of saddlery for riding horses.

Blacksmith The man who makes among other things horseshoes and then fits them to each foot of the horse. This is a skilled craft and one that seemed for some time to be dying out. Farriery, as the craft is more specifically called, is now on the increase and apprentice-training schemes are in operation.

Blaze A white mark running down the centre of a horse's face.

Blemish Any scar left by an injury or wound.

Blind bucker A horse which bucks indiscriminately, heading into anything, when ridden.

Blinkers A pair of leather eye-shields fixed to the bridle or on a head-covering, used to prevent a horse from looking anywhere other than in front of it.

Blister A form of medication; by rubbing an irritant on to an affected area, the blood supply to the injured area is increased, thereby hastening recovery.

Blood The amount of blood in a horse's body is made up of approximately one-eighteenth of its total body weight.

Blood horse An English Thoroughbred.

Bloodstock Thoroughbred horses, particularly race and stud animals.

Blow a stirrup To lose a stirrup iron. If this happens in a rodeo contest the rider is disqualified.

Blow away To send hounds after a fox by blowing a given signal on the hunting horn.

Blow up (a) A term used in the dressage arena or the show ring when a horse either breaks from the pace at which it is

meant to be going or misbehaves generally. (b) (US) To start bucking.

Body brush A soft-bristled brush essential for the grooming of a horse, as it removes the dirt and sweat from the body. It is normally used in conjunction with a curry comb, which is used at regular intervals to clean the brush.

Boil over To start bucking.

Bolt A dangerous vice in any horse, causing it to gallop in an uncontrolled manner with little regard either for its own safety or for that of its rider. This is highly dangerous, especially in a child's pony.

Bookmaker A professional betting man who is licensed to accept the bets placed by others on horses, etc.

Boot jack A wooden device to aid in the removal of hunting boots by fitting the heel into a shaped piece of wood and then pulling.

Boundary rider Station (ranch) worker whose task it is to ride round all the fencing on the huge Australian cattle and sheep properties, to find holes and to repair them.

Bran The husk of the wheat grain that is separated after milling. This bulk food is an essential part of a horse's diet, especially if the horse is off work for any period of time. It acts as a laxative when given as a hot mash with Epsom salts.

Break down To lacerate the suspensory ligament or fracture a sesamoid bone, so that the back of the fetlock drops to the ground.

Breaking in A term used to describe the early education of a young horse from the time it is first subjected to human influence until it has become a mannered and rideable animal.

Breastplate A device, usually of leather, attached to the saddle to prevent it from slipping back on the horse.

Breeder (a) The owner of a mare which gives birth to a foal. (b) The owner of a stud farm where horses are bred.

Bridle The equipment that fits over the horse's head, with a bit in the mouth to enable the rider to control the movement of the horse and guide the direction of movement. Bridles take many forms, the simplest being a snaffle bit with a plain noseband, one pair of reins, a throat latch, headpiece, cheekpieces and a browband. This equipment is normally made of leather.

Bridlepath A path over which there is a right-of-way for horses, as opposed to a footpath which is restricted to walkers on foot.

Broken-kneed A horse with blemishes on both knees showing that it has at some stage in its past been 'down' on its knees. A definite disadvantage in selling a horse.

Broken-winded A horse is said to be broken-winded when the air sacs in the lungs have been ruptured for any one of a variety of reasons, one being over-exertion of an unfit horse. Often the horse will have a chronic cough and will clearly be unable to perform any really hard and fast work.

Bronco An unbroken or imperfectly broken wild horse.

Bronco-buster A person who breaks and trains broncos.

Bronc riding One of the standard rodeo events. The only piece of tack worn by the horse is a wide leather band round its middle, from which a leather handhold protrudes.

Brood mare A mare used solely for breeding purposes.

Browband The part of the bridle which lies across the horse's forehead below the ears.

Brumby Australian wild horse.

Brumby runner Australian bush horseman who captures wild horses.

Brush The tail of a fox.

Brush 'Brushing' is a faulty action in a horse where the inside of one foot knocks into the lower part of the other leg and causes injury. 'Brushing boots' can be used to prevent injury.

Brush fence A fence built to simulate a hedge.

Buck A leap into the air by a horse keeping its back arched, and coming down with its forelegs stiff and its head held low.

Buckaroo (a) A cowboy. (b) A bronco-buster.

Bulldogging See Steer wrestling.

Bull riding One of the standard events in a rodeo, in which the contestant has to ride a bull equipped only with a rope round its middle, which the rider may hold with only one hand.

Bumper (a) An amateur race rider. (b) An amateur race.

Bush track An unofficial race meeting in the United States.

By Sired by.

Bye-day An extra meet held by a hunt, usually during the Christmas school holidays or to compensate for days lost through bad weather.

Calf horse A specially trained horse used for calf roping.

Calf-roping One of the standard events in a rodeo in which the rider ropes a calf and then swiftly dismounts to tie the calf by three legs.

Calkin A projecting piece of metal positioned at the end (heel) of a horseshoe to give extra grip, rather like a stud that can be inserted into a specially prepared hole in the shoe.

Call over The naming of the horses in a race, when the latest betting odds on each horse are given.

Camera patrol Equipment for the filming of a race while it is in progress.

Camp drafting A uniquely Australian rodeo contest in which a rider separates a large bullock from a group of cattle and drives it at the gallop around a course marked with upright poles.

Cannon bone The lower bone in the horse's front leg, the equivalent of the shin bone in the human.

Canter A pace of three-time in which the hoofs strike the ground in the following order: near hind, near fore and off hind together, off fore (leading leg): or off hind, off fore and near hind together, near fore (leading leg).

Cap The fee payable by a visitor for a day's hunting.

Capriole An air above the ground in which the horse half rears with the hocks drawn under, then jumps forward and high into the air, at the same time kicking out the hind legs with the soles of the feet turned upwards, before landing collectedly on all four legs.

Cast Said of a horse that lies down in a stable, usually to roll, and finds that it has not got enough room to stand up again without aid.

Catchweight The random or optional weight carried by a horse when the conditions of a race do not specify a weight. Except in matches, this does not occur now.

Cavalletti A series of small wooden jumps used in the basic training of a riding horse in order to encourage it to lengthen its stride, improve its balance and loosen up and strengthen its muscles.

Cavesson The standard bridle noseband; also a specially constructed noseband used in lungeing, with a centre swivel ring.

Cayuse An Indian horse or pony.

Certainty A horse regarded as certain to win a particular race (may or may not be the official favourite).

Chaff Meadow hay or green oat straw cut into short lengths for use as a feedstuff.

Charley A fox.

Check A halt in hunting when hounds lose the scent.

Cheekpiece (a) The leather part of the bridle to which the bit is attached at one end and the headpiece at the other. (b) The side pieces of a bit which lie outside the mouth and to which the reins are attached.

Chef d'équipe The manager of an equestrian team responsible for making all the arrangements, both on and off the field, for a national team competing abroad.

Chestnut (a) A horse with a gold to dark reddish-brown coat, usually having a matching or slightly lighter or darker mane and tail, or sometimes with a flaxen coloured mane and tail. (b) Redundant bony growth found on the inside forearm and near the hock on the inside of the leg.

Chime Hounds giving tongue in unison when on the line of the quarry.

Chukka A period of play in polo lasting seven and a half or eight minutes, depending on the country in which the game is being played.

Classic Any one of the five chief English flat races for three-year-old horses: that is, the Derby, the Oaks, the St Leger, the 1000 Guineas and the 2000 Guineas.

Clear round A show jumping or cross-country round which is completed without jumping or time faults.

Clench That part of the nail holding the shoe to the horse's foot visible on the outer hoof wall. Risen clenches indicate that the horse needs to have its shoes removed and renewed or refitted.

Clip The process of removing the horse's winter coat with electric clippers to enable it to work through the winter without sweating unduly and so losing condition or catching a chill. Once clipped, horses have to be kept in stables and clothed adequately to compensate for the loss of the winter coat.

Cob A type rather than a breed. A short-legged animal with a maximum height of 15·1 hands, with the bone and substance of a heavyweight hunter and capable of carrying a substantial weight.

Co-favourite One of two or more horses equally favoured to win a race and given the same shortest price in the betting odds.

Colic Sharp abdominal pains, often the symptom of flatulence, an obstruction created by a mass of hard food, or faeces in the bowel, and which can lead to a twisted gut.

Collection Shortening the pace by a light contact from the rider's hands and a

steady pressure with the legs to make the horse flex its neck, relax its jaw and bring its hocks well under it so that it is properly balanced.

Colt An ungelded male horse less than four years old.

Combination obstacle In show jumping, an obstacle consisting of two or more separate jumps judged as one obstacle.

Combined training competition A comprehensive test of both horse and rider, consisting of the following three phases: dressage, cross-country and show jumping, held over a period of one, two or three days depending on the type of competition.

Conformation The make and shape of a horse.

Contact The link between the rider's hands and the horse's mouth made through the reins.

Corn Bruising of the sole in the angle between the wall of the hoof and the heel.

Corral A pen or enclosure for animals, usually made of wood and always circular in shape, so that the animals cannot injure themselves.

Counter-canter A dressage movement in which the horse canters in a circle with the outer rather than the inner leg leading.

Country The area over which a certain pack of hounds may hunt.

Couple Two hounds; hounds are always counted in couples: thus 4½ couple, not 9 hounds.

Courbette An air above the ground in which the horse rears to an almost upright position, and then leaps forwards several times on its hind legs.

Course (a) A racecourse. (b) In show jumping and cross country a circuit consisting of a number of obstacles to be jumped in a particular order within a specified time limit. (c) For hounds to hunt by sight rather than by scent.

Course builder The person responsible for designing and building a show jumping or cross-country course.

Covert A hunting term for a thicket or small area of woodland.

Cow horse The horse which a cowboy rides while working cattle.

Crib-biting A vice which is often developed through boredom, when the horse grabs with its teeth any available fixed object, e.g. the manager or crib, and sucks wind through its open mouth. This can cause harm to the wind and digestion and is therefore extremely undesirable.

Croupade An air above the ground in which the horse rears, and then jumps vertically with the hind legs drawn up towards the belly.

Crupper A strap with a loop which fits round the horse's tail, the other end being attached to the saddle to keep it in place.

Cry The noise made by hounds when they are hunting their quarry.

Cub A young fox.

Curb bit Type of bit used in conjunction with a snaffle bit in a double bridle, consisting of two metal cheekpieces and mouthpiece with a central indented section (called the port).

Curb chain A metal chain which is fitted to the eyes of a curb or pelham bit and lies in the curb groove of the horse's jaw, acting in conjunction with the bit.

Curb groove The groove of the lower jaw just behind the lower lip.

Curry comb A piece of grooming equipment used to remove dirt and scurf from a body brush. It has a flat back, while the front consists of several rows of small metal teeth.

Cut To geld or castrate a colt or stallion.

Cutting horse A horse trained for separating selected cattle from a herd.

Dam The female parent of a foal.

Dandy brush The long-bristled brush for removing the surface dirt or mud from a horse's coat.

Dark horse In racing, a horse whose form is little known outside its own stable.

Dead heat In racing, a tie for first, second or third place.

Declaration A statement made in writing by an owner, trainer or his representative, a specified time before a race or competition, declaring that a horse will take part.

Dirt track A race track, the surface of which is a combination of sand and soil.

Dividend The amount paid to a person who has backed a winner or a placed horse on the totalizator. In the US called the pay-off.

Dishing An exaggerated movement of the front legs where the feet describe an outward movement as well as the normal forward action.

Dock The root of the tail.

Docking The cruel cutting of the bone of a horse's dock to give him a fashionably short tail; particularly applied to cobs, this is now illegal in many countries.

Dog fox A male fox.

Dog hound A male hound.

Dope To administer drugs to a horse, either to improve or to hinder its performance in a race or competition. It is an illegal practice and carries heavy penalties in all forms of equestrian sport.

Double (a) The backing of two horses to win in separate races, the winnings of one race being carried as a stake onto the second. If either horse fails to win the bet is lost. (b) In show jumping a combination obstacle consisting of two separate jumps; a horse refusing the second element has to approach both elements again.

Double bridle A bridle with two bits, a snaffle and a curb bit, normally used for showing horses and in advanced dressage as it demands a greater degree of collection and flexion than an ordinary snaffle bridle.

Drag An artificial scent for a hunt made by trailing a strong-smelling material such as a piece of sacking impregnated with aniseed or a fox's dropping over the ground.

Draghound A hound trained to follow a drag.

Draghunt A hunt with a drag or artificial scent.

Drain An underground pipe, ditch or watercourse in which a fox may hide during a hunt.

Dressage The art of training horses to perform all movements in a balanced, supple, obedient and keen manner.

Drover Australian horseman who herds cattle or sheep over long distances.

Dun The yellowish colour often found in the Connemara breed. Frequently there is a dorsal stripe in black, but a true dun must have black skin under the hair and a black mane and tail. A blue dun is, as its name suggests, a variation with a grey/blue coat colour.

Each way In racing, to back a horse to win and to finish in the first three.

Earth The lair of a fox which it digs below ground level or in the side of a bank.

Elimination The excluding of a competitor from taking further part in a particular competition.

Enteritis Inflammation of the intestinal or bowel lining which may be set up by bacteria, chemical or vegetable poisons, or mouldy or damaged food containing harmful fungi.

Entire A stallion.

Equestrian (a) Of, or pertaining to, horsemen or horsemanship. (b) A rider or performer on horseback.

Equestrienne A female rider or performer on horseback.

Equine (a) Of, or pertaining to, the horse. (b) A horse.

Equitation The art of riding, particularly applied to dressage.

Ergot The horny growth often apparent in ponies at the back of the fetlock joint.

Evens In racing, the betting odds given on a horse when the person who places the bet stands to win the same amount as his stake. In the US known as even money.

Event horse A horse which competes or is capable of competing in a combined training competition.

Extensions The exaggeration of the normal paces, i.e. an extended trot is an extended version of the trot pace, when the horse deliberately points its toes and really stretches its limbs.

Fall A horse is considered to have fallen when the shoulders and quarters on the same side touch the ground. A rider is considered to have fallen when there is separation between him and his horse which necessitates his remounting.

Fancied Said of a horse likely to win a particular race. In the US called favourite.

Farrier A person who makes horseshoes and shoes horses.

Fault In show jumping, a scoring unit used to record any knockdown, refusal or other offence committed by a competitor during his round.

Favourite The horse in a race having the shortest odds offered against it.

Feather The hairs growing down the back of the horse's lower leg and round the fetlock and pastern, particularly evident on heavy horse breeds.

Feed General term given to all horse fodder.

FEI The Fédération Equestre Internationale (International Equestrian Federation) which is the governing body of international equestrian sport and was founded in 1921 by Commandant G. Hector of France. It has its headquarters in Brussels. The FEI makes the rules and regulations for the conduct of the three equestrian sports which comprise the Olympic Equestrian Games – show jumping, three-day event and dressage – as well as international driving competitions. All national federations are required to comply with these rules and regulations in any international event.

Fence (a) Any obstacle to be jumped in steeplechasing, cross-country, show jumping or hunting. (b) In racing, to jump over an obstacle.

Field (a) The mounted followers of a hunt. (b) In racing, (i) all the horses running in a particular race; (ii) all the horses not individually favoured in the betting.

Filly Female horse under four years old.

Finish A horse is said to finish a race when it passes the winning post mounted, providing, in the case of a steeplechase or hurdle race, it has jumped all the obstacles with its rider.

Firing A process of applying hot irons to the horse's legs to help repair broken-down tendons. The act of firing sets up scar tissue that acts as a permanent bandage. Many racehorses and hunters are fired and continue to work adequately.

First jockey The principal person engaged by an owner or trainer to ride for him.

Flapping An unofficial race meeting, not held under the rules of racing.

Flat racing Racing in which there are no obstacles for the horses to jump.

Flying change A school movement involving a change of leading leg at the canter without a break into trot to strike off on the new lead.

Foal A young horse up to the age of twelve months.

Forehand The part of the horse which is in front of the rider: that is the head, neck, shoulders, withers and forelegs.

Forelock The lock of hair that falls between the ears. It is an extension of the mane.

Form The past performances of a horse in racing.

Forward seat A style of riding introduced by Federico Caprilli in which the rider maintains his weight over the horse's centre of balance, shifting further forward as the horse increases speed.

Foxhound One of a breed of swift, keen-scented hounds bred and trained for hunting foxes.

Foxhunting The hunting of the fox in its natural state by a pack of foxhounds, followed by people on horses or on foot.

Frog The part of the horse's foot that acts as the concussion pad during work.

Full Ungelded.

Fullering To put a groove into the horse shoe to aid its grip on slippery roads. Most hunter shoes are fullered.

Full mouth The mouth of a horse at six years old, when it has grown all its teeth.

Full pass An advanced dressage movement in which the horse moves laterally without gaining any forward ground.

Furniture Any item of harness or saddlery put on a horse.

Fuzztail running The act of herding and catching wild horses.

Gad A spur.

Gag bridle A severe form of bridle: cheekpieces are made of rounded leather and pass through holes at the top and bottom of the bit rings, before attaching directly to the reins.

Gall A sore produced by saddlery or harness rubbing on parts of the body, most common around the girth or under the saddle in riding horses.

Gallop The fastest pace of a horse.

Galloway An Australian show ring category based upon an animal's height: a Galloway measures from 14 to 15 hands (in Australia ponies are under 14 hands).

Gamgee A form of cotton wool for use under exercise or travelling bandages.

Garron Any native pony of Scotland or Ireland.

Gate Frequently used as an upright obstacle in show jumping competitions.

Gelding A male horse which has been castrated.

Gestation The period between conception and foaling, normally about eleven months.

Get The offspring of a stallion.

Girth (a) The circumference of a horse, measured behind the withers round the deepest part of the body. (b) A band, usually of leather, webbing or nylon, passed under the belly of the horse to hold the saddle in place.

Give tongue For hounds to bark or bay when in full cry after a quarry.

Going The condition of a race track or other ground over which a horse travels; variously classified as soft, good, etc.

Gone to ground A fox having taken refuge in an earth or a drain.

Good mouth A horse with a soft, sensitive mouth.

Go short Said of a horse which is lame or restricted in its action.

Green (a) A horse which is broken but not fully trained, an inexperienced horse. (b) A trotter or pacer which has not been raced against the clock.

Grey A dark-skinned horse with a coat of black and white hairs mixed together; the white ones become more predominant with each change of coat, so old horses appear almost white.

Groom (a) Any person who is responsible for looking after a horse. (b) To clean the coat and feet of a horse.

Grooming kit Collectively, the brushes and other items of equipment used to groom a horse.

Ground To let the reins touch the ground after dismounting so that the horse will stand without having to be tied up.

Ground money In a rodeo the entry fee and purse money split equally among all the contestants in an event where there is no outright winner.

Gymkhana Mounted games, most frequently for children under sixteen, many of which are adaptations of children's party games.

Habit The dress worn by a woman riding side-saddle, consisting of a jacket and matching long skirt or shaped panel worn over the breeches and boots.

Hack (a) A riding horse for hire. (b) A pleasure ride. (c) A type of horse, nowadays usually a show horse, in which elegance, manners and quality of conformation are paramount.

Hackamore A bitless bridle, mostly used in Western riding.

Hackney A specialized breed of driving horse or pony, characterized by the exaggerated action at the trot.

Half-halt A momentary check in pace to collect a horse before applying aids for a change of pace or movement.

Half-pass A lateral movement used in schooling the horse to a fairly high standard, where the horse moves both sideways and forwards.

Halter or headcollar Made of either leather or hemp rope, it is fitted on the horse's head and is used for leading horses to and from fields and stables, and for tying up, etc. It has no bit, and is usually used in conjunction with a headcollar rope or chain.

Hand The accepted measurement for horses, a hand measuring 10 cm (4 in). A horse is said to be 15·2 hands, meaning 15 hands two inches, and is measured to its withers from the ground.

Handicap (a) The weight allocated to a horse in a race. (b) A race in which the weights to be carried by the horse are estimated so as to give each horse an equal chance of winning.

Harriers Hounds similar to, but smaller than, foxhounds, used to hunt the hare.

Haunches The hips and buttocks of a horse.

Haute école The classical art of equitation.

Hay Grass cut and dried at a particular time of the year for use as fodder.

Hay net A string or rope net which contains the hay and prevents wastage.

Head One of the measurements of distance by which a horse may be said to have won a race: the length of a horse's head.

Heavy horse Any horse belonging to one of the breeds of large draught horses, such as Clydesdale, Percheron, Shire or Suffolk Punch.

Height The height of a horse is measured in a perpendicular line from the highest part of the withers to the ground.

High School (haute école) The classical art of equitation.

Hindquarters The rear end of the horse, including the back legs.

Hitch up To harness a horse or horses to be driven.

Hit the line For hounds to pick up the scent of the quarry.

Hobday A form of operation on the horse's larynx to assist breathing.

Hock The large joint on the hind leg between the second thigh and the hind cannon, which corresponds to the human heel.

Hogged mane A mane cut short, level with the neck, popular for cobby types.

Hog's back In show jumping, a spread obstacle in which there are three sets of poles, the first close to the ground, the second at the highest point of the obstacle and the third slightly lower than the second.

Holloa The cry given by a person out hunting to indicate that he has seen the fox.

Hood (a) A fabric covering which goes over the horse's head and ears and part of its neck, and is used when travelling, most usually in cold weather. (b) Blinkers.

Hoof (a) The insensitive horny covering which protects the sensitive parts of a horse's foot. (b) A term used to describe the entire foot.

Hoof pick A hooked metal instrument used for removing stones and dirt from a horse's foot.

Horse (a) The general term for an equine animal, whether it be a stallion, mare or gelding. (b) A stallion or uncastrated horse. (c) To provide a person with a horse to ride. (d) To ride on horseback.

Horseman (a) A rider on horseback. (b) A person skilled in the training and management of horses. (c) A farm labourer who works with horses.

Horserace A competition for horses ridden by jockeys which takes place on the flat or over obstacles within a given area and over a prescribed distance, under the control of appointed officials.

Horseshoe A shaped metal band nailed to the base of riding and harness horses' hoofs to protect them and prevent them from splitting.

Horse show A meeting at which competitions are held to test or display the qualities and capabilities of horses and their riders.

Horse-tailing Taking charge of the band of horses used by drovers when herding cattle or sheep over long distances.

Hull A term for a saddle.

Hunt button A button with the symbol or lettering of a particular hunt on it.

Hunter A type of horse rather than a breed, suited for hunting over varied terrain and capable of jumping and galloping for long distances. Hunter classes take up a large portion of the major horse shows and champion horses in these classes frequently fetch high prices when sold.

Hunter trials A type of competitive event held by most hunts and other organizing bodies during the hunting season, in which horses are ridden over a course of obstacles built to look as natural and similar to those encountered out hunting. The course has to be completed within a specified time.

Hunting The sport of following different types of hound, either mounted or on foot, in pursuit of the fox, the stag or the hare or an artificially laid drag line.

Hunting cap A velvet-covered protective riding hat.

Hunting horn A cylindrical instrument, usually 23–25 cm (9–10 in) long, made of copper with a nickel or silver mouthpiece, used by huntsmen to give signals, both to hounds and to the field.

Hunt livery The distinctive coat of a particular hunt worn by the staff of the hunt.

Hunt secretary A person who carries out the normal duties of a secretary in connection with the hunt; he is also responsible for keeping close contact with farmers and landowners within the area of the hunt, and collects the cap money at the meet.

Hunt servant Any salaried employee of a hunt, such as the huntsman, kennel huntsman or whipper-in.

Huntsman The person in charge of hounds during a hunt, whether the Master or someone employed by the Master.

Hunt subscription The fee payable by a person who is a member of a hunt.

Hunt terrier A small, short-legged terrier kept by a hunt and used to bolt foxes from earths, drains or other places which are inaccessible to hounds.

Hurdle One of a series of wattle fences over which a horse must jump in hurdle racing. In the US the fences are made of brush.

Impulsion The urge to move forward, in a correct and controlled fashion, of a well-schooled horse.

In blood Said of hounds having made a kill.

Inbreeding The mating of related individuals, such as brother and sister, sire and daughter or son and dam.

Independent seat The ability to maintain a firm, balanced position on a horse's back, without relying on the reins or stirrups.

In foal Pregnant.

In full cry A pack of hounds in strong pursuit of the quarry and giving tongue.

In-hand Leading a horse from the ground.

In-hand class Any of various show classes in which the animals are led,

usually in a show bridle or headcollar, but otherwise without saddlery (except for draught horses which are often shown in their harness), and are judged chiefly for conformation and/or condition.

In the book Accepted for, or entered in, the General Stud Book.

Irish martingale Two rings joined by a short leather strap that slip over the reins to prevent the horse from confusing the reins if he tends to throw his head about.

Irons The stirrup irons, part of the saddlery for a riding horse.

Jibbing Refusal of a horse to pass a certain point or object. The horse remains rooted to the spot or runs backwards.

Jiggle The ordinary gait of a cow horse, averaging about 8 kmh (5 mph).

Jockey (a) A person engaged to ride a horse in a race. (b) Formerly a dealer in horses, especially a disreputable one.

Jog A short-paced trot.

Jogging An annoying habit often found in excitable horses that refuse to walk or trot properly but insist on jogging, a most uncomfortable pace.

Joint Master One of two or more people who share the mastership of a pack of hounds.

Jumper Any horse trained to compete over jumps, such as a steeplechaser or show jumper.

Jumping lane An enclosed lane for loose schooling a horse over jumps without the rider.

Jump jockey A jockey who races horses over hurdles or steeplechase fences.

Jump-off In show jumping, a round held to decide the winner of the competition from competitors who have tied for first place in the previous round.

Jute rugs Most stable rugs are made of jute (a form of sacking), lined with wool.

Kaolin poultice A fine clay-type poultice that is invaluable in reducing

inflammation and swelling on horses' legs when applied hot.

Keep A grass field which is used for grazing. Known as pastures in the US.

Kennel huntsman A person employed by a hunt which has an amateur huntsman to manage the hounds and to act as first whipper-in on hunting days.

Kennels The buildings and yards where a pack of hounds is housed.

Keys Pieces of metal loosely attached to the mouthpiece of a breaking bit which help the horse to accept the bit by encouraging him to mouth and play with it.

Kicking A dangerous vice, especially when aimed at humans or other horses, and most dangerous when out hunting or with a gathering of other horses.

Knee caps Protective covering made of leather and rugging for the knees, used when travelling or occasionally when working on slippery road surfaces.

Lad (a) A boy or stableman who works in a stables of any kind. (b) A girl who works in racing stables. Known as a groom in the US.

Lash The small piece of silk attached to the end of the thong on a hunting whip which makes the cracking sound.

Laminitis Inflammation of the sensitive laminae which lie between the horny wall of the hoof and the pedal bone. It is a very painful condition, generally found in ponies which have been allowed to eat too much rich new grass.

Lawn meet Any meet of a hunt held at a private house by invitation of the owner.

Leathers The stirrup straps.

Length One of the measurements of distance by which a horse may be said to win a race; the length of a horse's head and body.

Levade A high-school movement in which the horse rears, drawing its forefeet in, while the hindquarters are deeply bent at the haunches and carry the full weight.

Light A term meaning to dismount.

Light horse Any horse, except a Thoroughbred, used or suitable for riding such as a hack or hunter.

Line The direction in which a fox is travelling with hounds in pursuit.

Linseed The seed of flax, generally used in the form of linseed jelly, oil or tea both as a laxative and to improve the condition and gloss of the coat.

Litter Another term for the bedding used in stables.

Livery A horse at livery is one which is boarded at a stable away from the owner's home; a livery fee will be charged.

Loose box A stable where a horse can wander at will rather than being restrained as in a stall.

Loriner A person who makes the metal parts of saddlery and harness such as bits, curb chains and stirrup irons.

Lungeing An important part of the horse's training; the horse circles the trainer on the end of a lunge rein, learning obedience and improving in suppleness and muscular development.

Lunge rein A piece of cotton or nylon webbing, usually about 2·5 cm (1 in) wide and 7·5 m (25 ft) long, which is attached by a buckle and leather strap to one of the rings on the noseband of a breaking cavesson and is used in training horses.

Made Said of a horse when it is properly schooled and obedient, and reasonably experienced in the tasks required of it.

Maiden A horse of either sex which to date has not won a race of any distance.

Maiden mare A mare which has not had a foal, though she may be carrying one.

Maiden race A race in which only horses which have never won a race may be entered.

Mane The long hair growing on the top of a horse's head and down the neck.

Manège The schooling area.

Mare A female horse aged four years or over.

Markings The distinguishing marks, usually white, of a horse on its face and legs, e.g. star, blaze, socks and stockings.

Martingale A device used to help in keeping a horse's head in the correct position. It generally consists of a strap, or arrangement of straps, fastened to the girth at one end, passed between the forelegs and, depending on the type, attached at the other end to the reins, noseband or directly to the bit.

Mask The head of a fox.

Master The person appointed by a hunt committee to have overall responsibility for the running and organization of all aspects of the hunt.

Meet (a) The place where the hunt servants, hounds, followers, etc., assemble before a hunt. (b) The hunt meeting itself.

Mixed meeting A race meeting at which both flat and steeplechase or hurdle races are held on the same day.

Mixed stable A racing stable where both flat race and National Hunt (steeplechase) horses are kept.

Montura (a) A riding horse. (b) A saddle.

Mount (a) A horse used for riding. (b) To get up on to the back of a horse.

Mount money The money paid in a rodeo to a performer who is riding, roping or bulldogging in exhibition but not in competition.

Muck out To clean out a box or stall in which a horse has been stabled, removing the droppings and soiled bedding.

Mudder A racehorse which performs well on a muddy track.

Mud fever An inflammation of the upper layer of skin on the legs and belly, caused by muddy and wet conditions.

Music The cry made by hounds when they are hunting.

Mustang A wild horse.

Nap (a) A horse is said to nap if it fails to obey properly applied aids, as in refusing to go forward or to pass a certain point. (b) In racing a good tip.

National federation The governing body of equestrian affairs in any country affiliated to the FEI.

Natural aids The body, hands, legs and voice as used by the rider to give instructions to the horse.

Navicular disease An incurable disease of the navicular bone and deep flexor tendon affecting the forefeet of riding horses; it results in acute lameness.

Near side The left-hand side of a horse. This is the side from which it is usual to mount and lead a horse.

Neck One of the measurements of distance by which a horse may be said to win a race; the length of a horse's head and neck.

Neck reining Method of guiding a horse by pressure of the reins on one or other side of its neck.

New Zealand rug A form of rug with a waterproof canvas outside and rugging inside, used to turn horses out in winter if they are clipped or in bad weather.

Nicking An operation involving the cutting of the small tendons under a horse's dock in order to make it carry its tail higher; mostly used on American gaited horses.

Nose The shortest measurement of distance by which it is possible for a horse to win a race.

Noseband The leather band that forms part of the bridle and which is fixed around the horse's nose. There are various forms of noseband: the standard type is a cavesson; others act as extra restraint on the horse, such as the drop noseband, the grakle, or the Kineton.

Numnah A pad placed under the saddle to prevent undue pressure on the horse's back. Cut to the shape of the saddle but slightly larger, it may be made of felt, sheepskin or cloth-covered foam rubber.

Nuts (or cubes) A concentrated compound food for horses (and for cattle), often fed instead of cereal concentrates, particularly to horses which tend to 'hot up'.

Oats A cereal crop used as part of a horse's feed. May be given either whole, bruised or boiled.

Objection In racing, an objection may be made against any of the placed horses, and must be heard by the stewards at the meeting where it was raised.

Odds The betting quotation on a horse in a particular race.

Odds on Betting odds of less than even money.

Off side The right-hand side of a horse.

On its toes Said of a horse eager and keen to move on.

On terms Said of hounds able to keep hunting steadily because there is a strong scent.

One-day event A combined training competition consisting of dressage, show jumping and cross-country phases and completed in one day.

Opening meet The first meet of the regular hunting season.

Outfit (a) A ranch with all its equipment and employees. (b) The personal equipment of a cowboy.

Outlaw A horse which is particularly vicious and untameable.

Outsider A racehorse which is given long odds in the betting as it is thought to have little chance of winning the race.

Overreach An injury to the back of the foreleg, caused by a horse striking itself with a hind foot.

Owlhead A horse which is impossible to train.

Owner The person in whose name a racehorse runs, irrespective of whether that person is the sole owner of the horse or is a member of a syndicate.

Pace A lateral gait in two-time, in which the hind leg and the foreleg on the same side move forward together; in horses the normal gait is diagonal.

Pacemaker In racing, a horse which takes the lead and sets the speed for the race.

Pad The foot of a fox.

Paddock (a) A grassy enclosure near a stable or house in which horses can be turned out. (b) The enclosure at a racecourse in which the horses are paraded and then mounted before a race.

Palomino A colour rather than a breed or horse, except in the United States where a specific breed is recognized, it is a beautiful golden shade made all the more striking as it is accompanied by a creamy mane and tail.

Parabola The arc made by a horse from the point of take-off to the point of landing as it jumps an obstacle.

Parallel bars A type of spread fence used in both show jumping and cross-country courses, consisting of two sets of posts and rails.

Parimutuel The US and continental equivalent of the totalizator; a form of betting in which the total amount wagered, after a deduction of a percentage for costs, etc., is divided among the holders of the winning and place tickets. An electro-mechanical apparatus is used for recording the number and amount of bets staked by this method.

Passage One of the classical high school airs, comprising a spectacular elevated trot in slow motion. There is a definite period of suspension as one pair of legs remains on the ground with the diagonal opposites raised in the air.

Pelham bit A bit designed to produce with only one mouthpiece the combined effects of the snaffle bit and the curb bit. Normally made of metal, vulcanite or rubber and used either with two reins, or with one rein linked to the two rings of the bit by a leather couplet.

Penalty In racing, an additional weight handicap carried by a horse, usually imposed when it has won a race since the weights for the race in which the penalty is given were published.

Photo-finish The result of a race photographed by a camera with a very narrow field of vision situated at the winning post on a racecourse. A camera was first used for recording a photo-finish in 1890 by John Hemment at Sheepshead Bay in the United States.

Piaffe A classical high school air, comprising a spectacular trot with great elevation and cadence performed on the spot.

Picnic races Meetings held in Australia's outback, when amateur riders and their grass-fed mounts compete against each other for small prizes on primitive bushland racetracks.

Piebald A horse whose coat consists of large irregular and clearly defined patches of black and white hairs.

Pinto A piebald or skewbald horse.

Pirouette In dressage, a turn within the horse's length, that is, the shortest turn it is possible to make. There are three kinds of pirouette – the turn on the centre, the turn on the forehand and the turn on the haunches.

Place To finish second in a horserace.

Plaits A decorative way of tying the hair of the mane and tail. It is seen most often in horses groomed for the show ring and out hunting, and serves no purpose other than to make the horse look more beautiful.

Planks A show jumping obstacle made up of painted planks about 30 cm (1 ft) wide.

Plug Any slow or broken-down horse.

Point-to-point A kind of steeplechase, run under National Hunt rules but organized by local hunts; runners qualify by hunting a given number of days in the season.

Points of the horse Names given to the various parts of the horse.

Pointing In lameness of the foreleg, a horse may be seen to rest the affected leg by 'pointing' it forward, with just the toe touching the ground.

Polo A mounted game bearing a resemblance to hockey, played between two teams of four a side. Popular in many parts of the world, it is recorded as having been played as long ago as the reign of Darius I of Persia (521–486 BC).

Polocrosse Australian mounted game which is rather like a horseback version of lacrosse: the ball is scooped up in a small net at the end of a long stick and is then carried or thrown.

Pony (a) A horse not exceeding 14·2 hands at maturity. (b) The sum of £25 in gambling.

Pony speed test The racing of ponies ridden by light boy riders around the quarter-mile circuit at showgrounds in Australia.

Post (a) Either the starting or winning post in racing. (b) To rise from the saddle at the trot.

Post and rails A type of obstacle in show jumping and cross-country courses consisting of upright posts between which are laid a number of horizontal posts. In show jumping the rails are simply supported by the posts, whereas in cross-country events they are fixed to the posts.

Price The odds quoted by a bookmaker at a race meeting for a particular horse.

Prix des Nations An international team show jumping competition held at an official international horse show. Four members in each team compete, jumping the course twice, and the three best scores of the team are counted in each round. In the event of equality after the two rounds a jump-off is held in which faults and time are totalled to give the final result. Again only the three best scores and times are counted.

Puissance A jumping competition in which the fences are raised higher for each round, rather than a speed competition in which time is the crucial factor in deciding jump-offs.

Punter A person who bets regularly on horses.

Quadrille A dressage display given by four horses and riders, or by a multiple of four.

Quarters The area of a horse's body extending from the rear of the flank to the root of the tail and downwards on either side to the top of the leg: the hindquarters.

Quidding A horse dropping partially chewed food out of its mouth; it is an indication that the teeth are in need of attention.

Race card The printed programme of a race meeting giving information, including the name and time of each race, and the names of all horses, their owners and trainers and the weights to be carried.

Racecourse A race track properly constructed for flat and/or steeplechasing and hurdle racing, together with all the relevant facilities, such as grandstands, paddock, stables, office buildings, etc. and administered by appointed officials.

Racehorse A horse bred and trained for racing, either on the flat or over hurdles or steeplechase obstacles.

Race meeting (a) A meeting at a given place for the purpose of holding a fixed number of horseraces. (b) The period during which this meeting takes place.

Racing plate A thin, very lightweight horseshoe used on racehorses.

Rack The most spectacular movement of the five-gaited American Saddlebred horse, it is a very fast, even gait in which each foot strikes the ground separately in quick succession.

Range horse A horse born and brought up on the range, and which is never handled until it is brought in to be broken.

Rear For a horse to rise up on the hind legs.

Red flag A marker used in equestrian sports to denote the right-hand extremity of any obstacle. It is also used to mark a set track and must always be passed on the left-hand side.

Red ribbon A piece of red ribbon tied round the tail of a horse, especially when hunting, to indicate that it is a known kicker.

Refusal (a) In racing, the failure of a horse to attempt to jump a hurdle or steeplechase fence. (b) In show jumping and combined training, either the act of passing an obstacle which is to be jumped, or stopping in front of it.

Rein back To make a horse step backwards while being ridden or driven.

Reins A pair of long narrow straps attached to the bit or bridle and used by the rider or driver to guide and control the horse.

Renvers A dressage movement on two tracks in which the horse moves at an angle of not more than 30 degrees along the long side of the arena with the hind legs on the outer and the forelegs on the inner track, looking in the direction in which it is going and being bent slightly round the inside leg of the rider.

Rep A cowboy employed to search for and round up cattle which have strayed from the ranch of his employer. Such cattle would be recognizable by their brand.

Resistance The act of refusing to go forward, stopping, running back or rearing.

Ride off In polo, to push one's pony against that of another player in order to prevent him from playing the ball.

Riding school An establishment where people are taught to ride and horses can be hired for riding, or may be taken for livery, or both.

Rig A male horse in which one or both testicles are retained in the abdomen; used also of a horse on which the operation of gelding has been incompletely or unsuccessfully performed.

Ringer A horse entered in a race under the name of another horse, the object being to win bets illegally on a good horse, which the public and bookmakers believe to be an inferior one.

Roan A horse having a black, bay or chestnut coat with an admixture of white hairs (especially on the body and neck), which modifies the colour.

Roaring A disease of the wind, due to paralysis of the larynx.

Roller A leather belly band to keep rugs in place; those with an arch over the withers both keep pressure off the withers and discourage the horse from rolling.

Rope horse Any horse which is especially trained and used for roping cattle.

Rubber A stable rubber is a cloth used for final polishing of the horse after thorough grooming to remove the final layer of dust and grease from the surface of the coat.

Run mute Said of hounds which are running very fast and thus have no time to speak.

Runner Any horse taking part in a particular race.

Run out (a) In show jumping and combined training, to avoid an obstacle which is to be jumped by running to one side or the other of it. (b) In racing, to avoid an obstacle which is to be jumped or to pass on the wrong side of a marker flag.

Saddle A seat for a rider on horseback, made in various designs according to the purpose for which it is required.

Saddle bronc riding One of the standard rodeo events. The rider has to use a regulation saddle; he is allowed to use only one rein attached to a simple halter and is not allowed to touch the saddle, the horse or himself with his free hand. He must remain mounted for ten seconds and is judged according to how hard the horse bucks and how well he rides.

Saddle furniture The metal parts of a saddle.

Saddler A person who makes or deals in saddlery and/or harness.

Saddlery The bridle, saddle and other items of tack used on a horse which is to be ridden as opposed to driven.

Sand crack A dry crack that forms in the wall of the horse's hoof; it can be eradicated by careful treatment by the farrier.

Scent The distinctive odour of the fox which is given off by the glands under the tail and from the pads.

School (a) To train a horse for whatever purpose it may be required. (b) An enclosed area, either covered or open, where a horse may be trained or exercised.

Scratch (a) To withdraw a horse from an equestrian event after it has been officially entered. (b) (US) to spur vigorously.

Scrub dashing Galloping after half-wild cattle in timbered country in Australia in order to round them up into a herd.

Selling race A race immediately after which any runner, if a loser, may be claimed for a previously stated price, or, if the winner, must be offered for sale at auction.

Service The mating of a mare by a stallion.

Shoeing The act of putting shoes on a horse. Normally a horse needs its shoes renewed every four to eight weeks depending on the type of work it is required to do, whether it is worked on soft or hard ground and how fast its feet grow.

Shoulder-in A school movement on two tracks, in which the horse is bent while moving sideways and forwards.

Show (a) To compete in a horse show. (b) (US) To finish third in a race.

Show class Any of various competitions held at horse shows in which the animals are judged for their conformation, condition, action and/or suitability for whatever purpose they are used, or intended to be used.

Shy For a horse to swerve away suddenly in fear (or occasionally from mere high spirits) from an obstacle or sound.

Side saddle A saddle designed for women on which the rider sits with both feet on the same side, normally the nearside. On that side, the saddle has two padded projections placed diagonally one above the other. The rider hooks her right leg over the upper one and places the left leg under and against the lower one resting her left foot in the single stirrup iron.

Silks The peaked cap and silk or woollen blouse, both carrying the colours of the owner, worn by a jockey in racing.

Sire The male parent of a foal.

Skate A horse of poor quality.

Skewbald A horse whose coat consists of large irregular and clearly defined patches of white and of any other colour, except black (when it is known as a piebald).

Sleeper A horse which unexpectedly wins a race having previously shown poor form.

Slow gait One of the gaits of the five-gaited American Saddlebred. It is a true prancing action in which each foot in turn is raised and then held momentarily in mid-air before being brought down. Similar to the rack and also called the single foot.

Slug A term used to describe a lazy horse.

Snaffle bit The oldest and simplest form of bit, available in a variety of types, but consisting chiefly of a single bar with a ring at each end to which one of a pair of reins is attached.

Sock The white marking on a leg extending from the coronet a short way up the leg. A longer marking is known as a stocking.

Sound Said of a horse which is free from any illness, disease, blemish, physical defect or imperfection which might impair in any way its usefulness or ability to work.

Speak The bark or bay of a hound on finding a scent.

Splint A bony growth which gradually forms between a horse's cannon bone and one of the splint bones as a result of excess strain or concussion, particularly in horses worked hard when young.

Spread fence In show jumping and cross-country events, any of various obstacles which are wide as opposed to simply high, such as a hog's back, parallel bars, triple bar or water jump.

Sprinter A horse which is able to move at great speed over a short distance but is seldom able to maintain the pace over a long distance.

Spur A pointed device strapped on to the heel of a rider's boot and used to urge the horse onwards.

Stable (a) A building in which one or more horses are kept. (b) A collection of horses belonging to one person, such as a racehorse owner or riding-school proprietor, or kept at one establishment.

Stale To pass urine.

Stale line The line of a fox which has passed some time previously.

Stallion An ungelded male horse aged four years or over.

Stallion hound A male hound used for breeding purposes.

Standard event Any of the five rodeo events recognized by the governing body, the Rodeo Cowboys Association. These are bareback riding, bull riding, calf-roping, saddle bronc riding and steer wrestling.

Starter's orders When the starter of a race has satisfied himself that all runners are present and ready to race, a flag is raised to show that the horses are 'under starter's orders'.

Stayer A term applied to a horse which has great strength and power of endurance and is therefore likely to be successful over a long distance.

Steeplechase A race over a certain course of a specified distance and on which there are a number of obstacles to be jumped.

Steer wrestling One of the standard events in a rodeo. The contestant rides alongside a running steer, and jumps from the saddle on to the head of the steer, the object being to stop the steer, twist it to the ground, and hold it there with the head and all four feet facing in the same direction. The contestant completing the event in the shortest time is the winner. The event is also called bulldogging.

Steward An official at a race meeting appointed to see that the meeting is conducted according to the rules.

Stirrup iron A loop, ring, or similar device made of metal, wood, leather, etc., suspended from a saddle to support the rider's foot.

Stirrup leather The adjustable strap by which the stirrup iron is attached to the saddle.

Stock (a) A white neckcloth worn for hunting and formal occasions. (b) The handle of a whip.

Stock class A show class for stock or ranch ponies.

Stock saddle The high-pommelled, high-cantled Australian cowboy's saddle which has long flaps.

Straight fence In show jumping and cross-country courses, any obstacle which has all its component parts in the same vertical plane, such as a gate, post and rails or planks.

Strangles An infectious and highly contagious disease caused by the organism *Streptococcus equi* and occurring most commonly in young horses. The symptoms include a rise in temperature, a thick nasal discharge and swelling of the submaxillary and other lymphatic glands of the head in which abscesses eventually form.

Strike a fox To find a fox.

Stud (a) An establishment at which horses are kept for breeding purposes. (b) Any large establishment of racehorses, hunters, etc., belonging to one owner. (c) (US) A studhorse or stallion. (d) A metallic head screwed into a horseshoe to give the horse a better grip on a slippery surface; used particularly in show jumping, etc.

Stud groom A senior groom, especially at a stud farm.

Surcingle A webbing belt usually 6 to 8 cm (2½ to 3 in) wide, which passes over a racing or jumping saddle and girth and is used to keep the saddle in position, or which can be used in place of a roller to secure a day or night rug.

Sweat scraper A curved metal blade with a wooden handle used to scrape sweat from a horse.

Sweet itch A dermatitis usually found in horses that are allergic to a particular pasture plant, and therefore most likely to occur in the spring and summer months. It particularly affects the crest, croup and withers causing intense irritation and producing patches of thick, scaly, sometimes ulcerated skin, which the horse often rubs bare in its attempts to get relief.

Tack Saddlery.

Tail The tail of the horse includes the dock together with all the hair, which is usually allowed to grow about 10 cm (4 in) below the point of the hock.

Technical delegate The person at an international horse show or three-day event who is responsible for seeing that the competition is run according to international rules and that the course is correct. He is usually from a country other than the host nation.

Teeth When fully mouthed the horse has 40 teeth: 12 incisors (6 in each jaw), 4 canines (1 in each side of the upper and lower jaw), and 24 molars (6 above and 6 below on each side). Females lack canines.

Temperature The normal temperature of a horse is 38°C (100·5°F).

Tetanus An infectious, often fatal, disease caused by the micro-organism *Tetanus bacillus* which lives in the soil and enters a horse's body through wounds, especially of the foot. One of the first visible signs is that the horse will stand with its head pointed forwards, its front legs wide apart, its hind legs straddled with the hocks turned outwards and its tail raised. If made to move the animal will walk stiffly. As the disease advances the horse may become nervous and excited, and the facial muscles become so rigid that the animal is unable to open its mouth – hence the familiar name for the disease, lockjaw.

Three-day event A combined training competition completed over three consecutive days. It consists of a dressage test, a speed and endurance section, which includes a steeplechase course and two circuits of roads and tracks as well as a course of cross-country obstacles, and finally a show jumping event.

Throatlatch A strap which is part of the headpiece of a bridle. It fastens under the horse's throat so as to prevent the bridle from slipping over the head.

Thrush Inflammation of the frog of a horse's foot, characterized by a foul-smelling discharge.

Time allowed The prescribed period of time in which a competitor must complete a show jumping course if he is not to incur time faults.

Time limit The prescribed period of time in which a competitor must complete a show jumping course if he is not to be eliminated.

Tipster In racing, a person who makes a business of providing information or tips about the chances of horses in races.

Totalizator An electromechanical apparatus used for a form of betting in which the total amount wagered, after a deduction of a percentage for costs, etc., is divided among the holders of winning and place tickets.

Trail horse A horse trained, bred or used for cross-country rides.

Trainer A person qualified to superintend the training of a horse for a particular sport or pursuit; most often used of racehorse trainers.

Training tracks Concentric tracks inside the racecourse proper at Australian racetracks, on which the great majority of Australian racehorses are trained.

Transition A change of pace.

Travers A dressage movement on two tracks in which the horse moves at an angle of not more than 30 degrees along the long side of the arena with the forelegs on the outer and the hind legs on the inner track, looking in the direction in which it is going and bent slightly round the inside leg of the rider.

Treble In show jumping, a combination obstacle consisting of three separate jumps.

Triple bar In show jumping, a spread fence consisting of three sets of poles built in staircase fashion with the highest at the back.

Triple Crown The three Classic races in Great Britain: the 2000 Guineas, the Derby and the St Leger. The American Triple Crown comprises the Kentucky Derby, the Preakness Stakes and the Belmont Stakes.

Trot A pace of two-time, in which the legs move in diagonal pairs but not quite simultaneously.

Turf (a) Any course over which horse-racing is conducted. (b) In the US turf races are held over grass courses as opposed to dirt tracks. (c) The world of horseracing in general.

Turn on the forehand A movement in which the horse pivots on the forehand while describing concentric circles with the hind legs.

Turn on the quarters A movement in which the horse pivots on the hind legs while describing concentric circles with the forelegs.

Unentered Said of a hound which has not completed a cubhunting season.

Unseated A rider who has in some way been put out of the saddle.

Unsound A horse which has any defect which makes it unable to function properly.

Unwind To start to buck.

Vixen A female fox.

Vice Vices in horses are objectionable habits, often dangerous to horse and rider – as in rearing, shying, bucking; or injurious to the health of the horse – as in wind-sucking, weaving, crib-biting, etc.

Volte In dressage a full turn on the haunches; the smallest circle a horse is able to execute on either one or two tracks, the radius being equal to the length of the horse.

Walk A pace of four-time in which the hoofs strike the ground in the following sequence: near hind, near fore, off hind, off fore.

Walking Horse class Any of various competitions held for Tennessee Walking Horses at horse shows in the US.

Walkover A race in which only one horse has been declared to start. To qualify for the prize money the horse has to be saddled, paraded in front of the stand and then has to walk past the winning post.

Wall of the hoof That part of the hoof which is visible when the foot is placed flat on the ground. It is divided into the toe, the quarters (sides) and the heel.

Water brush (a) A brush used to wash the feet and to dampen the mane and tail. (b) In show jumping, a small sloping brush fence placed in front of a water jump to help a horse take off.

Weaving A nervous habit that becomes a vice. The horse transfers its weight alternately from one foot to the other and weaves its head back and forth over the stable door, losing condition and often passing the habit on to other horses.

Weigh in In certain equestrian sports where a specified weight has to be carried, such as racing, combined training and show jumping, the rider has to be weighed immediately after completion of the race, or of his round in the competition, to ensure that the correct weight was carried throughout the event.

Weight allowance A weight allowance in racing which may be claimed by a jockey or apprentice who has not ridden a certain number of winners.

Whip There are various forms of this aid, including cutting, hunting, dressage, show cane, and driving.

Whipper-in The huntsman's assistant with a pack of hounds.

Whistling A disease of the wind, like roaring caused by paralysis of the larynx, but higher than roaring in pitch.

Windgall A puffy elastic swelling of a horse's knee or fetlock joints caused by an over-secretion of synovia, a fluid similar to joint oil.

Windsucking A harmful habit in which a horse draws in and swallows air, causing indigestion.

Wing One of a pair of upright stands with cups or similar fittings used to support the poles or other suspended parts of a show jumping obstacle.

Winter out For a horse to be left out in the field during the winter rather than to be brought into the stable.

Wisp A plait of hay made to muscle up and tone the horse during grooming.

Withers The point at which the neck of the horse joins the back above the shoulder. Horses are measured from the ground to the withers.

Worms All horses carry worms and it is only by a regular programme of dosing that they can be kept under control. If allowed to get out of hand, the horse rapidly loses condition and may die.

INDEX
(Page numbers in italics refer to illustrations)

ACKNOWLEDGMENTS

Drawings by John Lobban.

The publishers would like to thank the following organisations and individuals for their kind permission to reproduce the photographs in this book:

Animal Photography 56, 60, 77, 78, 79, 80, 154, 196, 270, 271, 326, 327; Arthur Bailey, Wyoming 305; Barnaby's Picture Library 308; John Carnemolla 307, 346–347, 348; Colorsport 366; Colour Library International 345; Gerry Cranham 97; Anne Cumbers 176; Daily Telegraph Colour Library, Patrick Thurston, title; Findlay Davidson 368; Robert Estall 272; James Fain, Logan, Utah 306, 325; Sonia Halliday contents; Robert Harding Associates half title; Keystone Press Agency 100, 120; Ed Lacey 365, 367; London Express News & Features 99; Leo Mason ends; Jane Miller 59, 117, 155, 173, 249, 252; John Moss 175; Pictor International Limited 156; Rapho Agence de Presse 250–251; Realites (M. Desjarding) 98; Peter Roberts 195; Iantha Ruven 174, 193; Spectrum Colour Library 21, 118, 153, 269; Margie Spence 328; Tony Stone Associates 119, 213, 214–215; Syndication International 194, 216; Van Phillips 24; Zefa 58;